# Charmaine Solomon's
## COMPLETE
# VEGETARIAN
# COOKBOOK

# *Charmaine Solomon's*
## COMPLETE
# VEGETARIAN
## COOKBOOK

Angus&Robertson
An imprint of HarperCollins*Publishers*

ACKNOWLEDGEMENTS

Thanks to the following contributors for supplying props for photography:
Accoutrement Cook Shops, Albi Imports, Appley Hoare Antiques, David Jones,
Georg Jensen Silver, Hampshire & Lowndes, Incorporated Agencies, Lifestyle
Imports, Made In Japan Imports, Made Where, Orrefors Australia, Royal Copenhagen,
Royal Doulton, Strachan, Studio Hans, Vasa Agencies, Waterford Wedgwoood,
and Whitehill Silver & Plate Company.

Thanks also to the following people for their assistance:
Robert Carmack, food stylist; Darlene Macklyn, personal assistant to Charmaine
Solomon; Kathy Metcalfe, editor; Margaret Fulton and The Banjo Paterson Cottage
Restaurant for locational photographic assistance.

**Angus & Robertson**
An imprint of HarperCollins*Publishers*, Australia

First published in Australia in 1990
This paperback edition published in 1996
by HarperCollins*Publishers* Pty Limited
ACN 009 913 517
A member of the HarperCollins *Publishers* (Australia) Pty Limited Group

**HarperCollins*Publishers***
25 Ryde Road, Pymble, Sydney NSW 2073, Australia
31 View Road, Glenfield, Auckland 10, New Zealand
77–85 Fulham Palace Road, London W6 8JB, United Kingdom
Hazelton Lanes, 55 Avenue Road, Suite 2900, Toronto, Ontario M5R 3L2
*and* 1995 Markham Road, Scarborough, Ontario M1B 5M8, Canada
10 East 53rd Street, New York NY 10032, USA

National Library of Australia Cataloguing-in-Publication data:

Solomon, Charmaine,
Charmaine Solomon's complete vegetarian cookbook.

Includes index.
ISBN 0 207 18436 4
1.Vegetarian cookery. 2.Cookery (vegetables).
I.Title. II.Title: Complete vegetarian cookbook.
614.5'636

Typeset in Goudy Oldstyle by Midland Typesetters Australia
Cover photograph by George Seper; photograph taken at 'The Banjo Paterson Cottage Restaurant'.
Printed in Singapore

9 8 7 6 5 4 3 2 1      95 96 97 98 99

# CHARMAINE SOLOMON

Charmaine Solomon is an international cookery writer whose books have won her popular acclaim in many parts of the world. Of her many cookbooks, she is especially well-known for her enduring classic, the *Complete Asian Cookbook*.

Her son's strict preference for vegetarian food inspired her to embark on the compilation of her favourite vegetarian recipes from all over the world. The result is the *Complete Vegetarian Cookbook*, a definitive book of vegetarian cuisine.

She believes that food should be fun, enjoyable and relaxing, and something you share with family and friends. 'One thing I know,' she says, 'life's too short to force down a meal you don't really enjoy. Perfecting and using these recipes, we relished every bite and if you cook with love and care, you will too.'

# CONTENTS

INTRODUCTION  viii

# WESTERN INFLUENCE

Entrees and Appetisers  2
Soups  55
Main Dishes  82
Complementary Dishes  132
Salads and Dressings  156
Desserts  188


# EASTERN INFLUENCE

Snacks and Appetisers  230
Soups  250
Asian Staple Dishes  259
Complementary Dishes  278
Accompaniments  349
Desserts  367


# EAST MEETS WEST

Breakfast and Brunch  378
Breads  396
Beverages  421
The Basics  435


GLOSSARY  457

INDEX  460

# INTRODUCTION

## A GUIDEBOOK FOR THE MIDDLE-OF-THE ROAD VEGETARIAN

Here is a book which doesn't go to extremes, a book anyone can enjoy cooking and eating from.

The recipes made it into this book for one reason—they are delicious, the sort of food you would be happy to serve family and guests. They just happen to be vegetarian.

Friends who have noticed my preference for vegetarian food have urged me to collect my recipes in a book. But that alone would not have made such a book a reality. It took an imaginative publisher who is aware that many people, even if not wholly vegetarian, are looking for a way of eating that does not rely on meat.

Vegetarian food has become fashionable. No longer are you considered the odd one out if you request a meal without meat. Big meat eaters are dwindling in number and, like smokers, finding themselves somewhat out of fashion. They have as much right as the next person to eat what pleases their tastebuds, but wouldn't it be great if they discovered that vegetarian food can be equally enjoyable.

This book is for everyone who loves cooking and eating good-tasting food. It is for "youngies" who have more awareness of the wisdom of eating low on the food chain; "oldies" who have been influenced by recent medical and nutritional advice; hosts and hostesses who find their guests are nibbling half-heartedly at meats and appreciating the vegetable accompaniments.

There are many schools of thought about how to combine foods, even for the non-vegetarian. One school is obsessed with getting enough protein, another says cut down on protein and get lots of complex carbohydrates, yet another says eat both but not at the same meal.

I won't buy into any of those arguments, being neither a dietitian nor a health fanatic. I'm not here to persuade you about anything except that, if you want to eat vegetarian, you can enjoy flavours you never dreamed of on a meat-and-three-veg way of eating. Want high protein dishes? They're here. Want others that don't combine protein with carbohydrates? They're here too. This really is a recipe book with something for everyone.

Eating raw fruits and vegetables has its following, but while enjoying some uncooked dishes (and you'll find many in these pages), I cannot banish from my life the free-wheeling creation of a recipe from whatever the marketing has yielded. There's the joy of stirring a pot and smelling the aromas which rise when onions and garlic are gently cooked in oil or butter, and the pleasure of seeing greens turn even greener when short-cooked just enough to make them tooth-tender. There is so much enjoyment in cooking the offerings of the garden (yours or someone else's), and producing meals which leave nothing to be desired by the most dedicated gourmets.

For someone who is timidly approaching vegetarian food and cannot imagine what to substitute for meat, be prepared to change your perception of what constitutes a meal. There does not have to be a great, hearty serving of something to take the place of the meat you're not having. A delightful and varied platter can be composed of various kinds of vegetables prepared in different ways. A small mound of tomato mousse, slices of raw marinated mushrooms, a timbale of spinach and leeks, a little celeriac remoulade. Flavours and textures contrasting and complementing, what a great way to eat!

There are, without apology, many international dishes—Indian, Chinese, Middle Eastern, Mexican. The reason is obvious. These cultures have depended on meatless meals for centuries, and it would be impossible, in a book that aims to present the whole gamut of vegetarian cooking, not to draw on such a rich source. Besides, more often than not, our vegetarian meals at home are Indian, Chinese or Thai—those being our favourite flavours.

But what governs me (and I hope will be your main guide too) are fruits, vegetables and herbs in season. I love to visit the markets, and the very sight of the bounty of the earth is an inspiration . . .

piles of green and purple artichokes, scarlet radishes, green avocados, shiny red, yellow and green capsicums (peppers), earthy potatoes, purple eggplants, the subtle pink of mushrooms, feathery dill, fragrant thyme, the pretty mauve flowers of chives, juicy apples, russet or green or yellow pears, perfumed peaches, velvety raspberries—what a feast of colour and texture! Buy seasonal vegetables and fruits, and build your meals around them. Become familiar with various grains too. These can be the mainstay of a meal and are filling and sustaining.

One thing I know. Life's too short to force down a meal you don't really enjoy. Perfecting and using these recipes, we relished every bite and if you cook with love and care, you will too. Happy cooking and eating!

# WESTERN
## INFLUENCE

# ENTREES & APPETISERS

Appetisers are ideal when entertaining, because most of them are finger food, can be eaten while standing talking and are absolutely perfect for serving to a sizable crowd.

On the other hand, I remember a wonderful meal I had in a restaurant in Versailles where one course was a selection of tiny tastes of vegetables prepared in various ways. Many of them could have been dips, but instead they had been prettily piped or spooned onto a dramatic black dinner plate, and I did enjoy the contrasting colours, flavours and textures. It is an idea worth copying.

Entrées. Now there's a word which bears examining. In Australia, Britain and Europe it denotes a light course preceding the main course. But in the United States it means the main course of the meal. Happily, the recipes in this chapter could fit into either category, because while I have chosen them with a first course in mind, there is absolutely nothing to prevent you serving them as a main course. They will yield fewer large servings, or may be served with a complementary dish or two for a very satisfying meal.

## FELAFEL

### INGREDIENTS

250 g (8 oz) dried chick peas

•

4 tablespoons cracked wheat (burghul or bulgur)

•

1 or 2 cloves garlic, crushed

•

2½ teaspoons salt

•

3 tablespoons wholemeal (whole wheat) flour

•

1 teaspoon ground cumin

•

1 teaspoon ground coriander

•

½ teaspoon ground black pepper

•

4 tablespoons finely chopped spring onions (scallions)

•

2 tablespoons finely chopped fresh coriander

•

1 tablespoon lemon juice

•

1 egg, beaten

•

oil, for deep-frying

Soak the chick peas in plenty of water overnight or preferably for 24 hours. Drain well and grind in a food processor. Soak the cracked wheat in cold water for 1 hour, squeeze out all moisture.

Combine all the ingredients, except oil, in a bowl. Mix thoroughly with the hands to a moulding consistency. If too moist, sprinkle in a very little more flour, and if it is too dry, add a little more beaten egg. Shape into walnut-sized balls.

Fry in hot, deep oil over medium heat for 5 minutes or until golden brown all over and cooked in the centre. Do not crowd them into the pan. Drain on absorbent paper and serve warm or at room temperature.

MAKES: about 30

# CREAMY CUCUMBER MOULDS

*An ideal first course if served in individual moulds with Melba toast. Or chill in a single mould, turn out and serve as a party dip, surrounded by crisp toast or crackers.*

### INGREDIENTS

1 cup (5 oz) diced cucumber

•

2 teaspoons gelatine

•

½ cup (4 fl oz) water

•

1½ teaspoons sugar

•

½ teaspoon salt

•

1 teaspoon cider vinegar

•

½ cup (4 fl oz) sour cream

•

2 tablespoons finely chopped pimiento

•

1 tablespoon chopped chives (optional)

Peel the cucumber, scoop out any seeds and finely dice enough cucumber to give 1 cup.

Sprinkle the gelatine over a tablespoon of water in a cup and leave for a few minutes to soften, then stand the cup in a saucepan of simmering water until the gelatine has completely dissolved. Alternatively, heat in a microwave oven for 30 seconds on full power. Cool to lukewarm then stir into the ½ cup water with sugar and vinegar. Chill until thick, then stir in the sour cream, cucumber, pimiento and chives. Pour into 4 individual *oeuf en gelée* moulds or other small moulds, and chill until set. Unmould onto plates, garnish with watercress or other fresh greens and serve with Melba toast.

SERVES: 4

# MUSHROOMS WITH TOMATO MOUSSE AND FRESH CORIANDER

### INGREDIENTS

250 g (8 oz) small, white button mushrooms

•

1 cup (8 fl oz) tomato purée

•

1 tablespoon tomato paste

•

2 teaspoons gelatine

•

¼ cup (2 fl oz) cold water

•

½ teaspoon hot pepper sauce or sweet chilli sauce

•

salt and white pepper to taste

•

few sprigs fresh coriander for garnish

Gently wipe mushrooms with a paper towel and remove stems with a little twist. Combine tomato purée with tomato paste, stirring to disperse tomato paste evenly. Sprinkle the gelatine over cold water and leave to soften, then dissolve over simmering water, or in a microwave. Mix into the tomato purée and add sauce and seasonings to taste. Chill until mixture starts to firm, then drop by small spoonfuls to fill mushroom caps. Decorate with coriander leaves and refrigerate.

NOTE: It is possible to substitute agar-agar (vegetable gelatine) in both recipes on this page. Use 1 teaspoon agar-agar powder in place of 2 teaspoons gelatine. Boil with the water to ensure it is dissolved, then stir quickly into the other ingredients as it sets almost immediately.

MAKES: about 25

# HUMMUS BI TAHINI

*This Lebanese chick pea dip with sesame paste will appeal to those who
like a tangy lemon flavour.*

## INGREDIENTS

250 g (8 oz) dried chick peas

•

½ cup (4 fl oz) lemon juice

•

3 large cloves garlic

•

1½ teaspoons salt, or to taste

•

½ cup (4 oz) tahini
(sesame seed paste)

•

olive oil

•

paprika or chopped parsley

Soak the chick peas overnight or for 24 hours in plenty of cold water to cover. Drain, put into saucepan or pressure cooker with fresh water and boil until soft enough to be mashed between the fingers, about 2 hours in a saucepan or 35 minutes under pressure. Drain peas, reserving liquid. Set aside a few whole peas for garnishing.

Purée chick peas in an electric blender or food mill, adding some of the cooking liquid if necessary. Mix in lemon juice and the garlic crushed with salt. Add tahini and mix well. Taste and add more lemon juice or salt if necessary— the flavour should be decidedly tangy with lemon and the consistency should be that of thick mayonnaise. If too thick, add a little water.

Spread on a plate, pour a little oil over the surface and garnish with reserved whole peas and a sprinkling of paprika or parsley.

SERVES: 6–8

# MUSHROOMS WITH GUACAMOLE

## INGREDIENTS

250g (8 oz) small, white button mushrooms

•

2 firm, ripe avocados

•

1 tablespoon finely chopped
white onion

•

1 tablespoon lemon juice

•

1 tablespoon finely chopped
fresh coriander

•

1 teaspoon finely chopped
chilli or hot chilli sauce,
optional

•

1 firm, red tomato,
peeled and seeded

Wipe over the mushrooms gently with a tissue, so the skins are not bruised, then remove stems with a little twist. These may be used in another dish. Peel and mash the avocados smoothly, then mix in the onion, lemon juice, coriander and chilli or sauce. Fill the mushrooms and garnish each one with a small triangle of tomato.

MAKES: about 25

## GUACAMOLE DIP

Make the avocado filling as for this recipe, but instead of using it to fill mushroom cups, mix in finely chopped tomato and serve it in a bowl with corn chips for dipping. Keep it closely covered with plastic to eliminate air, so the colour doesn't darken.

HUMMUS BI TAHINI

# CHEESE TRIANGLES

30 g (1 oz) butter

•

2 tablespoons flour

•

¾ cup (6 fl oz) milk

•

1 egg yolk

•

125 g (4 oz) feta cheese

•

90 g (3 oz) mature cheddar cheese

•

freshly ground pepper to taste

•

1 packet filo pastry

•

125 g (4 oz) butter, melted

Melt the butter and add the flour, stirring, over low heat for 1 minute. Whisk in the milk and cook the sauce for 2 minutes. Remove from the heat and add the egg yolk. In a medium-size bowl, place the crumbled or grated feta and cheddar cheese, then beat in the sauce. Season with freshly ground pepper to taste.

Take 12–15 sheets of filo pastry and put the rest away. Cover the pastry with dampened tea-towels to prevent drying out. Cut each sheet in half to give you a piece measuring approximately 24 × 30 cm (9½ × 12 in). Brush the centre third with melted butter and fold over the pastry on the left. Brush again with melted butter and fold over the pastry on the right, forming a strip approximately 8 cm (3¼ in) wide and 30 cm (12 in) long.

Brush lightly with butter and place a teaspoon of the cheese mixture on one end of the strip. Fold the corner over to enclose the mixture in a triangle. Continue to fold over and over, keeping the triangle shape, to the end of the strip. Place the pastry, seam side down, on a greased baking sheet.

Continue with the rest of the pastry until the filling is used up, then brush the tops of the triangles with melted butter. Bake in an oven preheated to 180°C (350°F) for 15 minutes or until golden. Serve while warm.

MAKES: about 25–30

# QUICK SAVOURIES

If friends are dropping in for a drink, serve easy savouries such as prunes filled with a piece of tasty (sharp) cheese and dab of fruit chutney.

If the vegetable crisper in the refrigerator holds such items as carrots, zucchini (courgettes), celery, or capsicums (peppers), cut them into thin strips and soak in iced water for 30 minutes or until crisp. Drain and dry the vegetable strips and serve with a dip, such as Pesto Dip (page 10), Skorthalia (page 12), or Savoury Cheese Dip (page 14).

# MUSHROOM CANAPÉS

Just about any filling goes with the delicate flavour of young mushrooms. Here are two which are particularly good.

Cream cheese, softened and spiced with a little mustard or horseradish cream (or bottled horseradish).

Cream cheese, softened and seasoned with pepper and salt, then given an extra lift with a few toasted cumin seeds. Toast the seeds in a dry pan, shaking the pan or stirring constantly, until the seeds are fragrant. Allow to cool.

Pipe or spoon the fillings into the hollows of small mushrooms which have had the stalks removed. Serve chilled.

# TOMATO AND MUSHROOM MINI QUICHES

*Surprise your guests with tasty appetisers. Party fare should be tempting.*

## INGREDIENTS

2 eggs

½ cup (4 fl oz) cream

60 g (2 oz) feta cheese, diced

½ cup (4 oz) cottage cheese

1½ cups (6 oz) grated cheddar cheese

1 tablespoon chopped parsley

¼ teaspoon black pepper

2 small, firm ripe tomatoes

2 teaspoons dried tarragon or basil

2 or 3 small mushrooms

garlic salt to taste

### PASTRY

1 cup (4 oz) wholemeal (whole wheat) flour

1 cup (3 oz) rolled oats

125 g (4 oz) butter

1 cup grated tasty (sharp) cheese

To make the pastry, put flour and rolled oats into food processor fitted with a steel blade and process for 30 seconds. Add butter, cut into pieces, and the grated cheese. Process until mixture forms a ball. Remove and wrap in plastic, chill for 20 minutes.

Meanwhile, prepare the topping. Lightly beat eggs and cream together and mix in the cheese, retaining 1 cup of the cheddar. Add parsley and pepper.

Roll out pastry between two sheets of plastic until thin. Cut out circles using a 7 cm (2¼ in) plain or fluted cutter. Place circles in lightly greased patty tins making sure there are no cracks in the pastry. Spoon 2 teaspoons of cheese filling into each pastry case. Top with a thin slice of tomato dusted with dried tarragon, which has been rubbed between the hands first to reduce it to a powder. Top with a few shreds of grated cheddar. Half the pies may be topped with a slice of fresh mushroom dusted with garlic salt before sprinkling with cheese.

Bake in an oven preheated to 190°C (375°F) for 12–15 minutes or until topping is puffed and golden and the pastry crisp. Serve warm or cold.

MAKES: about 36

# VINE LEAVES WITH RICE, CHICK PEAS AND CURRANTS

*If you have access to a grape vine, the fresh leaves are tender and delicious
in spring and early summer. You may also use leaves packed in brine.*

### INGREDIENTS

36 small, tender vine leaves and
a few large leaves for lining the pan

•

4 tablespoons olive oil

•

1 cup (5 oz) finely chopped onion

•

2 cloves garlic, finely chopped

•

¾ cup (5 oz) long grain rice

•

1¼ (10 fl oz) cups water

•

1 teaspoon salt

•

¼ teaspoon pepper

•

¼ teaspoon ground cinnamon
or mace

•

2 tablespoons currants or sultanas
(golden raisins)

•

2 tablespoons chopped parsley

•

1 cup cooked chick peas,
roughly mashed (3 oz dried)

•

approximately 1½ cups (12 fl oz)
water or stock

•

2 teaspoons tomato paste (optional)

•

few cubes of feta cheese for garnish

Pour boiling water over the leaves and allow to cool.

Meanwhile make the filling. Heat oil in a frying pan. Add the chopped onion and garlic to the oil and cook slowly, stirring, until it is pale gold. Add the rice and fry, stirring, for 2–3 minutes, then add the water, salt, pepper and cinnamon. Cover and cook on very low heat for 15 minutes, or until the rice is just tender. Cool slightly, mix in the currants or sultanas, parsley and chick peas.

Lay grape leaves one at a time, smooth side downward, on working surface. Pinch off any stems and place a spoonful of the filling near the site of the stem. Fold top of leaf over, then turn in both sides of leaf to enclose the filling. Continue to roll up to form a neat cylinder. Repeat until all leaves have been filled.

Line base of a heavy saucepan with large leaves and arrange the filled leaves in tightly packed rows. Pour over just enough stock to almost cover, dissolving the tomato paste in it first. Place a small plate on the rolls to stop them unwinding, then simmer very gently for 45–60 minutes, depending on size. Serve warm or cold and garnish with cubes of feta cheese.

SERVES: 6

# ONION TARTLETS

### INGREDIENTS

1 kg (2 lb) onions
•
4 tablespoons oil
•
1 tablespoon soy sauce
•
2 tablespoons tomato sauce
•
salt and pepper to taste
•
4 large eggs, beaten
•
1 cup (8 fl oz) pouring (light) cream
or evaporated milk

### PASTRY

3 cups plain (all-purpose) flour
•
¼ teaspoon baking powder
•
1 teaspoon salt
•
1 tablespoon caster (superfine) sugar
•
185 g (6 oz) butter
•
2 tablespoons lemon juice
•
approximately 6 tablespoons
iced water

To make the pastry, combine flour, baking powder, salt, sugar and butter in a food processor until the mixture resembles crumbs. Add lemon juice and water and process for a few seconds longer, until mixture forms a mass. Remove, knead lightly to form a ball, wrap and chill for 30 minutes. Meanwhile, to prepare the filling, peel and halve onions, then slice very finely. Heat oil in a heavy-based frying pan and fry onions, stirring frequently, until soft and golden brown. Add soy and tomato sauce, season to taste and mix well. Beat the eggs well, add the cream and a little salt and pepper.

Roll pastry out thinly and line small tartlet pans, lightly greased. Put a spoonful of the onion mixture in each one, then pour in a little beaten egg and cream mixture. Bake in an oven preheated to 220°C (425°F) until pastry is golden and the filling firm. Serve warm or cold.

MAKES: about 45

# LIMA BEAN PURÉE

*This is a versatile dish which can be served as a dip, a hot vegetable or cold as a companion to leafy salads—the flavour is so good you'll probably use it in more ways than one.*

### INGREDIENTS

375 g (12 oz) dried lima beans
•
10 whole black peppercorns
•
2 teaspoons salt
•
2 bay leaves
•
1 onion, peeled and quartered
•
2 cloves garlic, peeled and sliced
•
¼ cup (2 fl oz) olive oil
•
2 onions, finely chopped
•
2 cloves garlic, crushed
•
2 hot chillies, seeded
and chopped (optional)

Wash the dried beans well and soak overnight in plenty of water. If needed the same day, bring to a boil in a saucepan with water to cover by at least 3 cm (1¼ in). When they boil, turn off the heat, cover with a well fitting lid, and allow to soak for 2 hours. The beans may then be pressure cooked for 15 minutes or cooked in a saucepan with 4 cups (32 fl oz) fresh water, the peppercorns, salt, bay leaves, quartered onion and sliced garlic. When beans are very tender, remove from heat and drain off any excess liquid. Discard the bay leaves. For the simplest version, the beans may now be puréed in a blender with just enough olive oil to facilitate blending.

In a large saucepan, heat the olive oil and cook the chopped onions until soft and translucent. Add crushed garlic and the chillies and cook, stirring, for a further 1–2 minutes, then add the drained beans and stir well until mixed and partially mashed. Serve hot or at room temperature.

VARIATION: For a change, add 4 tablespoons of chopped fresh basil or 2 teaspoons ground cumin or 2 tablespoons tomato paste and 1 of sliced pimiento-stuffed olives.

SERVES: 6–8 (as part of a meal, many more as a party dip)

# PESTO DIP

*The wonderful herb flavour of pesto is too good to be confined to just a couple of dishes. Mix pesto with cream cheese or ricotta cheese, serve with fresh raw vegetables or grissini (Italian bread sticks).*

### INGREDIENTS

250 g (8 oz) ricotta cheese
•
½ cup (4 fl oz) Pesto Sauce
(see page 442)
•
salt and pepper to taste
•
¼ cup (1 oz) finely grated parmesan
cheese

Beat all ingredients together until smooth, or use a food processor. Turn into a bowl and chill until serving time.

MAKES: about 2 cups (16 fl oz)

# NUTTY NIBBLES

*Roasted nuts, salted nuts, smoked nuts—nuts of all kinds are just the thing to have around at a party, but it's so easy to eat too many. That's one reason for mixing the nuts with other not-so-rich items that are also crisp and delicious. Give the mixture exciting flavour with chilli and spice.*

### INGREDIENTS

¼ cup (2 fl oz) sunflower oil
•
1 cup (6 oz) roasted chick peas
(available at Greek delicatessens)
•
1 teaspoon salt
•
1 teaspoon ground cumin
•
1 teaspoon Garam Masala
(see page 456)
•
½ teaspoon chilli powder
or to taste
•
1 cup (5 oz) salted peanuts
•
1 cup (5 oz) salted cashews
•
4 cups (4 oz) rice bubbles
(puffed rice) or other crisp,
bite-size cereal (unsweetened)
•
1 cup (1 oz) potato straws (sticks)

Heat the oil in a wok or large, deep frying pan. Toss the roasted chick peas in the oil briefly. Turn off heat and add salt and spices to the oil.

Mix well, then add the nuts and cereal to the flavoured oil and toss well together. Taste and add extra salt and spices if liked. Stir in potato straws. Cool and store in an airtight container.

MAKES: 8 cups (20 oz)

# CHEESE PUFFS

*Easy, deliciously savoury, and all those odds and ends of cheese find a good home.*

### INGREDIENTS

2–3 cups (8–12 oz) finely
grated cheese
•
1 egg, beaten
•
1 teaspoon prepared mustard
•
pepper to taste
•
slightly stale sliced bread
•
butter or margarine

Put the cheese into a bowl and mix in just enough beaten egg to moisten. Stir in the mustard and seasoning. Trim crusts off bread, butter the slices, then spread thickly with the cheese mixture and cut with a sharp knife into triangles or fingers. Place on a baking tray and bake in an oven preheated to 190°C (375°F) until the cheese topping is puffed and golden. Serve warm.

MAKES: about 24 bite-size savouries

# SKORTHALIA

*This is a favourite Greek sauce for cooked vegetables, and it also makes
a robustly flavoured dip for raw vegetables served as an appetiser.*

### INGREDIENTS

3 thick slices stale white bread
•
3 cloves garlic
•
salt to taste
•
¼ teaspoon white pepper
•
2 tablespoons white vinegar
•
¹/₃ cup (3 fl oz) olive oil
•
½ cup (2 oz) walnut kernels

Trim crusts off bread and soak the slices in cold water for
10 minutes. Drain off water. Crush garlic with salt. Put
bread, garlic, pepper and vinegar into a food processor and
mix to a purée. With the motor running, add the olive
oil in a thin stream. Finally add the walnuts and process
for a few seconds. The sauce should be the consistency of
thick but runny cream. If necessary, add a little water or
lemon juice. Serve in bowls as a dip, or spoon it over fried
eggplant or other cooked vegetables.

# MUSHROOMS WITH CREAM CHEESE

### INGREDIENTS

250 g (8 oz) small, white
button mushrooms
•
125 g (4 oz) cream cheese
•
2 tablespoons finely chopped chives
•
salt and white pepper to taste
•
good squeeze lemon juice
•
1 teaspoon onion powder or
horseradish cream (bottled horseradish)
•
extra snipped chives for garnish

Wipe and prepare mushrooms as above. Soften cream cheese
at room temperature and beat until smooth. Add chives,
salt and pepper, lemon juice, onion powder or horseradish
cream, and mix well. Spoon into mushrooms, rounding the
tops neatly. Garnish with a sprinkling of snipped chives.
Cover and chill until serving time.

MAKES: about 25

PESTO DIP AND SKORTHALIA

# BLUE CHEESE LOG WITH WALNUTS

*This is ideal for a party, since a little goes a long way when spread on water crackers or Melba toast. If you don't need it all at one time, form half into a log and freeze, wrapped in foil. Thaw and roll in chopped walnuts to serve as part of a cheese board.*

### INGREDIENTS

100 g (3½ oz) blue vein cheese

•

100 g (3½ oz) cream cheese

•

2 tablespoons thick sour cream

•

1 tablespoon cognac (optional)

•

¾ cup (3 oz) chopped walnuts

Mash the cheese until smooth, add the cream cheese and sour cream and combine thoroughly. Stir in the cognac and form the cheese mixture into a cylinder.

Spread the finely chopped walnuts on a sheet of plastic or greaseproof paper. Place the cheese log on the nuts, then roll it over so the entire surface is coated. Press lightly to ensure the nuts stay on, cover with plastic wrap and chill until serving time. Remove from refrigerator 30 minutes before serving for cheese to come to room temperature and develop full flavour. Serve with water crackers or a home made crispbread like Lavosh (see page 401) broken in pieces.

MAKES: 1 medium or 2 small logs

# SAVOURY CHEESE DIP

*With a food processor, you can whip up this easy dip in minutes.*

### INGREDIENTS

250 g (8 oz) cottage cheese

•

2 tablespoons soft butter (optional)

•

1 teaspoon paprika

•

½ teaspoon caraway seeds

•

1 tablespoon chopped capers
or gherkin

•

1 teaspoon horseradish cream
(bottled horseradish) or mustard

•

½ teaspoon salt, or to taste

•

1 tablespoon finely chopped chives
or spring onion (scallion)

Put all ingredients except chives into a food processor and process until smooth and well mixed. This keeps well in the refrigerator for up to a week but add the onion-flavoured herbs on the day it is required.

MAKES: about 2 cups (16 fl oz)

# MUSHROOM AND CHEESE RAMEKINS

*A nice starter to a meal, or present them as a vegetarian main course,*
*accompanied by crusty wholemeal (whole wheat) rolls and a green salad.*

### INGREDIENTS

500 g (1 lb) fresh mushrooms

•

1 large onion, finely chopped

•

2 tablespoons butter

•

salt and freshly ground pepper
to taste

### CHEESE SAUCE

2 tablespoons butter

•

3 tablespoons flour

•

2 cups (16 fl oz) milk

•

2 cups (8 oz) grated mild cheddar
or Gruyère cheese

With a stainless steel knife, cut the mushrooms into fairly thick slices. Sauté the onion in butter until soft, then add the mushrooms and cook, stirring, for a few minutes until the mushrooms are also slightly soft. Season with salt and pepper and set aside while making sauce.

Melt the butter in a heavy-based saucepan, stir in the flour and cook, stirring constantly over low heat for 1 minute. Add the milk and whisk until smooth, then cook, stirring, until the sauce boils and thickens. Remove from heat and stir in the mushrooms and half the cheese. Taste and correct seasoning.

Divide the mixture between 4 individual ramekins, sprinkle remaining cheese on top and bake in an oven preheated to 180°C (350°F) just until cheese melts to a golden colour. Serve hot.

SERVES: 4

# CRISP SPICY TOAST

*These tasty morsels of toast are so more-ish one can keep eating a whole plateful.*

### INGREDIENTS

3 rounds of flat middle eastern bread

•

2 cloves garlic

•

1 teaspoon salt

•

1/3 cup (3 fl oz) olive oil

•

1 teaspoon paprika

•

2 teaspoons cumin seeds

•

2 tablespoons sesame seeds

With a pointed knife, slit the bread around the edges and gently pull apart so you have 6 very thin rounds instead of 3 double thickness loaves.

Crush the garlic with the salt on a wooden chopping board, pressing firmly with the flat of a knife until you have a smooth purée. Pour the olive oil into a shallow bowl or saucer and whisk in the garlic, salt and paprika. Brush the flavoured oil lightly over the inner surfaces of all the bread. Cut each circle into 8 or more wedges and place on flat baking trays. Sprinkle with the cumin and sesame seeds. Bake in an oven preheated to 160°C (325°F) until they are crisp and dry. Cool on a wire rack and store airtight until they are served.

SERVES: 6–8

# SPRING

*Fettucine tossed with butter and freshly grated parmesan is a classic Italian pasta dish which fits right into a vegetarian menu. Serve with a selection of vegetables and follow with a refreshingly lemony hot pudding.*

Fettucine Alfredo *page 84*

Green Beans with Mushrooms *page 138*

Tomatoes Provencale *page 154*

Sherry-glazed Carrots *page 151*

Lemon Delicious Pudding *page 212*

# SUMMER

*Depending on how hungry the crowd is that you're cooking for, serve ice-cold borsch either as a first course on its own or accompanied by freshly boiled potatoes.*

Mischa's Borsch *page 59*

Stuffed Cabbage Rolls *page 120*

Glazed Yams *page 152*

Raspberry Sherbet *page 216*

# MAKE-AHEAD MENUS

*Not only can this menu be made ahead and reheated before serving, it is also suitable for serving cold if the weather dictates.*

Carrot and Orange Soup *page 79*

Soft Pretzels *page 416*

Creamed Mushroom Roulade *page 18*

Green Salad or Braised Green Beans
*page 150*

Buttermilk Moulds *page 206*

*A very eclectic menu indeed, ending on a high note with a wonderful English pudding that is internationally popular.*

Cold Jellied Borsch *page 63*

Vine Leaves with Rice, Chick Peas and
Currants *page 8*

Orange Rice with Pinenuts *page 138*

Summer Pudding *page 208*

# CREAMED MUSHROOM ROULADE

*Like a Swiss roll but savoury instead of sweet, the roulade may be served
hot or cold. It even freezes well.*

## INGREDIENTS

60 g (2 oz) butter

•

½ cup (2 oz) plain (all-purpose) flour

•

2 cups (16 fl oz) milk

•

½ teaspoon salt

•

4 large eggs

### FILLING

1 cup (2 oz) finely chopped spring
onions (scallions)

•

1 tablespoon each of butter and oil

•

500 g (1 lb) finely sliced
button mushrooms
(if using larger mushrooms, dice them)

•

salt and white pepper to taste

•

60 g (2 oz) butter

•

3 tablespoons plain flour

•

1 cup (8 fl oz) milk

•

¼ cup (2 fl oz) cream

To make the roulade, melt the butter in a heavy-based saucepan over medium heat. Stir in all the flour and cook for 1–2 minutes stirring constantly, and not letting the mixture brown. Add milk and salt, and whisk constantly over heat until the mixture comes to the boil and becomes smooth and thick. Remove pan from heat. Separate the yolks from the whites of the eggs and beat the yolks into the hot mixture one at a time.

Prepare a Swiss roll (jelly roll) tin 25 × 37.5 cm (10 × 15 in), lining it with oiled baking paper. Alternatively, brush pan with oil, then line with oiled greaseproof paper. Sprinkle lightly with flour, shake to coat paper, then tip out excess flour.

In a clean, dry bowl whisk the egg whites until stiff and stir a quarter into the yolk mixture to lighten it. Gently fold in the rest of the whites.

Spread mixture into the prepared tin and bake in an oven preheated to 180°C (350°F) for 45 minutes or until well risen and golden. The top should be firm when touched lightly with a fingertip. Remove from oven, turn out onto a sheet of baking or greaseproof paper and quickly trim off edges with a sharp knife.

To make the filling, sauté the spring onions in butter and oil over low heat until soft but not brown. Add the mushrooms and cook, stirring, until soft. Add salt and pepper to taste. Set aside while making cream sauce.

Melt butter in a saucepan, stir in flour and cook over medium heat for 1–2 minutes, then briskly stir while adding milk and cream. Cook, stirring, until the sauce boils and is thick and smooth. Add salt and pepper to taste, then mix the mushrooms into the sauce.

To assemble, spread the roulade with the creamed mushroom filling and roll up lengthways as for a Swiss roll, using the paper to lift the roulade over the filling. Place on serving dish with the seam underneath. Allow to cool, or serve warm.

SERVES: 6–8

# BOILED ARTICHOKES

Buy artichokes which look good—fresh and green with no withered, leathery looking leaves. Some people go to a lot of trouble snipping off the end of each petal and slicing off the top of the artichoke but this isn't strictly necessary and it looks prettier as is.

If you decide to trim the artichokes, have a bowl of water with the juice of a lemon in it (or a good splash of vinegar) to drop the vegetable in and stop it discolouring. Or rub over with a cut lemon.

Use only a stainless steel knife as other metals can turn the cut surface black. Wash artichokes well, plunging them up and down in cold water.

Bring a saucepan of salted water to the boil and drop in the artichokes. When the water returns to the boil, turn the heat lower and simmer, covered, for about 40 minutes or until tender. You can tell by tugging on a leaf; if it comes off easily, the artichoke is ready.

Most important, don't leave the artichokes sitting in the water but drain them immediately, turned upside down in a colander so the water runs out. A soggy artichoke has no charm.

Serve warm or cold with Hollandaise Sauce (see page 440) or melted butter. I like to mix lemon juice with the melted butter.

# SPICED MUSHROOMS AND EGGS

*This quickly made meal has a few curry spices in it but is not a curry.*

### INGREDIENTS

2 tablespoons oil
•
1 onion, finely sliced
•
1 teaspoon crushed garlic
•
1 teaspoon finely grated ginger
•
2 teaspoons ground coriander
•
1 teaspoon ground cumin
•
½ teaspoon turmeric
•
½ teaspoon chilli powder, optional
•
250 g (8 oz) mushrooms, sliced
•
2 teaspoons tomato paste dissolved
in ¾ cup (6 fl oz) hot water
•
freshly ground pepper and
salt to taste
•
4 small eggs

Heat the oil in a wok (if using a frying pan slightly more oil will be needed) and fry the onion, garlic and ginger until soft. Add spices and fry again, stirring constantly, for 4–5 minutes.

Add the mushrooms and toss with spice mixture, then add the tomato paste, pepper and salt. Cover and cook for 8–10 minutes, stirring once or twice. With the back of a spoon, make indentations in the mushroom mixture and break in the eggs. Cover and simmer on low heat for a further 8 minutes or until the eggs are cooked as you like them. Serve with Chapatis (see page 398) or rice.

SERVES: 4

# CAULIFLOWER IN GREEN SAUCE

## INGREDIENTS

1 cauliflower, steamed
•
60 g (2 oz) butter
•
1 cup (1½ oz) finely shredded green leaves
of leek or spring onion (scallion)
•
2 cups (12 oz) frozen peas
•
1 sprig fresh mint
•
½ teaspoon sugar
•
salt and pepper to taste
•
buttered crumbs (optional)

The easiest way to steam a cauliflower, I find, is in about a cupful of water in a wok. Cut a few slits in the stem so it will become tender in the same length of time as the flower. Bring the water to a boil and place the cauliflower in it, cover and cook for 10 minutes. The wide, open shape of the wok enables it to be lifted out easily, without breaking.

Meanwhile, melt the butter in a heavy-based pan and cook the leek or onion leaves gently until soft. Add the peas, mint, sugar and seasonings and cook, covered, for 7–8 minutes. Push through a sieve or purée in a blender, adding a little milk or cream to facilitate blending. Reheat and spoon over the well drained cauliflower in a serving dish. Serve hot.

Pass a small bowl of fresh breadcrumbs fried in butter until crisp and golden, to be sprinkled over if desired.

SERVES: 6

# MUSHROOM PUFFS

*Few recipes could be simpler or prepared in shorter time. This quantity makes two individual soufflé dishes and is perfect for a light lunch or supper.*

## INGREDIENTS

1 medium onion
•
2 cloves garlic
•
60 g (2 oz) butter
•
250 g (8 oz) mushrooms
•
salt and freshly ground black pepper to taste
•
2 slices wholegrain bread
•
2 large eggs
•
½ cup (4 fl oz) milk

Peel and finely chop onion and garlic. In a stainless steel or enamel saucepan, melt the butter, add onion and garlic and cook over low heat until soft and translucent.

Meanwhile, dice the mushrooms. Toss them into the pan and stir over medium high heat for 2 minutes, or until they are soft. Season to taste with a good grinding each of sea salt and black pepper.

Trim the crust from the bread and cut into small dice. Beat the eggs briskly, stir in the milk, and leave the diced bread to soak in the mixture for 10 minutes.

Add the mushroom mixture and mix well, adjust seasoning, then divide between two buttered soufflé dishes. Bake in an oven preheated to 190°C (375°F) for 25–30 minutes or until well puffed, golden brown and firm to the touch. Serve warm, accompanied by a green salad.

SERVES: 2

CAULIFLOWER IN GREEN SAUCE

# VEGETABLE SPAGHETTI CHEESE

*Have you seen or tasted vegetable spaghetti, or spaghetti squash as this unusual vegetable is called? When the pale yellow squash is cooked, the flesh separates into crisp strands of what looks very much like spaghetti, hence its name. Like all members of the squash or marrow family, it does need some added flavour.*

### INGREDIENTS

400–500 g (about 1 lb) cooked
vegetable spaghetti
(spaghetti squash)
•
2 large eggs, beaten
•
½ cup (4 fl oz) milk
•
salt and pepper to taste
•
3 tablespoons finely grated
Romano or parmesan cheese
•
100 g (3½ oz) grated cheddar cheese

Combine all the ingredients in a bowl, reserving about ½ cup (2 oz) of the grated cheddar for topping. Put into a lightly buttered ovenproof dish, sprinkle with the reserved cheddar and bake in an oven preheated to 180°C (350°F) for 25 minutes or until golden brown on top. Serve warm with a tossed green salad.

SERVES: 4

# MUSHROOM SCALLOP

### INGREDIENTS

250 g (8 oz) mushrooms
•
500 g (1 lb) potatoes
•
60 g (2 oz) butter
•
salt and pepper to taste
•
1½ cups (12 fl oz) hot milk
•
2 eggs
•
nutmeg
•
½ cup (2 oz) dry breadcrumbs

Wipe mushrooms with a damp paper towel and slice thickly. It is not necessary to wash mushrooms, a lot of flavour and food value is lost. Peel potatoes and slice thinly. Butter a large, flat ovenproof dish with a little of the butter and arrange a layer of potato slices, then a layer of mushroom slices, seasoning each layer lightly. Finish with a layer of potatoes.

Combine milk, eggs and seasonings, and pour over. There should be just enough liquid to show through the top layer. Dot rest of the butter over the top and bake in an oven preheated to 190°C (375°F) for an hour or until potatoes are cooked and the top is light brown.

The dish may be given a crusty finish by adding half a cup each of breadcrumbs and grated cheese before dotting the butter over.

SERVES: 4

# SPINATSPATZLE

*Spatzle is a cross between pasta and dumplings, and originated, I believe, in Austria. Don't be put off by the fact that the mixture has to be pushed through a perforated spoon into boiling water. Once a rhythm has been established, the cooking is really no trouble.*

## INGREDIENTS

1 bunch English (flat) spinach

•

½ cup (4 fl oz) milk

•

3 eggs, beaten

•

1¼ cups (5 oz) plain (all-purpose) flour

•

½ teaspoon salt

•

100 g (3½ oz) coarsely grated Emmenthal cheese

•

3 tablespoons finely grated parmesan cheese

### SAUCE

30 g (1 oz) butter

•

1 onion, finely chopped

•

1 stalk celery, finely chopped

•

150 ml (5 fl oz) dry white wine

•

150 ml (5 fl oz) cream

•

½ teaspoon salt

•

¼ teaspoon white pepper

•

¼ teaspoon grated nutmeg

Wash the spinach thoroughly, discard stems and cook the leaves in lightly salted, boiling water for 3 minutes or until softened and a brilliant green. Lift out and plunge into cold water to refresh. Drain off water and put the spinach into an electric blender. Blend to a smooth purée, then measure out 200 ml (6½ fl oz).

Mix the milk with the beaten eggs. Put flour into a large bowl and add the milk, eggs, spinach and salt. Beat the batter until smooth and of a thick dropping consistency. Set the batter aside.

Bring a large amount of lightly salted water to the boil. Make the spatzle by pushing the spinach mixture through a spoon or other utensil with perforations, into the boiling water. I found a potato masher to have the ideal size holes.

Cook about half a cup of mixture at a time. The little spatzle will float to the surface of the water when they are ready. Skim them out on another perforated spoon and drop into a bowl of cold water. It may sound difficult, but it isn't and once you get into a rhythm the whole operation takes just minutes. Continue until all the mixture has been cooked. Drain in a colander and shake to get rid of as much of the water as possible.

To make the sauce, melt the butter in a heavy-based saucepan and cook the onion and celery until soft and translucent. Add the wine and cream and cook, stirring frequently, until it has reduced by one third. Stir in salt, pepper and nutmeg. Reserve.

Reheat the spatzle in the sauce, then spoon into an ovenproof dish or individual dishes. Sprinkle cheese over the top and bake in an oven preheated to 200°C (400°F) for 15 minutes or place under a preheated grill (broiler) until heated through and the cheese has melted. Serve hot.

SERVES: 4 as a main dish, 6 as a first course

# ASPARAGUS WITH POLONAISE SAUCE

*Polonaise sauce is simply browned butter with breadcrumbs crisped in it,*
*but it dresses up cooked vegetables like you wouldn't believe.*

## INGREDIENTS

2 bundles fresh asparagus
(about 500 g or 1 lb)
•
salt and pepper to taste
•
2 hard-boiled eggs
•
60 g (2 oz) butter
•
4 tablespoons fresh breadcrumbs

Prepare the asparagus, snapping off tough ends of stems and peeling the bottom half of the stalks. Wash well. Sometimes there is fine sand lurking in the tips.

In a pan large enough to accommodate the spears lying down, bring to the boil enough lightly salted water to cover the asparagus. Drop in the spears, and cover the pan to bring water back to the boil quickly, then uncover and simmer until just tender. (Cooking greens uncovered helps keep the colour bright.)

Drain well, season to taste, then serve sprinkled with finely chopped hard-boiled eggs (some people prefer just the yolk, pushed through a sieve). Heat the butter until nut brown, then quickly fry the breadcrumbs and sprinkle over the asparagus.

SERVES: 4

# TOASTED MUSHROOM SANDWICHES

## INGREDIENTS

250 g (8 oz) mushrooms
•
30 g (1 oz) butter
•
1 small onion, finely chopped
•
salt and freshly ground pepper
to taste
•
butter for spreading
•
4 slices wholegrain bread
•
4 slices cheese
•
1 small avocado, peeled and sliced

Wipe over the mushrooms and slice. Melt the butter in a heavy-based pan and cook the onion over low heat until soft and translucent. Add the mushrooms, stir and cook over medium heat until soft. Season with salt and pepper, and allow to cool slightly.

Butter slices of bread on one side and place under preheated griller (broiler) until golden. Turn slices over, spread cooked mushrooms on two of the slices and cheese on the other two. Grill (broil) to heat the filling and melt the cheese. Place slices of avocado on the mushrooms and top with the grilled cheese slice. Remove to heated plates and cut each sandwich diagonally.

SERVES: 2

ASPARAGUS WITH POLONAISE SAUCE

# RAINBOW LAYER CRÊPES

*A colourful combination of wholemeal (whole wheat) crêpes with varied vegetable fillings. This stack of savoury crêpes would make an elegant entrée or star as the main dish for a light meal.*

## INGREDIENTS

### CRÊPES

1 egg

•

½ cup (4 fl oz) water

•

¾ cup (2 fl oz) milk

•

1 cup (4 oz) fine wholemeal (whole wheat) flour

•

¼ teaspoon salt

•

1 teaspoon oil or melted butter

### CAPSICUM LAYER

1 large or 2 small red capsicums (peppers)

•

1 tablespoon oil

•

1½ cups (12 fl oz) Pizzaiola Sauce (see page 441)

### ZUCCHINI LAYER

750 g (1½ lb) dark green zucchini (courgettes)

•

½ teaspoon salt

•

2 tablespoons oil or butter

•

1 onion, finely chopped

•

1 cup cooked, drained spinach (12 oz uncooked)

•

pepper to taste

### EGGPLANT LAYER

500 g (1 lb) eggplant (aubergine)

•

1 tablespoon olive oil

•

1 onion, finely chopped

•

1 teaspoon finely chopped garlic

To make the crêpes, combine egg, water, milk, flour and salt in electric blender or whisk together in a bowl until smooth. Stir in oil or melted butter. Strain, cover and set aside for at least 30 minutes, then stir well before starting to cook the crêpes. If batter thickens too much to flow easily over pan, add a little extra milk or water. Heat a heavy crêpe pan, rub surface with a little butter or oil, then pour in just enough to cover pan base, swirling the pan to spread mixture evenly. Cook until golden brown underneath. Turn the crêpe and cook the other side briefly. Flip onto a plate. Continue until all the crêpes are made. You will need 6 for this dish.

Capsicum layer: Reserve one section of a capsicum for garnish and finely chop the rest, removing seeds. On low heat, sauté the capsicum in oil until soft. Add the pizzaiola sauce and cook, uncovered, until very thick. Serve extra sauce alongside if desired.

Zucchini layer: Wash and trim the ends of the zucchini. Slice one finely, blanch in boiling water for 1 minute, drain and refresh in cold water. Set aside for garnishing. Grate the remaining zucchini coarsely, sprinkle with salt, mix well and leave aside at least 20 minutes for excess liquid to drain out. Squeeze firmly in both hands to eliminate as much liquid as possible. In a heavy-based saucepan, heat oil and fry chopped onion until soft and golden. Add the zucchini and stir over medium high heat until fairly dry. Add the finely chopped spinach and mix well, season to taste.

Eggplant layer: Wash the eggplant but do not peel, then roast in a hot oven until soft. Heat 1 tablespoon oil and cook the onion and garlic over low heat until soft, translucent and starting to turn golden. Peel the eggplant and add the flesh to the pan with the onions. Add salt and pepper to taste, the finely diced potato and hot water. Stir, cover and cook until potato is soft. If necessary, add a little extra hot water but cook until all liquid has evaporated and the mixture forms a thick, dry purée.

To assemble, place one of the crêpes on a platter and spread with a layer of capsicum filling, taking it right to

salt and pepper to taste

•

1 small potato, finely diced

•

½ cup (4 fl oz) hot water

the edges. Cover with another crêpe and spread that with a layer of zucchini, then cover it with the next crêpe. Spread with a layer of eggplant filling. Repeat the first two layers, cover with a crêpe, and garnish the top with blanched zucchini slices and red capsicum slices. Cut in wedges to serve.

SERVES: 6–8

# CARROT AND CAULIFLOWER TIMBALES

*Made with cream, this is a rich and delicious timbale, yet light in texture. If weight or other considerations get in the way of your enjoying the dish, simply substitute non-fat evaporated milk. Another benefit is that this dish cooks equally successfully in a microwave oven. Serve on its own as a first course, or as part of a variety of vegetables as a main meal.*

## INGREDIENTS

CAULIFLOWER MIXTURE

250 g (8 oz) trimmed cauliflower florets

•

200 ml (6½ fl oz) cream

•

1 egg, beaten

•

⅛ teaspoon nutmeg

•

⅛ teaspoon white pepper

•

½ teaspoon salt

CARROT MIXTURE

100 g (3½ oz) carrot, cooked

•

1 small beet, cooked

•

1 egg, beaten

•

2 tablespoons cream

•

¼ teaspoon salt

•

pepper to taste

Wash, drain and trim the cauliflower, then put into a saucepan with the cream. Cook, uncovered, over low heat until the cauliflower is tender. Cool, then purée in a blender with the remaining ingredients. Purée the ingredients together for the carrot mixture.

Grease timbale moulds with melted butter or oil, and line bases with greaseproof paper. Fill moulds by first placing a teaspoonful of carrot mixture in the base and carefully spooning the cauliflower mixture over and around.

Place timbales in a baking dish with hot water to reach halfway up the sides of the moulds, and cook in an oven preheated to 180°C (350°F) for 20–25 minutes or until just firm when lightly touched. Remove from water bath and let stand for 5 minutes, then run a knife around the edge and turn out. Remove greaseproof paper and garnish with a sprig of fresh coriander. Serve warm or cold with very thin Melba toast.

NOTE: If cooking in a microwave oven, arrange mixture in china ramekins, and place the timbales at equal distance around the turntable. Cook on 30 per cent power for 8 minutes, then let the timbales stand for 3 minutes before turning out. This timing applies to a 700 watt oven. For ovens of lesser or greater power, adjust timing accordingly.

MAKES: 6–8 timbales

# LEEK AND SILVERBEET (SWISS CHARD) SOUFFLÉ

*Silverbeet is sometimes called spinach but is actually what is known as Swiss chard in some countries. It is much coarser than spinach, but can be combined with other vegetables to advantage, as in this unmoulded soufflé.*

### INGREDIENTS

1 bunch silverbeet (Swiss chard)

•

2 large leeks

•

60 g (2 oz) butter

•

1 tablespoon oil

•

2 tablespoons flour

•

¾ cup (6 fl oz) milk

•

3 eggs, separated

•

salt and pepper to taste

•

½ cup (4 fl oz) cream

•

½ cup (4 fl oz) tomato purée

•

½ cup (2 oz) finely grated parmesan cheese

Wash the silverbeet thoroughly in several changes of cold water. With a sharp knife, strip the leaves off the centre ribs. (The ribs may be steamed and served with melted butter or a cheese sauce.) Put the leaves into a large, stainless steel pot with the water that clings to them, cover and cook on low heat for 10 minutes, or until wilted. Drain thoroughly. When cool, press out excess moisture, chop leaves finely and measure out 1 cup, about 3 oz.

Wash the leeks, then slice finely, using only the white portion. Heat half the butter with the oil in a heavy-based saucepan. Add the leeks, stir well, then cover and cook on very low heat, stirring occasionally, for 12–15 minutes, or until tender. They should not brown. Cool.

Make the soufflé base, which is simply a thick white sauce with eggs added. Melt the remaining butter in a heavy-based saucepan, then sprinkle in the flour and cook over low heat, stirring constantly, for 2 minutes. Add the milk and whisk until the sauce boils and thickens. Remove from the heat and add the egg yolks one at a time to the sauce, whisking well. Mix in the leeks and the silverbeet, then add salt and pepper to taste.

Generously butter a ring mould with about a 4 cup (32 fl oz) capacity. Whisk the egg whites until stiff, then stir in a third to lighten the sauce and vegetable mixture. Gently fold in the remaining two-thirds of the egg whites. Spoon the mixture into the mould, stand it in a roasting tin and place on the oven shelf, then pour in enough hot water to come halfway up the sides of the mould. Bake in an oven preheated to 180°C (350°F) for 25 minutes, or until well risen and firm.

Remove from oven, allow to cool for 15 minutes, then unmould onto a shallow baking dish. Turn oven temperature to 220°C (425°F). Combine the cream with the tomato purée and half the cheese, then pour it over the soufflé. Sprinkle with remaining cheese and return to the oven for 15 minutes, or until golden brown. Serve hot.

SERVES: 6

CARROT AND CAULIFLOWER TIMBALES

# SPINACH AND LEEK TIMBALES

## INGREDIENTS

1 bunch spinach

•

1 large leek

•

1 tablespoon oil

•

1 tablespoon butter

•

½ teaspoon white pepper

•

½ teaspoon salt

•

¼ teaspoon nutmeg

•

3 eggs

•

½ cup (4 fl oz) cream

•

pimiento strips for garnish

## PUMPKIN PURÉE
500 g (1 lb) pumpkin

•

2 teaspoons butter, optional

•

salt, pepper and nutmeg to season

## CAPSICUM PURÉE
2 or 3 large red capsicums (peppers)

•

salt and pepper to taste

Wash spinach well in several changes of cold water. Remove stems and choose 4 large leaves for lining the moulds. Bring a large pan of water to the boil, blanch the 4 leaves for 1 minute, then remove from water and drop into cold water. Carefully line four oiled individual ramekins, allowing the ends of the leaves to hang over the side. Cook the rest of the leaves for 3 minutes and drain well.

Slit the leek lengthways and wash under cold running water, making sure any sand or grit is rinsed away. Slice very thinly. Heat the oil and butter, and cook the leek until soft but not brown, stirring frequently. Remove from heat. Squeeze spinach to rid it of excess moisture, chop and mix into the leeks. Add pepper, salt and nutmeg, and purée in a food processor or with a hand-held blender wand.

Beat the eggs, add the cream and stir into the vegetable purée. Spoon the mixture into the leaf-lined ramekins and cover with the overhanging portion of the spinach leaves. Place in a baking dish with hot water to come halfway up the sides of the ramekins. Bake in an oven preheated to 160°C (325°F) for about 25 minutes or until set.

Meanwhile, make the pumpkin purée. Peel and slice the pumpkin and cook until tender, then purée with butter until smooth and season to taste. For the capsicum purée, grill capsicums until skins are blistered all over. Put into a paper bag or cover with foil and leave until cool, then peel off the thin, tough skin and discard the seeds and stems, saving any juices from inside the capsicums. Push through a sieve or whiz in a blender to make a smooth purée.

Allow timbales to cool slightly, then unmould and garnish with strips of pimiento. Spoon pumpkin and capsicum purée around each mould.

SERVES: 4

# SEMOLINA GNOCCHI

*Crusty on the surface and creamy within, this savoury semolina and cheese dish becomes a favourite with everyone. Serve as a light meal or as an entrée.*

### INGREDIENTS

2½ cups (20 fl oz) milk

•

1 onion, peeled

•

1 bay leaf

•

½ teaspoon salt

•

¼ teaspoon white pepper

•

½ cup (3 oz) semolina

•

1 egg, beaten

•

¾ cup (3 oz) grated parmesan cheese

•

30 g (1 oz) butter

Put the milk, onion, bay leaf, salt and pepper into a saucepan and place over very low heat. Bring to simmering point to infuse milk with the flavours, then remove the onion and stir in the semolina. Cook, stirring constantly for 10–15 minutes until thick. Remove from heat and beat in the egg and ½ cup (2 oz) of the parmesan cheese. Pour into a greased flat dish and spread to 1 cm (¼ in) thickness. Cool completely.

Cut rounds or squares or, if you want a fancy effect, use a heart-shaped cutter. Put all the leftover pieces at the bottom of a shallow, well-buttered heatproof dish and arrange the nicely shaped pieces on top, overlapping slightly. Dot with the butter and sprinkle with remaining ¼ cup (1 oz) of cheese. Place under griller (broiler) to heat through, then bring closer to the griller or increase heat until bubbling and golden brown on top. Serve hot.

SERVES: 6

# GRILLED MUSHROOMS WITH GARLIC CRUMBS

### INGREDIENTS

18 medium-sized mushrooms

•

1 large clove garlic

•

½ teaspoon salt

•

60 g (2 oz) butter

•

½ cup (2 oz) coarsely chopped pecans or unblanched almonds

•

2 cups (4 oz) loosely packed fresh breadcrumbs

•

4 tablespoons chopped parsley

•

freshly ground black pepper to taste

Wipe over the mushrooms, remove stems and chop them finely. Crush garlic with salt. In a frying pan, melt the butter and cook the mushroom stems for a minute, stirring. Add the garlic and cook for a minute longer. Add chopped pecans and stir over moderate heat until they are golden. Remove from heat and stir in the breadcrumbs and parsley, mixing well. Add freshly ground pepper to taste.

Fill the mushroom caps, pressing the mixture in firmly. Place in a well buttered baking dish and bake in an oven preheated to 200°C (400°F) for 20 minutes or until filling is crisp and golden on top.

SERVES: 6

# TOMATOES WITH GARLIC CROÛTON FILLING

## INGREDIENTS

6 firm ripe tomatoes

•

salt

•

5 tablespoons olive oil

•

1 large clove garlic, bruised

•

1 cup (2 oz) diced wholemeal
(whole wheat) bread

•

1 cup (2 oz) soft wholemeal
(whole wheat) breadcrumbs

•

2 tablespoons finely chopped parsley

•

2 teaspoons chopped fresh
oregano or marjoram

•

½ cup (2 oz) finely grated parmesan
cheese

•

freshly ground black pepper

Cut off the stem ends of the tomatoes and, with a teaspoon, scoop out the pulp and seeds. (The pulp may be added to a sauce or soup but the seeds should be discarded.) Sprinkle cavities lightly with salt and turn the tomatoes, cut-side down, to drain for about 15 minutes.

Heat 3 tablespoons of the olive oil in a frying pan and on low heat, fry the clove of garlic to flavour the oil. (For a strong garlic flavour, peel and crush the clove instead of merely bruising it.) Fry the diced bread, stirring constantly, until golden brown. Remove to a paper towel and leave until cool and crisp. Add remaining 2 tablespoons of oil to the pan and toss the breadcrumbs in it. Remove from the heat and stir in the chopped herbs and the Parmesan cheese. Season to taste with freshly ground pepper. Combine with the garlic croûtons and lightly pack into the centre of each tomato. Place in an oiled ovenproof dish and bake in an oven preheated to 190°C (375°F) for about 20 minutes or until top of filling is browned and crisp. Serve warm.

SERVES: 6

# ARTICHOKE STRUDEL

*An elegant and delicious dish to serve at a dinner party.*

## INGREDIENTS

1 × 400 g (13 oz) can artichoke hearts

•

1 cup (8 oz) cottage cheese

•

1 cup (4 oz) freshly grated parmesan
cheese

•

1 egg

•

½ cup (3 oz) finely sliced spring
onions (scallions)

•

¼ cup (2 oz) chopped red
capsicum (pepper)

Drain the artichokes and pat dry on paper towels. Cut each artichoke into quarters. Combine with both kinds of cheese, egg, onions, capsicum, breadcrumbs, tarragon and pepper. Mix well.

Lay a sheet of filo pastry on a work surface, brush lightly with melted butter and cover with another sheet of pastry. Continue until all the pastry has been used.

Place filling on the pastry, starting 8 cm (3¼ in) from one of the short ends and leaving 2.5 cm (1 in) on each side. Fold the pastry over at the starting point and turn the sides in over the filling. Roll up like a Swiss roll (jelly roll). Brush top with melted butter and place on a baking tray with the join underneath. Bake in an oven preheated

¼ cup (½ oz) fresh white breadcrumbs

•

1 teaspoon dried tarragon leaves

•

½ teaspoon freshly ground black pepper

•

6 sheets filo pastry

•

60 g (2 oz) butter, melted

to 200°C (400°F) for 20–25 minutes or until golden brown. Allow to stand 5 minutes before cutting into thick slices.

SERVES: 6

ARTICHOKE STRUDEL

# CAMEMBERT IN PORT WITH GREEN PEPPERCORNS

*When eating soft, ripe cheeses like camembert and brie, timing is of the utmost importance. Too young and they're firm and chalky in the centre, with not much flavour; too old and they're strong enough to knock you over. Observe the "use by" date, and eat the cheese as close to this time as possible, but test the cheese for ripeness yourself. It should feel tender and springy when gently pressed, should not be shrunken or smell of ammonia. The crust should be creamy white and is perfectly edible.*
*I wouldn't do anything to a really splendid camembert in its prime, but this treatment improves a cheese that is perhaps a little too young or too old.*

## INGREDIENTS

1 small camembert
•
approximately ¼ cup (2 fl oz) port
•
125 g (4 oz) softened cream cheese
•
1 teaspoon green peppercorns
in brine
•
½ cup (2 oz) flaked, toasted almonds

Cut the camembert into wedges, place in a small bowl and pour port wine over to cover the cheese. Cover bowl tightly with plastic wrap and leave to soak in the refrigerator for 8 hours or overnight.

Lift the camembert out of the port and mash it with a fork on a flat plate. Mix in the cream cheese and then fold in the green peppercorns. Shape once again into the flat round shape typical of camembert cheese. Coat the surface with lightly browned flaked almonds, cover with plastic wrap and refrigerate until needed. Serve with plain biscuits.

SERVES: 8

# STUFFED ARTICHOKES

*The first time I saw artichokes receive the full treatment, a good Italian cook was lovingly preparing them, her nimble fingers tucking a little bit of the filling between each petal.*

## INGREDIENTS

6 large artichokes
•
2 cups (8 oz) finely grated parmesan
and pecorino cheese in equal parts
•
1½ cups (6 oz) fine dry breadcrumbs
•
½ teaspoon salt
•
½ teaspoon freshly ground
black pepper
•

Wash the artichokes in cold water, shake off water and turn upside down to drain. Combine cheese, breadcrumbs, salt, pepper and parsley and, starting at the outer edge, fill the artichoke.

Gently pull petals outward and in the hollow of each, put about half a teaspoon of the stuffing. If you have removed the inner petals and choke, it is possible to put a good spoonful of the mixture in the centre, otherwise stop when you reach the tightly packed centre and sprinkle a spoonful of mixture over.

½ cup (1 oz) finely chopped parsley

•

2 tablespoons olive oil

•

2 large ripe tomatoes

Place the artichokes in a stainless steel or enamel saucepan just large enough to hold them comfortably, and pour in 2 cm (¾ in) water. Add salt, a tablespoon of olive oil and a little chopped garlic if liked and tomatoes. Bring to the boil, then turn heat low, cover tightly and simmer for 35–45 minutes depending on the size of the artichokes. When a petal comes away easily, they are done. Lift out with a slotted spoon and serve warm or at room temperature.

SERVES: 6

# BUCKWHEAT CRÊPES WITH CREAMED LEEKS

*The special flavour of buckwheat crêpes will make this a favourite. Other vegetables in season may be used instead of leeks.*

### INGREDIENTS

2 eggs

•

½ cup (4 fl oz) water

•

½ cup (4 fl oz) milk

•

¼ cup (1 oz) buckwheat flour

•

¼ cup (1 oz) plain (all-purpose) flour

•

¼ teaspoon salt

•

1 tablespoon melted butter

•

sour cream and chives for garnishing

### FILLING

2 large leeks

•

30 g (1 oz) butter

•

2 tablespoons flour

•

½ cup (4 fl oz) milk

•

½ cup (4 fl oz) cream

•

salt and pepper to taste

Combine all the ingredients for the crêpes in a bowl and whisk until smooth, or blend in an electric blender. The batter should be quite thin. Cover and leave for at least 30 minutes. Cook in a lightly greased or non-stick heated crêpe pan. This quantity makes 10 fine crêpes about 12 cm (5 in) in diameter. Stack and reserve.

To prepare the filling, halve the leeks and wash very thoroughly, separating the leaves under cold running water to get rid of all sand. Shake off water, lay cut side down on a wooden board and cut into very fine slices. Use the white portion of the leeks and some of the tender green part but not the tough ends of the leaves.

In a heavy-based saucepan, heat the butter and cook the leeks over very low heat, stirring occasionally, until they are soft, but not brown. Sprinkle in the flour and cook for 2 minutes, then add the milk and cream gradually, stirring until thickened and smooth. Season to taste. Put a generous spoonful of filling on each crêpe and roll up. Spoon sour cream over and sprinkle with snipped chives.

SERVES: 4

# POTATO GNOCCHI

*Italians love this dish, and so does anyone else who tastes it properly made.*
*It is a little difficult, but well worth the trouble.*

## INGREDIENTS

90 g (3 oz) spinach leaves

•

2 tablespoons finely chopped
fresh basil or oregano

•

1 kg (2 lb) floury potatoes

•

1 teaspoon salt

•

1 egg, beaten

•

2 cups (8 oz) plain  (all-purpose) flour

•

¼ cup (2 fl oz) Pesto Sauce (optional)
(see page 442)

•

90 g (3 oz) Pecorino cheese, grated

•

1 small mozzarella cheese, sliced

Wash spinach thoroughly and boil for 3 minutes. Drain, refresh in cold water, then squeeze out all the moisture and chop the spinach finely. Set aside with the basil or oregano. Scrub the potatoes, boil until tender, then drain. When cool enough, peel them and return to the pan to dry off well. Mash until smooth. Add salt to the beaten egg, mix with the spinach and herbs, and work into the potato. Apart from adding flavour, the gnocchi will be prettily speckled with green.

Have ready a large saucepan of lightly salted boiling water before starting to mix and shape the gnocchi, as the mixture goes sticky unless you work quickly.

Add the flour to the potato mixture to make a soft dough. It may be necessary to add a little extra, depending on how moist the potatoes are. Form oval shapes about the size of an almond in its shell, and place them on a floured surface to ensure they do not stick. Drop a few at a time into the boiling water and cook for 3–4 minutes, or until they rise to the surface. Remove on a slotted spoon, draining the gnocchi well before putting them into a buttered, ovenproof dish.

Drizzle a little pesto sauce over the gnocchi if liked. Sprinkle with the grated cheese, then cover with slices of mozzarella. Bake in an oven preheated to 200°C (400°F) for about 7 minutes or until cheese has melted. Serve at once.

SERVES: 6

# GOLDEN NUGGETS WITH VEGETABLE RAGOÛT

### INGREDIENTS

6 golden nugget pumpkins

•

1 bundle asparagus

•

2 small carrots

•

1 onion, cut in thin wedges

•

1 medium potato

•

2 small zucchini (courgettes)

•

50 g (1½ oz) snow peas (mangetout)

•

100 g (3½ oz) button mushrooms

•

½ cup (4 fl oz) cream

•

2 tablespoons chopped fresh dill

•

2 tablespoons chopped fresh parsley

•

1 tablespoon snipped chives

•

few sprigs thyme and basil

•

60 g (2 oz) butter

Cut the tops off the pumpkins and remove seeds and membranes with a spoon. Place on a baking tray with the tops alongside. Pour 3 tablespoons of water onto the tray and cover completely with foil. Bake in an oven preheated to 200°C (400°F) for 20 minutes or until tender. Remove foil and cool.

On another baking tray, place the prepared vegetables, cut into bite-size pieces. Add 3 tablespoons of water to make steam, cover with foil and cook for no more than 8–10 minutes.

Meanwhile, bring cream to the boil with the herbs and cook until reduced by half. Whisk in the butter until it thickens. Add the lightly cooked vegetables to the sauce and heat through, then place vegetables in the hollowed out pumpkins and arrange the lid on top. Brush pumpkins with melted butter to give them a nice shine. Serve hot.

SERVES: 6

# CAPSICUM CUPS WITH TOASTED ALMOND RICE

*Some vegetables are perfect containers for tasty fillings.*

### INGREDIENTS

4 large or 6 medium
capsicums (peppers)

•

2 tablespoons olive oil

•

1 large onion, finely chopped

•

1 cup (7 oz) long grain rice

•

1½ cups (12 fl oz) Vegetable Stock
(see page 448) or water

•

1 teaspoon salt

•

3 tablespoons currants

•

½ cup (2 oz) roughly chopped
almonds

•

2 tablespoons chopped fresh herbs

•

freshly ground pepper to taste

Cut off the tops of the capsicums, then remove the central membrane and seeds. Blanch the capsicums in lightly salted boiling water for about 4 minutes, lift out on a slotted spoon and drain upside down.

Heat the oil in a small saucepan and fry the chopped onion, stirring occasionally, until soft and starting to turn golden brown. Add the rice and stir over medium heat until all the grains are coated with oil. Add stock or water, salt and currants, then bring to the boil. Turn heat very low and cook, covered, for 15 minutes if using white rice or 35 minutes if brown rice is used. While rice is cooking, toast almonds on a baking tray until golden. Mix with the rice and stir in the chopped herbs and pepper.

Fill capsicums, place in a lightly oiled baking dish with ¼ cup (2 fl oz) water poured in and bake in an oven preheated to 200°C (400°F) for 25 minutes or until capsicums are tender but still holding their shape.

SERVES: 4–6

# TEMPEH STUFFED GRILLED MUSHROOMS

*Tempeh is a fermented soy bean cake sold frozen in Asian stores, and is Indonesian in origin. It can be adapted to many recipes as it provides protein and good flavour.*

### INGREDIENTS

8 medium-sized mushrooms

•

1 tablespoon melted butter or oil

•

1 teaspoon finely chopped parsley

•

1 quantity Savoury Tempeh
(see page 436)

•

salt and pepper to taste

Wipe over mushrooms with damp paper and remove stems with a gentle twist. Brush outside of mushrooms with a little melted butter or oil.

Mix the parsley with the tempeh mixture, taste for seasoning and fill the mushroom caps, mounding it slightly. Brush filling with beaten egg or milk and dip into crumbs mixed with chopped almonds. Place on griller (broiler) rack and top each with a tiny piece of the cold butter. Put under preheated griller, watching carefully and removing them just

1 tablespoon beaten egg or milk

•

2 tablespoons dry breadcrumbs

•

1 tablespoon coarsely
chopped almonds

•

1 tablespoon cold butter
cut into 8 pieces

as they sizzle and turn golden. Serve immediately as part of a vegetable variety or as a first course.

NOTE:   Small mushrooms make delicious bite-size savouries.

SERVES: 4–8

# MUSHROOM AND HAZELNUT TERRINE

*A richly flavoured dish which is ideal for a party.*

## INGREDIENTS

500 g (1 lb) mushrooms

•

250 g (8 oz) onions

•

2 or 3 cloves garlic

•

2 teaspoons sea salt

•

60 g (2 oz) butter

•

50 g (1½ oz) hazelnuts, chopped

•

1 teaspoon dried thyme

•

1½ cups cooked rice (5 oz uncooked)

•

2 eggs

•

1 cup (8 fl oz) cream

•

freshly ground black pepper

Wipe over the mushrooms and chop coarsely, using a stainless steel knife. Chop the onions finely. Crush garlic with half a teaspoon of the salt.

In a heavy-based pan, melt the butter and cook the onions and garlic until soft and golden brown. Add the mushrooms, hazelnuts and thyme. Continue cooking and stirring to brown the mushrooms. Turn into a large bowl and mix in the rice.

Beat the eggs lightly and mix in the remaining salt, cream and pepper to taste. Pour over the mushroom and rice mixture and mix thoroughly. Butter a 6–8 cup (48–64 fl oz) pâté mould or other ovenproof dish and bake, uncovered, in an oven preheated to 180°C (350°F) for approximately 1 hour or until firm and brown. Serve hot or at room temperature with crusty wholemeal (whole wheat) bread and a green salad.

SERVES: 6–8

# BABA GHANNOUJ

*A full-flavoured appetiser with eggplant as a base. This has been popularised
by every Lebanese restaurant.*

### INGREDIENTS

2 medium-sized, firm eggplants
(aubergines)
•
3 cloves garlic
•
1 teaspoon salt
•
¼ cup (2 fl oz) lemon juice, strained
•
¼ cup (2 oz) tahini
(sesame seed paste)
•
finely chopped parsley for garnish

Grill the eggplants directly over a gas flame, over coals or bake in a hot oven until the skin blackens and the eggplants are soft. Turn them so that every part of the skin is in contact with the heat. Cool, then remove the skin under cold running water.

Mash the eggplant or put it in a food processor with the other ingredients and blend to a soft purée. It should have the consistency of thick mayonnaise. Spread the purée smoothly on a serving plate, sprinkle with parsley and serve with flat middle eastern bread as an appetiser or first course.

SERVES: 6–8

# WHITE AND GREEN BEAN SALAD

*This came about because I happened to have some cooked haricot beans
on hand, and unexpected guests to lunch. It will stay on my files as a perfectly
delicious salad. Incidentally, cooked beans and lentils freeze very well.*

### INGREDIENTS

3 cups cooked haricot beans
(8 oz dried)
•
¼ cup (2 fl oz) lemon juice
•
½ cup (4 fl oz) olive oil
•
freshly ground sea salt and pepper
•
1 small onion, finely chopped
•
½ cup (1 oz) chopped parsley
(optional)
•
250 g (8 oz) tender green beans
•
few slices of mild purple
onion to garnish

Make sure the haricot beans are cooked through and very tender. Put them in a bowl and make a dressing of the lemon juice, oil, salt, pepper, onion and parsley. Pour over the beans while still warm, tossing to distribute flavour.

Top and tail the green beans and cut them in half, making bite-size pieces. Drop into boiling, lightly salted water for 4–5 minutes, just until tender and still bright green. Drain, refresh under cold water and add to the haricot beans in the dressing. Toss well. Garnish with onion rings.

SERVES: 4–6

BABA GHANNOUJ AND FELAFEL

# HOT BAKED POTATO VARIETY

Very few people can resist a baked potato hot from the oven, with its crisp skin and fluffy interior. Here is how to present this favourite vegetable as the main attraction, topped off in style. Allow one large (400 g/13 oz) potato per serving for an entrée and two for a main course. The toppings are sufficient for 6 potatoes.

Choose large, evenly sized potatoes and try to get long, rather flat shaped spuds because they are better suited to this treatment.

Scrub the potatoes, dry them well and rub lightly with vegetable oil. Bake in an oven preheated to 220°C (425°F) (directly on the oven shelf) for 50 minutes or until done. There are special metal holders for baking potatoes, but if you don't have one, a heavy metal skewer passed through the centre of each potato will act as a heat conductor and speed things up a bit.

Use mitts to take the potatoes from the oven and remove the skewers. With a small knife, make a cross cut in each potato and press inwards so they open up and make room for the filling to be spooned in and over. Have the filling or fillings ready (most of them need only to be combined), top the potatoes and serve piping hot.

### COTTAGE CHEESE AND CHIVES
500 g (1 lb) cottage cheese
1/3 cup (2 oz) corn relish
2 tablespoons finely snipped fresh chives
freshly ground pepper and salt to taste
Combine and chill until required.

### SOUR CREAM AND ONION
300 ml (10 fl oz) thick sour cream
4 tablespoons finely chopped spring onions
(scallions), including green leaves
4 tablespoons finely chopped red capsicum
(sweet pepper)
1/8 teaspoon white pepper
Combine and chill until required.

### CHILLI, TOMATO AND BEANS
1¼ cups bottled pasta sauce
1 × 400 g (13 oz) can red kidney beans, drained
1 teaspoon Mexican style chilli powder

Combine in a small saucepan and heat until bubbling.

### COLESLAW AND CHEESE
2 cups Coleslaw (see page 158)
1 cup coarsely grated sharp cheddar cheese
paprika or grated nutmeg

Fill potato lavishly with coleslaw and cover thickly with cheese. Sprinkle with a little paprika or nutmeg and place under a preheated grill until the cheese melts. Serve at once.

### MUSHROOMS, TOMATOES AND OLIVES
1 tablespoon butter
1 clove garlic, crushed
2 cups (8 oz) thickly sliced fresh mushrooms
4 tablespoons chopped parsley
1 cup (8 oz) drained canned tomatoes, chopped
6 pitted black olives, cut into rings
salt and pepper to taste

Heat butter and sauté garlic and mushrooms until soft. Add parsley, tomatoes, olives and seasoning, cook for 5 minutes and keep warm. Top hot potato with a spoonful of sour cream or pat of butter and spoon mushroom mixture over the top.

### CUCUMBER, DILL AND YOGHURT
1 cup (2 oz) finely sliced cucumber
¼ teaspoon salt
1 cup (8 fl oz) natural yoghurt
2 tablespoons fresh dill, chopped
good squeeze of lemon juice
extra dill sprigs to garnish

Put sliced cucumber into a bowl, sprinkle with salt and leave for 20 minutes. Rinse and pat dry on paper towels. Combine with yoghurt, dill and lemon juice to taste. Chill until required.

# CHICORY, LEEK AND POTATO CUSTARD

*This is a delicious testament to the validity of the rule never to throw out leftovers or little bits of vegetables until you've given them the benefit of your creative imagination. Not much of anything, but combined they make an entrée for two people which I'll certainly be cooking again.*

### INGREDIENTS

90 g (3 oz) chicory
•
90 g (3 oz) green portion of leek
•
150 g (5 oz) potatoes
•
30 g (1 oz) butter
•
¼ teaspoon each salt and pepper
•
½ teaspoon sugar
•
¼ cup (2 fl oz) hot water
•
¾ cup (6 fl oz) cream
•
4 large, unpeeled cloves garlic
•
1 small egg

Wash, dry and chop the chicory. Wash the leek thoroughly to ensure all sand has been rinsed away. Shred very finely. Peel and dice the potato. Heat the butter in a stainless steel saucepan with a heavy base. Add the leeks, stir well and cook over the very lowest heat, covered, for 5 minutes. Add the chicory, stir again, cover and continue cooking on low heat for a further 5 minutes.

Meanwhile, peel the potatoes and cut them into very tiny dice. Add to the pan, stir and season with salt, pepper and sugar. Pour in the hot water, cover pan tightly and steam for 8–10 minutes or until potatoes are tender.

Heat the cream in a small saucepan with the garlic until the cloves are soft and cream has reduced to half its original quantity. Press the garlic out of their skins and mash to a purée, then mix into the cream. Beat the egg well and mix in, seasoning to taste with salt and pepper.

Butter 2 ramekins or a shallow dish and put the vegetable mixture in. Gently pour or spoon over the garlic custard. Place on a baking tray and bake in an oven preheated to 180°C (350°F) for 20–25 minutes or until the custard is just firm in the centre when touched, and golden brown on top. Serve hot, warm or at room temperature.

SERVES: 2

# GARLIC AND RIPE OLIVE TART

### INGREDIENTS

1 × 25 cm (10 in) partly baked Tart
Shell of shortcrust pastry or
pizza dough (see page 447 or 446)

•

1 quantity Garlic Custard
(see page 441)

•

2 tablespoons olive oil

•

1 large onion, finely sliced

•

2 cups (10 oz) pitted ripe olives

•

strips of bottled capsicums
(pepperoni grossi) for garnish

Prepare the tart shell and the garlic custard. Heat the olive oil and cook the onion until soft and translucent. Spread it on the pastry and pour the garlic custard over. Arrange the olives in rings.

Bake in an oven preheated to 180°C (350°F) for 35–40 minutes or until the custard is firm. Cover the top with foil if the olives start to look dried out. At the end of cooking, brush olives with olive oil and garnish with strips of red and yellow capsicums (pepperoni grossi).

SERVES: 6

# RICE WITH PEAS

*A popular dish from Venice known as Risi e Bisi, this is considered a "soup"*
*by Italians, but is not in the least liquid and is eaten with a fork.*

### INGREDIENTS

2 tablespoons butter

•

2 tablespoons olive oil

•

2 spring onions (scallions),
finely chopped

•

500 g (1 lb) shelled peas

•

8 cups (64 fl oz) Vegetable Stock
(see page 448)

•

1½ cups (10 oz) rice

•

salt to taste

•

½ cup (2 oz) finely grated parmesan
cheese

Heat the butter and oil in a heavy-based saucepan and gently cook the spring onions until soft. Add the peas, stir well, pour in about ½ cup (4 fl oz) stock, cover and cook on low heat for 15 minutes.

Add the rice and remaining stock, salt to taste, and bring to the boil. Cook on low heat, stirring frequently, for about 20 minutes or until the rice is tender and creamy. Stir in the Parmesan cheese or serve it separately in a bowl.

SERVES: 4

GARLIC AND RIPE OLIVE TART

# VEGETABLE MOSAIC TERRINE

*Colourful vegetables set in a creamy custard. Do not cook the terrine for
too long or the custard will separate.*

### INGREDIENTS

2 long carrots

•

1 large parsnip

•

1 red capsicum (sweet pepper)

•

1 cob sweetcorn or 1 cup
drained canned whole kernel corn

•

250 g (8 oz) green beans

•

3 large leeks

•

5 egg yolks

•

¼ cup (2 fl oz) milk

•

¼ cup (2 fl oz) cream

•

¼ teaspoon white pepper

•

1 teaspoon salt, or to taste

•

1 teaspoon dried tarragon
leaves, crushed

•

1 teaspoon dried ground thyme

Peel carrots and parsnip, and cut in strips lengthways, keeping them as even as possible—about 6 mm (¼ in) thick. Blanch the carrot and parsnip strips for 2 minutes or cover with plastic and cook in a microwave until barely tender. Cut the red capsicum in similar strips. Shave the corn kernels from the cob with a sharp knife, cook and drain well. Trim the beans and blanch for 2 minutes, drain.

Halve the leeks, wash well, then discard any tough leaves and blanch in lightly salted boiling water for 5 minutes. Drain well on absorbent paper.

Brush a loaf pan with oil or melted butter and line with 3–4 of the best leek leaves, reserving some for the top of the terrine. Make a layer with half the carrot and parsnip strips, then capsicum, corn kernels and beans. Make another layer of leeks and repeat the layers. Beat egg yolks with the milk and cream, stir in seasonings and herbs, and pour gently over the layers. Lay the reserved leek leaves over the top, cover with foil and place in a roasting pan with hot water to come more than halfway up the sides of the loaf pan. Bake in an oven preheated to 160°C (325°F) for 1¼ hours or until the custard is set. Cool, then turn out and cut in slices to serve.

SERVES: 6–8

# CHEESE FONDUE WITH GREEN PEPPERCORNS

*One of the most entertaining ways to entertain! You and your guests sit
around the melted cheese which is kept warm over low heat. The spearing
and dipping of crusty bread cubes requires a knack and some skill,
because it is all too easy to drop the morsel into the pot. This is a favourite
après ski supper in Switzerland and it is traditional for the person who drops
the bread to pay a forfeit—a man buys wine for the assembled company,
a woman has to pay up with kisses for the men at the table.
I have varied the recipe and made it more of a complete meal by adding
a platter of crisp young vegetables for dipping or simply eating alongside.*

## INGREDIENTS

500–600 g (1 lb–1¼ lb)
Swiss cheese (mixture of
Gruyère and Emmenthal)

•

1½ tablespoons cornflour
(cornstarch)

•

1 large loaf of crusty bread

•

vegetables, such as carrot sticks,
broccoli florets, canned artichokes
drained and halved, button
mushrooms, sliced zucchini
(courgettes), cherry tomatoes,
celery sticks

•

1 clove garlic, bruised

•

30 g (1 oz) butter

•

2 cups (16 fl oz) dry white wine

•

1 tablespoon kirsch (optional)

•

¼ teaspoon nutmeg

•

¼ teaspoon black pepper

•

1–2 tablespoons green peppercorns

Peel off any rind from the cheese and grate coarsely, then toss in a bowl with the cornflour. With a sharp knife, cut the bread into small cubes and pile in a basket. Remember to keep a bit of crust on each bread cube to hold the prongs of the fork firmly. Wash and prepare the vegetables, topping and tailing where necessary, or cutting into bite-size pieces. Arrange on a separate platter.

Cook garlic in the melted butter just until golden brown. Add wine and kirsch, and when wine is at simmering point, add the cheese by handfuls, stirring all the time and adding more as soon as the first batch has melted. Stir constantly over medium heat until the cheese has melted and is smooth. Add remaining ingredients and mix, then set over a small table burner with heat adjusted so the fondue barely simmers.

SERVES: 6–8

# EGGPLANT FRITTERS

## INGREDIENTS

2 medium eggplants (aubergines)

•

salt

•

1 cup plain flour

•

1 egg, separated

•

½ cup water

•

1 clove garlic, crushed

•

½ teaspoon finely grated ginger

•

pinch of salt

•

½ teaspoon turmeric, optional

•

oil, for deep frying

Wash but don't peel eggplants. Cut into thin circular slices, sprinkle with salt and leave aside for 30 minutes, then drain and dry on kitchen paper. Meanwhile, make a batter with the flour, egg yolk beaten with water, garlic, ginger, salt and turmeric. Just before using, beat egg white until stiff and fold in.

Heat oil for deep frying and when it is very hot, dip slices of eggplant into the batter and drop them into the oil. Fry a few at a time. Lift out on a perforated spoon and drain on absorbent paper. Serve immediately. These are so tasty they don't need a dipping sauce, but if you wish, serve a tempura dipping sauce or a sweet chilli sauce alongside.

SERVES: 6

# CAPONATA

*A cold dish, ideal as part of an antipasto selection.*

### INGREDIENTS

1 kg (2 lb) firm eggplants (aubergines)
•
salt
•
½ cup (4 fl oz) olive oil
•
1 cup (6 oz) finely diced celery
•
1 cup (8 oz) finely chopped onion
•
3 teaspoons sugar
•
3 tablespoons wine vinegar
•
½ cup (4 fl oz) dry white wine
•
salt and freshly ground
pepper to taste
•
½ cup (2½ oz) sliced green olives
•
1 tablespoon chopped capers
(optional)

Wash eggplants well, cut into 1 cm (½ in) cubes and sprinkle generously with salt. Set aside in a colander for about 1 hour. Gently press out liquid, then dry on paper towels.

Heat the olive oil in a large, heavy-based frying pan and cook eggplant until a light gold colour. Add the celery and onion and continue cooking, stirring frequently, until soft and golden.

Dissolve the sugar in the vinegar and add to the pan, together with wine. Let it bubble up, then lower heat and simmer for 15 minutes, stirring now and then.

Remove from heat, add salt and pepper to taste, stir in olives and capers, adjust seasoning. Put caponata into a serving dish, cover and chill before serving.

SERVES: 6

# CHEESEBOARD PIZZA

### INGREDIENTS

2 cups (1 lb) ricotta cheese

•

1 cup (4 oz) finely grated parmesan
or romano cheese

•

good grinding of black pepper

•

2 eggs, beaten

•

2 or 3 large red capsicums
(sweet peppers), roasted and peeled

•

200 g (6½ oz) red cheddar cheese

•

200 g (6½ oz) mozzarella cheese

•

1 × 200 g (6½ oz) camembert

---

### PIZZA DOUGH

1½ cups (6 oz) flour—white,
wholemeal (whole wheat), or half
and half

•

½ teaspoon salt

•

1 sachet (envelope) active dry yeast

•

½ cup (4 fl oz) lukewarm water

•

1 teaspoon sugar

•

2 tablespoons oil or melted butter

To make the pizza dough, put flour and salt into a large bowl. Sprinkle yeast over the water in a small bowl and leave a few minutes to soften, then add the sugar and stir to dissolve. Sprinkle a teaspoon of flour over the top and leave it in a warm place for 10 minutes until it froths.

Pour yeast mixture over the flour and add the oil or butter. Beat with a wooden spoon until well mixed. Turn dough onto a floured board and knead for 10 minutes or until smooth and elastic. Form into a ball and place in a greased bowl, turning it so the top surface is greased. Cover and put in a warm place until doubled in bulk, about 1 hour.

When dough has risen, punch it down and divide into 2 equal portions. Roll each piece out to a 22 cm (8½ in) circle, lift onto two greased baking sheets and make a slight rim around the edges. Leave in a warm place to prove while making the filling.

In a large bowl, combine the ricotta, finely grated parmesan cheese, the pepper and eggs. Mix well.

Grill the capsicums under a preheated griller (broiler) for about 5 minutes on each side, turning them with tongs so the skin is blistered all over. Put them into a paper bag and leave until cold. This makes it easy to peel away the thin skin. Remove and discard seeds and stem, and slice the capsicums into thin, even strips.

Cut the red cheddar into even-sized strips and slice the mozzarella to give circular slices. Cut the camembert into 16 wedges.

Divide the ricotta mixture between the 2 bases and spread within the rim. Arrange alternate strips of cheddar and capsicum like the spokes of a wheel at the outer edge, leaving space in the centre. Cover this space with a circle of mozzarella slices.

Bake the pizzas in an oven preheated to 200°C (400°F) for 15–20 minutes until the cheese is bubbly and brown, and the base is firm. Remove from the oven and place the camembert wedges in the centre. They will soften and become delightfully runny in the few minutes it takes to cut the pizzas into wedges and serve.

NOTE: Ready made pizza bases can also be used.
MAKES: 2 large pizzas

# THREE POTATO OMELETTE

*Try combining the orange coloured kumara, sweet potatoes and regular
potatoes in this variation on the Portuguese favourite.*

### INGREDIENTS

5 tablespoons olive oil

•

1 large onion, finely chopped

•

1 cup (5 oz) peeled and diced kumara
(yam)

•

1 cup (5 oz) peeled and diced sweet
potato

•

1 medium potato, peeled and diced

•

½ teaspoon crushed garlic

•

½ teaspoon ground cumin

•

1 teaspoon salt

•

½ teaspoon ground black pepper

•

3 tablespoons toasted sesame seeds

•

3 large eggs

•

salt and pepper to taste

•

chopped parsley to garnish

Heat 2 tablespoons of the oil and gently fry the onion, stirring occasionally, until soft and translucent. Meanwhile, cook the kumara, sweet potato and potato in lightly salted boiling water until tender. Drain.

Add the garlic, cumin, salt and pepper to the onions, then add the kumara (yam), sweet potato and potato, and cook for 2 minutes longer. Turn off heat, stir in sesame seeds.

Beat the eggs with salt and pepper. Heat remaining olive oil in a large frying pan, swirling to coat the pan, then pour in the eggs. Allow to set on bottom, then spread the potato mixture evenly over the eggs. When browned on the bottom, place the pan under a preheated griller (broiler) (protect handle of pan by wrapping in foil) until top is set and lightly browned. Cut into wedges, garnish with parsley and serve.

SERVES: 4

# SAVOURY CHEESE BISCUITS

### INGREDIENTS

185g (6 oz) butter

•

185g (6 oz) tasty cheddar

•

¼ cup (1 oz) finely grated parmesan
cheese

•

1½ cups (6 oz) plain flour

•

½ teaspoon salt

•

1 teaspoon paprika

•

small pinch of chilli powder, optional

Soften butter to room temperature. Finely grate both kinds of cheese. Sift flour with salt, paprika and chilli powder. Cream butter and grated cheese until smooth, add flour and mix well. Wrap in plastic and chilli for 20 minutes, then roll out on a floured surface.

Cut pastry into thin strips, then cut across to make finger length straws. Transfer to a foil-lined baking sheet and bake in an oven preheated to 180ºC (350ºF) for 8 minutes or until firm and golden. Cool on the baking tray, then transfer to an airtight container.

MAKES: approximately 45

# BROCCOLI AND CAPSICUM SOUFFLÉS

*Use large, well-shaped capsicums (sweet bell peppers) halved horizontally as
individual, edible soufflé "dishes". Serve as a first course or use small capsicums
and present as part of a degustation with other vegetables.*

## INGREDIENTS

4 capsicums (sweet peppers)
•
185 g (6 oz) broccoli
•
90 g (3 oz) butter
•
1 medium onion, finely chopped
•
5 tablespoons plain flour
•
1¼ cups (6 fl oz) milk
•
3 egg yolks
•
½ cup (2 oz) finely grated tasty
(sharp) cheese
•
¾ teaspoon salt, or to taste
•
½ teaspoon white pepper
•
½ teaspoon ground mace or nutmeg
•
4 egg whites

Wash the capsicums and dry them. Cut in half horizontally and remove the seeds. Trim the stem with a sharp knife or scissors but do not remove it or there will be a hole in the "soufflé dish".

Peel any tough stems and trim the broccoli. Blanch in boiling water for 3 minutes, drain and plunge into iced water to stop the cooking and set the colour. Drain, squeezing out excess water, and chop very finely.

In a heavy-based saucepan, melt half the butter and cook the chopped onion over low heat, stirring frequently, until soft and starting to turn gold. Remove from the pan. Melt remaining butter, add flour and cook, stirring constantly, for 1 minute. It should not brown. Add the milk and whisk until it boils and thickens. Continue to cook, stirring, for 1 minute longer.

Remove pan from heat and beat in the egg yolks, one at a time. Cool the mixture slightly. Stir in the cheese and seasonings, then add the broccoli and onion. Whisk the egg whites until stiff and fold in. Fill the halved capsicums, place in a greased, shallow baking dish and bake in an oven preheated to 210°C (425°F) for about 25 minutes or until the mixture is well risen and golden. Serve at once.

SERVES: 4–8

# CREAMED SPINACH AND CORN

*A light, very delicately flavoured dish which I like to use in many ways.*
*Try it as the filling for Buckwheat Crêpes (see page 35) or serve with*
*crisp, hot, lightly buttered toast points.*

### INGREDIENTS

1 bunch spinach
•
2 tender cobs of corn or
1 × 440 g (14 oz) can whole
kernel corn
•
1 large onion
•
1 tablespoon oil
•
2 teaspoons butter
•
2 teaspoons finely chopped fresh dill
•
½ teaspoon salt
•
¼ teaspoon black pepper
•
1 cup (8 fl oz) milk
(or evaporated milk)
•
½ teaspoon cornflour (cornstarch)
•
2 tablespoons thick cream

Wash the spinach well in several changes of cold water. Pick leaves off for this dish and save the stems for stir fry dishes. Cook the leaves in just the water that clings to them in a saucepan or in the microwave oven (on full power for 3 minutes). Do not overcook or spinach will lose its colour. Drain, and chop roughly.

Cook the corn in a little water without salt, or in the microwave oven (on HIGH for 6 minutes). When cool enough to handle, cut off the niblets with a sharp knife and scrape the cob so that none of the golden goodness is wasted. If using canned corn, drain well.

Finely chop the onion. Heat oil and butter in a heavy-based saucepan and cook the onion, stirring frequently, for 1 minute. Put lid on pan, turn heat very low and cook for 5 minutes, stirring once or twice to ensure onion doesn't brown. Stir in dill and corn and cook for 5 minutes longer. Add spinach, season with salt and pepper, then stir in milk and bring to simmering point. Mix cornflour with a spoonful of cold water and stir into the liquid in the pan to thicken slightly. Turn off heat and stir in the cream.

SERVES: 4

# FETTUCINE IN CREAMY CAPSICUM (PEPPER) SAUCE

*This is a subtle sauce, yet with a flavour and tang that come from using*
*the merest touch of hot chilli.*

### INGREDIENTS

2 onions, chopped
•
1 teaspoon chopped garlic
•
1 small red chilli, chopped

In a medium-sized, heavy-based saucepan, cook the onions, garlic and chilli in the olive oil over low heat until the onions are soft and translucent. Add the tomatoes, capsicum and other ingredients except for the fettucine and cream. Cook uncovered, stirring now and then, until reduced and thickened.

2 tablespoons olive oil

•

1 × 400 g (13 oz) can
peeled tomatoes

•

1 large red capsicum (sweet pepper),
chopped

•

2 tablespoons chopped fresh basil

•

½ teaspoon salt

•

½ teaspoon sugar

•

¼ teaspoon white pepper

•

250 g (8 oz) fettucine

•

150 ml (5 fl oz) cream

Put a large pan of lightly salted water on to boil for cooking the noodles. A small splash of oil in the water prevents boiling over. Boil the pasta while sauce is cooking, and when tender but still firm to the bite, pour cold water into the pan to stop the cooking. Drain noodles in a colander.

Add cream to the sauce, stir and heat through without boiling. Taste and adjust seasoning. Toss the pasta in the sauce and serve at once.

SERVES: 4

# CHICK PEA AND CORIANDER PÂTÉ

### INGREDIENTS

1 cup (6 oz) dried chick peas
•
1 small onion
•
2 whole cloves
•
8–10 black peppercorns
•
1 bay leaf
•
1 teaspoon salt
•
4 tablespoons lemon juice
•
2 tablespoons olive oil (optional)
•
2 tablespoons finely chopped
red onion
•
½ cup (1 oz) chopped fresh coriander

Wash chick peas well and soak overnight, or use the quick soak method. Bring to the boil with water to cover, turn off heat and allow to soak for 2 hours. Drain peas, add fresh water to cover, the onion stuck with the cloves, peppercorns, bay leaf and salt. Pressure cook for 15 minutes, or simmer in a saucepan, covered, for 1 hour or until very tender. Drain and discard spices and bay leaf.

Purée the chick peas in a food processor or blender with the lemon juice and olive oil. Stir in the chopped onion and fresh coriander, and serve with triangles of flat middle eastern bread dried out in a slow oven until very crisp.

SERVES: 4 (as a first course, many more as a party dip)

# WHOLEMEAL GOUGÈRE

*Crisp choux pastry made with wholemeal flour and Gruyère cheese encircles lightly cooked seasonal vegetables.*

### INGREDIENTS

½ cup (2 oz) wholemeal
(whole wheat) flour
•
½ teaspoon mustard powder
•
½ teaspoon white pepper
•
½ teaspoon salt
•
¾ cup (6 fl oz) water
•
75 g (2½ oz) butter
•
3 eggs, beaten
•
75 g (2½ oz) Gruyère cheese cut in
tiny dice

Mix together the dry ingredients on a sheet of paper. Bring the water and butter to a rolling boil in a heavy-based saucepan and add all the flour mixture at once. Beat well with a wooden spoon until mixture forms a ball and comes away from sides of the pan. Remove pan from heat.

Reserve a tablespoon of the beaten egg and gradually add the rest, beating well after each addition. Stir in two thirds of the diced Gruyère cheese. Drop tablespoons of the mixture around edge of a greased quiche dish or in a circle on the baking tray. Brush with reserved beaten egg and sprinkle with remaining cheese. Bake in an oven preheated to 200°C (400°F) for 20 minutes, then lower heat to 190°C (375°F) and continue baking for a further 10 minutes or until gougère is well puffed and golden brown.

While gougère is baking, prepare a selection of seasonal vegetables, steam them until just tender, then toss in a tablespoon of butter and season to taste. Fill the centre of the ring.

SERVES: 4–6

# SOUPS

Soups are so versatile. Luxurious or economical, they can be either the first course or the main dish. You'll find a large variety, ranging from hot and hearty soups that need only a crusty loaf to complete the meal, to ice-cold and refreshing soups that tempt appetites in summer.
Vegetable stock can be made according to the recipe given on page 448 or it can be the collected cooking liquids from vegetables that are boiled or steamed. Never throw all that goodness down the sink—collect it and refrigerate it or freeze it until needed.

## CREAM OF TOMATO SOUP

*When tomatoes are at their best in summer make use of them in soups and sauces.*

### INGREDIENTS

750 g (1½ lb) ripe tomatoes
•
30 g (1 oz) butter
•
1 medium onion, finely chopped
•
1 carrot, finely chopped
•
4 cups (32 fl oz) Vegetable Stock
(see page 448)
•
⅛ teaspoon mace
•
½ teaspoon dried basil
•
1 bay leaf
•
¼ teaspoon white pepper
•
1 teaspoon salt
•
2 teaspoons sugar
•
3 teaspoons cornflour (cornstarch)
•
½ cup (4 fl oz) cream

Peel tomatoes. To do this, immerse in boiling water for 30 seconds, then plunge into cold water. Or impale each tomato on a fork and hold over a gas flame until the skin splits and blisters, then hold under cold tap. Halve tomatoes crossways, gently squeeze out and discard seeds, then chop roughly.

In an enamel or stainless steel saucepan, heat the butter and fry onion and carrot on low heat until soft. Add tomatoes and vegetable stock together with mace, basil, bay leaf, pepper, salt and sugar. Bring to the boil, then simmer 30 minutes. Remove bay leaf.

Cool slightly and purée in an electric blender or push through a nylon sieve. Return to pan, bring back to the boil and thicken slightly with the cornflour mixed smoothly with a little cold water. Remove from heat, stir in the cream, taste and correct seasoning. Serve hot, accompanied by Melba toast or cheese puffs.

CHEESE PUFFS: Beat one small egg and stir into 1½ cups (6 oz) grated, sharp cheese. Add one teaspoon made (prepared) mustard. Spread on fingers or rounds of fresh bread and bake in a hot oven for a few minutes until puffed and golden.

SERVES: 4–6

# SUMMER BERRY SOUP

*This refreshing soup is suitable both as a first course or dessert.*

### INGREDIENTS

½ cup (3 oz) sago or minute tapioca

•

250 g (8 oz) ripe red strawberries

•

250 g (8 oz) raspberries

•

250 g (8 oz) mulberries
(or blackberries)

•

250 g (8 oz) blueberries

•

4 tablespoons sugar, or to taste

•

4 cups (32 fl oz) pure apple juice

•

crushed ice or ice cubes

Bring at least 6 cups (48 fl oz) of water to the boil and sprinkle in the sago. Boil, uncovered, for 7 minutes, then cover the pan, turn off the heat and leave for 10 minutes. By this time all the grains should be perfectly clear. (Use the small tapioca with grains about the size of a pin head, not the larger variety.) Run cold water into the pan, drain through a fine sieve and leave to cool.

Wash the berries and drain. Hull the strawberries and snip the stems off the mulberries. Set aside some perfect berries of each variety for garnishing and purée the rest with the sugar. Stir in the apple juice, then add 1 cup of the cooked sago. Cover and chill for 1 hour or longer. Ladle into soup plates and serve with crushed ice or ice cubes added, with a few berries floating on top.

SERVES: 8

SUMMER BERRY SOUP

# WATERCRESS SOUP

*Watercress has a peppery tang which works well as a flavour accent in salad but needs toning down in soup. It is only at the end of this recipe, when milk is added, that the taste smooths out, as it were.*

## INGREDIENTS

150 g (5 oz) watercress leaves

•

125 g (4 oz) spring onions (scallions), including green tops

•

200 g (7 oz) potatoes

•

1 cooking apple

•

4 cups (32 fl oz) water

•

1 cup (8 fl oz) milk

•

½ teaspoon sugar

•

salt and white pepper to taste

•

¼ teaspoon ground nutmeg

Wash the watercress thoroughly and pick only the leaves and tender stems for the soup. Chop roughly. Wash the spring onions, discarding any tough leaves, and slice into rounds. Peel the potatoes and cut into thin slices. Peel, core and slice the apple. Put all the vegetables and the apple into a saucepan with the water. Bring to the boil, then cover and simmer for 15–20 minutes or until potatoes are soft. Cool until lukewarm, then purée in an electric blender or food processor. Push through a sieve. Stir in the milk, add sugar, salt, pepper and nutmeg, and mix well. Taste and correct seasoning if necessary. Chill in a covered bowl for several hours if serving cold, or heat through without boiling if serving hot. Crisp croûtons go well with this soup.

SERVES: 6

# COLD ZUCCHINI SOUP

*In summer, a cold soup is always welcome. This one has a pretty colour and very delicate flavour. In winter, serve it hot.*

## INGREDIENTS

1 kg (2 lb) dark green zucchini (courgettes)

•

4 cups (32 fl oz) Vegetable Stock (see page 448)

•

4 cups (32 fl oz) milk

•

60 g (2 oz) butter

•

salt and white pepper to taste

•

½ cup (4 fl oz) light sour cream

•

chopped chives for garnish (optional)

Wash zucchini well, cut off stem ends and discard. Cut zucchini into thick slices.

Bring vegetable stock to boil, drop in zucchini slices and cook, covered, for 8 minutes or until zucchini are just tender and still bright green. Remove from heat, add milk and butter, allow to cool.

Purée soup in an electric blender on high speed, not filling the blender more than half full. Turn into a large bowl, season to taste with salt and pepper, and chill well.

At serving time, pour soup into a large tureen or glass bowl. Swirl sour cream through and sprinkle with finely snipped chives. Serve very cold.

SERVES: 8–10

# MISCHA'S BORSCH

*Taught me by an old friend, Mischa Borsteinas, who played in the same orchestra as my husband. It is the recipe his mother used to make in his native city of Vilnius, in Lithuania. Mischa says it is best served with steaming hot potatoes which must be boiled with an onion in the cooking water. He was most insistent about the onion and indeed it does make a difference. The cooking liquid can be saved for soup stock.*

## INGREDIENTS

1 × 850 g (1½ lb) can sliced beets

•

2 × 300 ml (10 fl oz) cartons thick sour cream

•

2 green cucumbers, peeled and diced

•

½ cup finely chopped spring onions (scallions)

•

4 cups (about 24) ice cubes

•

salt and freshly ground black pepper to taste

•

4 hard-boiled eggs, sliced

•

6 large or 12 small potatoes

•

1 large onion

Put beetroot and liquid from can into food processor and purée coarsely. Turn into a large bowl and stir in the sour cream, cucumber, spring onions and ice cubes. Season to taste. Cover and refrigerate overnight to allow flavours to blend.

Pour into deep bowls. Arrange the egg slices on top and serve accompanied by the hot, freshly boiled potatoes (boiled with an onion) on side plates.

SERVES: 8–10 as a first course and 6 as a light meal

# CREAM OF BROCCOLI SOUP

*As its name suggests, this is a rich-tasting, smooth soup but not high in calories—it actually has no cream in it.*

## INGREDIENTS

500 g (1 lb) broccoli

•

2 stalks celery, sliced

•

1 medium onion, chopped

•

4 cups (32 fl oz) Vegetable Stock (see page 448)

•

salt and pepper, to taste

•

1 cup (8 fl oz) milk

In a saucepan, simmer the broccoli, celery and onion in the stock until just tender. Don't overcook or broccoli will lose its green colour.

Cool to lukewarm, then purée in an electric blender until smooth. Return to pan, season to taste with salt and pepper, then add milk. Reheat without boiling and serve.

SERVES: 6

# SPRING VEGETABLE SOUP

*A delicious mixture of root and leaf vegetables which is hearty enough to
warm and sustain on chilly spring nights.*

### INGREDIENTS

1 tablespoon butter
•
1 large onion, chopped
•
1 cup (5 oz) diced carrot
•
1 cup (8 oz) peeled and diced potato
•
1 cup (5 oz) diced celery
•
¼ cup (2 oz) white or brown rice
•
6 cups (48 fl oz) cold water
•
1 tablespoon miso
•
4 cups (5 oz) finely chopped
raw spinach
•
1 bunch asparagus,
washed and base of stalk peeled
•
½ cup (4 fl oz) cream or evaporated
milk
•
generous pinch of nutmeg
•
salt and pepper to taste

In a large heavy-based saucepan, melt the butter and gently
sauté the onion until soft. Add the carrot, potato and celery,
cover and cook on very low heat for 10–15 minutes, stirring
occasionally. This brings out the flavour of the vegetables.
Add the rice. White rice breaks up and thickens the soup,
brown rice stays in shape and gives a thinner soup. Add
water to cover vegetables and stir in the miso.

Simmer until vegetables are tender, then add the spinach
and the sliced asparagus. Simmer again until spinach and
asparagus are just tender. Stir in cream or milk and a good
grating of nutmeg. Season to taste with salt and pepper.
Serve with crusty bread and butter.

SERVES: 6

# EGG AND LEMON SOUP

*Freely translated from the Greek.*

### INGREDIENTS

6–8 cups (48–64 fl oz) Vegetable Stock
(see page 448)
•
1 cup cooked rice (3 oz uncooked)
•
3 or 4 eggs
•
¼ cup (2 fl oz) strained lemon juice
•
salt and pepper to taste
•
finely chopped fresh mint
(optional)

Bring the stock to the boil, add the rice (cooked rice keeps
well in a plastic container in the fridge) and simmer until
it is very soft. Beat the eggs until frothy, stir in the lemon
juice and a ladle of the hot soup. Slowly pour the egg mixture
into the soup, stirring constantly over low heat. Do not
boil or the eggs will curdle. Season to taste with salt and
pepper. When heated through and slightly thick, serve at
once, garnished with the chopped mint.

SERVES: 6–8

SPRING VEGETABLE SOUP

# FRENCH ONION SOUP

*There are many versions of onion soup. Perhaps the best known is Soupe
à l'Oignon Gratinée with its topping of toasted bread and melting cheese.
Originally a peasant dish, it has become popular with all classes.*

## INGREDIENTS

1 kg (2 lb) brown onions
•
90 g (3 oz) butter
•
2 tablespoons oil
•
1 teaspoon sugar
•
1 tablespoon flour
•
8 cups (64 fl oz) hot Vegetable Stock
(see page 448)
•
1 cup (8 fl oz) dry white wine
•
salt and pepper to taste
•
thick slices of French bread
•
250 g (8 oz) Swiss cheese
•
125 g (4 oz) parmesan cheese
•
¼ cup (2 fl oz) cognac or brandy
(optional)

Peel onions and cut into thin, uniform slices so they will cook evenly. In a heavy fireproof casserole or large heavy-based saucepan, heat the butter and oil but don't let the butter brown. Add sliced onions and cook on low heat, stirring now and then until they are soft and golden. This could take about half an hour and must not be hurried if the soup is to have a good flavour. Sprinkle the sugar and flour over and stir for a few minutes longer or until they are golden brown.

Pour in the boiling stock, the white wine, salt and pepper to taste. Cover and simmer for 30 minutes. While soup is simmering, toast the sliced bread to a pale golden brown. If liked, brush each slice with a little olive oil and rub lightly with a cut clove of garlic.

Grate the Swiss cheese coarsely and parmesan cheese finely, mix together and sprinkle generously on the toasted bread. Return bread to preheated griller (broiler) or oven for a few minutes to melt the cheese.

Put bread into a large tureen or in individual soup bowls. Add brandy to soup and ladle over the bread, which will float to the top.

If soup is to be served in an oven-to-table casserole, it may be returned to the oven and kept hot. Pass extra bread and cheese separately.

SERVES: 8

# COLD JELLIED BORSCH

*Ideal for a dinner party as it may be made well ahead of time. But I've also found that any left over is much in demand for cool summertime snacking.*

### INGREDIENTS

2 tablespoons gelatine

•

4 cups (32 fl oz) Vegetable Stock
(see page 448)

•

1 × 850 g (1½ lb) can sliced beetroot
(beets)

•

1 small onion, finely grated

•

1 teaspoon salt, or to taste

•

1 cup (8 fl oz) thick sour cream
or yoghurt

•

3 tablespoons finely snipped chives

Sprinkle gelatine over ½ cup (4 fl oz) of Vegetable Stock and leave to soak for 5 minutes, then stand cup in a saucepan of simmering water until gelatine dissolves. Add gelatine to remaining vegetable stock and stir. Drain liquid from beetroot and add 1½ cups (12 fl oz) to the stock.

Cut beetroot slices into very fine julienne strips and add to the stock together with the grated onion and salt.

Pour into a large bowl and chill overnight. Before serving, chop the jelly roughly and pile into chilled soup bowls. Top each serving with a tablespoon of sour cream or yoghurt and sprinkle with chives.

SERVES: 8–10

# CARROT AND SAFFRON SOUP

*Carotene and vitamin A never tasted so good. This is adapted from a seafood soup featured in an exclusive establishment in France.*

### INGREDIENTS

250 g (8 oz) carrots

•

1 stalk celery

•

250 g (8 oz) leeks

•

30 g (1 oz) butter

•

¼ teaspoon Spanish saffron strands

•

1½ cups (12 fl oz) water

•

½ cup (4 fl oz) white wine (optional)

•

1 teaspoon salt

•

¼ teaspoon white pepper

•

1½ cups (12 fl oz) milk

•

1 cup (8 fl oz) cream

Wash, peel and finely grate the carrots. Finely chop the celery. Slit the leeks, wash well under cold water, separating the leaves and making sure all sand is removed. Shake off the water, then slice the leeks finely.

Melt butter in a heavy-based saucepan, add the leeks and stir to coat with butter, then turn heat very low. Cover pan with a well fitting lid and sweat the leeks for about 8 minutes until soft but not brown. Add carrots and celery, stir well, cover and cook for a further 5 minutes.

Meanwhile, toast saffron in a small, dry pan for about 1 minute, just to make it brittle enough to grind to a powder in a mortar and pestle. Dissolve ground saffron in 2 tablespoons hot water and add to vegetables in pan. Add the water, wine, salt and pepper.

Cook, covered, for 10 minutes or until carrots are very tender. Add milk and cream, and heat through without boiling. Taste and correct seasoning and serve hot.

SERVES: 4–5

# GUACAMOLE SOUP

*A delicious cold soup which has the same flavours as that famous
Mexican dip, Guacamole.*

### INGREDIENTS

1 medium green cucumber

•

2 cloves garlic, chopped

•

3 spring onions (scallions),
including half the green tops

•

half each red and green capsicum
(sweet pepper), roughly chopped

•

1 tablespoon chopped dill,
parsley and chives

•

1 tablespoon cider vinegar

•

2 teaspoons sugar

•

1 cup (8 fl oz) Vegetable Stock
(see page 448)

•

1 ripe avocado

•

2 tablespoons white wine

•

1 teaspoon salt

•

¼ teaspoon white pepper

•

2 teaspoons olive oil

•

1 firm red tomato, diced

•

2 tablespoons lemon juice

•

1 extra teaspoon chopped chives

•

garlic croûtons to serve

Peel and seed the cucumber and chop roughly. Put cucumber, garlic, spring onions, capsicum, herbs, vinegar, sugar, stock and half the peeled and chopped avocado into a food processor fitted with a steel blade. Blend well, then pour into a large serving bowl and add white wine, salt and pepper, olive oil and diced tomato. From now on it must be stirred, not blended. Just before serving, stir in the remaining avocado, diced and tossed in lemon juice. Sprinkle with remaining chives. Serve with garlic croûtons.

SERVES: 4

GUACAMOLE SOUP

# FRESH PEA SOUP

*For the most delicate flavour and prettiest jade colour, use fresh young peas.*

### INGREDIENTS

1 kg (2 lb) peas in the pod

•

1 tablespoon butter or olive oil

•

2 or 3 spring onions (scallions),
including green tops

•

½ teaspoon salt or to taste

•

¼ teaspoon white pepper

•

½ cup (4 fl oz) cream or sour cream

•

4 mint sprigs, finely chopped

### STOCK

2 handfuls pea pods

•

several green leaves, such as spinach,
lettuce, cabbage

•

3 celery tops with leaves

•

1 onion

•

handful of parsley sprigs

•

1 bay leaf

•

6 cups (48 fl oz) water

Shell the peas and measure them. There should be around 2½ cups (10 oz) of shelled peas. Reserve some of the best pea pods for making the stock. To make the stock, put all the ingredients into a large saucepan and bring to the boil, then cover and simmer for 30 minutes. Strain and cool.

Blanch ¼ cup (2 oz) of the smallest, sweetest peas for 1 minute in boiling water, drain and refresh in iced water to set the colour. Reserve for garnish.

Melt butter and sweat the spring onions over very low heat in a covered pan. Add raw peas and 2 cups (16 fl oz) stock, then simmer until tender but still a good green colour, about 8 minutes. Pour into cold stock (this helps to set the colour), blend to a purée or push through a fine sieve. Season with salt and pepper. Reheat to serve, or in summer chill the soup well.

To serve, combine cream and freshly chopped mint and place a spoonful in each bowl of soup. Add 4–5 peas to each bowl to garnish.

SERVES: 4–6

# CREAM OF MUSHROOM SOUP

*For soup, mushrooms need not be the choicest buttons. Large, flat mushrooms
will have better flavour.*

### INGREDIENTS

500 g (1 lb) mushrooms

•

60 g (2 oz) butter

•

1 clove garlic, crushed

•

1 onion, finely chopped

Wipe over the mushrooms and slice or dice with a stainless steel knife. Heat the butter in a heavy-based saucepan and gently sauté the garlic and onion until soft. Add the mushrooms and cook, stirring, for 2 minutes. Grind plenty of black pepper over the top and sprinkle with salt. Cover with a well fitting lid and cook on very low heat, shaking the pan from time to time, for 10 minutes. Add all the

freshly ground black pepper

•

1 teaspoon salt or to taste

•

1 × 375 ml (12 fl oz) can evaporated milk

•

2 cups (16 fl oz) milk

•

2 cups (16 fl oz) water

•

1 tablespoon cornflour (cornstarch)

•

2 tablespoons chopped fresh coriander

liquid and stir as it comes to a simmer. Mix cornflour with a little cold water and stir into the soup until it thickens. Simmer, stirring, for 1 minute, then stir in the coriander. Serve garnished with coriander leaves.

SERVES: 6

# GREEN AND GOLD SOUP

*Food should look good as well as taste good, and this simple soup does just that.*

### INGREDIENTS

6 spring onions (scallions)

•

2 tablespoons butter or oil

•

1 cup (5 oz) finely chopped carrot

•

1 teaspoon ground cumin

•

2 cups (1 lb) cooked, mashed pumpkin (retain cooking water)

•

1 × 440 g (14½ oz) can creamed corn

•

1 teaspoon salt or to taste

•

freshly ground pepper

•

3 cups (24 fl oz) water or Vegetable Stock (see page 448)

### CHEESE CROÛTONS
half a French bread stick or baguette

•

¾ cup (3 oz) finely grated natural cheese

•

cayenne pepper or paprika

Finely slice the spring onions and set aside the green tops. Melt butter and cook the white parts until soft. Add carrot and sauté for 3–4 minutes with cumin. Add remaining ingredients except onion tops. Simmer for 8–10 minutes, then add onion tops and simmer 1 minute longer. Serve with cheese croûtons.

To make the croûtons, have bread stick semi-frozen and slice as thinly as possible. Place on greased trays. Top each slice with cheese and dust with a very little cayenne pepper or paprika. Bake in an oven preheated to 180ºC (350°F) until golden.

SERVES: 6

# BREAD AND ALMOND SOUP

*Wonderful for summer, and there's no cooking involved in making this chilled
soup. The contrast of savoury soup and seedless grapes is delightful.
If you want a creamy white soup use blanched almonds and crusty Italian
type bread. For a soup with high fibre content and more flavour and nutrition,
use natural unblanched almonds and wholemeal (whole wheat) rolls, giving
a pale brown colour. Sliced, soft bread is not suitable.*

### INGREDIENTS

125 g (4 oz) almonds
•
125 g (4 oz) crusty bread
•
1 clove garlic
•
1 teaspoon sea salt
•
2 tablespoons olive oil
•
1 tablespoon tarragon or
other herb vinegar
•
¼ teaspoon white pepper
•
½ teaspoon ground cumin
•
¼ teaspoon ground nutmeg or mace
•
1 teaspoon vegetable seasoning
(or powdered vegetable soup)
•
250 g (8 oz) grapes, seedless if possible
•
1 cup (2 oz) diced bread
•
3 tablespoons olive oil or butter

Soak the almonds in 1 cup (8 fl oz) hot water for 15 minutes
and soak the bread in 2 cups (16 fl oz) cold water for the
same length of time. Drain off the water from the almonds
and bread, and reserve for adding later. In a blender or
food processor, purée the almonds, bread, garlic crushed with
salt, olive oil, tarragon vinegar, spices and vegetable seasoning.
Add the reserved soaking water gradually. Let the motor
run until the mixture is very smooth.

Pour into a bowl, cover and chill for at least 2 hours
or until very cold. Peel, halve and seed large grapes, or use
small seedless grapes whole.

Fry the diced bread in olive oil or butter, turning
frequently, until an even golden brown. Drain on absorbent
paper. Serve the soup in chilled cups with a few grapes in
each serving. Serve the croûtons separately so they will be
very crisp when eaten.

SERVES: 4

# CUCUMBER YOGHURT SOUP

*There are so many varieties of cucumber, some much stronger tasting
than others. The variety used in this recipe is what is known as a
telegraph cucumber, English cucumber, European cucumber and probably
a few other names as well. Long and slender, it has a very thin dark green
skin, delicate flavour and seeds that are barely formed.*

## INGREDIENTS

1 large green cucumber, about
400 g (14 oz)
•
2 cups (16 fl oz) water
•
1 tablespoon chopped chives
•
¼ teaspoon ground cumin
•
½ cup (4 fl oz) natural yoghurt
•
½ teaspoon salt, or to taste
•
pinch white pepper

Wash but don't peel the cucumber. Put into a saucepan with the water, bring to the boil and boil for 5 minutes. Purée in a blender or with a hand-held wand. Mix in the chives, cumin and yoghurt, then whisk until smooth. Refrigerate until thoroughly chilled, then serve.

SERVES: 6–8

# MUSHROOM SOUP WITH MISO

*When mushrooms are cheap make a batch of this and freeze what you don't
want immediately.*

## INGREDIENTS

500 g (1 lb) mushrooms
•
2 tablespoons butter
•
6 spring onions (scallions), sliced
•
2 cloves garlic, crushed
•
2 tablespoons parsley
•
1 teaspoon miso paste
•
6 cups (48 fl oz) water or Vegetable
Stock (see page 448)
•
2 slices white or wholemeal
(whole wheat) bread
•
½ cup (4 fl oz) evaporated milk
•
thickened cream, for garnish
•
2 tablespoons finely chopped parsley
or chives

Wipe over the mushrooms with a damp paper towel, retain 1 mushroom for garnish and slice the rest. Melt butter in a large, heavy-based saucepan and cook the onions on low heat until soft. Add garlic, parsley and miso paste, and stir for 3 minutes over moderate heat. Add mushrooms and cook, covered, for 8–10 minutes over low heat. Add stock and the bread with the crusts trimmed off. Simmer for 25–30 minutes. Cool slightly and purée in a blender.

Reheat without boiling and stir in evaporated milk just before serving. Top each bowl with a teaspoon of thickened cream poured in a swirl from the tip of the teaspoon. Draw the tip of a knife through the cream in spokes from the centre, to form a decorative "web". Sprinkle the chopped parsley over and lay a thin slice of mushroom on top.

SERVES: 8–10

69

# BEAN SOUP

*A wonderfully high fibre soup with beans and grain in addition to vegetables.*

### INGREDIENTS

1 cup (5 oz) dried haricot beans
•
2 large leeks
•
2 carrots
•
2 potatoes
•
2 beets
•
2–3 tablespoons oil
•
¼ cup (2 oz) brown rice
•
4 cups (32 fl oz) Vegetable Stock
(see page 448) or water
•
salt and pepper to taste
•
dash of vegetable seasoning
(or powdered vegetable
soup) (optional)

Wash the beans and put them into a small pan with cold water to cover. Bring to the boil, then turn off the heat and leave beans in covered pan for 2 hours to soak.

Wash the leeks well, slitting them to remove all the sandy grit, then slice them finely. Scrub and dice the carrots and potatoes, peel and dice the beets.

In a large, heavy-based saucepan, heat oil and cook the vegetables, stirring for about 5 minutes, then cover pan tightly with lid and cook on very low heat for 10–15 minutes so the vegetables develop good flavour without browning. Add rice, stock or water and the beans, together with their soaking liquid. Bring to boil, then lower heat and simmer for 45 minutes or until beans, rice and vegetables are very tender. Add more stock or water if the liquid cooks down.

Season to taste with salt and pepper and vegetable seasoning, if wished. Serve bowls of soup with wholegrain rolls heated in the oven until crust is crisp, or croûtons made from sliced wholegrain bread.

SERVES: 6–8

# GAZPACHO ANDALUZ

*On a hot day this chilled tomato soup is very refreshing and makes
a light meal in itself.*

### INGREDIENTS

1 kg (2 lb) firm ripe tomatoes, peeled,
seeded and diced
•
2 green cucumbers, peeled,
seeded and diced
•
2 small onions, peeled and
finely chopped
•
1 red capsicum (sweet pepper),
chopped
•
1 green capsicum (sweet pepper),
chopped
•

Put aside 1 cup (8 oz) each of the diced tomatoes and cucumbers and half the chopped onions and capsicums for garnishing the gazpacho.

Put remaining tomatoes, cucumbers, onions, capsicums, garlic and breadcrumbs into the container of a food processor and process until smooth, adding some of the water if necessary.

Turn into a bowl and mix in the water, wine or vinegar, olive oil and seasonings. Taste the mixture and add the sugar if necessary. Cover and chill for at least 2 hours.

Put the reserved tomatoes, cucumbers and onions into

1 teaspoon finely chopped garlic

•

1 cup (2 oz) fine white fresh
breadcrumbs made from the inside
of crusty bread

•

3 cups (24 fl oz) cold water

•

1 cup (8 fl oz) white wine or
3 tablespoons red wine vinegar

•

3 tablespoons olive oil

•

1 teaspoon salt or to taste

•

freshly ground black pepper, to taste

•

1 teaspoon sugar (optional)

•

3 hard-boiled eggs

•

extra olive oil, for frying

•

1 cup finely diced white bread,
trimmed of crust

separate bowls, cover and chill. Chop the hard-boiled eggs
with a stainless steel knife and put into a bowl.

Heat a little olive oil in a pan and fry the diced bread
until golden, lift out on a slotted spoon and drain on
absorbent paper. Do this just before serving. If liked, a bruised
clove of garlic may be added to the oil to flavour it.

Serve the soup in chilled bowls with ice cubes added
and surround with the bowls of garnishes to be added to
individual servings as desired.

NOTE: The breadcrumbs will not be evident but simply give
the soup more substance.

SERVES: 6

# CREAMY CARROT SOUP

*A simple carrot soup which most children enjoy.*

### INGREDIENTS

2 tablespoons butter
(or half butter, half oil)

•

1 large onion, finely chopped

•

500 g (1 lb) carrots,
scrubbed and sliced

•

4 cups (32 fl oz) Vegetable Stock
(see page 448) or water

•

salt and pepper, to taste

•

1 cup (8 fl oz) milk

•

pinch of grated nutmeg

•

½ cup (4 fl oz) cream or evaporated
milk

In a large, heavy-based saucepan, cook the butter, onion
and carrots over low heat, tightly covered, for 15–20 minutes.
Stir now and then. The vegetables must not brown, but
this slow cooking brings out the flavours and makes all the
difference to the soup.

Add the stock or water, bring to the boil, then simmer
for 30 minutes or until carrots are quite tender. Cool slightly,
then purée in a blender or food processor, return to heat
and season to taste. Stir in milk, nutmeg, cream or evaporated
milk and bring almost to the boil. Serve with crisp, freshly
made croûtons.

NOTE: If liked, rub the croûtons lightly with a cut clove
of garlic.

SERVES: 5–6

# BUTTERNUT PUMPKIN SOUP

*This soup is a favourite with most people just as it is, straightforward and simple. But if preparing it for a gourmet gathering, add ⅛ teaspoon each of freshly ground cardamom, clove and nutmeg when cooking the pumpkin. The spicing should be subtle.*

### INGREDIENTS

1 tablespoon butter
•
6 spring onions (scallions),
finely chopped
•
1 kg (2 lb) butternut pumpkin
(squash)
•
3 cups (24 fl oz) Vegetable Stock
(see page 448)
•
2 cups (16 fl oz) milk
•
white pepper and salt to taste
•
½ cup (4 fl oz) cream
•
2 tablespoons finely chopped parsley
•
croûtons, to serve

Melt the butter and fry spring onions over low heat until soft and golden. Cut pumpkin into pieces and peel. Add to pan with the spices (see above), cover and cook on very low heat for 10 minutes, stirring once or twice. Add stock and cook until pumpkin is tender.

Cool until lukewarm, then purée in an electric blender or push through a fine sieve. Return to pan, add milk and season with salt and white pepper.

Heat almost to boiling. Whip cream until thick and put a spoonful of cream on top of each serving of soup. Sprinkle with parsley and serve with small croûtons.

SERVES: 6

# BEETROOT AND ORANGE SOUP

### INGREDIENTS

3 medium beets
•
4 cups (32 fl oz) Vegetable Stock
(see page 448)
•
1 × 750 ml (24 fl oz) can
mixed vegetable juice
or tomato juice
•
1 cup (8 fl oz) orange juice
•
salt to taste
•
fine strips of orange rind (optional)

Scrub the beets well but don't peel them. Grate coarsely. If you own a food processor use it for this job because beets can be rather hard to grate. Put beets and stock into a stainless steel or enamel pan and bring to the boil, then turn heat low and simmer for 20 minutes. Strain and discard the beets. Cool the liquid. Add the vegetable juice, orange juice, orange rind and salt to taste. Serve hot or cold.

NOTE: If using orange rind to garnish, blanch the strips in boiling water 3 times to get rid of excessive bitterness. Drain and scatter a few strips on the soup.

SERVES: 6

BUTTERNUT PUMPKIN SOUP

# CREAMY ONION SOUP

*The soup of Paris that rose from being a cheap meal for the market workers at Les Halles to the most famous of French soups, is indeed worthy of its popularity. But there are other versions in other parts of France, and here is the onion soup of Bordeaux.*

### INGREDIENTS

2 tablespoons oil or butter

•

750 g (1½ lb) brown onions, finely chopped

•

1 teaspoon chopped garlic

•

2 tablespoons flour

•

4 cups (32 fl oz) Vegetable Stock (see page 448) or water

•

3 egg yolks

•

½ cup (4 fl oz) thickened cream or crème fraîche

•

good squeeze of lemon juice

•

salt and pepper, to taste

•

30 g (1 oz) butter, cut in small pieces

•

6 thick slices crusty French bread, toasted

Heat oil or butter in a large, heavy-based saucepan and gently fry the onions and garlic until soft and transparent, without letting them brown. Sprinkle in the flour and stir for a minute. Add the stock or water and stir until it comes to a boil. Partially cover the pan with a lid and simmer for 30 minutes.

Meanwhile, beat egg yolks with cream and lemon juice. Remove pan from heat and stir 1 cup (8 fl oz) of hot soup into the yolk mixture, adding gradually to prevent curdling. Slowly stir it back into the pan of soup over low heat, taking care it does not boil. Season to taste with salt and pepper, then dot the butter over the soup and stir in. Put a slice of toasted bread into each soup bowl or into a tureen. Ladle the soup over and serve.

NOTE: Crème fraîche is not always available but it is easy enough to make. Into 300 ml (10 fl oz) of cream, stir 1 tablespoon of unflavoured yoghurt or buttermilk, and leave at room temperature overnight or until it has thickened and has a nutty taste. Or heat to body temperature in in a warm water bath or yoghurt maker, and leave for 5 hours. Crème fraîche can be stored in the refrigerator for up to 10 days.

SERVES: 6

# SPICY PARSNIP SOUP

*A thick soup that has wonderful flavour.*

### INGREDIENTS

500 g (1 lb) parsnips

•

2 stalks celery, including leafy tops

•

spring onion (scallion) or leek leaves

•

few parsley or coriander sprigs

Peel the parsnips and put the peelings into a saucepan with the celery tops, onion leaves, parsley or coriander sprigs and water. Bring slowly to boil, then cover and simmer for 30 minutes. Strain and discard solids.

Heat oil or butter and sauté onion and leeks or spring onions until golden. Add curry powder, chopped parsnips and celery, and cook for a further 2 minutes. Add strained

6 cups (48 fl oz) water

2 tablespoons oil or butter

1 onion, chopped

2 leeks or 6 spring onions (scallions)

1 teaspoon mild curry powder

5 cups (40 fl oz) water or stock

¼ teaspoon white pepper

1 teaspoon salt

½ cup (4 fl oz) evaporated milk
or cream, optional

2 tablespoons chopped coriander
or parsley

½ cup (4 fl oz) yoghurt

1 teaspoon toasted cumin seeds

fresh coriander leaves, to garnish

stock, pepper and salt, and simmer a further 25–30 minutes or until tender. Cool slightly and purée in blender. Reheat in a saucepan, but don't boil. Stir in milk, adjust seasonings and serve topped with chopped coriander or parsley and a spoonful of yoghurt sprinkled with crushed toasted cumin. Garnish with coriander sprigs. Nice served with curried croûtons.

NOTE: To make curried croûtons, cut 3 slices white or wholemeal (whole wheat) bread into small dice, fry in a very little oil or butter with ½ teaspoon of curry powder added, until golden. Drain on absorbent paper.

SERVES: 4–6

# BLUEBERRY WINE SOUP

*Use any berries which are plentiful, or even stoned cherries.*

### INGREDIENTS

200 g (6½ oz) blueberries

1 cup (8 fl oz) sauterne

1 cup (8 fl oz) water

3 tablespoons sugar

half a vanilla bean

1 tablespoon arrowroot

4 tablespoons light sour cream
or whipped cream

Wash and drain the berries. Put wine, water, sugar and vanilla bean into an enamel or stainless steel pan and bring to the boil, stirring to dissolve the sugar. Simmer for 10 minutes, then add the berries, reserving a few for decoration. Cook gently for a few minutes longer, or just until the berries are tender and the liquid has taken on a pretty colour. Pick out the vanilla bean, split it and scrape the tiny black seeds into the soup.

Mix the arrowroot with a little cold water and stir it into the simmering soup for a minute or two, until it is clear and slightly thick. Pour into a bowl and chill.

If liked, a spoonful of light sour cream or whipped cream can be swirled through, and the reserved berries placed on top.

SERVES: 4

# STRAWBERRY AND ORANGE SOUP

*When strawberries are in season and cheap, make this fragrant, fruity soup.*

### INGREDIENTS

¼ cup (1½ oz) sago or minute tapioca

•

400 g (13 oz) ripe strawberries

•

3 tablespoons sugar, or to taste

•

1 cup (8 fl oz) fresh orange juice

•

ice cubes or crushed ice

Boil the sago as described in Summer Berry Soup (see page 56). Wash the strawberries well, hull and drain them, and set aside 8 berries for garnish. Purée the remaining berries with sugar and orange juice in a blender or food processor. Stir in cooked sago and the reserved berries, sliced. Cover and chill the soup so that the sago grains absorb colour from the strawberry purée. Ladle over a little crushed ice if the day is really hot.

SERVES: 4

# MINESTRONE

*The dried beans, pasta and chunky vegetables almost make this soup a meal
when it is served with lots of crusty bread.*

### INGREDIENTS

250 g (8 oz) dried haricot beans

•

2 tablespoons olive oil

•

1 cup (5 oz) chopped onion

•

3 cloves garlic, finely chopped

•

1 stalk celery, finely diced

•

1 large carrot, diced

•

1 small can tomatoes

•

8 cups (64 fl oz) Vegetable Stock
(see page 448)

•

½ cup (2½ oz) soup pasta
(fine, small pasta)

•

1 cup (4 oz) sliced or diced zucchini
(courgettes)

•

½ cup (2 oz) grated parmesan cheese

•

4 tablespoons finely chopped parsley

Soak the dried beans in cold water to cover overnight. Some versions mix various types of dried beans, such as haricots, chick peas and brown lentils, about 250 g (8 oz) altogether. Next day, drain and cover with fresh water and simmer until almost tender.

In a heavy-based saucepan, heat the olive oil for a few minutes. Add the onion, garlic, celery and carrot. Cover and cook over very low heat, stirring occasionally, for about 10 minutes. Add the tomatoes and stock, then cover and simmer for 1 hour.

Add the pasta, zucchini and more boiling stock if necessary. When pasta is tender the soup is ready to be served with parmesan cheese and parsley sprinkled over.

SERVES: 6–8

STRAWBERRY AND ORANGE SOUP

# CORN CHOWDER

*I've yet to meet the person who doesn't like corn chowder with its natural
sweetness. All that fibre is so beneficial too!*

### INGREDIENTS

1 tablespoon butter or olive oil
•
2 stalks celery, finely chopped
•
1 carrot, finely diced
•
1 small onion, finely chopped
•
2 cups (16 fl oz) water
•
2 tablespoons plain (all-purpose)
flour
•
1½ cups (12 fl oz) milk
•
1 small bay leaf
•
1 × 440 g (14½ oz) can creamed corn
•
½ cup (4 fl oz) cream
•
¾ cup (3 oz) grated cheese or
cottage cheese
•
chopped parsley, for garnish

Melt butter and sauté celery, carrot and onion until golden.
Add water and simmer for 20 minutes. Meanwhile, blend
flour with a little cold milk and heat remaining milk with
the bay leaf. Pour the hot milk onto the flour, stirring to
mix smoothly. Return to pan and cook for 3 minutes, stirring
constantly. Stir in the creamed corn, cream and cheese.
Combine both mixtures and reheat carefully if necessary.
Do not boil. Garnish with chopped parsley.

NOTE: If a smoother result is desired the celery, carrot and
onion may be puréed before combining with corn mixture.

SERVES: 4

# ASPARAGUS SOUP

*When fresh asparagus is in season, try this delicate soup.*

### INGREDIENTS

500 g (1 lb) fresh asparagus spears
•
100 g (3½ oz) green beans
•
6 spring onions (scallions)
•
4 parsley sprigs
•
2 stalks celery, including tops
•
half a bay leaf
•
6 cups (48 fl oz) water

Trim the asparagus and set aside a few perfect tips for garnish.
Use any tough ends of stalks for making the stock and put
them into a saucepan with the green beans, the green parts
of the spring onions, parsley sprigs, celery, bay leaf, water
and peppercorns. Bring to a boil, then lower heat and simmer
for 25–30 minutes. Strain, discarding solids.

Slice the white part of the spring onions and cook gently
in the butter or oil until soft but not brown. Add the
asparagus roughly chopped into about 1 cm (½ in) pieces,
4 cups (32 fl oz) stock, parsley, and salt and pepper. Cook,
uncovered, for 10 minutes or until asparagus is tender and
still bright green. Cool slightly, then place in blender and

10 whole peppercorns
•
2 tablespoons butter or oil
•
1 tablespoon finely chopped parsley
•
salt and pepper to taste
•
¼ cup (2 fl oz) cream or evaporated milk
•
4 teaspoons sour cream or whipped cream (optional)

purée. Strain to remove fibres. Return strained purée to the pan and thin if necessary with a little extra stock. Stir in cream, taste and adjust seasoning.

Cook the reserved asparagus tips in a small quantity of water until tender. Drain. Put a teaspoonful of sour cream or whipped cream on each serving of soup and garnish with the asparagus tips.

SERVES: 4

# CARROT AND ORANGE SOUP

*A delicious soup to serve hot or cold, refreshing and with a creamy texture, although it contains no cream at all. If serving hot, reduce orange rind to 1 teaspoon or it may be too strong, whereas cold soups need the extra flavouring.*

### STOCK

trimmings from carrots and 1 extra carrot, chopped
•
2 stalks celery with tops, chopped
•
1 onion, unpeeled
•
several parsley stalks
•
6 cups (48 fl oz) water
•
½ teaspoon salt

### INGREDIENTS
2 tablespoons butter or olive oil
•
1 onion, roughly chopped
•
500 g (1 lb) carrots
•
3 cups (24 fl oz) stock (see above)
•
1 teaspoon salt
•
¼ teaspoon white pepper
•
2 teaspoons finely grated orange rind
•
1 cup (8 fl oz) strained orange juice
•
sprig of parsley or coriander, for garnish

Make the stock first. Bring all the ingredients to the boil, cover pan, reduce heat and simmer for 30 minutes. Strain.

Heat butter or olive oil in a heavy-based saucepan and cook onion gently until golden. Add chopped carrots and sauté for 2–3 minutes longer. Add the stock, salt and pepper, then cover and simmer for 20–25 minutes. Cool slightly and purée in a blender. Stir in orange rind and juice and adjust seasoning if necessary. Chill, or reheat without boiling. Serve garnished with a sprig of parsley or fresh coriander.

SERVES: 4–5

# VICHYSSOISE VERTE

*It is with very good reason that vichyssoise has become so famous—its flavour is unrivalled. This version has a pretty green colour because of the added peas, but if you prefer it to be the traditional creamy white, simply omit them.*

## INGREDIENTS

4 leeks or 12 large spring onions (scallions)
•
4 medium potatoes
•
2 tablespoons butter
•
1 cup (6 oz) frozen peas
•
6 cups (48 fl oz) Vegetable Stock (see page 448)
•
salt and pepper, to taste
•
½ cup (4 fl oz) cream (optional)
•
2 tablespoons finely chopped chives

Wash leeks well, using the white part and 5 cm (2 in) of the green leaves. With a sharp knife, make a cross cut into leeks and separate leaves while washing to make sure no grit remains. Peel and cut potatoes into thin slices.

Heat butter in a saucepan and when melted, put in the sliced leeks or spring onions and cook over low heat, covered, until soft but not brown. Add potatoes, peas and stock, salt and pepper. Cover and simmer for 15 minutes.

Cool the mixture, put into a blender and purée until smooth. Pass through a nylon sieve and chill for at least 2 hours. Stir in cream and taste for seasoning.

Serve in chilled soup cups. If liked, swirl a little extra cream on top of each serving and sprinkle with chopped chives.

NOTE: For weight watchers, the cream content of the soup may be omitted and no one would notice, the soup is so rich in flavour and texture.

SERVES: 6

VICHYSSOISE VERTE

# MAIN DISHES

These recipes are for the hearty eater and can either take their place in a menu or be the one and only featured dish when there is neither the time nor the inclination to provide a number of courses.

## FRESH HOMEMADE PASTA

*Purists about pasta say this is the only kind worth eating. I wouldn't go so far, but there is no doubt that freshly made pasta is in a class of its own. Besides, you can invest it with flavours and colours using fresh herbs and vegetables, custom-made to your own taste.*

## PLAIN PASTA

### INGREDIENTS

1½ cups (6 oz) plain (all-purpose) flour
•
½ cup (3 oz) fine semolina
•
½ teaspoon salt
•
3 × 55 g (medium) eggs
•
2 tablespoons oil
•
1 tablespoon water

Mix flour, semolina and salt together on a smooth surface, make a well in the centre and add the eggs, oil and water. Mix and knead for at least 10 minutes. The dough should be smooth, non-sticky and elastic. Cover with a bowl and allow to rest for 20–30 minutes.

Roll out half the dough at a time on a floured surface, as thinly as possible. Leave to dry for 15 minutes. Sprinkle with flour and fold three or four times, then cut into strips of the required thickness. Shake the strands loose and boil in lightly salted water. Drain, and serve immediately with Tomato Sauce (page 86) or with grated cheese, seasoned cream, or simply tossed with 2 tablespoons of pure olive oil in which a clove of crushed garlic has been cooked.

SERVES: 4

## HERB PASTA

Blanch a few sprigs of basil or parsley for 1 minute in boiling water. Drain well, squeezing out the moisture. Chop finely and add to the basic pasta recipe. The pasta will have a speckled effect.

# FRESH SPINACH PASTA

*Yes, there is plenty of spinach pasta sold both dried and "fresh" but unless you have made your own you cannot imagine what a difference there is in texture, flavour and colour.*

## INGREDIENTS

few leaves spinach
(not silverbeet or chard)
•
1 tablespoon water
•
1½ cups (6 oz) plain
(all-purpose) flour
•
½ cup (3 oz) fine semolina
•
½ teaspoon salt
•
2 × 60 g (large) eggs
•
2 tablespoons oil

Wash the spinach and blanch it in boiling water for less than 1 minute, then plunge it into iced water to set the colour. Drain well and chop. Put a tablespoon of the spinach into a blender jar with the tablespoon of water and blend to a smooth purée. If more liquid is needed to facilitate blending, add one of the eggs.

Mix the flour, semolina and salt together on a smooth surface, make a well in the centre and add the eggs, oil and puréed spinach. Knead for 10 minutes or until the dough is smooth and elastic. Cover with a bowl or wrap in plastic and let the dough rest for 20–30 minutes.

Roll out half the dough very thinly on a lightly floured board, or use a pasta machine, starting at the thickest setting and working progressively through to the finest. Leave the sheets of pasta to dry for 15 minutes, then cut into thin strips with a sharp knife or fix the cutting attachment to the pasta machine and cut into fettucine strips or vermicelli.

Have ready a large pan of boiling, lightly salted water with a splash of oil added. Drop in the pasta and when it returns to the boil cook for just 1 minute. Drain and serve immediately with some finely grated parmesan cheese, a knob of butter or a little cream.

NOTE: You don't need to invest in machinery—a rolling pin and pastry board are enough. But, being honest, using a hand-turned pasta machine does make it easier. If the pasta craze really gets to you, it would be a worthwhile investment.

The machine may also be used to "knead" the dough, by passing the dough through the rollers eight times on the widest setting. Take a small portion at a time and fold it in three each time before passing it through to keep it a manageable size.

I also use my pasta machine for making the paper-thin Armenian crispbread, Lavosh (see page 401).

SERVES: 4

# ASPARAGUS WITH PASTA

*Vegetable sauces for pasta are more in vogue now than the tired old Bolognese.*

## INGREDIENTS

2 bundles asparagus,
about 500 g (1 lb)

•

2 small white onions

•

90 g (3 oz) butter

•

freshly ground sea salt and
black pepper to taste

•

375 g (12 oz) small shell pasta

Snap off ends and peel asparagus spears if necessary. Wash well. Cut spears into small pieces, starting from the base and leaving the tips whole. Reserve the tips separately. Peel, halve and chop the onions finely.

Melt butter in a saucepan, add the onion and sliced asparagus and cook over very low heat until the vegetables are soft. Add salt and pepper to taste, then put in the tips to cook. Meanwhile, cook pasta in a large amount of fast boiling salted water with a dash of oil added.

When pasta is tender but still firm when bitten, add cold water to pan to stop cooking, and drain the pasta in a colander. Shake the colander to get rid of as much water as possible. Add to the pan with the asparagus and toss until thoroughly mixed. If a richer sauce is preferred, add a generous ½ cup (4 fl oz) of cream and heat through before tossing with the pasta.

SERVES: 4–6

# FETTUCINI ALFREDO

## INGREDIENTS

1 quantity Plain or Herb Pasta Dough
(see page 82) or 375 g (12 oz)
fettucine noodles

•

90 g (3 oz) soft butter

•

1 cup (4 oz) freshly grated parmesan
cheese

Divide pasta dough into two portions and roll out one portion on a lightly floured board until paper thin. Dust lightly with flour, roll up like a Swiss roll (jelly roll) and with a very sharp knife, cut into narrow slices. Quickly unroll strips to prevent sticking together. Repeat with the other half of dough.

Bring a large amount of salted water to the boil and cook fettucine until just tender. Do not overcook. Drain immediately.

Serve in a warm dish, add butter and half the cheese and toss until strands are coated with the mixture. Serve at once. Pass around extra cheese for sprinkling and a pepper mill for freshly ground black pepper.

SERVES: 4

ASPARAGUS WITH PASTA

# BEETROOT PASTA

*Don't panic when you see the colour of the pasta dough! It fades to a pretty pink when cooked.*

## INGREDIENTS

1½ cups (6 oz) plain
(all-purpose) flour

•

½ cup (3 oz) fine semolina

•

½ teaspoon salt

•

2 × 55 g (medium) eggs

•

2 tablespoons oil

•

50 g (1½ oz) cooked beets
(not canned)

Combine the dry ingredients. In an electric blender process the eggs, oil and beetroot, pour onto the flour mixture and knead 10 minutes or until smooth. Cover and rest 30 minutes before rolling out thinly. Make fettucine, vermicelli, ravioli or little bows.

For bows, simply cut with a pastry wheel into strips about 3 cm (1¼ in) wide, then across into 6 cm (2½ in) lengths and pinch together in the middle.

Cook until tender in boiling water with a little oil, drain and serve with a sauce or grated cheese.

SERVES: 4

# EGGPLANT LASAGNE

## INGREDIENTS

2 large eggplants (aubergines)

•

½ cup (4 fl oz) French Dressing
(see page 184)

•

1 clove garlic, crushed

•

1 packet instant lasagne noodles

TOMATO SAUCE

3 tablespoons olive oil

•

2 large onions, finely chopped

•

2 cloves garlic, crushed

•

1 large can peeled tomatoes, or
1 kg (2 lb) ripe tomatoes,
peeled and chopped

•

1 teaspoon dried oregano

•

1 teaspoon dried basil

•

3 tablespoons tomato paste
dissolved in ½ cup (4 fl oz) of water

Wash the eggplants but do not peel them. Cut crossways into slices about 1 cm (½ in) thick and brush both sides of each slice with French dressing mixed with the garlic. Preheat griller (broiler), place eggplant slices on a tray lined with foil and grill until golden brown on one side, then turn over and grill other side.

To make the tomato sauce, heat oil in a saucepan and cook the onions and garlic over low heat, stirring frequently, until they are soft and golden. Add tomatoes, herbs, the tomato paste dissolved in ½ cup (4 fl oz) of water, sugar and seasonings. Cover and simmer for 30 minutes, or until slightly thickened.

In a well buttered, ovenproof dish (preferably a square or rectangular shape because the lasagne noodles will fit more easily), ladle in just enough tomato sauce to cover the base. Place a layer of lasagne noodles in the sauce. Make a layer of the grilled eggplant slices, cover with tomato sauce, then more lasagne and so on until the dish is three-quarters full. There should always be sufficient sauce on either side of the noodles to moisten them thoroughly. Bake in an oven preheated to 180°C (350°F) for 20 minutes.

1 tablespoon sugar

•

1 teaspoon salt

•

¼ teaspoon pepper

CHEESE SAUCE

2 tablespoons butter

•

2 tablespoons flour

•

1¼ cups (10 fl oz) milk

•

salt and pepper to taste

•

2 eggs, separated

•

250 g (8 oz) tasty (sharp) cheese,
finely grated

Meanwhile, make the cheese sauce for topping lasagne. Melt butter in a saucepan, add flour and stir over low heat for 2 minutes. Whisk in milk and stir constantly until it boils and thickens. Remove from heat, season to taste, then beat in the egg yolks, one at a time. Reserve 3 tablespoons of cheese for topping lasagne and stir in the rest. Whip the egg whites until stiff and fold into the sauce.

Remove lasagne from oven and pour the sauce over the top, taking it right to the edges of the dish. Sprinkle with reserved cheese and return to the oven for a further 25 minutes, or until well puffed and browned. Serve hot, with crusty bread and a green salad.

SERVES: 6–8

# PASTA WITH MUSHROOMS AND PEAS

INGREDIENTS

250 g (8 oz) button mushrooms

•

2–3 tablespoons olive oil

•

outer leaves from 2 cos (romaine)
lettuce

•

white portion of 1 leek, finely sliced

•

1½ cups (6 oz) shelled fresh peas

•

1 teaspoon sugar

•

sprig of fresh mint

•

2 cups (16 fl oz) water or stock

•

1 cup (8 fl oz) milk or half cream,
half milk

•

salt and freshly ground
black pepper to taste

•

1 tablespoon soft butter mixed
with 1 tablespoon flour

•

500 g (1 lb) pasta

•

finely grated cheese for serving

Wipe over the mushrooms and if they are small, leave them whole, otherwise cut them in halves or quarters. Heat the olive oil in a saucepan and on low heat, cook the finely shredded lettuce and leek, covered, for 10 minutes or until soft.

Add the peas, sugar, mint, water or stock, cover and cook for 15 minutes or until peas are tender. Meanwhile, cook the pasta in lightly salted boiling water until just tender, drain and have ready.

Add mushrooms, milk and cream to the vegetables and bring to a simmer, season to taste with salt and pepper, then add small bits of butter and flour mixture to the sauce, stirring so they dissolve and thicken the liquid. Simmer for a few minutes. Turn the pasta into the vegetable mixture and heat through without boiling. Serve with a bowl of finely grated cheese for sprinkling over.

SERVES: 4–6

# SPAGHETTI SQUASH MEDLEY

## INGREDIENTS

800 g (1 lb 12 oz) cooked
spaghetti squash
•
1 or 2 corn cobs
•
2 or 3 young carrots
•
3 tablespoons olive oil
•
1 medium onion, very finely chopped
•
1 clove garlic, crushed
•
1 teaspoon dried sweet basil or
1 tablespoon chopped fresh basil
•
1 cup (4 oz) fresh or frozen (6 oz)
green peas
•
¼ teaspoon finely grated nutmeg
•
salt and pepper to taste

Cook the spaghetti squash until tender, drain and allow to cool. With a sharp knife, cut the corn kernels from the cob. Slice the carrots finely. Heat the olive oil in a large saucepan and, on gentle heat, cook the onion and garlic for a few minutes, then add the basil and vegetables.

Cover and cook on low heat for 10 minutes or until just tender. Meanwhile, scoop the spaghetti-like strands from the cooked vegetable, add to pan and toss until heated through. Add nutmeg, taste for seasoning and serve hot.

SERVES: 6

# SPANISH OMELETTE

## INGREDIENTS

6 eggs
•
salt and pepper to taste
•
3 tablespoons olive oil
•
cold cooked potatoes, sliced
•
1 medium onion, finely chopped

Beat the eggs lightly and add salt and pepper to taste. Heat half the oil in a large, heavy-based frying pan and fry the potato slices until golden brown. Remove from pan. Add remaining oil and fry the onions until soft and golden, pour in the eggs and return the potato slices to the pan. Cook on low heat until eggs are set, then run a spatula around edge of pan to loosen the omelette and turn it over onto a large plate. If necessary, heat a little more oil and slip the omelette back into the pan to brown the other side. Serve hot, cut in quarters and accompanied by tomato wedges and crusty bread.

SERVES: 4

SPAGHETTI SQUASH MEDLEY

# SPINACH RAVIOLI

*Ravioli, little pasta parcels with fillings, is no quick and easy meal, but
it is very satisfying to make and tastes infinitely better than bought ravioli.*

### INGREDIENTS

1 quantity of Spinach Pasta
(see page 83)

### FILLING

1 cup cooked, drained and
finely chopped spinach
(about 12 oz uncooked)
•
2 tablespoons finely grated
fresh parmesan cheese
•
salt, white pepper and
ground nutmeg to taste

extra grated parmesan for serving

Roll the pasta dough very thinly by hand or with a pasta machine. Lay the strip on the work surface and lose no time in filling and sealing the ravioli while the dough is still moist.

Mix together the spinach, parmesan and seasoning. Put half-teaspoons of the mixture along one edge of the dough at regular intervals, brush with cold water between each mound, and fold the strip in half lengthways. Press firmly to seal and use a pastry cutter to separate the little squares, or cut into round shapes with a small biscuit (or scone) cutter.

Lay the ravioli in a single layer on a lightly floured tea-towel and cover with another tea-towel. Repeat until all the dough and filling are used up. Cook as soon as possible in lightly salted boiling water with a splash of oil added to prevent boiling over. Drain when just tender, which will depend on how finely you have rolled the pasta. Serve immediately, with extra grated parmesan passed separately.

# MUSHROOM LASAGNE

### INGREDIENTS

375 g (12 oz) fresh mushrooms
•
60 g (2 oz) butter
•
2 tablespoons oil
•
salt and pepper to taste
•
½ cup (4 fl oz) cream or sour cream
•
150 g (5 oz) lasagna noodles
•
250 g (8 oz) ricotta cheese
•
1 cup grated (4 oz) sharp cheese

Wipe over and slice mushrooms, heat butter and oil in a heavy-based frying pan and toss in the mushrooms. Stir briefly over the heat, then season generously with salt and freshly ground pepper. Pour in the cream, stir well and turn off the heat.

For speed I prefer the lasagne which needs no pre-cooking. If you cannot obtain this, cook lasagne in lightly salted boiling water until just tender. Run cold water into the pan to stop it cooking further.

Grease a large ovenproof dish, put in a half cup of Pizzaiola or pasta sauce, then a layer of drained lasagne noodles. Crumble ricotta cheese over, then cover with mushroom mixture. Repeat with more noodles, tomato sauce and so on until you finish with a layer of tomato sauce. Sprinkle

extra tablespoon butter
•
2 cups (16 fl oz) Pizzaiola Sauce
(see page 441) or bottled
pasta sauce

thickly with grated cheese, dot with butter and bake in an oven preheated to 190°C (375°F) for 45 minutes or until golden brown.

SERVES: 4–6

# LEEK AND BROCCOLI FLAN

### INGREDIENTS

1 quantity No-roll Pastry
(see page 447)
•
1 large or 2 medium leeks
•
3 tablespoons butter
•
375 g (12 oz) broccoli
•
3 large or 4 medium eggs
•
½ cup (4 fl oz) milk
•
90 g (3 oz) grated Cheddar cheese

salt and pepper to taste

Make pastry and line a 23 cm (9 in) pie plate. Wash the leeks well, slitting them in half to make sure all sand and grit between the leaves are rinsed away. Slice the white parts and tender portion of the green leaves very finely.

Heat the butter in a heavy-based saucepan and on low heat, cook the leeks, covered, until soft but not brown. Meanwhile, cut the broccoli into florets, peel the stems and cut into slices. Bring 1 cup (8 fl oz) water to the boil with a half teaspoon of salt. Drop in the broccoli and cook for 2–3 minutes, until half tender and still bright green. Drain, reserving liquid. Beat the eggs, add milk and cheese, and season to taste. Stir in the leeks and half cup of the broccoli cooking liquid. Arrange broccoli in the pastry-lined plate, pour the milk mixture over and bake in an oven preheated to 190°C (375°F) for 20 minutes. Lower heat to 180°C (350°F) and bake for a further 20 minutes or until filling is firm and pastry nicely browned.

SERVES: 6

# CHEESE SOUFFLÉS

*The best standby ever for impressive meals without meat. If you've never tried a soufflé before, think of it as nothing more intimidating than a well-flavoured white sauce into which eggs are incorporated. Nothing to be afraid of. If you have individual soufflé moulds, use them because they will cook more quickly than a large one. If you have no soufffflé mould at all, don't be put off because the mixture will rise just as well in a casserole dish (a deep shape rather than a large shallow one).*

## INGREDIENTS

1 tablespoon butter and dry breadcrumbs, flour or grated parmesan cheese for preparing dish
•
60 g (2 oz) butter
•
3 tablespoons plain flour
•
1¼ cups (10 fl oz) milk
•
1 teaspoon prepared mustard
•
½ teaspoon salt
•
¼ teaspoon white pepper
•
¼ teaspoon ground mace or nutmeg
•
3 egg yolks
•
4 egg whites
•
125 g (4 oz) tasty (sharp) cheese, finely grated

Butter a 4 cup soufflé mould or individual moulds and dust with breadcrumbs or parmesan, shaking out excess. Preheat the oven to 200°C (400°F).

Melt the butter in a heavy-based saucepan and when foaming, sprinkle in the flour and stir over low heat for 1–2 minutes, not letting it brown. Heat the milk and pour it onto the butter and flour all at once, whisking vigorously with a wire whisk until smooth. Add seasonings and cook, stirring constantly. Bring to the boil and allow to boil for 1 minute.

Remove pan from heat and beat in the yolks one at a time. Let mixture cool slightly while whisking whites and pinch of salt to a stiff froth. (A pinch of cream of tartar added while beating helps stiffen the albumen.) Stir a quarter of the whites into the sauce to lighten the mixture, then stir in the cheese, reserving 1–2 tablespoons for the top. Lightly fold in the remaining egg white, taking care not to over-mix and lose the air you've beaten in. Pour mixture into the soufflé dish or divide between the individual dishes. Put into preheated hot oven, and immediately lower the temperature to 190°C (375°F).

Bake single soufflé for 25 minutes or until well risen and golden brown. Individual soufflés will require about 12–15 minutes. Serve at once with a tossed green salad.

SERVES: 4–6

CHEESE SOUFFLÉS

# BRUSSELS SPROUTS TIMBALE

*Turned out on a serving dish surrounded with bright carrot slices, green peas and button mushrooms, this mould makes an impressive main dish. Cooked, well-drained broccoli could be used instead of the Brussels sprouts if preferred.*

### INGREDIENTS

750 g (1½ lb) Brussels sprouts
•
salt and pepper to taste
•
¼ teaspoon ground mace or
freshly grated nutmeg
•
1 egg
•
¾ cup (1½ oz) fresh, soft
breadcrumbs
•
1½ tablespoons butter
•
¼ cup (2 fl oz) hot milk
•
Mornay Sauce (see page 106) or
Sour Cream Sauce (see page 126)

Wash and trim the sprouts and cook in boiling water until tender. Drain well, pressing out as much excess liquid as possible. Purée in a food processor and season to taste with salt, pepper and spice. Add the well beaten egg, then stir in the breadcrumbs. Melt the butter in the hot milk and mix in.

Turn the purée into a well buttered mould, preferably a straight-sided soufflé dish or timbale. Place in a pan of hot water. Cut a piece of greaseproof paper to fit the top of the mould, butter it and place on the surface of the purée, pressing it down right to the edges. Bake in an oven preheated to 180°C (350°F) for 40 minutes or until firm.

Remove from the oven, leave 10 minutes or so, then run a knife around the edge of the mould to ensure it turns out cleanly. Invert the serving dish over the mould, grasp both with a tea towel or oven mitts and turn over so the mould slides out. Serve with hot sauce poured over.

SERVES: 4–6

# GREEN PASTA WITH PUMPKIN AND WALNUT SAUCE

### INGREDIENTS

500 g (1 lb) pumpkin
•
1 tablespoon butter
•
¼ teaspoon white pepper
•
¼ teaspoon salt
•
1 teaspoon finely chopped dill
•
1 tablespoon finely chopped chives

Cut pumpkin in wedges, scoop out and discard the centre membrane and seeds. Steam, boil or microwave until tender. When cool enough to handle, cut away the skin with a sharp knife. Mash the pumpkin with the butter, pepper and salt. Stir in the dill and half the chives and walnuts.

Cook the pasta in a large amount of lightly salted boiling water with a teaspoon of oil added to keep it from boiling over. Freshly made pasta will be ready in 1 minute from when the water returns to the boil, but dried pasta will take longer. Test every 2 minutes and stop cooking when

½ cup (2 oz) coarsely chopped walnuts

•

250 g (8 oz) capelli d'angelo spinach pasta or homemade spinach pasta

•

1 tablespoon olive oil

•

1 clove garlic, crushed

tender but still slightly firm. Remove from heat, run cold water into the pan to stop the cooking, and drain immediately in a colander.

Heat olive oil in the saucepan, add the garlic and stir over low heat for a minute or two, not allowing the garlic to brown. Return the pasta and toss to distribute the oil and garlic.

Put the pasta in a serving dish and pile the pumpkin mixture in the centre. Sprinkle with remaining chives and walnuts and serve at once.

NOTE: Either make spinach pasta or buy the fine, 'angel hair' variety. For convenience, cut the unpeeled pumpkin in wedges and cook in the microwave oven on HIGH for 6–8 minutes, or until tender, while boiling the pasta on the stove.

SERVES: 4

# SAVOURY PECAN LOAF

*Serve this high protein loaf with cooked vegetables or a green salad.*

### INGREDIENTS

250 g (8 oz) pecan kernels

•

3 cups (6 oz) fresh wholegrain breadcrumbs

•

2 tablespoons butter or oil

•

1 cup (5 oz) finely chopped onions

•

1 cup (5 oz) finely chopped celery

•

1 cup (2 oz) finely grated carrot

•

1 cup (8 oz) cottage cheese (optional)

•

1 teaspoon dried oregano

•

3 eggs, beaten

•

1 teaspoon salt

•

½ teaspoon pepper

•

½ cup (1 oz) chopped parsley

Finely chop the pecans—a food processor does this quickly. Combine in a bowl with the breadcrumbs. Heat the butter or oil and cook the onions over medium heat until soft and golden. Remove from heat, add to the pecans together with the rest of the ingredients and mix together thoroughly. Put into a greased loaf tin and bake in an oven preheated to 180°C (350°F) for 35–40 minutes or until firm.

SERVES: 6

# RATATOUILLE

*A highly-flavoured vegetable stew popular in French provincial cooking.*

## INGREDIENTS

750 g (1½ lb) eggplant (aubergine)
•
cooking salt
•
3 small zucchini (courgettes)
•
2 red or green capsicums (peppers)
•
3 cloves garlic
•
2 large onions
•
4 large ripe tomatoes
•
½ cup (4 fl oz) olive oil
•
1 teaspoon ground coriander
•
1 teaspoon dried basil
•
salt and freshly ground black
pepper to taste

Wash eggplant but do not peel. Cut into cubes, sprinkle with salt and set aside in a colander for an hour. Slice unpeeled zucchini and treat in the same way as the eggplant. Press out and discard liquid drawn out by the salt. Discard seeds and centre membranes from capsicums and cut into strips. Finely chop the garlic and onions. Peel, seed and chop the tomatoes.

Heat olive oil in a heavy-based saucepan and cook the onions and garlic until soft but not brown. Add eggplant, capsicums and zucchini, cover and cook on low heat for half an hour, then add the tomatoes, coriander, basil, salt and pepper and cook for a further 30–40 minutes or until the vegetables are very tender. Serve warm or cold, accompanied by flat middle eastern bread or crusty French bread, preferably wholemeal (whole wheat).

NOTE: To make a more substantial meal, put the cooked ratatouille into an ovenproof dish, make hollows with the back of a spoon and break in an egg for each person. Bake in an oven preheated to 180°C (350°F), until the eggs are cooked as desired. (*see photograph page 96*)

SERVES: 6

# BAKED EGGPLANT

## INGREDIENTS

2 medium eggplants (aubergines)
•
2 tablespoons oil
•
2 onions, finely chopped
•
½ teaspoon ground black pepper
•
1 teaspoon salt
•
½ teaspoon dried oregano
•
1 cup chopped raw cashews
•
1 cup (2 oz) fresh wholemeal
breadcrumbs

Slice stem ends off eggplants half and lengthways and score the flesh. Drop into boiling, lightly salted water for 7-10 minutes, or until just tender. Drain well with the cut sides downwards. When cool enough to handle, gently scoop out centres, leaving a fairly thick shell that will hold its shape.

Heat the oil and fry the onions over gentle heat until soft and golden. Add the scooped out eggplants, the seasonings and cashews and mix well. Fill the eggplants with the mixture and place in a lightly greased baking dish.

Mix breadcrumbs with the butter, garlic and cheese. Sprinkle over eggplants and bake in an oven preheated to 180°C (350°F) for 25-35 minutes or until tops are crisp and golden. Serve hot.

SERVES: 4

2 tablespoons butter or margarine,
melted

•

2 small cloves garlic, crushed

•

1 cup (4 oz) grated cheddar cheese

# RAVIOLI WITH NUT FILLING

DOUGH

1½ cups (6 oz) plain (all-purpose)
flour

•

½ cup (3 oz) fine semolina

•

½ teaspoon salt

•

2 × 60 g (large) eggs

•

2 tablespoons oil

•

1 tablespoon chopped fresh
basil or parsley

•

2 tablespoons water

•

melted butter and freshly
grated Parmesan for serving

NUT FILLING

1 leek

•

1 tablespoon olive oil

•

⅓ cup (1½ oz) ground Brazil nuts
or raw cashews

•

¾ cup (1½ oz) fresh wholemeal
(whole wheat) breadcrumbs

•

3 tablespoons wheatgerm

•

½ teaspoon dried sage

•

¼ teaspoon white pepper

•

¼ teaspoon salt

•

1 egg yolk

Put all the dough ingredients into the bowl of a food processor and process until it forms a mass, or mix on a smooth work surface. Knead for 10 minutes until smooth and elastic (see Note page 83). Cover with a bowl and let it rest for 20 minutes.

Meanwhile, make the filling. Wash the leek well, and finely chop the white portion. Heat the olive oil and cook the chopped leek until soft, stirring frequently. Remove from the heat and mix with the remaining ingredients.

Take a quarter of the dough at a time and roll out very thinly, (or use pasta machine as described in Note on page 83). Do the same with another portion. Put on a lightly floured work surface, and place teaspoonsful of the filling on one sheet at intervals. Moisten around the mounds of filling with a brush or finger dipped in cold water. Cover with the second sheet, pressing gently around the filling to seal, then cut out with a pastry wheel or a small biscuit (or scone) cutter. Repeat with remaining half of dough and filling.

Drop the ravioli into a large pot of lightly salted, fast-boiling water with a splash of oil added and cook until just tender. Drain and serve immediately, with melted butter and freshly grated Parmesan for sprinkling over.

SERVES: 4

# MUSHROOM RISOTTO

### INGREDIENTS

6 cups (48 fl oz) Vegetable Stock
(see page 448)

•

150 g (5 oz) butter

•

1 small onion, finely chopped

•

½ cup (4 oz) dry porcini mushrooms,
soaked in water until soft

•

2 cups (14 oz) short grain rice,

•

1 cup dry white wine

•

salt and pepper to taste

•

freshly grated parmesan cheese

Bring broth to a boil, keep simmering. In another saucepan, heat three quarters of the butter, add the chopped onion and cook over moderate heat, stirring constantly until onion is golden. Add the well-drained mushrooms, then the rice and stir for about 3 minutes. Add wine and cook until almost evaporated. Add salt and freshly ground pepper to taste. Now start adding broth, 1 cup (8 fl oz) at a time. Continue stirring until liquid has been absorbed. Remove pan from heat, stir in remaining butter and some freshly grated parmesan. Serve additional grated parmesan separately.

SERVES: 4–6

# RISOTTA ALLA MILANESE

*A favourite Italian dish, risotto should be moist and creamy but with the rice grains still holding their shape. The distinctive feature of Risotto alla Milanese is the flavour of genuine Spanish saffron.*

### INGREDIENTS

8 cups (64 fl oz) Vegetable Stock
(see page 448)

•

½ teaspoon Spanish saffron strands

•

125 g (4 oz) butter

•

1 cup (5 oz) finely chopped onion

•

2 cups (14 oz) short grain rice,
preferably arborio rice

•

½ cup (4 fl oz) dry white wine

•

½ cup (2 oz) grated parmesan cheese

Make a well-flavoured vegetable stock. Keep stock simmering so it is very hot when added to the rice. In a small, dry pan gently toast the saffron strands for a minute or two—this makes them brittle and easily ground to powder. Pound with a mortar and pestle, then dissolve in a tablespoon of boiling water.

Melt half the butter in a heavy-based saucepan and cook onion over low heat until soft and golden, stirring frequently. Add rice and cook, stirring with a metal spoon, until all the grains are coated with butter.

Add wine and 2 cups (16 fl oz) of stock and simmer, stirring occasionally, until liquid is almost absorbed. Add 2 more cups stock, stir and continue simmering. Add saffron to remaining stock and simmer for 5 minutes. Add to the rice and cook until stock has been absorbed, by which time the rice should be very tender and moist.

Add remaining butter and the grated Parmesan and mix in very gently. Serve with a green vegetable.

SERVES: 6

MUSHROOM RISOTTO

# BARBECUED TEMPEH PATTIES

### INGREDIENTS

1 teaspoon chopped fresh thyme
or mint

•

1 quantity Savoury Tempeh
(see page 436)

•

2 tablespoons wholemeal
(whole wheat) flour

•

1 egg, beaten

•

3 tablespoons dry breadcrumbs

•

5 tablespoons roughly chopped
almonds

•

1 tablespoon melted butter or oil

Mix fresh herb of your choice into the Savoury Tempeh and shape into flat round patties. Coat in flour, then dip in beaten egg and roll in the crumbs and almonds mixed together. Repeat egg and crumb coating for a really crisp texture. With a brush, gently dab on melted butter or oil, taking care not to brush off the chopped almonds.

Cook on a hot griddle plate over the barbecue and when firm and golden, place over the coals on rack or grill for a brief time to give them that smoky barbecue flavour. Serve with barbecue sauce and a salad.

NOTE: If you can't wait until the next barbecue these may be placed on greased foil and baked in a hot oven until golden brown, about 20 minutes, or shallow fried in a frying pan.

SERVES: 4–6

# HUNZA PIE

*Remember when every "alternative lifestyle" restaurant was serving Hunza
Pie? Frankly, I don't know if the Hunzas even heard of it, but it's a
good, filling meal.*

### INGREDIENTS

PASTRY
1 cup (4 oz) wholemeal (whole
wheat) flour

•

¾ cup (3 oz) plain (all-purpose) flour

•

1 tablespoon wheatgerm

•

½ teaspoon salt

•

125 g (4 oz) chilled butter,
cut into dice

•

2–3 tablespoons water

FILLING
1 bunch spinach or silverbeet
(Swiss chard)

To make the pastry, combine dry ingredients in a food processor for a few seconds. Add the butter and process until mixture resembles breadcrumbs. With the motor running, add water down the tube until the flour and butter form a ball of dough. Remove from processor, form into a ball, wrap in plastic and refrigerate.

To prepare the filling, wash the spinach or silverbeet in several changes of cold water. With a stainless steel knife, strip the leaves from the stems (save the stems to cook as a separate vegetable), then steam the leaves in a large, stainless steel pan for 10 minutes.

Peel and dice the potatoes, cook in lightly salted water until tender. Slit and wash the leek thoroughly, shred finely and cook in butter in a covered pan until soft. Combine all the vegetables, add salt and pepper and leave until cool.

1 kg (2 lb) potatoes

•

1 large leek

•

1 tablespoon butter

•

1 teaspoon salt

•

¼ teaspoon pepper

Fill a 22.5 cm (9 in) pie dish, packing it down well.

Roll out the pastry to cover the pie dish, trim and decorate the edge. Brush with milk and make a few slits in the top. Bake in an oven preheated to 200°C (400°F) for 15 minutes, then reduce heat to 180°C (350°F) and cook a further 25 minutes, or until pastry is golden.

SERVES: 6

# BRUSSELS SPROUTS AND PECAN FLAN WITH CRUMBLE TOPPING

### INGREDIENTS

500 g (1 lb) Brussels sprouts

•

1 medium onion

•

2 teaspoons butter

•

1 tablespoon oil

•

2 small eggs, beaten

•

salt and pepper to taste

•

1 cup (4 oz) roughly chopped pecans

### PASTRY AND CRUMBLE TOPPING

90 g (3 oz) butter

•

2½ tablespoons milk

•

½ cup (2 oz) wholemeal self-raising flour (or whole wheat flour with 1 level teaspoon of baking powder)

•

½ cup (2 oz) self-raising white flour

•

2 slices wholemeal bread

Wash and trim the vegetables and slice them finely. In a heavy-based saucepan, heat butter and oil, put in the sliced sprouts and onion and toss for a few minutes on medium heat, taking care not to brown them. Turn heat very low, cover with lid and steam for about 10 minutes, stirring once or twice.

Add about ½ cup (4 fl oz) water or just enough to prevent burning, and cook until tender. Cool, drain off any excess liquid, and purée in a food processor. Add eggs, pepper and salt and blend well. Stir in the pecans.

To make the pastry, put butter and milk into a saucepan and heat until butter melts. Remove from heat, add the two kinds of flour together and stir until it forms a ball. Take two thirds of the mixture and press into a lightly buttered 20 cm (8 in) pie plate to form a thin shell. This pastry doesn't need rolling out.

Remove crusts from bread and, in a food processor, make breadcrumbs. Add the remaining pastry mixture and process for 3–4 seconds until it is well distributed through the crumbs. Pour the vegetable mixture into the pie shell and sprinkle crumb topping evenly over the filling. Bake in an oven preheated to 180°C (350°F) 40–45 minutes or until golden. Cover top with foil if it browns before the pastry shell is cooked and the filling firm. (Using a glass pie plate enables you to check on the pastry.) Serve warm or cold, cut into wedges and accompanied by a side salad.

SERVES: 6

# AUTUMN

*As the weather cools down, appetites become more robust. Savoury Pecan Loaf is served with a piquant beet salad for flavour contrast. If fragrant quinces are available, they make a wonderful dessert, but if not, don't forget those old fashioned favourites, stewed rhubarb or apples with custard.*

Cream of Broccoli Soup *page 59*

Savoury Pecan Loaf *page 95*

Raw Beetroot Salad *page 162*

Quince with Dumplings *page 207*

# WINTER

*Winter is the time for thick soups, filling main dishes and hot puddings to sustain and comfort, all possible on vegetarian fare.*

Spicy Parsnip or Butternut Pumpkin
Soup *page 74 or 72*

Ravioli with Nut Filling *page 99*

Broccoli in Garlic Butter *page 136*

Apple Charlotte *page 202*

# SPECIAL OCCASIONS

*A special meal need not be elaborate, but each item is cooked with care and chosen for flavour and eye appeal.*

Asparagus Soup *page 78*

Mushroom and Hazelnut Terrine
*page 39*

Carrot Ring with Peas *page 155*

New Potatoes

Raspberry Mousse *page 196*

Mushroom and Cheese Ramekins *page 15*

or

Onion Tartlets *page 9*

Lentil Salad *page 159*

Crunchy Salad with Garlic Croûtons
*page 156*

Risotto or Pasta

Orange Blintzes *page 202*

# RICE AND VEGETABLE PATTIES

### INGREDIENTS

1 cup (7 oz) brown rice

2 zucchini (courgettes)

½ teaspoon salt

¾ cup (4 oz) corn niblets

½ cup (2 oz) grated cheese

1 cup (2 oz) grated carrot

1 tablespoon chopped parsley

1 tablespoon chopped dill

1 teaspoon salt

¼ teaspoon black pepper

3 eggs

4 tablespoons flour

1½ cups (6 oz) dry breadcrumbs

¾ cup (3 oz) sesame seeds

oil for deep- or shallow-frying

Cook rice by absorption method (see page 438). Coarsely grate zucchini, sprinkle with the salt and leave to drain in a colander for 15 minutes. Squeeze out excess liquid. Mix zucchini into cold cooked rice with corn, cheese, carrot, parsley, dill, salt, pepper and 1 beaten egg. Sprinkle in 1 tablespoon flour, mix well and divide into 12 equal portions. Form into round balls, compressing well. Coat in remaining flour, then dip in remaining eggs lightly beaten. Finally, coat patties in a mixture of breadcrumbs and sesame seeds. Allow coating to set slightly before firming on crumb coating, then leave to set for 10–15 minutes before frying until golden brown on both sides. Drain well on absorbent paper. Serve hot with chutney or fresh Tomato Sauce (see page 86).

NOTE: These patties are easier to mould and shape with white rice, but brown rice has more nutrition and is worth a little extra trouble if time permits.

SERVES: 6

# CAULIFLOWER CHEESE

*The secret of making this simple dish delicious is to steam the cauliflower to just the right degree of tenderness and not let it get water-logged. Try this method for any dish that requires pre-cooked cauliflower.*

### INGREDIENTS

1 firm white cauliflower

salt and white pepper to taste

### MORNAY SAUCE

1 tablespoon butter

2 tablespoons plain (all-purpose) flour

Trim off the stem close to the cauliflower and with a sharp pointed knife, cut a cone-shaped hollow in the main stem. Make slits in the other stems so they cook in the same time as the tender flower heads. One of the bugbears of cooking a whole cauliflower in a saucepan is that it is so difficult to lift out, so I use a wok as the wide shape makes it easy.

Bring about 2 cups (16 fl oz) of water to the boil, put the cauliflower in, stem down, season with salt and pepper,

1½ cups (12 fl oz) hot milk

•

185 g (6 oz) grated natural Cheddar
or Emmenthal cheese

•

3 tablespoons freshly grated Romano
or parmesan cheese

•

paprika for garnish

then cover and cook 8–10 minutes, depending on size. Don't overcook.

To make the sauce, melt the butter in a heavy-based saucepan and cook the flour, stirring, for a minute without browning. Add the hot milk and cook, whisking until smooth and thick. Remove from heat and stir in ½ cup (2 oz) of the cheddar or emmenthal and half the romano or parmesan.

As soon as the cauliflower is tender, lift out and drain. Place in a buttered baking dish, spoon sauce over to coat, sprinkle thickly with remaining cheese and bake in an oven preheated to 220°C (425°F) just until cheese is golden. Remove from oven, sprinkle lightly with paprika and serve.

SERVES: 4–6

# BROWN RICE BAKED WITH CHEESE

*A delicious and satisfying main dish that is very simple to prepare.*
*Follow with a salad.*

### INGREDIENTS

500 g (1 lb) natural brown rice

•

4 cups (32 fl oz) hot Vegetable Stock
(see page 448)

•

2 tablespoons vegetable oil

•

2 large onions cut in rings

•

salt and pepper to taste

•

1½ cups (6 oz) grated cheddar cheese

Put the rice into a saucepan that has a well-fitting lid. Add the strong, well-flavoured stock. Make stock strong, because rice absorbs extra salt. Bring to boil, then turn heat very low, cover and simmer for 40 minutes.

Meanwhile, heat oil in a frying pan and gently fry the onion rings until soft and golden, turning from time to time. Continue frying, stirring frequently, until they are nicely brown. Remove from heat.

Put half the rice into a greased ovenproof casserole (a deep one that is not too large) and spread a layer of half the onions over the base. Season with salt and pepper. Cover with remaining rice, smooth top and cover with remaining onions.

Sprinkle generously with pepper, then with grated cheese so that the onions are covered completely. Bake in an oven preheated to 180°C (350°F) for 20 minutes or until the cheese has melted and is golden. Garnish with parsley if liked. Serve hot.

SERVES: 4–5

# MEXICAN BEANS WITH CHILLI

*Serve this tasty mixture with hot rice for a filling meal.*

### INGREDIENTS

500 g (1 lb) dried borlotti
or red kidney beans
•
3 tablespoons olive oil
•
1 large onion, finely chopped
•
1 green or red capsicum (pepper),
diced
•
1 teaspoon chopped garlic
•
1 fresh green chilli or
canned jalapeno chilli, chopped
•
1 teaspoon oregano
•
2 teaspoons toasted, ground cumin
•
1 tablespoon paprika
•
½ teaspoon chilli powder (optional)
•
1 can peeled tomatoes
•
2 teaspoons brown sugar
•
1 teaspoon salt, or to taste
•
1 cup (4 oz) finely grated tasty
(sharp) cheese
•
1 cup (8 fl oz) sour cream
•
1 cup (2 oz) finely chopped spring
onions (scallions)

Wash the dried beans well and soak in plenty of water for some hours, or bring to the boil, turn off heat and leave covered for 2 hours. Drain, cover with fresh water and bring to the boil. If liked, a whole onion and a bay leaf may be added for flavour. Simmer until tender, about 1½ hours.

Drain, reserving a cup (8 fl oz) of the cooking liquid. Heat olive oil in a heavy-based saucepan and cook the onion, capsicum, garlic and chilli until the onion is soft and translucent. Add oregano and cumin and fry for 1 minute, then add the paprika, chilli, canned tomatoes with their juice, sugar and salt. Bring to the boil and simmer for a few minutes, stirring to break up the tomatoes. Return beans and reserved cooking liquid to the pan and simmer, covered, for 30 minutes longer.

Serve the beans ladled over rice and top each serving with a sprinkling of cheese, a spoonful of sour cream and chopped spring onions.

SERVES: 6

MEXICAN BEANS WITH CHILLI

# CHICK PEA AND NUT BURGERS

*Another barbecue bonanza!*

## INGREDIENTS

250 g (8 oz) dried chick peas
(garbanzo beans), soaked overnight

•

2 tablespoons oil

•

2 onions, finely chopped

•

1 clove garlic, crushed

•

2 teaspoons curry powder

•

salt and freshly ground black
pepper to taste

•

½ cup (2 oz) chopped almonds

•

½ cup (2 oz) chopped walnuts

•

½ cup (2 oz) toasted sunflower seeds

•

1 cup (4 oz) flour

•

2 eggs, beaten

•

1 cup (4 oz) dry breadcrumbs

•

oil for brushing

•

Mayonnaise (see page 180) to serve

Drain the soaked chick peas, put them into a saucepan with fresh water to cover and bring to the boil. Simmer in the covered pan for 2 hours or until very soft, then drain thoroughly in a colander.

Heat the oil and gently soften the onions and garlic, stirring occasionally until golden. This takes time, so don't rush it because it makes a great deal of difference to the flavour.

Mash the chick peas until smooth, using a food processor or blender if available. Mix in with the sautéed onions and garlic, curry powder, salt and pepper to taste, and the chopped nuts and sunflower seeds. Form into round patties and coat in the flour, then in beaten egg and finally in dry breadcrumbs.

Heat and lightly oil the griddle plate on your barbecue, or use a large iron frying pan and coat the base with a little oil. Cook the burgers over medium hot coals until golden on one side, then flip over with a frying slice (spatula) and cook the other side. Serve warm or cold, topped with a spoonful of creamy mayonnaise.

SERVES: 6

# CHICK PEA AND CAULIFLOWER FRICASSÉE

*This creamy, herb-flavoured dish is a true fricassée—first sautéed, then simmered with liquid, and finished with milk or cream. Serve with crusty bread for taking up the sauce or with a light grain accompaniment such as cous-cous, burghul (bulgur) or rice.*

## INGREDIENTS

1 cup (6 oz) dried chick peas

•

300 g (10 oz) cauliflower

Wash and soak the chick peas overnight or use quick soaking method, bringing to the boil, leaving for 2 hours, then cooking in fresh water until tender, either in a saucepan or pressure cooker. Drain the peas and save the cooking liquid.

250 g (8 oz) tender green beans
or broccoli

•

1 stalk celery

•

1 large onion

•

2 tablespoons olive oil

•

2 teaspoons finely chopped garlic

•

½ teaspoon dried oregano

•

½ teaspoon dried thyme

•

½ teaspoon paprika

•

1 teaspoon salt, or to taste

•

¼ teaspoon white pepper

•

¾ cup (6 fl oz) evaporated milk
or mixture of milk and cream

•

2 teaspoons cornflour (cornstarch)

Cut cauliflower into florets, keeping a bit of the stem on each. Do the same with the broccoli if used, or top and tail beans and string them if they are not the stringless variety. Cut the celery into thick slices. Peel and slice the onion thinly.

In a large, heavy-based saucepan, heat the oil and fry the onion over medium heat, stirring frequently, until the slices take on a translucent appearance and start to turn golden. Add the garlic and stir for a minute, then add the prepared vegetables and fry, stirring, for a few minutes.

Add 1½ cups (12 fl oz) cooking liquid, herbs, paprika, salt and pepper and the cooked chick peas. Bring to the boil, cover and simmer gently for 15 minutes or until cauliflower and beans or broccoli are tender but not mushy. Add milk and when it boils stir in the cornflour mixed with a tablespoon of cold water. It will thicken almost immediately. Remove from heat and serve with crusty bread or a pilaf of fluffy grain as suggested above.

SERVES: 6

# BROWN RICE AND CHICK PEA PILAF

*This combination of rice and chick peas, served with a green vegetable, is*
*a nutritionally balanced meal in itself.*

### INGREDIENTS

1 cup (6 oz) dried chick peas

•

1 teaspoon turmeric

•

½ teaspoon salt

•

1 onion, finely chopped

•

2 tablespoons olive oil

•

500 g (1 lb) long grain brown rice

•

4 cups (32 fl oz) hot water or stock

•

salt to taste

Wash the chick peas, cover with cold water and bring to the boil. Turn off heat and leave covered for 2 hours to soak. Bring to the boil once more, adding turmeric and salt, then simmer for 45 minutes or until tender. Drain. In a heavy-based saucepan, fry the onion in the oil, stirring, until soft and golden. Add the rice and fry for a couple of minutes, then add 4 cups (32 fl oz) boiling water or stock. Bring to a boil, stir in 1 teaspoon salt or to taste, cover and cook on very low heat for 40 minutes or until all the water has been absorbed. Fork the chick peas through the rice, cover and keep warm until serving time. Garnish with cooked green peas or chopped parsley, if liked.

SERVES: 5–6

# WALNUT AND RICE LOAF WITH CHIVE SAUCE

### INGREDIENTS

30 g (1 oz) butter
•
2 carrots, finely diced
•
2 teaspoons ground cumin
•
4 large spring onions (scallions),
sliced finely
•
250 g (8 oz) mushrooms,
coarsely chopped
•
3 eggs, lightly beaten
•
1 cup (8 fl oz) tomato purée
•
½ cup (2 oz) grated cheese
•
½ cup (2 oz) chopped walnuts
•
2 tablespoons finely chopped parsley
•
1½ teaspoons salt, or to taste
•
½ teaspoon black pepper
•
2½ cups cooked brown rice
(about 5 oz uncooked)

### CHIVE SAUCE

1 cup (4 fl oz) dry white wine
•
2 spring onions, chopped
•
2 tablespoons lime juice
or 1 tablespoon lemon juice
•
½ teaspoon grated lime or lemon rind
•
100 g (3½ oz) butter, softened
•
2 tablespoons chopped chives
•
sea salt and white pepper to taste

Melt butter in a frying pan and sauté carrots for 2 minutes, add cumin and stir well. Add spring onions and mushrooms and cook, stirring, for a further 2 minutes. Remove from heat.

Stir together the beaten eggs, tomato purée, cheese, walnuts, parsley, salt and pepper. Combine with the rice and cooked vegetables and mix thoroughly. Taste and correct seasoning as required.

Generously grease a 28 × 12 cm (11 × 4½ in) loaf tin and line base with greased greaseproof paper. Pack the mixture in well, being especially careful to fill the corners. Bake in an oven preheated to 180°C (350°F) for 50–60 minutes or until firm. Cool slightly before turning out. Serve sliced with chive sauce.

To make the sauce: In a small enamel or other non-aluminium saucepan bring to the boil the wine, spring onions and citrus juice and boil uncovered until reduced to about ¼ cup (2 fl oz) in volume. Strain into a bowl, allow to cool, and beat in the soft butter, a small piece at a time. Stir in the chives and season to taste with salt and pepper. If you feel the flavour is too sharp, stir in a little thickened cream.

SERVES: 4–6

# SPINACH AND CHEESE PIE

*Most recipes use filo pastry both under and over the filling, but there is no point putting filo pastry under the spinach filling as it goes soggy. I substituted a quickly-made wholemeal (whole wheat) pastry for lining the dish, used a leek and spinach combination for flavour and filo pastry for a flaky, golden top crust.*

## INGREDIENTS

### PASTRY
90 g (3 oz) butter

•

2½ tablespoons milk

•

¼ teaspoon salt

•

1 cup (4 oz) wholemeal self-raising flour (or whole wheat flour with 2 level teaspoons of baking powder)

•

6 sheets filo pastry

•

60 g (2 oz) melted butter

•

2 tablespoons olive oil

### FILLING
1 large bunch spinach or silverbeet (Swiss chard)

•

4 leeks

•

half bunch spring onions (scallions)

•

2 tablespoons olive oil or butter

•

250 g (8 oz) feta cheese

•

5 eggs

•

1 cup (8 oz) cottage cheese

•

1 cup (4 oz) finely grated sharp cheese such as Kefalotiri or tasty (sharp) cheddar

•

freshly ground pepper to taste

•

half teaspoon freshly grated nutmeg

To make the pastry, melt the butter in a saucepan. Remove from heat, add the milk and salt and stir in the flour, all at once. Place the lump of rather soft dough in a lightly buttered 23 cm (9 in) square oven-proof dish or large, deep pie plate. Pat out pastry to cover base and sides of dish very thinly, making the greatest thickness on the top edge. This pastry is so easily handled, you can pat and push it so there is no heavy crust on the base or in the corners. Chill the lined dish while preparing the filling.

Wash the spinach thoroughly in as many changes of water as necessary to get rid of the sand and grit that cling. If using silverbeet, discard the heavy white stems and centre veins. Put spinach into a stainless steel saucepan with just the water that clings, cover and cook gently until it has wilted. Drain well, pressing out as much liquid as possible.

Wash the leeks, slitting them and taking care that the sand is washed away. Slice thinly. Clean the spring onions, chop roughly and set aside. Heat the olive oil or butter in a heavy-based saucepan and toss the leeks in, stirring to coat with the oil. Cover and cook on very low heat for about 15 minutes or until tender, stirring now and then and taking care not to burn the leeks. Remove from heat, add the spinach and spring onions.

Cut feta cheese into small dice and sprinkle evenly over base of pastry. Beat the eggs, mix in the cottage cheese and grated sharp cheese, add pepper and nutmeg, stir in the vegetable mixture. Pour into dish.

Take filo from its packet just before using, return remaining sheets to plastic packet and seal to prevent drying out. Have ready the melted butter and olive oil mixed together, and brush over half of one sheet. Fold the sheet over to fit just inside the dish and place it so it covers the filling, pressing lightly. Continue brushing, folding and placing remaining sheets of filo pastry over the first one. Brush top with melted butter and with a very sharp knife, cut squares or diamond shapes in the top layer of pastry, then sprinkle lightly with a few drops of cold water. Bake in an oven preheated to 190°C (375°F) for an hour, covering top with foil if it browns too quickly.

SERVES: 6–8

# LENTIL, SESAME AND SUNFLOWER BURGERS

*Barbecue parties are what people feel they miss out on when they eat only vegetarian meals but recipes like this ensure they can still enjoy the outdoor cooking scene. Of course, you can also cook these nutty burgers in a frying pan and serve them with salad. Besides being delicious and satisfying, they are rich in protein and calcium.*

### INGREDIENTS

125 g (4 oz) brown lentils
•
125 g (4 oz) red lentils
•
2 cups (16 fl oz) water
•
1 tablespoon miso or yeast extract
•
2 tablespoons soy sauce
•
1 egg, beaten
•
1 teaspoon dried oregano or marjoram
•
1 teaspoon curry powder (optional)
•
1 tablespoon honey
•
1 clove garlic, crushed
•
1 large carrot, grated
•
1 large onion, grated
•
1 large potato, grated
•
1/3 cup (1½ oz) sunflower seeds
•
1/3 cup (1½ oz) sesame seeds
•
1 cup (3 oz) rolled oats
•
4 tablespoons wholemeal (whole wheat) flour

Spread the lentils on a flat tray and pick out any stones. Wash well and drain. Put into a saucepan with the water and bring to the boil, then turn off the heat and leave to soak for 2 hours. Add the miso or yeast extract and cook, covered, until all water has been absorbed and the lentils are soft.

Mix the soy sauce, egg, herbs and seasonings together. In a large bowl, combine all the remaining ingredients thoroughly, adding in the egg mixture.

Form the mixture into round patties. Heat the griddle plate of the barbecue, brush with a little oil and cook the the burgers over low coals until golden brown on both sides. For informal eating, serve in hamburger buns with shredded lettuce and mayonnaise. For a knife and fork meal, serve with thickly sliced tomatoes and other favourite salads.

SERVES: 6

# COUSCOUS

Made from semolina and fine wheat flour, this light, fluffy cereal is delicious as an accompaniment to the traditional stew or as a pilaf on its own. The most readily available and convenient form requires very little done to it. Check packet directions. Here is how I prepare it.

Put 1 cup (6 oz) of couscous into a bowl. Bring ¾ cup (6 fl oz) of water to a boil with ½ teaspoon salt and 2 teaspoons butter or oil. Pour over the couscous and leave for 10 minutes. Put the soaked couscous in a small saucepan with a well-fitting lid and steam over low heat for 4–5 minutes.

Alternatively, put the soaked couscous in a colander or steamer and place it over the simmering stew. Ensure there is plenty of liquid in the stew so it won't stick to the bottom of the pan, but the pot must be deep enough so the grain does not touch the bubbling liquid. The steam carries the flavours of the stew into the couscous.

# HARISSA

### INGREDIENTS

200 g (6½ oz) fresh or
100 g (3½ oz) dried hot red chillies
•
12 cloves garlic, peeled
•
1 tablespoon ground coriander
•
1 tablespoon ground cumin
•
1 tablespoon dried mint leaves
•
3 teaspoons salt
•
½ cup (1 oz) chopped fresh coriander

With kitchen scissors, snip off stems and remove seeds from the chillies. If using dried chillies rinse them, then put them in a bowl and pour boiling water over them. Leave to soak for an hour or longer. Drain, and put with all the other ingredients into a blender jar and purée to a paste, or pound in a mortar with a pestle. Store in a glass jar in the refrigerator, covering the top with a layer of olive oil. Use sparingly, replacing with a little oil to cover the surface each time.

NOTE: For a quick and easy way to make this hot sauce, combine in a small bowl 2 tablespoons hot chilli sauce and 1 teaspoon each of crushed garlic, ground coriander, ground cumin and dried mint. Add ½ teaspoon salt.

VEGETARIAN COUSCOUS

# VEGETARIAN COUSCOUS

*Originally a Berber dish and one of the most famous in North African cuisine, couscous refers to a semolina preparation which is served with a hearty stew. The stew is based on meat and poultry with an assortment of vegetables. There is another version in Tunisia and Sicily, where fish is the main ingredient. However, don't imagine you're missing out on anything. This recipe concentrates on vegetables with distinctive flavours, and contains all the herbs and spices which give the original Moroccan dish its appeal. While hearty and satisfying, it is much lighter on the digestion than the meat based version.*

### INGREDIENTS

2 cups (12 oz) dried chick peas
•
4 tablespoons oil
•
1 large onion, finely chopped
•
1 small stick cinnamon
•
1 large unpeeled eggplant (aubergine)
(about 350 g/12 oz), cut in cubes
•
3 medium carrots (about
300 g/10 oz), cut in thick rounds
•
2 potatoes (250 g/8 oz), peeled
and halved if large
•
250 g (8 oz) pumpkin, peeled
and cut in large cubes
•
2 large ripe tomatoes,
quartered and seeded
•
salt and pepper to taste
•
¼ teaspoon ground allspice
•
3 teaspoons Harissa or hot chilli sauce
(see page 116)
•
100 g (3½ oz) green beans
•
250 g (8 oz) zucchini (courgette)
•
2 tablespoons chopped parsley
•
2 tablespoons chopped
fresh coriander

Wash the chick peas thoroughly, put into a saucepan with cold water to cover and bring to the boil. Boil for 2 minutes, then turn off heat and leave in saucepan, covered, for 2 hours. Drain, replace with fresh cold water and bring to the boil again. Simmer for 1 hour or until chick peas are tender, adding salt to taste only when cooking time is almost complete. If using pressure cooker, 20 minutes should be sufficient. Drain the chick peas, reserving cooking liquid.

Heat the oil in a large, heavy-based saucepan and fry the onion and cinnamon stick over medium heat, stirring, until the onion is soft. Add the eggplant, carrots and potatoes, stir to coat with oil, cover and cook over low heat for 10 minutes, shaking the pan or stirring once or twice. Add the pumpkin, tomatoes, seasoning, spice and harissa.

Add water if necessary to the liquid drained from the chick peas to equal 2 cups and pour over the vegetables. Add cooked chick peas. Cover and simmer for 30 minutes or until the vegetables are almost tender. Add the green beans, trimmed and cut into short lengths and the zucchini, washed and not peeled, but cut into 2 cm (3½ in) lengths. Simmer, covered, for a further 15 minutes. Serve with couscous (see page 116) cooked separately.

If preferred, after the stew has simmered for 30 minutes, add the vegetables which need only a short cooking time and cover the pan with a colander in which the soaked couscous has been placed. Allow it to steam over the vegetable stew, uncovered, for 15 minutes until the vegetables are cooked and the grains tender and fluffy.

SERVES: 6

# ALMOND-CRUSTED POTATO CROQUETTES

*In this variation the amount of potato is increased but instead of being mixed with the tempeh, it is used to coat the savoury mixture, then double-crumbed in a crunchy almond mixture.*

## INGREDIENTS

1 quantity Savoury Tempeh (see page 436)
•
2 teaspoons chopped parsley
•
500 g (1 lb) floury potatoes
•
salt and pepper to taste
•
2 tablespoons plain (all-purpose) flour
•
1 egg, beaten
•
3 tablespoons dry breadcrumbs
•
5 tablespoons coarsely chopped almonds
•
oil for frying

Complete cooking of tempeh and onions, stirring in parsley when tempeh is returned to the pan.

Scrub the potatoes and boil in their skins, then peel and mash smoothly while still hot. Season mashed potato with extra salt and white pepper and divide into 6 equal portions. Divide the tempeh mixture equally too. Take one portion of potato in your palm and make a deep trough down the centre, adding the tempeh in a neat line. Close potato over the filling, shaping to a smooth cylinder. It is easy to do this if the potato is allowed to become quite cold after mashing.

When all are shaped, roll them in flour, then in beaten egg and thirdly in the breadcrumbs and chopped almonds mixed together. For a beautifully crisp, firm coating, repeat the egg and crumb layers. They may be deep fried or shallow fried in hot oil but either way, turn them gently as they cook so they don't darken too much on the underside. Drain on absorbent paper and serve hot with a salad or cooked green vegetable.

SERVES: 6

# EGGPLANT WITH CHEESE STUFFING

## INGREDIENTS

3 small eggplants (aubergines), each approximately 125 g (4 oz)
•
salt
•
2 tablespoons oil
•
2 medium onions, finely chopped
•
1 clove garlic, crushed
•
1 teaspoon dried oregano

Choose rounded eggplants rather than long shapes—they will be easier to fill. Halve the eggplants lengthways. Score each half lightly with a pointed knife but don't cut through to the skin. Sprinkle cut surfaces with salt and leave for 30 minutes for juices to be drawn out. Drop into a saucepan of boiling water and when water returns to the boil, cook for about 7 minutes, just until soft but not long enough for them to lose their shape. Drain and cool in a colander, cut sides down.

With a spoon, scoop out and reserve most of the flesh, leaving a thin layer in the shell. Heat the oil and fry onions

1½ cups minced Gluten
(see page 437)
•
1½ teaspoons miso
•
1 tablespoon tomato sauce or
barbecue sauce
•
salt and pepper to taste
•
1 large potato, peeled and diced
•
½ cup (4 oz) cottage cheese
•
1 egg
•
3 tablespoons finely grated
cheddar cheese
•
3 tablespoons breadcrumbs
•
1 tablespoon olive oil or
30 g (1 oz) butter

and garlic on low heat until soft and golden. Add the oregano and then the gluten.

Add the reserved eggplant, the miso and sauce, salt and pepper to taste, then cover and cook for 10 minutes on low heat. Meanwhile, boil the diced potato, drain and add to the filling. Remove from heat and when lukewarm, stir in the cottage cheese and egg, mixing well.

Put the eggplant halves into a greased ovenproof dish and fill with the seasoned mixture, rounding it slightly in the shells. Sprinkle with a mixture of cheese and crumbs, drizzle the olive oil over or dot with tiny bits of butter. Bake in an oven preheated to 180°C (350°F) for 45–50 minutes or until top is crusty and golden brown. Serve warm with brown rice pilaf and a green vegetable.

SERVES: 6

# STUFFED CABBAGE ROLLS

## INGREDIENTS

12 small or 6 large cabbage leaves
•
6 spring onions (scallions),
finely chopped
•
2 cups cooked brown rice
(about 4 oz uncooked)
•
½ cup (1 oz) coarsely grated carrot
•
1 tablespoon chopped dill
•
½ cup (2 oz) pine nuts, toasted
•
¾ cup (4 oz) currants
•
2 tablespoons tomato paste
•
2 teaspoons finely chopped garlic
•
1 tablespoon chopped mint
•
1 cup (8 fl oz) water
•
1 teaspoon sugar
•
salt and freshly ground black
pepper to taste

Carefully remove centre rib of cabbage leaves and wilt them in boiling water or in a plastic bag in the microwave oven. If the leaves are large, cut in half and if small, overlap at the base where the rib was removed. Combine spring onions, rice, carrot, dill, pine nuts and currants. Divide the filling evenly and place on the leaves. Roll each leaf like a parcel and arrange them, seam-side down, in a greased ovenproof dish.

Mix all the remaining ingredients together and pour over cabbage rolls. Cover dish and bake in an oven preheated to 180°C (350°F) for 35–40 minutes. If rolls tend to dry out, add a little water.

SERVES: 6

# CHILLI CON TEMPEH

*Served to dedicated meat eaters, this received rousing approval. Try it on friends who don't believe that meals without meat can be worth eating.*

### INGREDIENTS

2 tablespoons oil
•
2 stalks celery, chopped
•
2 large onions, finely chopped
•
2 cloves garlic, finely chopped
•
1 × 250 g (8 oz) pkt frozen tempeh
•
1 tablespoon Mexican chilli powder (please note this is mixed with cumin and nowhere near as hot as regular chilli powder, which cannot be substituted without dire results!)
•
1 red capsicum (sweet pepper), diced
•
1 × 400 g (13 oz) can peeled tomatoes
•
1 bay leaf
•
2 teaspoons brown sugar
•
2 tablespoons vinegar
•
2 tablespoons tomato paste
•
2 teaspoons salt
•
1 × 440 g (14½ oz) can red kidney beans

In a large, heavy-based saucepan, heat the oil and on low heat, fry the celery, onions and garlic until soft. Add the sliced tempeh and allow to brown slightly. Add Mexican chilli powder, capsicum, tomatoes with their juice, and bay leaf. Simmer, covered, for 30 minutes.

Add sugar, vinegar, tomato paste dissolved in a little hot water, and salt. Drain the canned beans and add them, simmer 10 minutes longer and serve with hot Corn Muffins (see page 418).

SERVES: 6–8

# BAKED CAPSICUMS WITH RICE, PINENUTS AND OLIVES

### INGREDIENTS

6 large red or green capsicums
(sweet peppers)
•
1 cup (7 oz) brown rice or
rice-shaped pasta
•
2 tablespoons olive oil
•
2 cloves garlic, finely chopped
•
1 onion, finely chopped
•
1 small can peeled tomatoes or
2 ripe tomatoes, peeled,
seeded and chopped
•
¼ cup (2 oz) chopped pimiento-
stuffed olives
•
6–8 black olives, seeded and chopped
•
2 tablespoons pine nuts (optional)
•
125 g (4 oz) mild cheese, diced
•
½ cup (2 oz) finely grated sharp
cheese, such as pecorino
•
salt and pepper to taste

Cut tops off capsicums and reserve to use as lids. Remove and discard the seeds and membranes. Parboil capsicums for 5 minutes in lightly salted boiling water, remove on slotted spoon and drain upside down while preparing filling.

Cook rice or pasta until just tender. Heat the oil and fry garlic and onion over low heat until soft and golden. Add tomatoes and cook for 10 minutes or until tomatoes are pulpy. Remove from heat, mix with the rice or pasta, olives, pine nuts, diced and grated cheese. Taste and add salt and pepper if necessary.

Fill the capsicums with the mixture and cover with the tops or, if preferred, with cheese. Place in a greased baking dish and bake in an oven preheated to 180°C (350°F) for 35–40 minutes. Serve warm or cold.

SERVES: 6

# LIMA BEAN AND VEGETABLE STEW

*Getting the right food combination is important and here is a dish that
meets the requirements.*

### INGREDIENTS

1½ cups (9 oz) dried lima beans
•
3 bay leaves
•
2 onions, finely chopped
•
3 cloves garlic, finely chopped

Wash the lima beans well and put into a pan with enough cold water to cover generously. Bring to the boil, turn off the heat and leave covered for 2 hours. Drain, cover with fresh water and return to the boil with the bay leaves and simmer for 35 minutes or until beans are very tender. Set aside, together with cooking liquid.

Gently fry onions and garlic in the oil until soft, add

2 tablespoons vegetable oil

•

1 green capsicum (pepper),
finely diced

•

1 red capsicum (sweet pepper),
finely diced

•

1 teaspoon dried oregano

•

1 teaspoon ground cumin

•

1 teaspoon celery salt

•

1 teaspoon garlic salt

•

2 stalks celery, sliced

•

handful of green beans

•

pepper to taste

•

½ cup (1 oz) finely chopped parsley
to garnish

green and red capsicums and fry, stirring occasionally, for a few minutes longer. Add the oregano, cumin, celery salt and garlic salt. Add the lima beans and 2 cups (16 fl oz) of the cooking liquid. Cover and simmer for 15 minutes.

Meanwhile, slice the celery and cut the green beans (topped, tailed and strings removed) into short lengths. Add to stew and cook, covered, for a further 10–15 minutes until the beans are tender but still bright green and crisp. Check seasoning and if the liquid needs thickening, mix together 1 tablespoon of soft butter and 1 tablespoon of flour and add it in small pieces, stirring until the gravy bubbles and thickens. Serve stew garnished with parsley and accompanied by hot brown rice.

SERVES: 6

# MILLET PILAF WITH NUTS

### INGREDIENTS

1 tablespoon butter

•

1 tablespoon olive or sunflower oil

•

1 onion, finely chopped

•

1 small stick cinnamon

•

1 cup (6 oz) hulled millet seed

•

2½ cups (20 fl oz) hot Vegetable
Stock (see page 448) or water

•

1 teaspoon salt

•

¼ teaspoon white pepper

•

½ cup (2 oz) roughly chopped nuts
(cashews, natural almonds or pecans)

•

¼ cup (2 fl oz) oil for frying

Heat the butter and 1 tablespoon oil in a heavy-based saucepan and fry the onion over medium heat, stirring occasionally, until soft and starting to colour. Add the cinnamon and millet, and fry for 2–3 minutes, stirring constantly. Pour in the stock or water and add salt and white pepper. Bring to the boil, cover with a lid and cook on very low heat for 25 minutes until the millet is tender and all the liquid has been absorbed. Uncover and leave for a few minutes to allow the steam to escape, then fluff with a fork.

Fry the nuts in hot oil and when just starting to turn golden, remove pan from heat, lift nuts out on a slotted spoon and drain on absorbent paper. Fork half the fried nuts through the millet pilaf. Sprinkle remaining nuts over the top and serve hot with a vegetable accompaniment such as beans in tomato sauce. In warm weather, serve the pilaf at room temperature accompanied by a tomato and spring onion salad or Parmesan cheese and lettuce.

SERVES: 4–5

# FIRESIDE WINTER DINNER PARTY

*Chick Pea and Coriander Pâté with raw vegetables and pitta bread* page 54

•

*Artichoke Strudel*
page 32

*Rainbow Layer Crêpes*
page 26

*Lima Bean and Vegetable Stew*
page 122

•

*Tarte Aux Pommes (sideboard)*
page 190

# BAKED POTATOES WITH SPICY CHEESE FILLING

*If you ever doubted that potatoes could be a main dish, one taste of this will convince you.*

## INGREDIENTS

8 large potatoes
•
oil for frying
•
2 leeks or large onions
•
1 tablespoon butter
•
2 cloves garlic, crushed
•
small bunch fresh coriander or mint, chopped
•
2 tablespoons chopped fresh dill
•
2 hard-boiled eggs
•
250 g (8 oz) ricotta cheese
•
½ teaspoon ground allspice or cinnamon
•
¼ teaspoon ground cloves
•
good grating of nutmeg
•
2 teaspoons prepared mustard
•
2 teaspoons Worcestershire sauce
•
1 teaspoon salt
•
freshly ground black pepper
•
½ cup (1 oz) fresh wholemeal (whole wheat) breadcrumbs

SOUR CREAM SAUCE
1 cup (8 fl oz) sour cream
•
1 cup (8 fl oz) natural yoghurt
•
1 clove garlic, crushed with ½ teaspoon salt
•
1 tablespoon chopped fresh dill

Try and buy flattish potatoes—they are so much easier to fill and sit steady on a baking tray and serving dish. Scrub the potatoes well and bring to the boil. Simmer for 10 minutes only, then drain and leave until cool enough to cut in half lengthways. Scoop out the centres, leaving shells about 1 cm (½ in) thick. (I used a grapefruit knife for this—its slightly curved blade makes it easy.) The centres can be boiled for a further 10 minutes or until done, then drained and mashed with a little butter, pepper and salt.

Heat oil for frying and fry the potato shells first on one side and then the other, until crisp and golden. Drain on absorbent paper.

If using leeks, wash very well and shred finely, or chop the onions. Heat 2 tablespoons oil and 1 tablespoon butter in a saucepan and fry the leeks or onions on low heat until soft. Add the crushed garlic and fry for a few minutes longer, then add the fresh herbs and stir over low heat for a couple of minutes. Dice the hard-boiled eggs and mash the ricotta cheese. Mix all the ingredients together, add the spices, plenty of freshly ground black pepper and salt to taste, the fresh breadcrumbs and mashed potato. Taste and adjust seasoning if necessary. Fill the potato skins, mounding the mixture slightly. Place on a baking tray and bake in an oven preheated to 220°C (425°F) for 20 minutes or until heated through.

To make the sauce, combine sour cream and yoghurt, stir in the crushed garlic, dill and, if liked, a squeeze of lemon juice. Taste and add more seasoning if necessary. Spoon over the potato halves just before serving and sprinkle with some fresh chives or place a small sprig of fresh coriander or dill on top to garnish. Serve with cooked green vegetables.

SERVES: 8

# CONFETTI VEGETABLE MOULD

*Specks of bright coloured, mixed vegetables in a cheese-flavoured sauce which may be simply baked in a shallow buttered dish. For a more impressive presentation the mixture may also be used to fill a mould decorated with fancy shapes or ribbons cut from the vegetables, then baked in a bain marie and unmoulded.*

### INGREDIENTS

600 g (1¼ lb) cauliflower, trimmed
•
300 g (10 oz) carrots
•
300 g (10 oz) dark green zucchini (courgettes)
•
60 g (2 oz) butter
•
½ cup (1 oz) chopped spring onions, including the green tops
•
2 tablespoons plain (all-purpose) flour
•
250 ml (8 fl oz) milk
•
1½ teaspoons sea salt
•
½ teaspoon white pepper
•
½ teaspoon ground nutmeg
•
3 eggs, beaten
•
½ cup (2 oz) finely grated parmesan or romano cheese

Separate the cauliflower into florets and cook in a microwave oven or in boiling salted water until tender, about 6 minutes. Drain well. Grate the carrots and blanch them for 2 minutes. Grate the zucchini and blanch for 1 minute. Melt 30 g (1 oz) of the butter in a heavy-based saucepan and cook the cauliflower, stirring and mashing, until it is quite dry. It should not brown. Add the carrots, zucchini and spring onions, and cook for a further 4–5 minutes, stirring.

In another saucepan, melt the remaining 30 g butter, stir in the flour and cook over medium low heat for 1–2 minutes, stirring constantly. Add the milk all at once and whisk until the sauce boils and thickens. Remove from heat and add the salt, pepper and nutmeg. Stir in the beaten eggs and the cheese. Turn the cooked vegetables into the sauce and mix well.

Butter an ovenproof dish, turn the vegetable mixture into the dish and bake in an oven preheated to 180°C (350°F) for 30 minutes or until firm to the touch. Serve in the dish.

For unmoulding, decorate the dish with strips of zucchini and carrot, in alternate ribbons, or make patterns with peas and corn. Pour the mixture into the dish, place a piece of buttered greaseproof paper on the surface and put the dish into a roasting tin with hot water in it. Bake for 45 minutes or until firm to the touch, then remove greaseproof paper and unmould onto serving dish. Serve warm or cold.

SERVES: 6

# FETTUCINE WITH ROSY MUSHROOM SAUCE

## INGREDIENTS

500 g (1 lb) fresh mushrooms

•

3 tablespoons olive oil

•

1 tablespoon butter

•

4 cloves garlic, finely chopped

•

freshly ground black pepper and
sea salt to taste

•

½ cup (4 fl oz) tomato purée

•

½ cup (4 fl oz) cream

•

dash of hot pepper sauce (optional)

•

500 g (1 lb) fettucine or vermicelli

•

2 teaspoons cornflour (cornstarch)

Wipe mushrooms and cut them in thick slices, then into large dice. Heat the olive oil and butter in a heavy-based saucepan, and cook on gentle heat until soft. Add the mushrooms and toss in the hot oil for 5 minutes. Add pepper and salt, then the tomato purée, cream and hot sauce. Simmer for 10 minutes while cooking the pasta in lots of fast boiling water. When pasta is done, pour some cold water into the pan to stop the cooking, and drain well in a colander. Stir the cornflour, mixed with 2 tablespoons cold water, into the simmering sauce and stir until it thickens slightly. Serve sauce over pasta and follow with a salad of assorted greens.

SERVES: 4–6

# EGGPLANT AND GARLIC TART

## INGREDIENTS

1 × 25 cm (10 in) partly baked
Tart Shell (see page 446)

•

1 quantity Garlic Custard
(see page 441), using oregano
as the herb

•

750 g (1½ lb) slender eggplant

•

salt

•

olive oil for frying

•

4 tablespoons finely grated kefalotiri
or other mature cheese

•

fresh Tomato Sauce (see page 86)
for serving

Have the tart shell and garlic custard ready. Wash but do not peel the eggplant. Cut in fairly thick slices, about 1 cm (just under ½ in) and sprinkle lightly with salt. Leave for 20 minutes, then pat dry with paper towels.

Heat enough olive oil to just cover the base of a heavy frying pan and fry the slices until golden on one side. Turn and fry other side. Alternatively, brush the slices with olive oil and grill under a preheated griller (broiler)—they will absorb less oil this way.

Lay the slices in the tart shell, pour the garlic custard over and sprinkle with the cheese. Bake in an oven preheated to 180°C (350°F) until set. Garnish the tart with sprigs of parsley and serve wedges with a spoonful of home made tomato sauce.

SERVES: 6–8

# "CHEESE AND CRACKERS" LOAF

*Everyone likes nibbling on cheese and crackers but would you believe they
make the base for a delicious main dish? Chop or dice the vegetables finely
but not so fine that their bright colours are indistinguishable.*

## INGREDIENTS

250 g (8 oz) wholemeal
(whole wheat) crackers

•

60 g (2 oz) very fresh walnuts
or pecans

•

250 g (8 oz) tasty Cheddar cheese

•

1 tablespoon butter

•

1 tablespoon olive oil

•

1 clove garlic, crushed

•

½ cup (3 oz) finely sliced spring
onions (scallions)

•

1 cup (5 oz) finely chopped celery

•

1 cup (5 oz) finely diced carrots

•

1 cup (4 oz) finely chopped broccoli

•

1 cup (4 oz) finely chopped
cauliflower

•

2 eggs, lightly beaten

•

1 tablespoon peanut butter

•

2 teaspoons finely grated lemon rind

•

¼ teaspoon black pepper

•

1 teaspoon salt

•

1 teaspoon liquid vegetable
seasoning (or powdered vegetable
soup) or miso

Crush the crackers finely (in a plastic bag with a rolling
pin is the quick way). Roughly chop the nuts. Dice the
cheese finely.

Heat the butter and oil in a heavy-based saucepan and
gently fry the garlic, spring onions, celery and carrots for
2 minutes. Add broccoli and cauliflower, stir well and reduce
heat to very low. Cover pan tightly and sweat vegetables
for 5 minutes, stirring now and then. This brings out their
flavour. Transfer to a bowl and cool slightly.

Mix together the beaten eggs, peanut butter, lemon rind,
pepper, salt and liquid vegetable seasoning or miso. (If the
cheese is a very salty variety, reduce or omit the salt.) Pour
over the vegetables and lastly, mix in the crushed crackers,
chopped nuts and cheese.

Pack into a lined and greased loaf tin or greased glass
loaf dish and bake in an oven preheated to 180°C (350°F)
for 40–45 minutes or until firm. Allow to stand for 5 minutes
before turning out. Serve cut in thick slices with Tomato
Cream Sauce, made by mixing 1½ cups fresh Tomato Sauce
(see page 441) with ½ cup cream or evaporated milk. Stir
over gentle heat but do not boil.

SERVES: 6

# SPIRALI WITH JULIENNE OF VEGETABLES

### INGREDIENTS

1 large or 2 medium carrots

•

half a celeriac

•

2 dark green zucchini (courgettes)

•

250 g (8 oz) pasta spirals

•

30 g (1 oz) butter

•

pepper and salt to taste

•

4 tablespoons finely grated Romano or Parmesan cheese

Wash, peel and slice the carrots into long diagonal slices, then cut the slices into julienne strips. Peel the celeriac, slice, and cut into similar sized strips. Wash the zucchini but don't peel. Top and tail them, then slice lengthways and finally cut the slices into strips roughly the same size as the other vegetables.

Bring a saucepan of lightly salted water to the boil and cook the pasta until tender but still holding its shape. Add some cold water to stop the cooking process, then drain in a colander. Melt the butter in the saucepan and return pasta, shaking to coat with the butter. Cover and keep warm.

Put a small amount of water to boil in a saucepan and cook the vegetables separately, since carrots will take longer to cook than celeriac and zucchini. Lift out on a slotted spoon and drain, then add next variety to the same water. (When all the vegetables have been cooked, save the water for stock—it will have good flavour.) Toss the drained vegetables with the pasta. Season with pepper and salt to taste and serve immediately, sprinkled with the grated cheese.

SERVES: 4–6

# KASHA WITH PEAS

### INGREDIENTS

60 g (2 oz) butter

•

1½ cups (8 oz) buckwheat

•

3½ cups (28 fl oz) hot water

•

2 teaspoons salt

•

pepper to taste

•

1½ cups (9 oz) shelled peas, cooked and drained

In a medium-size saucepan, melt the butter and toss the buckwheat, stirring constantly for 5 minutes or until the butter has been absorbed. Add the hot water and salt, and bring to the boil.

Turn heat very low, cover pan with well-fitting lid and cook for 25 minutes or until all the liquid has been absorbed. Uncover, season with pepper to taste and, if liked, add an extra knob of butter to kasha. Stir peas through and serve hot.

SERVES: 4

# SPRING VEGETABLE RISOTTO

*I watched Chef Luciano Parolari of the famous Hotel Villa d'Este demonstrate the technique of cooking a risotto, stirring almost constantly as he added wine, rice and vegetables. The creamy, moist result would have been memorable even without the fantastic setting of Lake Como and the charming chef.*

### INGREDIENTS

125g (4 oz) butter
•
2 onions, finely chopped
•
2 large cloves garlic, finely chopped
•
1 cup (4 oz) fresh green peas
•
1 cup (5 oz) diced zucchini
•
2 slender carrots, diced
•
1 tomato, peeled, seeded and diced
•
2 cups (16 fl oz) dry white wine
•
500g (1 lb) Italian arborio rice or short grain rice
•
6 cups (48 fl oz) boiling stock
•
½ cup (2 oz) finely grated parmigiano or romano cheese
•
freshly ground pepper

Divide butter into four equal pieces. In a small saucepan melt one piece of butter and on low heat cook half the chopped onion and garlic, the peas, zucchini, carrot and tomato, stirring frequently. When the onion is soft and golden, add 1 cup of the wine and simmer until the wine has evaporated. Set aside.

In a large saucepan melt two pieces of the butter and cook the remaining onion and garlic on medium heat, stirring, until the onion is soft. Add the rice and stir until it is well coated with the butter, then add the remaining cup of wine and stir until the wine has been absorbed.

Add boiling stock, one cup at a time, stirring until each cupful is absorbed before adding another. In about 20 minutes the rice should be completely cooked, tender and creamy. Stir in the vegetable mixture, the remaining piece of butter and half the cheese. Season to taste with freshly ground pepper. Serve at once, with the remaining cheese separate.

SERVES: 6

# — COMPLEMENTARY DISHES —

While these simple vegetable dishes are ideal to serve with a main course
pie or loaf, a selection of three or four could also constitute a main meal.

## ZUCCHINI WITH TOMATO AND GARLIC

### INGREDIENTS

6 medium zucchini (courgettes)

•

2 tablespoons butter or oil

•

2 cloves garlic, crushed

•

2 ripe tomatoes, peeled and diced

•

salt and freshly ground pepper

•

2 tablespoons finely chopped parsley

Wash zucchini and cut off ends. Do not peel but cut in fairly thick rounds.

Heat butter or oil in a heavy-based saucepan and fry the garlic on low heat. Add the tomatoes and stir well, add zucchini and season with salt and pepper.

Cover and cook on low heat for about 15 minutes or until zucchini is tender, stirring occasionally and adding a little water if mixture is dry. Serve hot, sprinkled with chopped parsley.

SERVES: 4

## RED CABBAGE WITH APPLES

*When cooked with acid the cabbage keeps a good colour. Cooking should
be done in enamel, stainless steel or other non-aluminium pan. Serve as a
side dish with croquettes or baked loaf-type dishes.*

### INGREDIENTS

1 small red cabbage

•

30 g (1 oz) butter

•

1 cup (8 fl oz) dry red wine

•

½ cup (4 fl oz) garlic vinegar

•

1 teaspoon salt

•

¼ teaspoon pepper

•

¼ cup (2 oz) sugar

•

¼ cup (2 fl oz) water

•

2 large green cooking apples

•

2 tablespoons cranberry or
redcurrant jelly

•

¼ teaspoon ground cloves

Cut cabbage into quarters, discard core and shred the leaves finely.

Heat butter in a large heavy-based pan and add the cabbage, ½ cup (4 fl oz) of red wine, the garlic vinegar, salt and pepper. Cook over low heat, stirring now and then.

Put the sugar and water into a small saucepan and cook over medium heat without stirring, until sugar starts to caramelise and turn golden brown. Add to cabbage, cover and simmer for 1½ hours or until tender.

Peel and core the apples and slice thinly. Add apples, remaining red wine, cranberry jelly and cloves to the cabbage, stir well, cover and simmer for 15 minutes, then uncover and cook until excess liquid has evaporated. Serve hot.

SERVES: 4

RED CABBAGE WITH APPLES

# BEANS WITH WALNUT DRESSING

*Use tender green beans, runner beans, yellow wax beans or string beans
and serve as a vegetable course on their own so the flavour of the dressing
is not confused with other flavours.*

### INGREDIENTS

500 g (1 lb) beans

•

½ cup (2 oz) walnuts, finely chopped
or ground

•

2 spring onions (scallions), chopped
very finely

•

1 clove garlic, crushed

•

1 teaspoon salt

•

1 teaspoon mild paprika

•

2 tablespoons red wine vinegar

•

½ cup (4 fl oz) water or Vegetable
Stock (see page 448)

•

1 tablespoon finely chopped
fresh basil leaves

Top and tail beans and remove strings if necessary. Cook in steamer or in lightly salted boiling water until tender but still crisp. Drain well.

While beans are cooking, combine all the other ingredients and pour over the drained beans in serving dish. Toss to mix and serve warm.

SERVES: 4–6

# SAVOURY ZUCCHINI PANCAKES

*Serve as part of a mixed platter. Best eaten while still hot and crisp.*

### INGREDIENTS

1 medium zucchini (courgette)
(about 2 cups grated)

•

1 onion, grated

•

1 egg

•

¼ teaspoon freshly ground
black pepper

•

¼ teaspoon salt

•

½ cup (2 oz) wholemeal
(whole wheat) flour

•

oil, for frying

Wash but do not peel zucchini, then grate on coarse grater. Combine in a bowl with the onion, beaten egg and seasonings. Stir in flour.

In a large, heavy-based frying pan, heat just enough oil to film the base of pan and when hot, put in the mixture in large spoonfuls. Spread mixture with back of spoon to form a well shaped pancake about 10 cm (4 in) across.

Cook over medium heat until golden brown, turn with egg slice and fry until other side is brown. Drain on paper towels and fry remaining mixture, adding more oil to pan if necessary. Serve pancakes hot.

VARIATION: Zucchini and potato pancakes are just as delicious and have an extra crispness with the addition of potato. Peel and grate potato and use 1 cup potato in place of 1 cup grated zucchini. Cook the pancakes as soon as mixture is made or it will discolour.

MAKES: about 8 small pancakes

# RIZ BI SH'ARIEH

*A Lebanese combination of rice and noodles cooked in the pilaf style. I have cut down on the amount of ghee (clarified butter) in the original recipe demonstrated by a Lebanese friend, but for those who watch their fat intake I suggest using 2 teaspoons ghee for flavour and light vegetable oil to make up the quantity.*

### INGREDIENTS

2 cups (14 oz) Basmati or other
long grain rice

•

½ cup (2½ oz) fine noodles
or vermicelli

•

½ cup (4 oz) melted ghee
(clarified butter)

•

1½ teaspoons salt

•

3½ cups (28 fl oz) water

•

pine nuts (optional)

Wash the rice thoroughly and drain for at least 30 minutes. Break the noodles into short pieces. In a large, heavy-based saucepan with a well fitting lid, heat the ghee and fry the noodles until deep brown. This browning brings out the flavour in the finished dish.

Add the rice and fry for a few seconds longer, then add salt and water, bring to the boil, turn heat low, cover and cook for 20 minutes without lifting lid. Fluff up with fork and serve. If liked, a few pine nuts fried in ghee may be used for garnish.

SERVES: 4

# GREEN BEANS WITH PINENUTS AND RASPBERRY VINAIGRETTE

### INGREDIENTS

500 g (1 lb) tender stringless beans

•

60 g (2 oz) pine nuts

### DRESSING

1 tablespoon raspberry vinegar

•

½ teaspoon dry mustard

•

1 teaspoon whole grain mustard

•

pinch salt

•

1 teaspoon honey

•

¼ cup (2 fl oz) pure olive oil

•

1 clove garlic, bruised

Make the dressing first and let it stand while preparing the beans. Whisk vinegar with mustards, salt and honey until blended. Gradually whisk in the oil. Add garlic and allow to stand for garlic to flavour the dressing.

Top and tail the beans and rinse in cold water. Cook beans in boiling water, steam in a basket, or cook in a microwave oven until just tender, bright green and crisp. Plunge beans into iced water to set the colour and stop further cooking. Drain well and just before serving, remove the garlic from the dressing, pour over the beans, sprinkle with pine nuts and toss to mix.

SERVES: 4

# BROCCOLI IN GARLIC BUTTER

*This is one of those vegetable dishes I could make a meal of, but it also makes a wonderful accompaniment to Risotto Alla Milanese (see page 100) or other grain dishes.*

### INGREDIENTS

1 large bunch broccoli

•

60 g (2 oz) butter

•

2 cloves garlic, crushed with ½ teaspoon salt

•

2 tablespoons lemon juice

Wash and trim broccoli. Cut slits in ends of stalks to speed up cooking. Put a very little lightly salted water into a heavy-based saucepan and bring to the boil. Immerse only the stalks, leaving flower heads to cook in the steam. Cover pan and cook for about 4 minutes or until just tender and brilliantly green. Drain immediately and arrange in a serving dish. (Overcooking will result in soggy broccoli and a poor colour.)

While broccoli is cooking, melt butter in a small saucepan and when it turns a nut brown, remove from heat and stir in the garlic. Add lemon juice. Pour the garlic butter over broccoli or serve it separately so broccoli may be dipped in it.

SERVES: 4

GREEN BEANS WITH PINENUTS AND RASPBERRY VINAIGRETTE

# ORANGE RICE WITH PINE NUTS

### INGREDIENTS

500 g (1 lb) long grain rice

•

3 large oranges

•

60 g (2 oz) ghee (clarified butter)
or butter

•

1 onion, finely chopped

•

4 vegetable stock cubes
(or 4 tablespoons of powdered
onion soup)

•

2 teaspoons salt, or to taste

•

2 teaspoons fresh thyme or
½ teaspoon dried thyme

•

½ cup (2 oz) pine nuts

•

2 tablespoons oil

Wash the rice well and leave to drain in a colander for at least 30 minutes. Grate orange rind on fine grater, taking care to avoid the white pith. Measure 2 teaspoons orange rind. Squeeze juice from oranges and add water to make 4 cups (32 fl oz).

In a heavy-based saucepan, heat the ghee and fry onion on medium heat, stirring occasionally, until soft and golden. Add rice and stir with a metal spoon for 4–5 minutes. Add orange juice, stock cubes and salt. Add grated orange rind and thyme, stir and allow to come to the boil. Cover pan with a well fitting lid, turn heat very low and cook for 20–25 minutes, not lifting lid for at least 20 minutes. If there is still moisture to be absorbed, continue cooking for a few minutes longer.

Uncover pan and allow steam to escape for a few minutes, then gently fluff up rice with a long pronged fork. Transfer rice to a serving dish using a metal spoon. Garnish with pine nuts fried in oil until golden.

SERVES: 6

# GREEN BEANS WITH MUSHROOMS

### INGREDIENTS

500 g (1 lb) tender green beans

125 g (4 oz) button mushrooms

2 tablespoons butter

salt and pepper to taste

Bring a large pan of lightly salted water to the boil and drop in the beans. Cover just until water returns to the boil, then cook, uncovered, on high heat for 4–5 minutes or just until beans are tender but still crisp. Be careful not to overcook. Drain immediately and refresh under cold water. This sets the brilliant green colour. Drain well on paper towels.

Slice the mushrooms thinly with a stainless steel knife. Heat butter and toss the mushrooms for 2–3 minutes, add salt and pepper to taste, turn in the beans and toss briefly just until heated through. Serve at once.

SERVES: 4

# BRAISED FENNEL WITH ONION

*The pleasant liquorice flavour of fennel is given more savoury overtones when cooked with onion.*

### INGREDIENTS

1 medium onion
•
3 bulbs fennel
•
2 tablespoons butter or margarine
•
black pepper and salt to taste

Peel the onion and slice into thin rings. Wash and slice fennel. Melt the butter or margarine in a saucepan, add the onion and fennel and toss over medium heat for a few minutes. Sprinkle liberally with freshly ground pepper and a little salt, cover pan, reduce heat and cook over low heat for 10 minutes or until fennel is tender. Serve hot.

SERVES: 6

# BAKED BUTTERNUT

### INGREDIENTS

1 kg (2 lb) butternut pumpkin (squash)
•
60 g (2 oz) butter
•
salt and pepper, to taste
•
¼ teaspoon ground mace or nutmeg
•
2 teaspoons honey (optional)
•
2 eggs, well beaten
•
½ cup (2 oz) grated cheese (optional)

Peel pumpkin, discard spongy centre and seeds, then cut into slices and cook in lightly salted boiling water until tender. Butternut pumpkin cooks quickly, so make sure it doesn't overcook and become mushy. Drain off liquid and mash smoothly. Add all other ingredients, mixing well. Turn into a buttered heatproof dish and bake in an oven preheated to 180°C (350°F) for about 25 minutes. Serve hot.

SERVES: 4–6

# HERBED GREEN PEAS

*This is the French style of cooking fresh young peas; surely one of the
best tasting vegetables.*

## INGREDIENTS

1 kg (2 lb) fresh peas in the pod
•
4 large leaves lettuce, finely shredded
•
3 spring onions (scallions),
finely chopped
•
few sprigs fresh mint
•
1 cup (8 fl oz) hot water or
Vegetable Stock (see page 448)
•
30 g (1 oz) butter
•
1 tablespoon plain (all-purpose) flour
•
salt and pepper to taste
•
½ cup (4 fl oz) cream or evaporated
milk (optional)

Shell peas and put into a saucepan with the lettuce, spring
onions, mint and about ¼ cup (2 fl oz) water. Cook on
low heat, tightly covered, until peas are tender, adding more
hot water or vegetable stock as liquid reduces.

Mix together the butter and flour and add, a little at
a time, to enrich and thicken the juices. Season to taste
with salt and pepper. If a creamy result is preferred, stir
in the cream at the end of cooking and heat through, but
do not boil. Serve hot.

SERVES: 4–6

# JULIENNE CARROTS

## INGREDIENTS

3 or 4 medium carrots
•
½ cup (4 fl oz) Vegetable Stock
(see page 448)
•
salt and pepper to taste
•
finely chopped parsley, for garnish

Peel the carrots and cut into julienne strips. Bring vegetable
stock to boil in a small saucepan, add carrots and season
to taste. Cover and cook on low heat until just tender.
If stock boils away, add a little more. Sprinkle with chopped
parsley just before serving.

SERVES: 4

HERBED GREEN PEAS

# BAKED POTATOES

*What makes these potatoes special is that they are peeled and sliced very finely, but because they are not sliced through, they hold their shape. I learned an easy way of doing this rather tricky slicing (how often the knife goes too far and the potato is divided in pieces). Simply place each potato in a spoon before slicing. The spoon prevents the knife going all the way through.*

### INGREDIENTS

6 large potatoes

•

2 tablespoons melted butter

•

paprika, for dusting

•

salt, to taste

Peel even-sized potatoes and cut in very, very fine slices almost to the bottom, as described above. Brush with melted butter and bake until soft in the centre and crusty on the surface. Dust lightly with paprika about 10 minutes before they are done.

SERVES: 6

# SOUTH SEA ISLAND SPINACH

*In the islands of the South Pacific, young taro leaves and coconut cream are wrapped in parcels of breadfruit leaves and cooked over the coals. This recipe can be re-created using spinach, but aluminium foil replaces the leaves for wrapping and stands up well to cooking over a barbecue. They may also be cooked in the oven.*

### INGREDIENTS

1 large bunch spinach or silverbeet
(Swiss chard)

•

1 large onion, thinly sliced

•

½ cup (4 fl oz) thick coconut milk
(see page 443)

•

salt to taste

Wash the spinach well in cold water, making sure all sand has been rinsed out. Cut off the stems. If using silverbeet, strip the leaves away from the white stalks. Bring a large pan of water to the boil and blanch the leaves a few at a time, holding them in the water for about 30 seconds. They don't have to be cooked, merely softened sufficiently to make compact parcels. Drain in a colander.

Take two lengths of heavy-duty aluminium foil. In the middle of each, place another piece of foil folded double to protect the bottom of the parcel from scorching. Put some spinach leaves on the double foil, bunching them in a neat pile in the centre. Add a few slices of onion on top, then season with a little salt.

Repeat until all the spinach and onion have been used. Do not use too much salt—the flavour should be mild and sweet. Spoon the coconut milk over the spinach. Bring the foil together at the top and fold over twice to seal the edges. Cook on the barbecue for 6–8 minutes.

SERVES: 4

# DEVILLED MUSHROOMS

## INGREDIENTS

500 g (1 lb) button mushrooms
or small caps

•

3 tablespoons vegetable oil

•

2 cloves garlic, finely chopped

•

1 fresh red chilli, seeded and chopped

•

salt and pepper to taste

•

2 tablespoons soy sauce

•

dash of hot chilli sauce

Wipe over the mushrooms and cut in halves or quarters. Heat the oil in a wok or large frying pan and cook the garlic and chilli over low heat until soft and golden. Add mushrooms and toss constantly until coated with oil. Season to taste, cover and cook for 3–4 minutes. Add sauces and stir to combine. If liquid has collected in the pan, thicken it slightly with 1 teaspoon cornflour (cornstarch) mixed with 1 tablespoon cold water. Serve with hot rice.

SERVES: 4–6

# POTATO DUMPLINGS

*In Bavaria, where I first tried these, dumplings are large, almost the size of tennis balls. Serve them with a vegetable stew or green beans, or for potato fanciers, as a light meal on their own, sprinkled with crisp, buttered breadcrumbs.*

## INGREDIENTS

3 or 4 large potatoes
(about 800 g/1 lb 6 oz)

•

½ cup (2 oz) plain (all-purpose) flour

•

½ cup (3 oz) semolina

•

1½ teaspoons salt

•

¼ teaspoon white pepper

•

1 egg, beaten with 2 teaspoons milk

Scrub potatoes and boil them in their skins until tender. Drain while hot. When cool enough to handle, peel and push through a potato ricer or mash and sieve.

Put a large pan of water on to boil, ready for cooking the dumplings. Combine the potatoes and other ingredients in a bowl, mixing with a wooden spoon until quite smooth. Dust hands with flour and form into balls of the required size. Make smaller ones if preferred.

Drop dumplings into boiling water and when the water returns to the boil, lower the heat so they simmer gently. Do not cover pan. Cook until they rise to the surface, then simmer a few minutes longer, about 15 minutes in all for large dumplings. Drain on a slotted spoon and arrange on a heated dish.

NOTE: If liked, sprinkle with fresh breadcrumbs which have been fried in butter until golden and crisp.

MAKES: 8 large dumplings

# BRAISED CELERY WITH ALMONDS

### INGREDIENTS

1 large or 2 small bunches
white celery
•
2 tablespoons butter
•
½ cup (2 oz) slivered blanched
almonds
•
salt and pepper to taste
•
¾ cup (6 fl oz) Vegetable Stock
(see page 448)

Wash celery well, separating stalks. Cut into finger lengths, stripping away the coarse strings from the outside of the stalks as you do so.

Heat butter in a heavy-based pan and toss the almonds over medium heat until golden. Remove with slotted spoon and set aside. If necessary, add more butter to the pan.

When butter is hot and just starting to brown, add the celery, season and sauté for a few minutes, then turn heat very low, add vegetable stock, cover and cook until tender but still slightly crisp. Serve hot, sprinkled with the fried almonds.

SERVES: 4–5

# LEBANESE POTATOES

*I learned this recipe when I saw a young couple at the markets pushing a pram filled with bunches of fresh coriander! Curiosity aroused, I ventured to ask what they would use such a quantity of the herb for, and they shared this delicious recipe.*

### INGREDIENTS

500 g (1 lb) potatoes
•
vegetable oil, for frying
•
4 cloves garlic, finely chopped
•
1 large bunch fresh coriander,
roughly chopped (about 2 cups)
•
¼ cup (2 fl oz) lemon juice
•
1 teaspoon salt

Peel and dice the potatoes. Heat enough oil to cover the base of a frying pan, then fry the potatoes over medium heat until crisp, brown all over and cooked through. Pour off any excess oil, move potatoes to one side and gently fry the garlic, taking care not to burn it.

Add the coriander leaves and toss potatoes with garlic and coriander. Sprinkle with lemon juice and salt, mix well. The flavour should be very lemony.

SERVES: 4–6

BRAISED CELERY WITH ALMONDS

# STUFFED CHOKOS (CHAYOTES) WITH MUSHROOMS

*Choko, chayote, christophene—they all mean one and the same thing. A prolific member (is there any other kind?) of the squash family that grows with abandon and could use some help when it comes to flavour.*

## INGREDIENTS

2 large chokos (chayotes), about 500 g (1 lb) each

•

250 g (8 oz) mushrooms

•

2 large onions

•

3 tablespoons butter

•

salt and freshly ground black pepper to taste

•

1 cup (2 oz) soft fresh breadcrumbs

•

2 tablespoons dry breadcrumbs

Wash chokos and halve lengthwise. Cook in lightly salted boiling water with lid on pan for 25 minutes or until chokos are just tender when tested with a knife. Turn the halves cut-side down on paper towels to drain. When cool enough to handle, scoop out pulp with a spoon, leaving a fairly thick shell so that it will hold its shape. Carefully peel away skin.

Wipe over mushrooms and chop finely. Peel and chop onions finely. Heat 2 tablespoons of the butter in a heavy-based frying pan and fry the onions over low heat until soft and golden. Add the mushrooms, season with salt and pepper and cook until mushrooms are soft. Remove from heat, cool slightly and stir in soft breadcrumbs. Taste and add more salt and pepper if required.

Divide the mushroom mixture between the choko shells and mound firmly into the hollows. Sprinkle with dry breadcrumbs, dot with remaining butter and bake in an oven preheated to 200°C (400°F) for 20 minutes or until tops are lightly browned. Serve hot.

The chokos may be baked in individual ovenproof dishes and served as a vegetable course on their own.

NOTE: Very young chokos may be quartered and cooked without peeling if the skin is tender enough. They should still be slightly crisp. Drain, toss with butter, pepper and salt. Serve right away.

SERVES: 4

# ROASTED CAPSICUMS

*Lucia, a wonderful Italian lady who cooked in her own family restaurant, taught me how to prepare many dishes, and this is one of them. I've been hooked on roasted capsicum ever since.*

### INGREDIENTS

8–10 large capsicums (sweet peppers)
•
olive oil to taste
•
sea salt to taste

Wash the capsicums and dry well. Place under a preheated griller (broiler) and grill until the skins are scorched and blistered, then turn them and keep grilling until all surfaces have been done. Wrap capsicums in a clean damp tea towel and leave to get cold. This makes it very easy to peel the thin, tough skin away. Remove and discard the seeds, then cut the flesh into strips. Pour over about 4 tablespoons of good quality olive oil. Grind sea salt over to season. Cover and chill. Serve with slices of crusty bread for dipping.

SERVES: 8

# BRAISED ENDIVE, LEBANESE STYLE

*When the mother of a family who run a Lebanese restaurant gave me the recipe for this dish, it became part of my repertoire.*

### INGREDIENTS

1 bunch curly endive (chicory)
•
½ cup (4 fl oz) oil
•
4 large onions, finely sliced
•
2 cloves garlic, finely chopped
•
lemon juice
•
salt and pepper, to taste

Wash the endive well and cook with very little water until tender. Drain well, pressing out excess moisture. Heat the oil in a saucepan and fry the onions and garlic until golden. Add the endive, season with lemon juice, salt and pepper and simmer for a few minutes. Serve warm or at room temperature.

SERVES: 4

# ARMENIAN POTATOES

*This recipe goes back a long way, and I remember being quite bowled over by the flavour when I first made it. Quite garlicky, but delicious.*

## INGREDIENTS

750 g (1½ lb) large, old potatoes

•

¼ cup (2 fl oz) vegetable oil

•

3 tablespoons tomato paste

•

generous ½ cup (4 fl oz) water

•

1 teaspoon salt

•

1 teaspoon paprika

•

freshly ground pepper to taste

•

6 cloves garlic, finely chopped

•

1 cup (2 oz) finely chopped parsley

Wash and thinly peel the potatoes and cut into small dice. Stir together the oil, tomato paste, water, salt and paprika and combine with the potatoes. Add pepper, garlic and parsley and toss to mix. Bake in a covered dish in an oven preheated to 160°C (325°F) for about 45 minutes or until potatoes are soft. Sprinkle with extra parsley to serve.

SERVES: 6

# POOR MAN'S CAVIAR

## INGREDIENTS

2 medium eggplants (aubergines)

•

1 large onion

•

3 cloves garlic

•

1 large red capsicum (pepper)

•

4 tablespoons olive oil

•

2 ripe tomatoes

•

1½ teaspoons salt or to taste

•

generous grinding of black pepper

•

lemon juice, to taste

Grill the whole eggplants until black all over and soft to the touch, turning them after 10-15 minutes on each side; or cook in a hot oven. The best flavour, of course, is if they are cooked over glowing-coals—remember the next time the barbecue fire is dying down.

Chop the onion, garlic and capsicum very finely. Heat oil in a heavy-based pan and cook the chopped vegetables until soft and golden, stirring now and then. When eggplants are cool enough, peel away the skin and mash the pulp.

Peel and seed the tomatoes and chop finely. Add eggplants and tomatoes to the mixture in the pan, season with salt and pepper and stir well. Cover and cook for 30 minutes on low heat, then uncover and cook until liquid in pan has evaporated, stirring frequently so it does not stick to pan. Add lemon juice and adjust seasoning. Serve chilled or at room temperature with slices of black or rye bread.

SERVES: 6-8

ARMENIAN POTATOES

# SWEET POTATO PUFFS

### INGREDIENTS

1 kg (2 lb) sweet potatoes

•

2 tablespoons melted butter

•

2 tablespoons grated tasty (sharp) cheese

•

1 egg yolk

•

½ teaspoon white pepper

•

½ teaspoon grated nutmeg

•

beaten egg, for glazing

Scrub the sweet potatoes and cook in their skins, then peel and mash. (I cook them in a microwave oven but they can also be baked or steamed. Try to avoid getting them waterlogged.) Because sweet potatoes are rather fibrous, push them through a coarse sieve so they will be smooth enough to pipe into swirls.

In a bowl, combine all the ingredients except egg for glazing. Mix well and fill a piping bag fitted with a large star nozzle. Pipe potato swirls on to a greased or non-stick baking tray.

Using a small pastry brush, coat the potato swirls with beaten egg and bake in an oven preheated to 180°C (350°F) for 25 minutes or until golden brown and firm.

# BRAISED GREEN BEANS

### INGREDIENTS

500 g (1 lb) tender beans

•

2 medium onions

•

2 cloves garlic

•

½ teaspoon salt

•

3 tablespoons olive oil

•

3 ripe tomatoes, peeled and diced

•

salt and pepper to taste

Top and tail the beans, then wash and cut into bite-size lengths. Finely slice the onions. Crush the garlic with salt. Heat the olive oil in a saucepan and cook the onions and garlic over low heat until soft and translucent. Add the beans and toss, then add the tomatoes. Cover and simmer for 20 minutes, or until beans are tender but still slightly crisp. Season to taste and serve.

SERVES: 6

# SHERRY-GLAZED CARROTS

*Adding extra flavour to a commonplace vegetable turns it into
something special.*

### INGREDIENTS

750 g (1½ lb) tender carrots

•

½ cup (4 fl oz) water or Vegetable
Stock (see page 448)

•

1 tablespoon butter

•

3 tablespoons sherry

•

1 tablespoon honey

•

1 teaspoon cornflour (cornstarch)
or arrowroot

•

finely chopped parsley, to garnish

If carrots are small, scrub them and leave whole. If large,
cut into diagonal slices or quarter them. Put carrots into
a pan with a well fitting lid. Add the water, butter, sherry
and honey. Bring to boiling point, then turn heat very low,
cover tightly and cook for 8–10 minutes or until just tender
but still crisp.

Using a slotted spoon, lift carrots onto a serving dish.
To make the glaze, stir cornflour mixed with about a
tablespoon of cold water into the liquid in pan. Cook until
it boils and thickens, then spoon over the carrots and sprinkle
chopped parsley over.

SERVES: 4

# KOHLRABI IN GARLIC BUTTER

### INGREDIENTS

4 kohlrabi (turnips, swedes or
parsnips may be used instead of
kohlrabi if liked)

•

2 tablespoons butter or margarine

•

1 small clove garlic

•

½ teaspoon salt

•

lemon juice

Remove leaves and stems and peel the kohlrabi. (Choose
medium-sized ones, large ones are apt to be woody.) Cut
into thin slices, then into julienne strips. Drop into lightly
salted boiling water and boil for about 15–20 minutes, until
just tender.

Melt the butter or margarine and add the garlic, crushed
with the salt (or use ½ teaspoon garlic salt). Leave on low
heat for 1–2 minutes, not long enough to brown the garlic.
Add a squeeze of lemon juice and toss the kohlrabi in the
butter. Serve hot.

SERVES: 4

# IRISH MASHED POTATOES

### INGREDIENTS

500 g (1 lb) old potatoes

•

half bunch spring onions (scallions),
including green leaves

•

¾ cup (6 fl oz) milk

•

salt and pepper to taste

•

100 g (3½ oz) butter

Boil the potatoes in their skins and while they are boiling, cut the spring onions into short lengths and simmer in the milk. When potatoes are tender, drain them and return to the pan to dry off over low heat. Peel and mash the potatoes smoothly, adding the hot milk strained from the onions. Season generously with salt and pepper.

Add the onions and half the butter, beating well until the potatoes are fluffy and pale green. Pile on 4 individual plates. Make a well in the centre of each serving and put a piece of the remaining butter in it to melt into a little golden pool. Eat from the outside, dipping the potato into the melted butter.

SERVES: 4

# GLAZED YAMS

*With orange rind and spice to flavour them, these are no ordinary yams.*
*Serve with a main dish or as part of an assorted vegetable platter.*

### INGREDIENTS

750 g (1½ lb) sweet potatoes
or kumara (bright orange
coloured yams)

•

½ cup (3 oz) brown sugar

•

finely grated rind of 1 orange

•

pinch of grated nutmeg
or dried ginger

•

¼ cup (2 fl oz) honey

•

2 tablespoons orange juice

•

30 g (1 oz) butter, cut in small pieces

Choose yams of an even size. Boil in plenty of lightly salted boiling water until almost tender. Drain immediately, peel, cut into thick slices and arrange in an oven-proof dish. Sprinkle with sugar mixed with orange rind and spice. Drizzle the honey and orange juice over and dot with butter. Bake in an oven preheated to 200°C (400°F) for 25 minutes or until glazed and golden.

SERVES: 6–8

IRISH MASHED POTATOES

# TOMATOES PROVENCALE

*With their garlic flavoured, crisp buttered-crumb topping, tomatoes cooked this way have always been popular.*

### INGREDIENTS

4 medium, firm, ripe tomatoes

•

1 clove garlic

•

½ teaspoon salt

•

2 tablespoons butter

•

4 tablespoons soft white breadcrumbs

•

½ cup (2 oz) finely grated sharp cheese

Wash and wipe tomatoes. Halve crossways and place on a foil-lined griller (broiler) tray. Preheat griller.

Crush garlic with salt. Heat butter in a small pan and add the garlic. Remove from heat before garlic has a chance to brown. Combine garlic butter with the breadcrumbs, mixing well.

Stir the cheese through the breadcrumb mixture and top the cut surfaces of the tomatoes with it. Place under the preheated griller for a few minutes until cheese mixture is golden. Serve hot.

SERVES: 4

# CARROTS AND MUSHROOMS

### INGREDIENTS

1 tablespoon butter

•

1 tablespoon oil

•

3 shallots or spring onions (scallions), finely chopped

•

500 g (1 lb) carrots, thickly sliced

•

250 g (8 oz) small mushrooms, halved or quartered

•

salt and pepper to taste

Heat butter and oil in a saucepan, add the shallots and stir for 1 minute, then add the carrots and mushrooms and toss in the butter until well coated and lightly browned. Season with salt and pepper, cover and cook until tender but not mushy. Serve hot.

SERVES: 4–6

# CARROT RING WITH PEAS

*When you want something that looks rather special for a festive table, turn
out a ring of carrot purée and fill it with fresh young peas or, if you prefer,
button mushrooms.*

## INGREDIENTS

1 kg (2 lb) carrots, washed
and trimmed

•

1 vegetable stock cube
(or 1 tablespoon of powdered
onion soup)

•

3 tablespoons butter

•

2 eggs, beaten

•

salt and pepper to taste

•

freshly cooked peas,
tossed with a little butter

Cook the carrots in just enough water to cover, with a
vegetable stock cube added for extra flavour. When tender,
drain the carrots, reserving the liquid to add to soup or
stock. Mash the carrots, mix in the butter and eggs, and
season well with salt and pepper.

Press into a well buttered ring mould and bake in an
oven preheated to 180°C (350°F) for 20 minutes or until
firm to the touch. Turn out on serving dish, fill the centre
with peas and serve hot.

SERVES: 6

# ARTICHOKE AND ONION PIZZA

## INGREDIENTS

1 Pizza Base or Tart Shell
(page 446)

•

1 x 425 g (14 oz) can artichoke hearts,
or 2 cups cooked artichoke bottoms

•

2 onions, finely sliced

•

3 tablespoons olive oil

•

salt and pepper, to taste

•

1 quantity Garlic Custard
(see page 441)

•

½ cup grated cheese

•

12 pitted black olives

•

strips of pimiento, for garnish

Make the pizza dough or use frozen bread dough to make
a quick pizza base or tart shell. Line a 25cm (10 in) flan
tin or pizza tray, building it up on the edges so it contains
the filling securely. Leave to prove while preparing filling.

Drain the artichoke hearts well and cut them into
quarters. In a heavy-based frying pan, cook the onions in
the olive oil until soft and golden. Season with salt and
freshly ground black pepper. Spread over the pizza base, then
place the artichokes evenly over the base and pour the garlic
custard over. Sprinkle lightly with grated cheese. Bake in
an oven preheated to 180°C (350°F) for 35-40 minutes and
serve warm, garnished with olives and pimiento strips.
Accompany with a green salad.

SERVES: 6

# SALADS AND DRESSINGS

Here you will find light side-salads or rather more filling salads based on pasta, potatoes or beans. Use these as main dishes for picnics if you like. They are eminently suitable, especially in warmer weather.

The dressings, however, are the strength of this chapter. With a good dressing, the humblest vegetable or salad greens take on a special importance. So when I specify balsamic vinegar or raspberry vinegar, hazelnut oil or walnut oil, don't immediately make the translation in your mind, saying "Oh, white vinegar and blended oil will do." They won't.

While these special oils and vinegars are more expensive, you use so little of them at a time that they'll go a long way, and they work miracles in flavouring your salads. They keep well—store the oils in the refrigerator once opened. Go on, treat yourself. Think of all the money you're not spending on meat!

## CRUNCHY SALAD WITH GARLIC CROÛTONS

*Do take a few minutes to make fresh croûtons—bought ones never taste quite as good.*

### INGREDIENTS

2 slices wholegrain bread
•
1 clove garlic
•
3 tablespoons olive oil
•
125 g (4 oz) button mushrooms
•
2 tablespoons wine vinegar
•
4 tablespoons salad oil
•
salt and pepper to taste
•
1 cos (romaine) lettuce, washed and dried

Trim crusts from bread and cut the slices into small cubes. Peel and crush the garlic and fry gently in the olive oil without browning. Toss in the bread and stir or shake so that all surfaces come in contact with the garlic oil. Place on a foil-lined baking sheet and bake in an oven preheated to 180°C (350°F) for about 8 minutes or until pale gold. Allow to cool and crisp.

With a sharp knife, cut the mushrooms into thin slices. Combine vinegar and oil, add salt and pepper to taste and marinate the mushroom slices for a few minutes.

Tear the washed and dried lettuce into a salad bowl, add the mushrooms and dressing, and toss well. Add the crisp garlic croûtons and toss again, then serve at once.

SERVES: 4

# GREEK COUNTRY STYLE SALAD

1 curly endive

•

1 cos (romaine) lettuce

•

1 cucumber

•

1 green capsicum (sweet pepper)

•

125 g (4 oz) feta cheese, cubed

•

125 g (4 oz) black olives

•

½ cup (4 fl oz) olive oil

•

¼ cup (2 fl oz) lemon juice

•

1 clove garlic, crushed with
¼ teaspoon salt

•

¼ teaspoon ground black pepper

Wash the endive and lettuce thoroughly, drain well and gently blot dry. Crisp in the refrigerator. Cut the cucumber into quarters lengthways, then into bite-size pieces. Halve the capsicum, remove core and seeds, then cut into thick slices. Tear the lettuce and endive into bite-size pieces and place in a serving bowl. Add the cucumber, capsicum, feta cheese and olives.

Combine the oil, lemon juice, crushed garlic and black pepper, whisking until thick. Just before serving, whisk again and pour over the salad, tossing gently to distribute dressing.

SERVES: 6

# BASIC COLESLAW

*The crunch of tender raw cabbage makes this a universally popular salad,
and with various additions, it can take on many flavours.*

INGREDIENTS

half a small white cabbage

•

half a small red cabbage (optional)

•

2 carrots

•

1 green capsicum (pepper)

•

½ cup (4 fl oz) French Dressing
(see page 184)

•

1 cup (8 fl oz) Mayonnaise
(see page 180)

Choose a tightly packed cabbage and shred very finely with a sharp knife. Soak cabbage in iced water for an hour, drain well.

Scrape and coarsely grate carrots. Cut capsicum into fine strips or dice finely. Combine all vegetables with French dressing and mayonnaise, and serve chilled.

Coleslaw can be as simple or as elaborate as you like. Some delicious additions are: fresh ripe pineapple, diced; or drained, canned pineapple; oranges, peeled and segmented; diced raw apples; sliced celery; walnuts or toasted almond slivers. If liked, some sour cream may also be added to dress the slaw.

SERVES: 6

# LENTIL SALAD

*Brown or green lentils from the supermarket shelves take on superb flavour
when simmered with a few simple ingredients.*

### INGREDIENTS

500 g (1 lb) green or brown lentils
•
8 cups (64 fl oz) water
•
2 carrots
•
2 onions
•
1 bay leaf
•
3 tablespoons red wine vinegar
•
salt and pepper to taste

### DRESSING

4 tablespoons red wine vinegar
•
1 tablespoon Dijon mustard
•
1 teaspoon salt, or to taste
•
good grinding of black pepper
•
½ cup (4 fl oz) olive oil
•
½ cup (4 fl oz) sunflower oil

Pick over lentils, discarding any unsound ones or little stones. Wash well and drain. Soaking is not necessary with these slender lentils, but a brief soaking will speed cooking.

Put the lentils into a saucepan with the measured water, carrots, onions, bay leaf, vinegar, salt and pepper. Bring to the boil over very low heat and cook until tender. Drain well. Pick out the bay leaf and vegetables, and season the lentils with pepper and salt.

To make the dressing, put the vinegar and mustard into a bowl and whisk together. Add salt and pepper. Whisk in the oil very gradually and dressing will thicken. Spoon over the lentils and toss gently. Serve warm or at room temperature.

SERVES: 8

# LIMA BEAN SALAD

*These large, mealy beans are a favourite because of their good flavour. Make
sure they are sufficiently cooked.*

### INGREDIENTS

375 g (12 oz) dried lima beans
•
1 teaspoon ground turmeric
•
salt
•
1½ cups (12 fl oz) Mayonnaise
(see page 180)
•
1 red capsicum (sweet pepper),
finely chopped

Soak the dried beans in water overnight. Drain, put into a pan or pressure cooker with enough fresh water to cover, add turmeric (this gives a rich golden colour as well as flavour) and salt to taste. Cook until tender.

Drain beans in a colander and cool until lukewarm. Toss with mayonnaise and some of the chopped red capsicum, reserving some for garnish. Serve warm or chilled.

SERVES: 4–6

# COOKED SALAD WITH SESAME DRESSING

*A robust flavoured salad. Use any combination of vegetables—beans, cabbage, cauliflower, okra, carrots, bamboo shoots, spring onions (scallions), bean sprouts, cucumber or zucchini (courgettes).*

## INGREDIENTS

6 cups (1½–2 lb) sliced vegetables
•
½ cup (4 fl oz) vegetable oil
•
1 tablespoon sesame oil
•
½ teaspoon ground turmeric
•
2 large onions, finely sliced
•
4 cloves garlic, finely sliced
•
2 tablespoons white vinegar
•
3 tablespoons sesame seeds

Cut vegetables into bite-size strips and boil for 1–2 minutes in lightly salted water, just until tender but still crisp. Drain vegetables in a colander and plunge into iced water to prevent overcooking. Drain again.

Heat the two oils in a small frying pan, add turmeric, onions and garlic, and fry over medium heat, stirring all the time, until the onions and garlic start to brown. Remove pan from heat and continue stirring until they are brown and crisp. When cool, pour a little of this oil over the vegetables, add onions and garlic and toss lightly but thoroughly, adding salt to taste, and vinegar. In a dry pan, roast the sesame seeds over medium heat until golden brown and sprinkle over the vegetables.

SERVES: 6

# MARINATED MUSHROOM AND AVOCADO SALAD

## INGREDIENTS

500 g (1 lb) button mushrooms
•
¼ cup (2 fl oz) lemon juice
•
½ cup (4 fl oz) salad oil
•
1 small clove garlic, crushed
•
salt and pepper to taste
•
2 teaspoons chopped
fresh marjoram or chives
•
2 firm ripe avocados
•
salad greens, washed, dried
and chilled

Wipe the mushrooms and slice thickly through the cap and stem. Blanch for 1–2 minutes in lightly salted boiling water. Drain and refresh.

Combine the lemon juice, oil, garlic, salt, pepper and herbs in a bowl, whisk well to make a dressing, and marinate the mushrooms in this for half an hour, turning them over after 10 minutes.

Halve avocados lengthways and remove seed. Peel, then slice evenly. Place alternate layers of salad greens, torn into bite-size pieces, mushrooms and avocados in a glass bowl, with mushrooms and avocados on top. Toss and serve.

SERVES: 6

# MUSHROOM AND BEAN SPROUT SALAD

## INGREDIENTS

500 g (1 lb) button or
cup mushrooms

•

250 g (8 oz) fresh bean sprouts

•

1 head lettuce

•

2 tablespoons toasted,
crushed sesame seeds

•

1 cup (8 fl oz) good Mayonnaise
(see page 180)

Wipe mushrooms with damp kitchen paper, then slice thinly with a stainless steel knife. Blanch for 1 minute in lightly salted boiling water. Drain and refresh.

Wash bean sprouts, drain, then pinch off straggly tails. Wash, dry and chill lettuce until crisp. Tear into bite-size pieces. Put mushrooms, bean sprouts and lettuce into a bowl and toss lightly. Serve with a dressing made by stirring the crushed sesame seeds into the mayonnaise. If liked, thin the dressing with a little milk.

NOTE:   Toasting sesame seeds is easily done in a dry frying pan. Heat pan with sesame seeds over medium heat, stirring or shaking pan to keep seeds from burning. They should be golden brown after 5–6 minutes. Immediately turn out on a plate to cool. Crush with a mortar and pestle or in an electric blender.

SERVES: 4

# RAW BEETROOT SALAD

*This is popular in east European countries, and I first tasted it when it was made by a good cook from that part of the world.*

## INGREDIENTS

4 tender young beets
•
1 small onion
•
½ cup (4 fl oz) French Dressing
(see page 184)
•
1 tablespoon bottled horseradish
•
1 cup (8 oz) sour cream
•
lettuce cups

Peel beets and grate coarsely. Peel and grate the onion. Combine in a small bowl. Pour dressing over the beet mixture, cover and chill.

Stir horseradish into the sour cream and chill separately. At serving time, put spoonfuls of grated mixture into crisp lettuce cups and top with a generous spoonful of cream.

SERVES: 4

# FATTOUSH — LEBANESE BREAD SALAD

*The distinguishing feature of this salad is the addition, just before serving, of pieces of crisply toasted flat bread.*

## INGREDIENTS

1 seedless cucumber, diced
•
2 large red or green capsicums
(sweet peppers), diced
•
3 large firm tomatoes, diced
•
half bunch spring onions
(scallions), chopped
•
small bunch parsley, chopped
•
¼ cup (2 fl oz) lemon juice
•
¼ cup (2 fl oz) olive oil
•
1 clove garlic, crushed
•
½ teaspoon salt
•
¼ teaspoon pepper
•
1 flat loaf middle eastern bread

If using a thin-skinned cucumber it is not necessary to peel it.

Put the diced and chopped vegetables into a bowl, cover and chill until shortly before serving time. Combine lemon juice, oil, garlic, salt and pepper, and pour over the vegetables. Split the round loaf of bread into two layers, gently pulling them apart and toast under a grill. It should be the palest gold colour, not brown. Break into large pieces and toss into the salad at the last minute so that bread will still be crisp when eaten.

SERVES: 6

# PASTA SALAD WITH PEAS

*Teenage boys love this salad and take it on picnics because it travels well.*
*Keep it cool in an insulated container.*

## INGREDIENTS

250 g (8 oz) pasta in the shape
of shells, twists, or any other desired
form
•
1 cup (8 fl oz) Mayonnaise
(see page 180)
•
1 small onion, finely chopped
•
1 cup (6 oz) shelled peas, cooked
and drained
•
½ cup (3 oz) diced red capsicum
(sweet pepper)
•
salt and freshly ground black
pepper to taste

In a large saucepan, bring to the boil enough lightly salted water to cook the pasta. Add a teaspoon of oil to prevent boiling over. When the water boils, add the pasta and stir until it returns to the boil. Cook 5–7 minutes or until it is just tender. Do not overcook—pasta must not be mushy. Run cold water into the pan to stop cooking, and drain well in a colander.

Mix together the mayonnaise, onion, peas and diced capsicum. Add to the well drained pasta in a bowl and toss to mix. Add salt and pepper to taste. Cover and chill until serving time.

SERVES: 4–6

# BEAN SPROUT SALAD

*As befits an ingredient associated with oriental food, the dressing has*
*subtle oriental flavours.*

## INGREDIENTS

500 g (1 lb) fresh mung or
soy bean sprouts
•
1 tablespoon sesame oil
•
1 tablespoon salad oil
•
1 tablespoon crushed, toasted
sesame seeds
•
3 tablespoons light soy sauce
•
1 clove garlic, crushed
•
2 spring onions (scallions),
very finely chopped
•
1 teaspoon honey or sugar
•
dash of chilli powder or
cayenne pepper

Wash bean sprouts. Bring a pan of lightly salted water to the boil, drop in the bean sprouts and return to the boil. Boil for less than a minute if using mung beans, longer for soy beans. The sprouts should be just tender, never overcooked. Drain at once and refresh in iced water. Drain well. Combine all other ingredients for the dressing and toss with bean sprouts. Chill before serving.

SERVES: 6

# CAULIFLOWER AND BROCCOLI SALAD

*These vegetables are plentiful in the colder months and, being members of
the Brassica family, are very good to eat.*

### INGREDIENTS

1 small cauliflower
•
500 g (1 lb) broccoli

### DRESSING

3 tablespoons white vinegar
•
6 tablespoons salad oil
•
salt and pepper to taste
•
1 clove garlic, crushed
•
3 tablespoons finely chopped
red capsicum (sweet pepper)

Trim cauliflower and broccoli, wash well and divide into florets. Bring a pan of lightly salted water to the boil and blanch the cauliflower for 3–4 minutes, just until tender. Lift out with a slotted spoon and drain. Cook the broccoli in the same way.

To make the dressing, whisk all the ingredients together thoroughly, reserving a little of the chopped capsicum for sprinkling over the top. Sprinkle dressing over and toss to distribute the seasoning. Serve warm or cold.

SERVES: 6

# PASTA, PECAN AND BEAN SALAD

*A substantial salad, one that could provide a well balanced light meal.*

### INGREDIENTS

250 g (8 oz) small shell pasta
•
3 cups cooked dried beans (8 oz dried)
or 1 large can 4 bean mix
•
1 cup (5 oz) finely diced celery
•
½ cup (2 oz) roughly chopped pecans
•
1 cup (6 oz) shelled peas, cooked
and drained
•
2 tablespoons finely chopped onion
•
½ cup (4 fl oz) Mayonnaise
(see page 180)
•
½ cup (4 fl oz) light sour cream
•
2 tablespoons tomato paste

Cook the pasta in a large amount of lightly salted boiling water, with a little oil added, until just tender. Run cold water into pan to stop cooking, drain pasta in a colander and cool. Rinse canned beans in cold water and drain. Combine with the pasta, celery, pecans, peas and onion. Stir together the mayonnaise, sour cream and tomato paste and, if necessary, thin with a little water to give the consistency of pouring cream. Pour over the pasta mixture and stir gently to coat. Serve at room temperature, or slightly chilled.

SERVES: 4–6

CAULIFLOWER AND BROCCOLI SALAD

# PAPAYA SALAD

## INGREDIENTS

1 medium, firm papaya (pawpaw)

•

1 small ripe pineapple,
peeled and diced

•

2 spring onions (scallions),
finely sliced

•

1 cooking apple, peeled and diced

•

½ cup (3 oz) thinly sliced celery

•

½ cup (4 fl oz) Salad Dressing or
Mayonnaise (see page 180)

•

salt and pepper to taste

Peel papaya, cut in half and scoop out seeds. Cut flesh into dice. Combine with all the other ingredients, cover and chill before serving.

SERVES: 6

# POTATO AND ARTICHOKE SALAD

*For those who like the flavour of artichokes, try this potato salad
with a delicious difference.*

## INGREDIENTS

1 kg (2 lb) small new potatoes

•

½ cup (1 oz) finely chopped spring
onion (scallion)

•

2 tablespoons cider vinegar

•

2 tablespoons water

•

1 teaspoon sea salt

•

¼ teaspoon freshly ground pepper

•

1 can artichoke hearts, drained

•

1 cup (8 fl oz) Mayonnaise
(see page 180)

•

½ cup (2½ oz) pimiento-stuffed
olives, sliced

•

3 tablespoons finely snipped chives
and parsley

Boil the potatoes in their skins. Peel and cut into halves or quarters. Combine the spring onion with vinegar, water, salt and pepper, and pour evenly over the potatoes, tossing to mix well. Cut the artichoke hearts into quarters, add to potatoes and pour the mayonnaise over. Sprinkle with sliced olives and fresh herbs and toss gently again. Serve with a spoonful of sour cream if liked.

SERVES: 6

# SPROUT AND WATER CHESTNUT SALAD

### INGREDIENTS

250 g (8 oz) fresh mung bean sprouts
•
2 cups (8 oz) finely shredded
Chinese white cabbage
(wongah bak)
•
6 spring onions (scallions),
finely sliced
•
1 small can water chestnuts, sliced
•
2 tablespoons toasted sesame seeds

### SESAME DRESSING

3 tablespoons peanut oil
•
2 teaspoons sesame oil
•
1 tablespoon vinegar
•
1 tablespoon light soy sauce
•
¼ teaspoon finely grated fresh ginger
•
1 small clove garlic, crushed
•
1 teaspoon sugar

Wash and drain fresh bean sprouts, pinching off any straggly tails. Combine bean sprouts in a bowl with all other ingredients except sesame seeds.

Combine the ingredients for the dressing. (Crushing the garlic is made easy if it is sprinkled with the sugar on a wooden board to prevent slipping.)

Just before serving, sprinkle salad with the sesame seeds, toasted until golden in a dry frying pan over medium heat for 5–6 minutes. Drizzle dressing over, toss and serve.

SERVES: 4

# JAPANESE RADISH AND CABBAGE SALAD

*To make the shreds of vegetables as fine as possible is to ensure the success of this salad. There is a very fine grater from Japan which makes incredibly delicate strips of carrot and radish.*

### INGREDIENTS

1 giant white radish (daikon)
•
¼ head firm white cabbage
•
1 tender carrot
•
Kimizu Dressing (see page 182)

Peel radish and cut into very fine strips. Shred cabbage finely, discarding leaf ribs and tough stalks. Scrape carrot and cut into very fine strips. Chill vegetables in iced water for 1 hour or until crisp. Drain well and serve with dressing.

SERVES: 6

# PINEAPPLE SALAD

## INGREDIENTS

half a firm, ripe pineapple
•
1 mild salad onion, finely chopped
•
1 small cucumber, thinly sliced
•
1 fresh chilli

## DRESSING

3 tablespoons light soy sauce
•
2 tablespoons lime or lemon juice
•
2 teaspoons sugar
•
1 small clove garlic, crushed
•
2 tablespoons crisply fried onions

Cut the half pineapple into three long spears. Discard core and slice pineapple spears across into thin, fan-shaped slices. Combine with finely chopped mild salad onion, cucumber, and a sliced fresh chilli, if a hot flavour is desired.

Make a dressing by mixing together the soy sauce, lime juice, sugar and garlic. Pour over the pineapple and cucumber and mix. Just before serving, sprinkle with the crisp fried onions, which can be bought in a packet from Asian food shops and stored in the freezer until required.

SERVES: 4–6

# MUSHROOM SALAD

## INGREDIENTS

500 g (1 lb) button mushrooms
•
1 teaspoon salt
•
juice of half a lemon
•
4–6 cups torn salad greens

## DRESSING

1 clove garlic, crushed
•
1 teaspoon salt
•
½ teaspoon freshly ground black pepper
•
¼ cup (2 fl oz) white vinegar
•
¾ cup (6 fl oz) olive oil
•
2 tablespoons finely chopped parsley or other fresh herbs

Wipe over the mushrooms with a damp paper towel. (Do not wash mushrooms, it is not necessary.) If mushrooms are small leave them whole, otherwise slice or cut in half. Blanch the mushrooms in batches, for just a couple of minutes, in boiling water with a little salt and lemon juice added. Drain well.

Whisk together all the dressing ingredients and pour over the mushrooms in a glass or china bowl. Cover and set aside for 10 minutes, then drain the mushrooms and arrange on salad greens.

SERVES: 6

# RED BEAN SALAD

### INGREDIENTS

500 g (1 lb) dried red kidney beans
or borlotti beans

•

salt

•

¾ cup (6 fl oz) French Dressing
(see page 184)

•

2 or 3 small white onions

•

4 tablespoons finely snipped chives

Soak beans in water overnight. Drain, put into a pan or pressure cooker with enough water to cover, add about 2 teaspoons salt, and cook until beans are tender. Drain in a colander.

While beans are still hot, toss in the dressing to coat thoroughly. Cut onions into thin slices and separate into rings. Reserve a few for garnishing and mix the rest, along with the chives, through the beans. Serve warm or chilled.

NOTE:   If time is short use canned beans, drained and rinsed.

SERVES: 6–8

# RAW MUSHROOM AND ZUCCHINI SALAD

### INGREDIENTS

300 g (10 oz) firm white mushrooms

•

250 g (8 oz) dark green
zucchini (courgettes)

### DRESSING

2 tablespoons walnut oil

•

¹/3 cup (3 fl oz) sunflower oil

•

3 tablespoons wine vinegar or
lemon juice

•

½ teaspoon salt

•

¼ teaspoon pepper

•

1 teaspoon honey

•

1 clove garlic, bruised

•

2 tablespoons finely
chopped parsley

•

1 tablespoon finely
chopped chives

Wipe over the mushrooms and slice thickly. Wash the zucchini, then trim stem ends and slice diagonally. Make a dressing by whisking all the ingredients together. Remove garlic clove before pouring dressing over the salad. Toss gently so that all ingredients are coated. Serve at once.

SERVES: 4–6

# SCANDINAVIAN CUCUMBER SALAD

*Here is a salad without a creamy dressing—very fresh tasting with its generous
component of fresh dill weed.*

### INGREDIENTS

2 large green cucumbers

•

3 teaspoons salt

•

½ cup (4 fl oz) white vinegar

•

3 tablespoons sugar

•

¼ teaspoon white pepper

•

2 tablespoons finely snipped fresh dill

Wash and dry cucumbers and score skin with a fork. Cut into thin slices and sprinkle with salt. Mix well, cover and leave for 2 hours, then drain away the liquid that gathers, pressing out as much as possible. Mix together the vinegar, sugar and pepper, stirring to dissolve the sugar. Pour over the cucumbers in a glass or enamel bowl, cover and chill overnight. Garnish with the dill and serve chilled.

SERVES: 6

# SPANISH EGGPLANT (AUBERGINE) SALAD

*Ideal for anyone who is trying to cut down on oil. Here is one of the few
recipes where eggplant is not cooked in oil, but in water. It is still full of
flavour and makes a wonderful diet lunch.*

### INGREDIENTS

2 medium, firm eggplants
(aubergines)

•

1 teaspoon salt

•

juice of half a lemon

•

1 small onion, very finely chopped

•

1½ cups (8 oz) finely sliced celery

•

½ cup (2 oz) walnuts, broken into
pieces

•

½ cup (4 fl oz) Garlic French
Dressing (see page 184)

•

lettuce

•

3 hard-boiled eggs, sliced

•

125 g (4 oz) olives

•

6 teaspoons Mayonnaise
(see page 180)

With a vegetable peeler, peel eggplants thinly and cut into medium-size cubes with a stainless steel knife. Bring to the boil a saucepan of water with the salt and lemon juice, drop in eggplants and cook uncovered until tender, about 10–12 minutes. Drain in a colander and cool.

Combine eggplant with the onion, celery, walnuts and dressing. Toss gently but thoroughly, cover and chill.

Serve in lettuce cups on a pile of torn lettuce leaves. Garnish each serving with slices of hard-boiled eggs and olives and top with a spoonful of mayonnaise.

SERVES: 6

# RUSSIAN TOMATO SALAD

*Large bowls of this combination are always on hand on the Russian cruise
ships which take holidaymakers to Pacific islands and other idyllic places.*

## INGREDIENTS

6 firm ripe tomatoes
•
6 tender spring onions (scallions),
including green leaves
•
2 tablespoons white vinegar
•
¼ cup (2 fl oz) olive oil
•
1 clove garlic, crushed
•
salt and pepper to taste
•
1½ cups (12 fl oz) sour cream

Scald and peel tomatoes, then cut into quarters. Wash the spring onions well, slice finely and combine with the tomatoes, reserving some of the green tops for garnish. Whisk together the vinegar, oil, garlic, salt and pepper. Pour over tomatoes and onions, toss, cover and chill. Prepare only shortly before serving for the freshest taste. To serve, spoon sour cream generously over salad and garnish with onion tops.

SERVES: 4–6

# RICE SALAD

*Colourful and filling, this salad looks good on the plate and tastes good too.*

## INGREDIENTS

500 g (1 lb) long grain rice
•
3½ cups (28 fl oz) Vegetable Stock
(see page 448) or water
•
½ teaspoon ground turmeric
•
2 teaspoons salt
•
1 red capsicum (sweet pepper),
chopped finely
•
1 green capsicum (sweet pepper),
chopped finely
•
3 small onions, cut into fine rings
•
2 small zucchini (courgettes),
sliced thinly
•
1 cup (5 oz) black olives
•
1 cup (8 fl oz) French Dressing
(see page 184)

Wash the rice thoroughly and drain in a colander.

Put rice, vegetable stock, turmeric and salt into a saucepan, bring to the boil over high heat, then lower heat to a simmer, cover and cook, without removing lid, for 20 minutes. Uncover, allow steam to escape for 5 minutes, then turn rice into a large bowl or tray and allow to cool completely. Chill, covered, until required.

Mix in the capsicums, onions, zucchini slices and olives, sprinkle dressing over and toss to mix.

SERVES: 6

# CARROT AND COCONUT SALAD

*Fresh coconut is delightful in this salad, but if not available, use desiccated coconut which has been sprinkled with a little water and tossed until moistened.*

## INGREDIENTS

4 cups loosely packed grated carrot (about 4 medium carrots)

•

½ cup (3 oz) sultanas (golden raisins)

•

½ cup (2 oz) toasted pecans

•

1 cup (4 oz) grated fresh coconut

•

½ teaspoon salt

•

3 tablespoons lemon juice

Choose fresh young carrots and grate coarsely shortly before using. Combine with the sultanas, the pecans broken roughly into pieces, and the coconut. Sprinkle with salt and lemon juice, toss together and serve chilled.

SERVES: 4

# TABBOULI

## INGREDIENTS

1 cup burghul (bulgur or cracked wheat)

•

½ cup (1 oz) finely chopped mint leaves

•

4 cups (about 2 large bunches) finely chopped parsley

•

6–8 spring onions (scallions), finely sliced

•

½ cup (4 fl oz) olive oil

•

¾ cup (6 fl oz) strained lemon juice

•

1 teaspoon salt, or to taste

•

crushed garlic (optional)

•

4 firm ripe tomatoes, diced

•

lettuce leaves (optional)

Wash and soak the burghul (bulgur) in cold water until tender, 15–25 minutes depending on the size of the grain. Squeeze out water and spread in a fine sieve or on paper towels. Combine the burghul (bulgur), mint, parsley and spring onions in a bowl and toss together.

Combine the oil, lemon juice, salt and garlic if used and pour over the parsley mixture, tossing well. Add the tomatoes and mix through lightly.

If you like, line a bowl with crisp lettuce, preferably cos (romaine), and pile the tabbouli in the centre. Alternatively, present individual servings in lettuce cups.

SERVES: 6–8

CARROT AND COCONUT SALAD

# RUSSIAN SALAD

*This is one of the golden oldies—I remember Russian salad from many years ago. One is inclined to forget some of the old favourites, so I include it here to remind you what good use can be made of leftover vegetables.*

### INGREDIENTS

3 cups boiled, diced potatoes
•
1 cup boiled, diced carrots
•
1 cup cooked, diced beets
•
½ cup cooked green peas
•
1 small onion, finely chopped
•
1 pickled cucumber, sliced
•
1 cup (8 fl oz) Mayonnaise
(see page 180)
•
salt and pepper to taste

Combine all vegetables with mayonnaise in a bowl, add salt and pepper to taste and toss well.

Press lightly into a bowl, cover and chill for 1–2 hours, turn out onto a serving plate and, if liked, spoon more mayonnaise over the top. Alternatively, spoon sour cream over and sprinkle with finely chopped parsley.

SERVES: 4–6

# CUCUMBER SALAD

*Don't be alarmed at the amount of salt—it will be rinsed off after it has drawn out excess juices from the cucumber.*

### INGREDIENTS

2 large green cucumbers
•
2 teaspoons coarse salt
•
2 tablespoons mild vinegar
•
1 teaspoon sugar
•
¼ teaspoon cayenne pepper
•
1 clove garlic, finely chopped
•
1 spring onion (scallion),
finely chopped
•
3 teaspoons toasted, crushed
sesame seeds

Peel cucumbers and cut across into thin slices. Put in a bowl, sprinkle with salt and leave for 15 minutes, then rinse in cold water and drain off all liquid. Combine other ingredients, pour over cucumbers, mix well and serve chilled.

SERVES: 6

# PINK PASTA SALAD

## INGREDIENTS

250 g (8 oz) pasta

•

1 cup (8 fl oz) Mayonnaise
(see page 180)

•

½ cup (4 fl oz) tomato purée

•

salt and pepper to taste

•

1 clove garlic, crushed

Cook pasta according to directions on package. Drain, cool quickly under cold tap, drain again.

Combine mayonnaise with tomato purée, seasonings and crushed garlic. Pour over the pasta and toss well.

SERVES: 4

# DIETER'S EGGPLANT SALAD, ITALIAN STYLE

*You will notice there is no oil in this recipe, but the dressing has good flavour and when eaten with low-fat cheese it makes quite a satisfying lunch for a dieter.*

## INGREDIENTS

2 medium eggplants
(aubergines), diced

•

salt

•

juice of half a lemon

•

½ cup (3 oz) finely chopped celery

•

1 small onion (optional)

•

2 large firm tomatoes, peeled
and diced

•

2 tablespoons red wine vinegar

•

2 teaspoons fresh oregano

•

parsley or chives, chopped

•

½ teaspoon crushed garlic

•

1 teaspoon capers, chopped

•

crisp lettuce or other salad greens

•

sliced stuffed olives for garnish

Cook the eggplant cubes in boiling water with a little salt and lemon juice added, until soft. Drain well. Combine eggplant, celery, onion and tomatoes in a bowl. Make a dressing with the vinegar, herbs, garlic and capers. If liked, a tablespoon or so of salad oil may be added to the dressing. Whisk the dressing with a fork and pour over the vegetables, toss lightly to mix, then arrange on the lettuce and garnish with olive slices.

SERVES: 3–4

# YOGHURT AND ONION SALAD

*A pungent salad to be served with rice and vegetable curries.*

### INGREDIENTS

3 medium onions

•

1 teaspoon salt

•

1 cup (8 fl oz) yoghurt

•

1 teaspoon finely grated fresh ginger

•

2 medium tomatoes, peeled and chopped

•

3 fresh green chillies, seeded and chopped

•

3 tablespoons chopped fresh coriander leaves

Thinly slice the onions, sprinkle with the salt and set aside for 20 minutes. Squeeze out as much liquid as possible. Mix together the yoghurt and ginger, then fold in the onions and the rest of the ingredients. Cover and chill thoroughly before serving.

SERVES: 6

# RASPBERRY, AVOCADO AND WATERCRESS PLATTER

*Not so long ago I threw together, with what was in the refrigerator, a most successful salad based on avocados and strawberries. When next I wanted to make it, there were no strawberries on hand, but I did find a punnet of raspberries . . . here is the result.*

### INGREDIENTS

2 firm ripe avocados

•

250 g (8 oz) raspberries

•

1 tablespoon raspberry vinegar

•

1 tablespoon walnut oil

•

2 tablespoons extra light olive oil
½ teaspoon sea salt

•

good grinding of black pepper

•

1 teaspoon liquid honey

•

4 cups lightly packed tender watercress sprigs

Quarter the avocados lengthways, remove skin and cut the flesh across into slices, dropping them into a bowl. Tumble the raspberries over the avocado. Whisk the vinegar, walnut oil, olive oil, salt, pepper and honey together until thick, and spoon over the fruit. Toss ever so gently—both avocado and raspberries are easily crushed. Line a platter with the watercress and pile the fruit on top.

SERVES: 6

RASPBERRY, AVOCADO AND WATERCRESS PLATTER

# FENNEL SALAD

## INGREDIENTS

3 bulbs fennel
•
3 tablespoons olive oil
•
1 tablespoon lemon juice or vinegar
•
salt and black pepper to taste
•
1 small clove garlic, crushed
•
fresh or dried oregano
(optional)

Wash the fennel well and slice crossways into 6 mm (¼ in) slices.

Make a dressing with the olive oil, lemon juice or vinegar, add salt and pepper to taste and mix in the garlic. Add a little oregano if liked. Pour dressing over fennel and toss well. Chill and serve by itself or with other salad greens.

SERVES: 4

# SUMMER SALAD

*The bright colour combination makes people notice, the flavours bring them back for more.*

## INGREDIENTS

4 cups (about 1 lb) julienne strips of carrots, green beans and red capsicum (sweet pepper)
•
1 cup (4 oz) grated fresh coconut
•
1 tablespoon finely grated onion
•
½ teaspoon cayenne pepper
(optional)
•
½ teaspoon salt, or to taste
•
2 tablespoons lemon juice
•
lettuce cups

Blanch carrots and beans separately for just 1–2 minutes until colour intensifies and they are tender but still crisp. Drain and refresh in iced water.

Combine coconut with the other ingredients and sprinkle over the mixed vegetables. Toss lightly but thoroughly to mix, taste for seasoning and add more salt and lemon juice if necessary. Pile into crisp lettuce cups.

SERVES: 4–6

# TOMATO AND BASIL SALAD

*A simple salad of tomatoes and basil may be served as a vegetable course
on its own, or as an accompaniment to a main dish.*

### INGREDIENTS

4 firm ripe tomatoes
•
salt and freshly ground pepper
to taste
•
2 teaspoons sugar
•
3 tablespoons finely chopped
fresh basil leaves
•
French Dressing (see page 184)

Pour boiling water over the tomatoes, leave for 1 minute, then plunge into iced water. Peel. Cut in thick slices and arrange on a serving dish.

Sprinkle with salt, pepper and sugar, then with the basil. Cover and chill until serving time. If liked, a little finely chopped onion or shallot may be added. Serve with French dressing drizzled over.

SERVES: 4

# RADISH AND APPLE SALAD

*The large radishes called daikon are now available in most fruit and vegetable
markets. Very mild and suitable for people who don't like the hotter radishes.*

### INGREDIENTS

2 giant white radishes (daikon)
•
1 or 2 crisp cooking apples
•
3 tablespoons lemon juice
•
3 spring onions (scallions)

### DRESSING

3 tablespoons light soy sauce
•
1 tablespoon salad oil
•
2 teaspoons sesame oil
•
3 tablespoons mild vinegar
•
3 teaspoons sugar
•
1 teaspoon salt
•
1 tablespoon toasted, crushed
sesame seeds
•
1 fresh hot red chilli, seeded
and finely chopped (optional)

Peel radishes and cut into matchstick strips. Peel apples and cut into similar strips, and soak in cold water with a good squeeze of lemon juice to prevent discolouration. Slice the spring onions very finely, including white and green portions. Combine ingredients for the dressing and toss with the radish, well-drained apple and spring onion. Cover and chill before serving.

SERVES: 4

# SALAD DRESSINGS
# CLASSIC MAYONNAISE

*To make mayonnaise successfully, have all ingredients at room temperature
and remember to add the oil very gradually at first.*

### INGREDIENTS

2 egg yolks

•

1 teaspoon French (Dijon) mustard
or ½ teaspoon dry mustard

•

½ teaspoon salt

•

½ teaspoon sugar

•

¼ teaspoon white pepper

•

2 tablespoons white vinegar

•

1¼ cups (10 fl oz) olive oil
or salad oil

Put egg yolks into a warm bowl with the mustard, salt, sugar
and pepper, and 2 teaspoons of the vinegar. Beat with a
wire whisk until the mixture thickens.

Start adding the oil, drop by drop at first, beating hard
all the time. When mixture thickens the oil may be added
more quickly, but make sure that at no stage does the
emulsion show signs of curdling.

Add a little of the vinegar from time to time after half
the oil has been added. When all the oil has been
incorporated, taste and adjust seasoning.

NOTE: If mayonnaise does curdle, start again with another
yolk and a clean bowl and add the curdled mixture drop
by drop, beating until the mixture is smooth and thick.

MAKES: about 1½ cups (12 fl oz)

# EASY MAYONNAISE

*This quickly made, delicious mayonnaise is one of the benefits of owning
an electric blender. Makes about 1¼ cups, which is all that most blenders
will handle at a time. If you need to make a larger amount, turn to that
other marvellous appliance, the food processor. Increase quantities to yield
the amount you need, and proceed as described, adding the oil through the
feed tube and using either the steel or plastic blade.*

### INGREDIENTS

1 egg

•

2 tablespoons vinegar

•

½ teaspoon salt

•

¼ teaspoon pepper

•

1 teaspoon dry mustard

•

1 teaspoon sugar

•

1 cup (8 fl oz) olive or salad oil

Warm egg to room temperature by standing it in warm water.
Even in a blender, ingredients straight from the refrigerator
can cause mayonnaise to curdle.

Put all ingredients, except oil, into the container of an
electric blender and blend for 10 seconds. Then start adding
oil through the hole in blender cover, in a very thin stream.
When mixture thickens, the oil may be added more quickly.

As soon as all the oil has been added, switch off blender.
Store mayonnaise in an earthenware or glass container in
a cool place.

MAKES: 1¼ cups (10 fl oz)

# VARIATIONS ON MAYONNAISE

### REMOULADE SAUCE

To 1 cup (8 fl oz) Mayonnaise stir in 1 tablespoon finely chopped pickled gherkins, 2 teaspoons chopped capers, 1 teaspoon French (Dijon) mustard, 1 teaspoon finely chopped parsley, half teaspoon each of chopped tarragon and chervil.

### SAUCE ANDALOUSE

Mix gradually into 1 cup (8 fl oz) Mayonnaise, 2 tablespoons tomato paste, a touch of crushed garlic and enough finely chopped canned pimiento (mild red peppers) to measure 2 tablespoons.

### SAUCE NOISETTE

To 1 cup (8 fl oz) Mayonnaise, add ½ cup (2 oz) toasted, finely ground hazelnuts. Makes a delicately flavoured dressing for cooked green vegetables such as asparagus or broccoli.

### SAUCE TARTARE

Add to 1 cup (8 fl oz) Mayonnaise 1 hard-boiled egg, finely chopped, 1 tablespoon each finely chopped parsley and pickled gherkin, 2 teaspoons each finely chopped shallot and capers, 1 teaspoon French (Dijon) mustard.

### SAUCE VERTE

Drop into boiling water a handful of parsley sprigs, 2 leaves of spinach and 6 spring onion (scallion) leaves or chives. Boil for 2 minutes, then lift out and run under cold water to set the colour. Purée in a blender with a very little water, or push through a sieve. Add a little of this green purée at a time to 1 cup (8 fl oz) Mayonnaise, until it is an attractive shade of green.

### MY FAVOURITE COMBINATION

Not a classic, but with flavours that are good with everything. To 1 cup (8 fl oz) Mayonnaise, add 2 tablespoons chopped fresh dill, 1 tablespoon chopped pickled gherkin, 2 teaspoons crushed green peppercorns and 1 teaspoon of bottled horse-radish.

# FRESH DILL AND GARLIC MAYONNAISE

### INGREDIENTS

1 egg at room temperature
•
2 tablespoons cider vinegar
•
½ teaspoon salt
•
1 teaspoon dry mustard
•
⅛ teaspoon ground pepper
•
1 or 2 cloves garlic
•
1 cup (8 fl oz) olive or salad oil
•
2 tablespoons finely snipped fresh dill

If egg has just been taken from the refrigerator, stand it in a cup of warm water for a few minutes—cold eggs tend to make mayonnaise curdle.

Break egg into the container of an electric blender and add the vinegar, salt, mustard, pepper and garlic. Blend on medium speed for 10 seconds, then start adding oil in a very thin stream through hole in cap of blender jar. If liked, use a small amount of olive oil and the rest in a light oil such as safflower, maize or sunflower oil. When oil is incorporated and mayonnaise is thick, switch off blender and turn mayonnaise into a bowl. Fold in the fresh dill and store in refrigerator. Serve with salads or as a dip for raw vegetables.

MAKES: about 1¼ cups (10 fl oz)

# KIMIZU — JAPANESE SALAD DRESSING

*A cooked salad dressing which is thick and smooth but which uses no oil to achieve this.*

### INGREDIENTS

3 egg yolks
•
¼ teaspoon salt
•
1 tablespoon sugar
•
3 tablespoons white vinegar
•
¾ cup (6 fl oz) water
•
1 tablespoon cornflour (cornstarch)
•
1 teaspoon wasabi

Put all ingredients into the container of an electric blender and blend until smooth, about half a minute. Or whisk in a bowl.

Pour into a small saucepan and cook over very low heat, stirring constantly with a wooden spoon, until mixture thickens and coats back of spoon. Do not allow it to boil or the eggs will coagulate. Remove from heat and keep stirring until lukewarm. Chill and serve with sliced raw or crisp-cooked vegetables.

NOTE: Wasabi is Japanese green horseradish, available in powder or paste form. If using powder, mix to a smooth paste with a little cold water. Prepared English mustard may be used instead.

MAKES: about 1¼ cups (10 fl oz)

# PIQUANT SALAD DRESSING

### INGREDIENTS

1 hard-boiled egg yolk
•
1 teaspoon English-style
prepared mustard
•
1 tablespoon vinegar
•
2 teaspoons Worcestershire sauce
•
pinch of sugar
•
2 tablespoons salad oil
•
salt and pepper to taste
•
2 finely chopped shallots
(optional)

Mash the yolk well in a bowl with the mustard, vinegar, Worcestershire sauce, sugar and add the salad oil gradually. Add salt and pepper to season well. Stir in shallots if used.

MAKES: ½ cup (4 fl oz)

# GREEN GODDESS DRESSING

*This is a richly flavoured dressing which makes any salad special. Particularly recommended for hard-boiled eggs and cooked vegetables.*

### INGREDIENTS

1 cup (8 fl oz) Mayonnaise
(see page 180)
•
½ teaspoon crushed garlic
•
2 tablespoons finely chopped
spring onions (scallions)
•
2 tablespoons finely chopped parsley
•
1 tablespoon tarragon vinegar
•
½ cup (4 fl oz) thick sour cream
•
salt and freshly ground pepper
to taste

Combine mayonnaise with other ingredients, making sure they are evenly distributed.

MAKES: about 1½ cups (12 fl oz)

# AIOLI

*This is a very garlicky mayonnaise-type sauce served as an accompaniment to many dishes in Provence, notably green vegetables. It also makes a wonderful substitute for the anchovy-butter-garlic dip that Italians serve with raw vegetables in Bagna Cauda. The classic version would use 3 egg yolks instead of 1 whole egg, but these days one has to be health conscious.*

### INGREDIENTS

1 slice crusty white bread
•
milk for soaking
•
1 egg at room temperature
•
1 tablespoon wine vinegar
or lemon juice
•
½ teaspoon salt
•
¼ teaspoon white pepper
•
4–8 cloves garlic
•
1¼ cups (10 fl oz) olive oil

Trim off crusts, break up the bread and soak in just enough milk to moisten. Put all ingredients, except oil, into the container of an electric blender and blend on high speed for 10 seconds.

Turn speed to medium and, through hole in blender lid, add the oil in a very thin stream. It is essential to add it very slowly at first and, as the mayonnaise thickens, add it more quickly.

NOTE: If a lighter version is preferred, use half olive oil, half safflower, sunflower or maize oil.

MAKES: about 1½ cups (12 fl oz)

# OIL AND VINEGAR DRESSINGS

*The classic dressing commonly called French dressing is a combination of 1 part vinegar and 3 parts oil. Be particular about using good quality oil and wine vinegar.*

If you like exotic flavours in your salads, keep a supply of walnut and hazelnut oils, storing them in the refrigerator once they have been opened. They give wonderful flavour to salads and though expensive, a little goes a long way, as they should be mixed with other light, flavourless oils, or their flavour will dominate the other ingredients.

Vinegars with the scent of herbs or fragrant fruits, such as raspberry or blackberry vinegar, are also an investment in flavour. Balsamic vinegar is another asset in the cupboard—admittedly expensive, but since only a few drops suffice to add flavour, it is not an expense you will meet up with frequently.

## BASIC FRENCH DRESSING

### INGREDIENTS

2 tablespoons wine vinegar
•
½ teaspoon salt
•
good grinding of pepper
•
¼ teaspoon dry mustard
•
6 tablespoons olive oil

In a small bowl, whisk together the vinegar, salt, pepper and mustard. Gradually add the oil, whisking until thick. Or shake all the ingredients together in a screw-top jar just before using the dressing on the salad.

MAKES: ½ cup (4 fl oz)

## GARLIC FRENCH DRESSING

For a gentle hint of flavour, bruise a clove of garlic with the flat of a knife and let it sit in the dressing for a few minutes. For the full flavour of this pungent bulb, which vitalises any salad into something quite exceptional, crush a clove of garlic with the salt until it is a smooth paste. Whisk with the other ingredients.

MAKES: ½ cup (4 fl oz)

## FRESH HERB DRESSING

Make either the basic dressing or Garlic French Dressing and add 2–3 tablespoons of finely chopped fresh herbs. Go easy on the dominant herbs such as sage and tarragon, use more of the gentler flavours and make a mixture to suit your taste and complement the salad you will be using it on. Parsley, chives, thyme, basil, coriander, oregano or marjoram, tarragon and dill are some of the most popular.

MAKES: ½ cup (4 fl oz)

# WALNUT OIL AND RASPBERRY VINEGAR DRESSING

### INGREDIENTS

2 tablespoons raspberry vinegar

•

1 teaspoon honey

•

1 small clove garlic, bruised
or crushed with salt

•

freshly ground pepper to taste

•

1 teaspoon prepared mustard

•

2 tablespoons walnut oil

•

4 tablespoons extra light olive
oil or maize oil

Whisk together all the ingredients until well combined and
thick. If not using immediately, whisk again before pouring
onto salad.

NOTE: If you don't have any raspberry vinegar in your
pantry, you can make a substitution if you're willing to
sacrifice some of the precious *Eau de vie Framboise* you may
have in your liquor cabinet. A teaspoonful in 2 tablespoons
of good wine vinegar will be sufficient to perfume the dressing.

MAKES: about ½ cup (4 fl oz)

# BALSAMIC VINEGAR DRESSING

### INGREDIENTS

1 tablespoon balsamic vinegar

•

1 teaspoon whole grain mustard

•

1 teaspoon honey

•

5 tablespoons extra virgin olive oil

•

sea salt and freshly ground pepper
to taste

Stir vinegar, mustard and honey together and whisk in the oil gradually. Season to taste.

MAKES: about ½ cup (4 fl oz)

# ORANGE AND HAZELNUT OIL DRESSING

### INGREDIENTS

finely grated zest of 1 orange

•

juice of 1 orange

•

2 tablespoons lemon juice or vinegar

•

1 teaspoon honey

•

1 teaspoon Dijon mustard

•

½ teaspoon salt

•

freshly ground pepper to taste

•

2 tablespoons hazelnut oil

•

4 tablespoons safflower or maize oil

Whisk together all the ingredients until thick, or shake in a screw-top jar. If not using all the dressing immediately, store in refrigerator.

MAKES: about ¾ cup (6 fl oz)

# YOGHURT DRESSING

*A quickly made dressing with less oil per spoonful than the usual salad dressing.*

### INGREDIENTS

1 cup (8 fl oz) yoghurt

•

3 tablespoons Mayonnaise
(see page 180) or salad oil

•

½ cup (4 fl oz) Garlic French
Dressing (see page 184)

•

1 tablespoon chopped fresh herbs

•

salt and pepper to taste

Beat yoghurt and mayonnaise together until smooth. Gradually add the French dressing, then stir in the herbs and season to taste with pepper and salt. Chill.

MAKES: about 1½ cups (12 fl oz)

# ORIENTAL DRESSING

### INGREDIENTS

3 tablespoons Chinese black vinegar

•

6 tablespoons peanut oil

•

2 tablespoons oriental sesame oil

•

2 tablespoons light soy sauce
or teriyaki sauce

•

1 teaspoon finely grated fresh ginger

•

½ teaspoon crushed garlic

Combine all the ingredients and whisk or shake together. The peanut oil should, if possible, be the unrefined variety which has a definite flavour of peanuts. Most of the supermarket oils are refined and have no flavour.

If serving a salad with bean sprouts, Chinese cabbage, water chestnuts, snow peas and similar ingredients with a Far Eastern character, season them with a matching dressing.

MAKES: about 1¼ cups (10 fl oz)

# DESSERTS

Now here's a chapter close to my heart. When your diet is wholly or largely vegetarian, it seems to leave more room for dessert. There's no rich, heavy, meaty main course to take up all the calories or kilojoules, and you can indulge with a clear conscience in luscious desserts . . . from apple dumplings in cold weather to velvety ice-creams and refreshing sorbets when the temperature rises.

## CRÈME BRÛLEE WITH GRAPES

### INGREDIENTS

300 ml (10 fl oz) cream
•
half a vanilla bean
•
3 egg yolks
•
4 tablespoons caster (superfine) sugar
•
2 teaspoons cornflour (cornstarch)
•
sultana (white seedless) grapes
•
extra caster (superfine) sugar

Put some of the cream and the vanilla bean, cut into pieces, into a blender container and blend at high speed until bean is pulverised. Pour into an enamel saucepan with rest of the cream and bring gently to the boil.

Whisk egg yolks with caster sugar and cornflour until thick and light. Pour on the boiling cream, whisking constantly, then return to saucepan and cook over low heat until custard thickens. Stand pan in a sink of cold water and stir until cool.

Put a layer of sultana grapes into 4 small ramekins, pour custard over them and leave in refrigerator until chilled. Using a fine sieve, sprinkle extra caster sugar over surface of the custard and place under a preheated griller (broiler) for a few minutes, until the sugar caramelises. Serve at once.

SERVES: 4

## AVOCADO FOOL

### INGREDIENTS

2 large, very ripe avocados
•
5 tablespoons caster (superfine) sugar
•
1 cup (8 fl oz) cream

The avocados you use for this recipe should be soft to the touch, but with no black spots on the flesh. Mash with a silver fork until very smooth, add the sugar and mix well. (If you have vanilla sugar, this makes it even nicer. Store vanilla beans in the jar of sugar to give subtle flavour.)

Whip the cream and fold into the avocado purée until evenly mixed, then spoon into small individual dessert dishes. Cover with plastic wrap and chill. Prepare shortly before serving, as after some hours the surface will discolour.

SERVES: 6

TARTE AUX POMMES

# TARTE AUX POMMES

PASTRY

2 cups (8 oz) plain (all-purpose) flour

•

3 tablespoons caster (superfine) sugar

•

pinch of salt

•

185 g (6 oz) chilled butter

•

approximately 2 tablespoons
iced water

FILLING

2 kg (4 lb) cooking apples

•

¾ cup (6 oz) caster (superfine) sugar

•

lemon juice

•

2 tablespoons butter

•

½ cup (6 oz) apricot conserve

•

¼ cup (2 fl oz) Calvados (apple
brandy), rum or Cognac or
3 teaspoons vanilla extract

To make the pastry, put flour, sugar and salt into a bowl and add butter, cut into small pieces. With cool fingertips, rub the fat into the flour quickly and lightly until the texture of rolled oats.

Add water and mix with one hand until the whole mass holds together, but do not make the pastry too wet. On a lightly floured surface, blend the flour and butter more thoroughly by a series of quick, smearing movements away from you until all the pastry has been worked over in this way. Scrape it together with a spatula and knead quickly and lightly into a ball, wrap in plastic and refrigerate until firm, about 1 hour.

To prepare the filling, peel, quarter and core apples, then slice about a third into thin, even slices and reserve for the top of the tart. Toss with ¼ cup (2 oz) caster sugar and a little lemon juice to prevent discolouring. Put the rest of the apples, thickly sliced, into a saucepan with a couple of tablespoons water. Cover and cook until tender. Add remaining sugar, butter, apricot conserve and Calvados or vanilla. Cook uncovered, stirring until the purée is thick enough to mound in the spoon.

Roll pastry out on a lightly floured board, flouring the rolling pin and using firm, even strokes always away from you, not back and forth. Sprinkle with more flour as necessary to prevent sticking and roll to a circle of even thickness and 5 cm (2 in) larger than the flan ring.

Place a 25 cm (10 in) flan ring on a level baking sheet and brush both with melted butter. Drape the pastry over the rolling pin and lift it so it is poised over flan rim, then gently unroll. Lift and press gently into the shape, taking care not to tear it. Allow a little extra pastry against sides of the flan ring so the sides do not collapse when the ring is removed.

Trim excess pastry by rolling the pin across the top of the flan ring. Decorate edge with a series of knife cuts and prick base of shell with a fork. Line with foil and fill with dried beans. Bake in an oven preheated to 200°C (400°F) for 10 minutes. Remove foil and beans, then return to oven for a further 3 minutes. This is partially baked and ready to take the apple filling.

Spread purée evenly in the pastry shell. Cover top with the thin slices of apple, starting in the middle and continuing outwards in circles. Bake at 190°C (375°F) for 30 minutes or until apple slices are golden. Remove from oven and slide onto wire rack, or serving dish if serving right away. Lift off flan ring. Brush over the apple slices with a glaze of warmed, strained apricot conserve. Serve warm or cold, with cream.

SERVES:   8

# CHOCOLATE MOUSSE CAKE

*The great thing about eating vegetarian meals is that you can indulge in rich desserts like this one without too many pangs of conscience, especially if the foregoing meal has been light. If you think the centre of this cake is too soft, have no fear—it is meant to be that way . . . half way between a mousse and a cake, as the name implies.*

### INGREDIENTS

2 tablespoons melted butter
and 1 tablespoon sifted cocoa
for preparing tin
•
450 g (15 oz) dark (semi-sweet)
cooking or eating chocolate
•
125 g (4 oz) unsalted butter
•
5 large eggs
•
¼ cup (2 oz) caster (superfine) sugar
•
2 tablespoons sifted flour
•
whipped cream and raspberry puree
for serving

Brush a deep 20 cm (8 in) cake tin with melted butter. Dust lightly with the sifted cocoa, then tap upturned tin on a hard surface to remove excess cocoa.

Chop the chocolate into small pieces and melt with the butter in a bowl placed over hot water. Stir until smooth, remove from hot water and cool slightly.

Beat eggs and sugar in a bowl over hot water until sugar dissolves. Transfer mixture to bowl of electric mixer. Use beater recommended for heavier mixtures and beat on high speed for 15 minutes, by which time it will have more than doubled in bulk. Fold in the flour.

Add a third of the egg mixture to the chocolate and stir well. Fold this thinned chocolate into the rest of the egg mixture until combined evenly. Pour into prepared tin and bake in an oven preheated to 260°C (500°F) for 15 minutes only.

Remove from oven and cool in tin, then cover top with foil and freeze cake in tin for at least 24 hours. To unmould, heat base of tin slightly on low heat for a moment. Turn on to serving plate and return to refrigerator. This cake should be served well chilled but never frozen. Cut in wedges and serve plain or with whipped cream and raspberry puree.

SERVES: 12–16

# FRENCH MENUS

*Serve French peasant fare with bowls of onion soup, and Ratatouille with crusty bread; or go haute cuisine with creamy individual timbales followed by freshly baked gougère.*

French Onion Soup *page 62*

Ratatouille *page 98*

Carrot and Cauliflower Timbales *page 27*

Wholemeal Gougère *page 54*

Raspberry, Avocado and Watercress Platter *page 176*

Frangipane Fig Tart *page 198*

# GREEK MENUS

*See for yourself, Greek food is not all souvlakia and stifatho. You will enjoy the flavours and feel satisfied savouring their other specialities.*

Egg and Lemon Soup *page 60*

Spinach and Cheese Pie *page 114*

Country Style Salad *page 158*

Baklava *page 210*


Skorthalia with raw vegetables *page 12*

Pocket Bread *page 416*

Vine leaves with Rice, Chickpeas and Currants *page 8*

Braised Green Beans *page 150*

Custard-filled Pastries *page 207*

# ITALIAN MENUS

*So much good Italian food is based on
colourful fresh vegetables that one hardly
realises the entire meal is vegetarian—just the
menus to serve friends who are convinced a
meal centres on meat.*

Minestrone *page 76*

Eggplant Lasagne *page 86*

Cassata à la Siciliana *page 210*


Roasted Capsicums *page 147*

Wholemeal Rolls *page 415*

Fettucine Alfredo *page 84*

Semolina Gnocchi *page 31*

Fennel Salad *page 178*

Watermelon and Raspberry Granita
*page 216*

# DANISH APPLE CAKE

## INGREDIENTS

1 kg (2 lb) Granny Smith apples

90 g (3 oz) butter

sugar to taste

2 cups (4 oz) fresh breadcrumbs

3 tablespoons sugar

½ cup (4 fl oz) cream, whipped

red currant jelly (or jam)

Peel and core apples and slice thinly. Put into a heavy-based stainless steel or enamel pan with a little water to cover the base. Cover with lid and cook gently until apples are soft, then purée. Stir in 1 tablespoon of butter and enough sugar to sweeten the purée slightly. Melt remaining butter in a frying pan, add breadcrumbs and sugar and stir until golden. Allow to cool.

Just before serving, arrange alternate layers of apple purée and crumbs in a serving dish or individual bowls. Finish with a sprinkling of crumbs, decorate with whipped cream and red currant jelly.

SERVES: 5–6

# APPLE PIE

## INGREDIENTS

2 cups (8 oz) plain (all-purpose) flour

1 tablespoon caster (superfine) sugar

¼ teaspoon salt

½ teaspoon baking powder

185 g (6 oz) cold butter

approximately 2 tablespoons cold water

1 kg (2 lb) Granny Smith apples

2 tablespoons plain (all-purpose) flour

1 teaspoon freshly grated nutmeg or ground cinnamon

¼ teaspoon ground cloves

¾ cup (6 oz) caster (superfine) sugar

1 tablespoon butter

1 egg white

Sift flour, caster sugar, salt and baking powder into a bowl and rub in butter, or combine in food processor. Add water and mix to a firm dough, wrap and chill for 1 hour.

Roll out two thirds of the pastry on a lightly floured surface and line a buttered 23–25 cm (9–10 in) pie plate. Leave pastry overlapping edge. Peel, core and slice apples, toss with flour, spices and caster sugar, reserving 1 tablespoon for sprinkling over pastry.

Fill the pastry and put dabs of butter over the apples. Roll out remaining third of pastry to cover pie. Trim edges and press firmly together, making a decorative rope edge or flutes. Brush top with slightly beaten egg white and sprinkle with reserved caster sugar.

Use a pointed knife to make slits at regular intervals in the top crust. This allows steam to escape and keeps the pastry crisp. Bake in an oven preheated to 200°C (400°F) for 40 minutes, then reduce heat to 180°C (350°F) and continue baking until pastry is golden brown, about 20 minutes more. Serve warm, with or without ice-cream.

SERVES: 8

# BAKED APPLES

## INGREDIENTS

2 large apples

•

2 fresh dates

•

grated rind of 1 lemon

•

juice of half lemon

•

1 cup (8 fl oz) natural apple juice

Remove a strip of apple skin all around or, if preferred, peel the apples completely. Use an apple corer to remove the core. Slit the dates, remove seeds and place the dates in the hole left by coring the apple.

Place apples in a baking dish and pour the combined grated lemon rind, lemon juice and apple juice over and around apples.

Bake in an oven preheated to 190°C (375°F) until the apples are tender or, if preferred, cook as directed in a microwave oven. With the latter method, use very little liquid. Serve warm.

SERVES: 2

# HOT STRAWBERRY SOUFFLÉS

*Use individual soufflé dishes of one cup (8 fl oz) capacity—
the soufflés rise better.*

## INGREDIENTS

butter and caster (superfine) sugar
for preparing dishes

•

400 g (13 oz) strawberries

•

2 tablespoons Grand Marnier
(optional)

•

4 tablespoons caster (superfine) sugar

•

5 egg whites

•

1 cup (8 oz) sugar

•

½ cup (4 fl oz) water

•

1 tablespoon cornflour (cornstarch)

Prepare soufflé dishes by smearing with soft butter and dusting with extra caster sugar. Wash and drain strawberries, remove hulls, purée in a blender or mash with a fork and add Grand Marnier and the 4 tablespoons of caster sugar.

Whip egg whites in a clean dry bowl until stiff, but not dry. Put sugar and water into a small heavy-based saucepan and cook over high heat until sugar has dissolved, then boil for 1 minute or until the syrup thickens and bubbles. Pour on to egg whites in a thin stream, beating all the while until thick and glossy. Continue to beat until lukewarm, then beat in cornflour.

Put strawberry purée into a large bowl, spoon the egg whites onto the purée and fold both mixtures together quickly and gently until mixed. It doesn't matter if there are a few streaks of egg white, but take care not to overmix.

Divide between the soufflé dishes and place in an oven preheated to 220°C (425°F). Immediately turn heat down to 190°C (375°F) and bake for 30 minutes or until well risen. Serve immediately. Whipped cream or ice-cream may be served in a separate bowl.

SERVES: 4

# RASPBERRY MOUSSE

## INGREDIENTS

500 g (1 lb) raspberries, fresh or frozen

•

1½ cups (7 oz) icing (powdered) sugar

•

1½ tablespoons gelatine

•

½ cup (4 fl oz) cold water

•

3 eggs

•

½ cup (4 oz) caster (superfine) sugar

•

300 ml (10 fl oz) milk

•

1 cup (8 fl oz) cream, whipped

•

Kiwi fruit (Chinese gooseberry) slices to decorate

Purée raspberries in a blender with icing sugar and strain through a fine nylon sieve, discarding the seeds. Sprinkle gelatine over cold water in a cup, leave to soften, then dissolve over boiling water. Cool and stir into raspberry purée. Chill until slightly thick.

Separate eggs and beat yolks with ¼ cup (2 oz) caster sugar until light. Bring milk to the boil and pour over yolks, stirring constantly. Return to pan and cook over very low heat, stirring, until the custard coats the back of a metal spoon. Do not boil or it will curdle. Stir over ice until cold. Combine with raspberry mixture.

Beat egg whites until stiff, add remaining caster sugar and beat until glossy. Fold whipped cream and egg whites into mixture, pour into a lightly oiled 20 cm (8 in) springform pan or large pie plate and chill until set.

Unmould on serving platter and decorate top with sliced kiwi fruit and more whipped cream if liked.

SERVES: 8–10

# ORANGES IN CARAMEL

*A delicious dessert which can be served at a barbecue or done under the grill (broiler).*

## INGREDIENTS

4 large seedless oranges

•

60 g (2 oz) firm, cold butter

•

4 tablespoons soft brown sugar

Peel the oranges with a small sharp knife, removing all the skin and white pith. Cut each orange into 4 thick slices and re-assemble each one on a square of double aluminium foil.

Cut the butter into 16 small, flat slices, then roll them in the sugar so they are thickly covered. Put a slice of butter between each slice of orange and one on top. Sprinkle the remaining sugar over and wrap the oranges in foil.

Place on the edge of the barbecue for 10 minutes or long enough to melt the butter and sugar, and serve hot with cream for those who want it. A spoon and fork are useful for breaking the orange slices and taking up the caramel syrup.

SERVES: 4

# CHAMPAGNE-GLAZED FRUIT

### INGREDIENTS

400 g (13 oz) strawberries

•

250 g (8 oz) raspberries

•

3 ripe guavas

•

¾ cup (6 oz) caster (superfine) sugar

•

2–3 tablespoons mandarin liqueur
or Curaçao

•

150 ml (5 fl oz) thick cream or
crème fraîche

•

3 egg yolks

•

150 ml (5 fl oz) champagne

•

icing (powdered) sugar

Wash and dry the fruit and sprinkle it with half the caster sugar and the mandarin liqueur or Curaçao. Leave for an hour or so.

When ready to serve, transfer the fruit to a shallow heatproof dish. Lightly beat the cream. Make the sabayon with the egg yolks, the remaining caster sugar and the champagne. To do this, whisk yolks and sugar in a bowl, place above a pan of simmering water, making sure it doesn't touch the water. Add champagne gradually while whisking, and keep whisking until doubled in volume, thick and fluffy.

Fold in the whipped cream and spread over the fruit. Sprinkle generously with icing sugar and put under a medium hot grill (broiler) until the sabayon is golden. Watch carefully to see that it does not burn. Serve at once.

NOTE:  Crème fraîche may be found at specialty markets or delicatessens but if not available, it is easy to make. Add 1 tablespoon cultured buttermilk or natural yoghurt to 300 ml (10 fl oz) fresh cream (35 percent milk fat), mix well and leave in a warm place for a few hours or out of the refrigerator overnight. Crème fraîche has a distinctive flavour and keeps well in the refrigerator for at least a week.

SERVES: 6

# PECAN PIE

### INGREDIENTS

PASTRY

1 cup (4 oz) plain (all-purpose) flour

•

pinch of salt

•

60 g (2 oz) cold butter

•

2 tablespoons water

FILLING

3 large eggs

•

½ cup (4 oz) sugar

•

3 tablespoons melted butter

•

1 cup (8 fl oz) dark or light corn
syrup or maple syrup

•

1 cup (4 oz) chopped pecans

•

whipped cream and pecan halves,
to decorate

Put all the pastry ingredients into a food processor fitted with steel chopping blade and process for the few seconds it takes to form a ball. Wrap in greaseproof paper or plastic and refrigerate for 20 minutes while making filling.

Beat the eggs, sugar, butter and syrup well with a wooden spoon or whisk, then mix in the chopped pecans.

Roll out pastry between sheets of greaseproof paper and rest it for 5 minutes, then line a 20–23 cm (8–9 in) pie plate. The pastry should be as thin as possible on the base but build it up on the sides and crimp the edges to give a decorative effect.

Pour filling into the pie shell and bake in an oven preheated to 180°C (350°F) for 1 hour. Cool, then make mounds of whipped cream around the edge and top each with a toasted pecan half.

SERVES: 8–10

# FRANGIPANE FIG TART

*To complement the delicate sweetness of figs, I chose a crisp almond pastry filled with frangipane (almond pastry cream) on which the fig slices sit in technicolour splendour. Either green or purple figs may be used.*

### INGREDIENTS

PASTRY

1½ cups (6 oz) plain (all-purpose)
flour

•

60 g (2 oz) ground unblanched
almonds

•

2 tablespoons caster (superfine) sugar

•

125 g (4 oz) cold butter

•

3 or 4 tablespoons iced water

Put flour, almonds, sugar and butter, cut in pieces, into a food processor and process for a few seconds until consistency of oatmeal. Add just enough water through tube until dough forms a ball. Knead lightly, wrap and chill at least 30 minutes.

Roll pastry out very thinly and line a 25 cm (10 in) flan tin. Prick base, weight with dried beans or rice and bake in an oven preheated to 220°C (425°F) for 10 minutes, then lower heat to 180°C (350°F). Remove beans and cook pastry for about 15 minutes longer. Cool.

To make the filling, beat yolks, egg and caster sugar until thick and light. Whisk in the flour. Bring milk to the boil

### ALMOND PASTRY CREAM

2 egg yolks

•

1 egg

•

¾ cup (6 oz) caster (superfine) sugar

•

²/₃ cup (3 oz) plain (all-purpose)
flour, sifted

•

500 ml (16 fl oz) milk

•

60 g (2 oz) unsalted butter

•

90 g (3 oz) ground blanched almonds

•

3 teaspoons vanilla extract

•

½ teaspoon almond extract

•

8 large ripe fresh figs to decorate

and add slowly, whisking constantly. Pour into an enamel saucepan and cook, stirring, until custard thickens and becomes smooth. Cook for 3 minutes, stirring briskly. Remove from heat, add the butter and stir well. When cool, add the almonds and flavourings. Cool completely.

Spoon the almond cream into the pastry case, slice figs across and arrange like spokes of a wheel, with smaller slices towards the centre. Chill and serve.

SERVES: 8

# PUMPKIN CARAMEL MOULDS

### INGREDIENTS

½ cup (4 oz) sugar

•

¼ cup (2 fl oz) water

•

4 large eggs

•

½ cup (3 oz) brown sugar

•

1 cup (8 oz) cooked, mashed
pumpkin

•

1 cup (8 fl oz) milk

•

1 cup (8 fl oz) cream

•

½ teaspoon freshly grated nutmeg

•

½ teaspoon ground mace

•

1 teaspoon vanilla essence (extract)

Put sugar and water into a small, heavy-based saucepan over medium heat without stirring until it turns a rich golden brown. Divide equally between 6 individual soufflé moulds or ramekins, pouring it in and rapidly rotating the moulds to coat bottom and sides with the caramel. Handle moulds with oven mitts as the caramel will be very hot.

Beat eggs with brown sugar until foamy, stir in the pumpkin, milk, cream, spices and vanilla. Ladle into the caramel-lined moulds, place in a baking dish in an oven preheated to 150°C (300°F). With dish firmly in place on oven rack, pour boiling water into the dish to almost half way up the moulds.

Bake for 35–40 minutes or until custards are firm and a knife inserted into the centre comes out clean. Remove from oven and cool, then cover with plastic wrap and refrigerate at least overnight. Unmould onto dessert plates and serve. It may be necessary to run a knife around edge of custards to help unmoulding.

SERVES: 6

# CHERRY CLAFOUTI

*This recipe, a real French country-style baked dessert, is very quick to make (if you don't count the time spent pitting the cherries). Tell you what— I'm not above making it without performing this chore. If you do the same, warn those who partake that they have to separate seeds from flesh as they eat, or you may be presented with a dentist's bill!*

### INGREDIENTS

2 teaspoons butter
•
300 g (10 oz) pitted cherries
•
2 eggs
•
¼ cup (2 oz) sugar
•
2 teaspoons kirsch or cherry brandy,
or ½ teaspoon vanilla
•
½ cup (2 oz) plain (all-purpose) flour
•
¾ cup (6 fl oz) milk
•
2 tablespoons icing (powdered)
sugar

Thickly butter an ovenproof dish—a flat oval one that allows the cherries to completely cover the base. Put the cherries into the dish and prepare the batter for pouring over. Whisk the eggs and sugar together well, add the cherry brandy or vanilla, whisk in the flour and then the milk. Pour this mixture over the cherries in the dish and dot the top with any remaining butter. Bake in an oven preheated to 180°C (350°F) for 45–55 minutes or until the batter has risen and is crusty and browned on the edges. Test with a fine skewer. It should come out clean to indicate the clafouti is done. Sift icing sugar over the top and serve hot.

SERVES: 6

# SHORTCAKE WITH BERRIES

### INGREDIENTS

1 cup (4 oz) wholemeal self-raising
flour (or whole wheat flour with
2 level teaspoons of baking powder)
•
1 cup (4 oz) plain (all-purpose)
flour
•
1 teaspoon bicarbonate of soda
•
1 teaspoon salt
•
1 tablespoon caster (superfine) sugar
•
60 g (2 oz) chilled butter
•
2/3 cup (5 fl oz) cream
•
250 g (8 oz) ripe strawberries and
blueberries
•
sugar to taste
•
whipped cream for serving

Mix the dry ingredients together in a bowl. Rub in butter with fingertips, then add cream to make a soft dough. Gather into a ball and divide in 4 equal portions. Lightly pat each to a round 2 cm (¾ in) thick. Place on baking tray and bake in an oven preheated to 200°C (400°F) for 25 minutes. Cool slightly on a wire tray (rack), split with a sharp knife and fill with sliced, sugared strawberries, whole blueberries and whipped cream. Serve warm.

SERVES: 4

SHORTCAKE WITH BERRIES

# APPLE CHARLOTTE

## INGREDIENTS

apple puree made with 3 kg (6 lb)
apples
•
approximately 12 square slices
of firm white bread
•
250 g (8 oz) unsalted butter, melted
•
apricot jam for glazing (optional)
•
whipped cream for serving
•
vanilla extract or rum
for flavouring

Peel, quarter and core the apples, and cook in a covered pan with a couple of tablespoons of water until tender. Add sugar to taste and a tablespoon of the butter and cook, stirring constantly, until the moisture has evaporated and the paste is very thick. The apple purée must be cooked until very thick and firm or the bread case will collapse when it is unmoulded. Flavour with vanilla extract or rum. Trim crusts from bread and cut some slices to fit the base of the charlotte mould exactly. Pour the melted butter into a flat dish, discarding the milky solids at base of pan. In 4 tablespoons of the butter, lightly brown the pieces of bread for the base of the mould and put them in place.

Cut remaining bread slices into 3 strips each. Dip bread strips in melted butter and place them, slightly overlapping, around sides of mould. Fill with apple purée, mounding it slightly in the centre, and cover with remaining strips of bread. Place on baking tray and bake in an oven preheated to 210°C (425°F) for 30–35 minutes. To test if it is done, insert a knife between side of mould and bread and see if it is deep gold in colour.

Remove from oven, cool for 20 minutes, then unmould onto serving plate. The longer the charlotte is left to cool, the more chance it has of unmoulding perfectly. If liked, brush over with strained, melted apricot jam flavoured with rum.

NOTE: Another way to present this dish is to make individual charlottes in small moulds.

SERVES: 8

# ORANGE BLINTZES

## INGREDIENTS

250 g (8 oz) ricotta cheese
•
finely grated rind of 2 oranges
•
½ cup (3 oz) icing (powdered) sugar

Beat ricotta cheese with grated rind and icing sugar until smooth. Peel and slice the two oranges, cut each slice into quarters and simmer briefly in the sugar and water. Fill the pancakes with the cheese mixture and fold over. Melt butter in a large frying pan, add the syrup from the orange slices and the orange juice. Reduce quickly until thick. Remove

½ cup (4 oz) sugar

•

¼ cup (2 fl oz) water

•

6 thin blintzes (crepes)
(see page 450)

•

90 g (3 oz) butter

•

½ cup (4 fl oz) orange juice

•

2 tablespoons Grand Marnier

from heat and stir in Grand Marnier. Arrange orange slices over blintzes and pour the sauce over.

NOTE: For a hot dessert during winter, heat the blintzes in an oven preheated to 180°C (350°F) for 10 minutes before adding the orange slices.

SERVES: 6

# COCONUT CHIFFON PIE

### INGREDIENTS

CRUMB CRUST
½ cup (2 oz) crushed plain biscuits
(cookies)

•

½ cup (2 oz) finely chopped Brazil
nuts

•

2 tablespoons caster (superfine) sugar

•

2 tablespoons melted butter

1 cup (4 oz) grated fresh coconut

•

2 teaspoons gelatine

•

¼ cup (2 fl oz) cold water

•

3 eggs

•

½ cup (4 oz) caster (superfine) sugar

•

½ cup (4 fl oz) coconut milk

•

4 tablespoons rum or orange
juice concentrate

First make the crust. Combine dry ingredients, add butter and mix well. Press crumb mix against base and sides of a 20 cm (8 in) pie plate and bake in an oven preheated to 190°C (375°F) for 10 minutes. Cool.

To prepare the coconut milk: Put half of the grated coconut and ½ cup (4 fl oz) hot water into a blender and blend on high speed for 30 seconds. Strain through muslin or press in fine strainer, extracting as much liquid as possible.

Sprinkle gelatine over the cold water in a cup, soak for 5 minutes, then stand the cup in a saucepan of simmering water until gelatine dissolves.

Separate yolks and whites of eggs. Beat yolks with ¼ cup (2 oz) caster sugar until thick and light. While whisking, add the coconut milk gradually, then turn mixture into an enamel saucepan and stir over very low heat until it thickens enough to coat the back of a spoon.

Do not boil or it will curdle. Remove from heat, stir in dissolved gelatine and rum (or orange juice). Chill, stirring occasionally, until thick but not set. Beat egg whites until stiff but not dry, gradually add the remaining ¼ cup (2 oz) caster sugar and beat until glossy. Stir a quarter of the egg whites into the gelatine mixture, then fold in the remaining grated coconut and the rest of the egg whites.

Pour into pie shell, smooth top and chill until firm. If liked, decorate with slightly sweetened whipped cream piped around the edge, or sprinkle with a little extra grated coconut.

SERVES: 6–8

# SOUFFLÉ OMELETTES

*Light, airy and flavoured with fruit or liqueurs, here are desserts that belong among the culinary classics. Compared to the time most desserts require, these are 10 minute wonders.*

## INGREDIENTS

4 egg yolks

•

4½ tablespoons caster (superfine) sugar

•

2 tablespoons unsalted butter

•

1 tablespoon plain (all-purpose) flour

•

5 egg whites

•

icing (powdered) sugar for dusting

Beat the yolks with 1½ tablespoons of the measured sugar until light. Heat butter in a heavy (cast-iron) frying pan, then allow to cool.

The pan should not be too hot or the base of the omelette will burn because of the sugar content.

Add 1 tablespoon of the melted, cooled butter and flour to the yolks with chosen flavouring (below).

In a clean, dry bowl whisk the egg whites to soft peaks, add the remaining sugar and beat until the meringue is stiff and glossy. Fold the yolk mixture into the whites quickly and gently, then pour into the heated frying pan. Level the top gently with a spatula. Cook for 1 minute over medium heat, then transfer pan to an oven preheated to 200°C (400°F) and bake for 10 minutes, or until well puffed and golden.

Using a thick oven mitt, remove pan from the oven and slide the omelette onto a heated serving dish. Spoon filling on top and gently fold in half. Sift icing sugar over and mark, if liked, with a metal skewer which has been heated on a gas flame for about 3 minutes. The hot skewer caramelises the sugar, giving both an interesting pattern and nice flavour.

SERVES: 4

### PASSIONFRUIT OMELETTE

To the yolk mixture, add ½ cup (4–5 oz) fresh passionfruit pulp. The tangy passionfruit makes this one of the most delicious of dessert omelettes.

### OMELETTE GRAND MARNIER

To the yolk mixture, add the finely grated rind of 1 mandarin (tangerine) or orange, using only the coloured zest, and 2 tablespoons of Grand Marnier. Segments of orange or mandarin, macerated in Grand Marnier and a little caster sugar to taste, may be used as a filling or garnish.

NOTE: If you don't own a cast-iron pan, use any heavy all-metal pan that can be placed in an oven.

# OMELETTE NORMANDY

*Apples and Calvados, the apple brandy of the Normandy region, are highlighted in many recipes from this part of France. Also, the best butter and cream are supposed to come from this area, so it is not surprising that the apples for the filling are cooked in butter.*

### INGREDIENTS

2 apples
•
lemon juice
•
30 g (1 oz) unsalted butter
•
1 tablespoon caster (superfine) sugar
•
2 tablespoons Calvados
•
½ cup (6 oz) apricot jam (jelly)
•
basic Soufflé Omelette (see page 204)

Peel and quarter the apples, then core them. With a sharp knife, cut each quarter into three slices. Squeeze lemon juice over to prevent discolouring.

Heat the butter in a frying pan and quickly fry the apples over medium-high heat, just until golden. Cover and cook on low heat for 3 minutes or until barely tender and still holding their shape. Remove from heat, sprinkle with caster sugar and 1 tablespoon of the Calvados. Heat the apricot jam.

Make the soufflé omelette, adding the remaining tablespoon of Calvados to the yolk mixture. Fill the omelette with the warm apples. Combine any buttery juices in the pan with the apricot jam and spoon over the folded omelette to become glaze and sauce in one.

SERVES: 4

# PEAR POACHED IN ORANGE JUICE

### INGREDIENTS

1 large, firm, ripe pear
•
juice of 1 orange
•
1 large mandarin (tangerine)

Peel the pear, halve lengthways and remove the seeds with a melon baller. Use a small, sharp knife to neatly remove the hard core leading to the stem.

Put the pear, cut side down, in a small saucepan with the orange juice, cover and bring to simmering point. Cook gently for 8–10 minutes, just until tender, turning the halves over after 5 minutes and spooning some of the juice over them.

Leave to cool in the juice. Peel the mandarin, divide into segments and remove the membrane covering each segment. Put pear half in each dessert dish and spoon pan juices over. Arrange mandarin segments around and decorate with a mint sprig. Serve at room temperature or chilled.

SERVES: 2

# GUAVA PIE

12–15 guavas

•

¾ cup (6 oz) sugar or to taste

•

juice of 1 lime or half a lemon

•

1 cup (8 fl oz) Pastry Cream (see page 199, omit ground almonds and almond extract)

•

1 baked 23–25 cm (9–10 in) Pie Shell (see page 447)

Halve the guavas and scoop out the seed ball with a teaspoon. Put seeds into a saucepan, cover with cold water, bring to the boil and simmer, covered, for about 25 minutes. Cool slightly then strain. Discard seeds and save the juice. There should be about 1½ cups (12 fl oz).

Put the guava juice and sugar into a saucepan and bring to the boil stirring until sugar dissolves. Add the guava shells (in more than one batch if necessary), cover and poach gently until just tender but still holding their shape—it will take 12–15 minutes depending on how firm or how ripe the guavas are. Cool until they are lukewarm. Drain the shells and set aside. Reduce the syrup by cooking until it is slightly thick. Add the lime juice.

Spoon the pastry cream into the pie shell, spreading it evenly. Let it set, then arrange the guavas on it, pink side upwards. Spoon the thickened juice over and allow to cool.

SERVES: 6–8

# BUTTERMILK MOULDS

500 ml (16 fl oz) cultured buttermilk

•

3 tablespoons sugar

•

½ teaspoon vanilla extract

•

1 tablespoon gelatine

•

¼ cup (2 fl oz) water

•

fresh berries for serving

Combine buttermilk, sugar and vanilla, stirring to dissolve sugar. Sprinkle gelatine over the cold water in a cup and leave to soften for a few minutes. Dissolve by standing the cup in simmering water or in the microwave oven for 30–40 seconds on full power. Stir until all gelatine granules have dissolved and let it cool to room temperature. Stir into the buttermilk.

Chill until thickened but not set. Whisk until smooth and aerated, then pour into wetted moulds and chill until set. To serve, dip the moulds in warm water for a few seconds, run a knife around the top and turn out. Decorate with fresh berries.

SERVES: 4

# QUINCE WITH DUMPLINGS

*These pale green or golden fruit are worth taking the trouble to experiment with. Besides having a wonderful perfume, they turn a beautiful port wine colour when cooked long and slowly.*

## INGREDIENTS

2 large quinces

•

1½ cups (12 oz) sugar

•

4 cups (32 fl oz) water

•

1½ cups (6 oz) self-raising flour

•

1 tablespoon icing (powdered) sugar

•

30 g (1 oz) butter

•

1 egg, beaten

•

½ cup (4 fl oz) milk

•

few drops lemon juice

With a sharp knife, cut the quinces into quarters, then carefully peel and core them. Put the sugar and water into a heavy-based saucepan and boil until sugar dissolves. Add the quinces and when they return to the boil, cover and simmer gently for 3–4 hours or until they have turned a deep red. The quinces will be tender in a short time but need long, slow simmering to develop colour. This can be done a day ahead if more convenient and heated up when ready to cook the dumplings and serve.

Make the dumplings just before serving. Sift flour and icing sugar into a bowl and rub in the butter. Combine egg, milk and lemon juice and add to the dry ingredients, mixing to form a thick batter of dropping consistency.

Gently remove the pieces of quince from the syrup on a slotted spoon, placing them in a serving dish. If the syrup is very thick, stir in a little extra water so there is sufficient liquid for the dumplings to float.

Drop dough from a soup spoon into the simmering quince syrup, leaving enough space for dumplings to expand. Cover and simmer for 8 minutes or until fluffy and well risen. Test with a wooden toothpick which should come out clean when they are done. Lift out and cook more dumplings. Serve hot with the quinces and their syrup. Pouring (light) cream or custard is optional.

SERVES: 8

# CUSTARD-FILLED PASTRIES

## INGREDIENTS

150 g (5 oz) unsalted butter

•

½ cup (2 oz) ground unblanched almonds

•

1 tablespoon caster (superfine) sugar

First make the custard. Mix a little cold milk with the cornflour and semolina to a smooth cream. Heat the rest of the milk in a non-aluminium saucepan with the sugar, stirring to dissolve. When milk is almost boiling, move the pan away from the heat and stir in the egg and the combined cornflour mixture. Cook on low heat, stirring constantly,

12 sheets filo pastry

CUSTARD

1½ cups (12 fl oz) milk

•

3 tablespoons cornflour (cornstarch)

•

1 tablespoon semolina

•

2 tablespoons sugar

•

1 egg yolk, beaten

•

1 teaspoon cognac or vanilla

until it boils and thickens. Remove from heat and stir occasionally as it cools. Flavour with cognac or vanilla.

Heat the butter in a saucepan and add the ground almonds. Stir constantly for 2 minutes, then remove from heat and stir in sugar. Lay a sheet of filo pastry flat on the work surface and brush with a tablespoon of the butter mixture. Place a second sheet on the first one and brush again. Fold the pastry in thirds, starting at a short edge. There will be six layers of pastry. Place ¼ cup (2 fl oz) of the custard near one end of the pastry, fold in the sides and roll up so custard is completely enclosed.

Repeat with the other sheets of pastry and remaining custard. Place the six rolls in a buttered baking tray (pan), brush top with almond butter and bake in an oven preheated to 180°C (350°F) for 12–15 minutes or until golden. Serve warm or at room temperature, preferably on the day it is made.

MAKES: 6

# SUMMER PUDDING

*The yeasty flavour of bread, the perfume of summer berries and the sweet and tart flavours, all combine to make this one of the best loved puddings.*

INGREDIENTS

500 g (1 lb) raspberries or mixture of red berries

•

125 g (4 oz) red currants

•

½ cup (4 oz) sugar or to taste

•

slices of day-old white bread

•

cream for serving

Put the berries into an enamel or stainless steel saucepan with the sugar and cook over low heat for a few minutes, until the juices run. No water will be necessary. Leave to cool.

Trim the crusts off the bread, halve the slices and neatly line the pudding bowl. Place a circle of bread in the bottom of the bowl, making sure it is completely lined, so the juices can't escape.

Fill with the fruit and reserve the juice left in the pan. Cover the fruit with a layer of bread so it fits snugly inside the rim of the bowl, then a plate with a weight on top. (A large can of fruit, perhaps.)

Chill pudding overnight. At serving time turn out onto a dish, pour the reserved juices over and pass a jug of cream separately.

SERVES: 6–8

# CASSATA À LA SICILIANA

### INGREDIENTS

500 g (1 lb) fresh ricotta cheese
•
½ cup (4 oz) caster (superfine) sugar
•
ground cinnamon or finely grated
lemon rind to flavour
•
250 g (8 oz) glacé fruit
•
150 g (5 oz) dark (semi-sweet)
chocolate, chopped
•
¼ cup (1 oz) chopped pistachios or
toasted almond slivers
•
500 g (1 lb) sponge cake
•
1/3 cup (3 fl oz) maraschino liqueur
or Amaretto
•
icing (powdered) sugar
•
extra glacé fruit

Beat the ricotta cheese with sugar and flavouring until creamy, or let the food processor do it for you. Finely chop the glacé fruit and fold in, together with the chocolate and nuts.

Cut the sponge cake into slices about 1 cm (½ in) thick. Sprinkle them with the liqueur. Line a deep bowl about 25 cm (10 in) in diameter with the strips of cake, then fill with the cheese mixture and cover with more slices of sponge. Cover with plastic wrap or foil and chill overnight or for several hours. Unmould on serving plate, sift icing sugar over the cassata and decorate with extra glacé fruit. Serve chilled. This dessert should not be prepared more than 24 hours ahead since it is the freshness of the ricotta that makes it so appealing.

SERVES: 8–10

# BAKLAVA

*When cooking with nuts, especially walnuts, make sure they are very fresh—few foods taste as nasty as a rancid walnut. If I cannot get to a shop where the nuts are sold loose and I can taste one before I buy, I prefer to buy the walnuts in vacuum-packed cans.*

### INGREDIENTS

FILLING
2 cups (8 oz) finely chopped almonds
•
1 cup (4 oz) finely chopped walnuts
•
¼ cup (2 oz) caster (superfine) sugar
•
2 teaspoons ground cinnamon
•
⅛ teaspoon ground cloves

SYRUP
2 cups (1 lb) sugar

Combine all the ingredients for the filling in a bowl. Place the ingredients for the syrup in a medium-sized pan. Bring to the boil, stirring to dissolve the sugar. Simmer for 10 minutes and leave to cool.

Brush a 30 × 25 cm (12 × 10 in) baking dish with butter and brush 10 sheets of filo with melted butter, laying them in the dish one by one. Spread the filling in the dish, then top with a further 10–12 sheets of pastry, buttering each sheet as needed. Trim the excess pastry and brush the top with melted butter.

With a sharp knife, score the top layers in large diamond shapes. Bake in an oven preheated to 160°C (325°F), for 1 hour, covering the top with foil if it browns too quickly.

2 cups (16 fl oz) water

•

1 stick cinnamon

•

1 tablespoon lemon juice

---

150 g (5 oz) unsalted butter, melted

1 × 375 g (12 oz) packet filo pastry

Remove from the oven and slowly pour the syrup over the top. Leave the baklava to stand for a few hours to absorb the syrup.

NOTE: If liked, make a third layer of pastry in the middle of the filling, using 3 sheets of filo and buttering each one.

MAKES: about 20 pieces

# CARAMEL APPLE DUMPLINGS

### INGREDIENTS

2 cups (8 oz) plain (all-purpose) flour

•

¼ teaspoon salt

•

2 tablespoons caster (superfine) sugar

•

125 g (4 oz) cold butter

•

1 egg yolk

•

2–3 tablespoons iced water

•

4 small apples

•

2 tablespoons toasted slivered almonds

•

4 tablespoons sultanas
(golden raisins)

---

CARAMEL GLAZE

²/₃ cup (4 oz) brown sugar

•

60 g (2 oz) butter

•

½ cup (4 fl oz) water

Sift flour, salt and sugar into a bowl, rub or cut in the butter and mix in the egg yolk beaten with iced water. Mixture should be just moist enough to hold together. If a food processor is available, use to make the pastry, whizzing the butter with the dry ingredients for a few seconds until evenly distributed, then adding the yolk and water just until the mixture forms a mass on the blades. Wrap and chill the pastry for 30 minutes or until firm.

Roll pastry out to a large square and divide into 4 squares, each large enough to enclose an apple. Peel and core the apples, place one on each square, then fill the hollows with almonds and sultanas mixed together. Bring the corners of the pastry up to meet over the apple and either press together or mould around the apple to give a round shape. Cut small leaves from scraps of pastry and decorate, pressing in a whole clove for the stem. Place in a large baking dish with space between the apples and bake in an oven preheated to 220°C (425°F) for 25 minutes.

Meanwhile, combine ingredients for glaze in a small saucepan and stir over heat until sugar dissolves. Simmer for 8 minutes or until slightly thick. Baste the half-cooked apples with the caramel syrup and return to the oven for 20 minutes longer, spooning remaining syrup over them every 10 minutes. Serve hot, with custard or cream.

NOTE: Cooking time depends on the apples. Pierce with a fine skewer to test if they are tender. If pastry browns before apples are soft, turn oven heat down and cover top loosely with foil.

SERVES: 4

# LEMON DELICIOUS

*This pudding needs no introduction. Its tart, refreshing flavour and the creamy
sauce that forms under the feather-light top makes it an all time favourite.
I've found that it can be prepared very quickly by doing the initial creaming
and blending in the food processor.*

### INGREDIENTS

60 g (2 oz) butter

•

1 cup (7 oz) caster (superfine) sugar

•

3 eggs, separated

•

2 teaspoons finely grated lemon rind

•

½ cup (4 fl oz) lemon juice

•

¹/₃ cup (1½ oz) plain (all-purpose)
flour, sifted

•

1¾ cups (14 fl oz) milk

•

⅛ teaspoon salt

Have butter softened at room temperature. Set aside ¼ cup
(2 oz) caster sugar and cream butter and remaining sugar
until light. Add egg yolks one at a time, incorporating each
one well before adding the next. Beat in the lemon rind,
then add the lemon juice. If using processor, stop at this
stage and pour mixture into a bowl. Fold in the flour
alternately with the milk to give a very liquid mixture. In
a clean bowl, whisk the egg whites with the salt until stiff
peaks form. Add reserved caster sugar and whisk until thick
and glossy. Gently fold into the first mixture, taking care
not to overmix.

Butter a deep, 6 cup (48 fl oz) baking dish or soufflé
dish and dust with caster sugar, tipping out excess. Pour
the lemon mixture into the dish and place it in a roasting
pan with hot water to come half way up the side of the
dish. Bake in an oven preheated to 180°C (350°F) for 30–35
minutes or until well risen and golden. Serve warm, each
portion including some of the cake-like top and the tangy
sauce underneath.

SERVES: 6

# FROZEN DESSERTS

The origin of this idea goes back to ancient Rome when Nero had runners bring snow from the mountains. Sweetened with honey and fruit juices, these prototypes of the modern sorbet were served between courses at their gargantuan feasts.

These days, thankfully, there are machines which freeze fruit pulp and syrup into delightful iced confections. In summer, granitas and sorbets are more refreshing than rich ices. Originally sorbets were simply made with crushed ice, fruit syrups and bits of fruit; often a drink rather than a dessert. Now they are as smooth as ice-creams, and made from the pulp or juice of fruit or from champagne or other wines. Take advantage of seasonal produce when fruit is plentiful and cheap, and enjoy *real* fruit ices.

The aim of keeping the mixture smooth has led to the electric ice-cream maker becoming one of the fastest selling kitchen appliances in recent years. There are many models in many price ranges, but it isn't mandatory that you rush out and buy one. Before I acquired mine, I used to make do very nicely. There are ways of smoothing out a frozen dessert that is not constantly churned while freezing, and over the years I've tried them all.

One method is to stir the mixture 3–4 times during freezing, starting when it is frozen about 2 cm (¾ in) in from the edge of the container. Another method is to let it freeze to the slushy stage, then beat it in a food mixer until smooth but not melted, and return it to the freezer. Most effective is to let it freeze firm, break the frozen slab into pieces and whiz them in a food processor using the steel chopping blade. Process until smooth but not melted, return to the container and freeze until needed. All these methods aim at one thing, breaking down large ice crystals so the mixture is smooth. Another approach is to inhibit their formation by adding gelatine or egg white to the mixture.

Don't overlook the charm of granitas or frappés; water ices with large, icy flakes. They could be smoothed out by beating or churning, but then they would lose their character. They are easiest of all to make.

Sorbets and ice-creams should be removed from freezer to refrigerator for about 20 minutes, or left at room temperature for a shorter time, to bring them to the right temperature and consistency for serving. They can be scooped or spooned with less effort, and they are not so cold that flavours cannot be appreciated.

Some rules stay constant, whatever type of ice you are making. These are to set the freezer at its coldest setting an hour before starting to freeze the mixture, and to have the mixture chilled. Electric churns too must be pre-cooled before adding the chilled syrup or custard.

When storing ice-creams and sorbets remember that excluding air is an important detail in keeping them from becoming icy. Place a sheet of freezer wrap directly on the surface of the mixture and press lightly to exclude air. Cover tightly and freeze. All frozen desserts are best eaten within a few days.

# SORBET SYRUP

*To be able to turn a batch of bargain-price fruit into sorbet, it helps if you have sorbet syrup ready in the refrigerator. Make it, then cool and bottle it ready for use. Label it clearly please, because it looks like water.*

## INGREDIENTS

4 cups (2 lb) white sugar
•
4 cups (32 fl oz) water

Put sugar and water into a saucepan and stir over medium heat until the sugar has completely dissolved. Let it come to a boil, then turn off the heat and leave until cold. Pour through a funnel into clean bottles and store in the refrigerator for approximately 6 weeks.

MAKES: about 5 cups (40 fl oz)

# RASPBERRY SORBET

## INGREDIENTS

500 g (1 lb) fresh or frozen raspberries
•
2 cups (16 fl oz) Sorbet Syrup
(see above)

If using fresh raspberries, purée in a food processor or blender with half the syrup. If frozen raspberries are being used, allow to thaw at room temperature or heat the raspberries and half the syrup just until the berries are soft, then purée.

Strain raspberries through a nylon or stainless steel sieve, pressing the seeds hard against the sieve with the back of a spoon. Discard the seeds. Mix in remaining syrup, chill the mixture and freeze.

SERVES: 6–8

# STRAWBERRY APPLE FREEZE

*Light and refreshing, freeze without churning for an icy granita. If a smooth texture is preferred, either freeze in an electric churn or purée the frozen mixture in a food processor.*

## INGREDIENTS

250 g (8 oz) ripe red strawberries
•
1 cup (8 fl oz) Sorbet Syrup
(see above)
•
250 ml (8 fl oz) clear apple juice

Wash, drain and hull the berries. Purée in a blender with the sorbet syrup and apple juice. Freeze according to result preferred. Scoop into balls and pile in a glass.

SERVES: 6

# GUAVA SORBET

## INGREDIENTS

750 g (1½ lb) ripe guavas

•

1 cup (8 oz) sugar or to taste

•

juice of 1 lime or 2 tablespoons
lemon juice

•

½ teaspoon salt

Halve the guavas and scoop out the seeds, then put the seeds into a pan. Add enough water to cover the seeds and bring to the boil. Lower heat and simmer for 20–30 minutes, then cool slightly and strain. Discard seeds and return strained liquid to the saucepan, add sugar and heat until sugar has dissolved. Add the guava shells to the syrup and simmer, covered, for 20 minutes. Reserve 8 halves for serving and put the rest into an electric blender with the syrup. Blend until smooth, then strain through a nylon sieve. (Avoid using metal sieves for fruit or any acidic food). Stir in the lime juice and salt, taste and add a little more sugar if necessary, remembering that freezing diminishes sweetness.

Pour the mixture into a freezing tray or other container and freeze until hard. Break up into chunks and process in a food processor until smooth and snowy. Return to tray and freeze until firm. Serve scoops in guava shells or in dessert dishes.

NOTE:  The salt and lime juice bring out the flavour in quite an extraordinary fashion.

SERVES: 8

# ROCKMELON AND GINGER SORBET

## INGREDIENTS

1 ripe rockmelon (cantaloupe)

•

1 cup (8 fl oz) Sorbet Syrup
(see page 214)

•

1 cup (8 fl oz) ginger ale

•

mint sprigs for decoration

Cut the rockmelon in half, scoop out seeds, make some melon balls for decorating and chill them. Peel the melon, cut up roughly and purée in a blender or food processor together with the sorbet syrup. There should be 3–4 cups (24–32 fl oz) of sweetened purée.  Stir in the ginger ale and freeze. When firm, break it into chunks and purée in a food processor until smooth but not melted. Return to the container and freeze again. To serve, soften slightly at room temperature, pile into glasses and decorate with melon balls and mint sprigs.

SERVES: 6

# WATERMELON AND RASPBERRY GRANITA

*Watermelon is refreshing but not always big on flavour, so I add a small amount of raspberry. Lime or lemon juice may be used instead, or a dash of rosewater.*

1 cup (8 fl oz) Sorbet Syrup
(see page 214)

•

90 g (3 oz) raspberries

•

500 g (1 lb) watermelon without
skin or seeds

Purée sorbet syrup and raspberries in a blender and strain through a nylon sieve, discarding seeds.

Put watermelon into a blender with the raspberry syrup and purée. Chill and freeze without churning. Break up roughly and pile into chilled glasses. Serve immediately.

SERVES: 4–6

# RASPBERRY SHERBET

*In a wonderful little old-fashioned ice-cream parlour in a small town in California, I discovered a world of ice-cream, sherbet and sundaes that would capture the imagination and taste buds of anyone without a will of iron. I swooned rapturously over their raspberry sherbet and wheedled the information that it was a close relative of the sorbet, with a very small amount (5 per cent to be exact) of cream. I managed to duplicate the recipe, and now people swoon rapturously over my raspberry sherbet.*

INGREDIENTS

400 g (13 oz) raspberries

•

2 cups (16 fl oz) Sorbet Syrup
(see page 214)

•

¼ cup (2 fl oz) cream

Purée raspberries through a nylon or stainless steel sieve to eliminate seeds. Or give them a quick whirl in the food processor or blender, then strain them. Stir in the sorbet syrup and cream. Chill mixture well before freezing it. Using an electric churn keeps the mixture very smooth and increases the volume by beating air into it. If using still-freeze method, remove from freezer when it has frozen hard and leave at room temperature for 10 minutes, then chop it into pieces and purée in a food processor until completely smooth but not melted. Return to container and freeze again until firm.

MAKES: about 8 servings

WATERMELON AND RASPBERRY GRANITA AND RICH
PINEAPPLE ICE-CREAM

# KIWI FRUIT SORBET

*The wonderful colour and flavour of Kiwi fruit make this a real treat.*

### INGREDIENTS

6–8 large, ripe Kiwi fruit

•

2 cups (16 fl oz) Sorbet Syrup
(see page 214)

Reserve 1 Kiwi fruit for decoration. Halve the remainder and scoop out the flesh with a spoon. Put into a food processor and use the plastic blades—they will crush the seeds less than the steel ones. Add the sorbet syrup and process just until mashed. Freeze in an electric churn or still freeze, then soften and beat with a rotary beater or in a food mixer until smooth but not melted. Return to the freezer for a short time to firm it up a bit without freezing hard. Put sorbet into a piping bag fitted with a large star nozzle and pipe into glasses. Top with a slice of peeled Kiwi fruit and serve right away.

SERVES: 6

# VELVETY ICE-CREAMS

There are ice-creams which are smooth and velvety with egg yolks and cream, and less rich formulas which still make very good ice-cream. I like to combine a small proportion of basic custard with fruit purée, milk, buttermilk or yoghurt for a lighter mixture and lower fat content.

# LIGHT CUSTARD

### INGREDIENTS

4 cups (32 fl oz)) milk

•

half a vanilla bean

•

1¼ cups (10 oz) sugar

•

5 egg yolks

•

1¼ cups (10 fl oz) cream

Heat the milk with the vanilla bean and half the sugar, stirring constantly until sugar dissolves and milk is almost at simmering point. Whisk the yolks, add remaining sugar and whisk until thick and light. Add some of the hot milk, stir well, then pour the egg mixture into the pan with the rest of the milk and stir constantly over very low heat until the custard thickens and coats the back of a metal spoon. Remove from heat at once, stir in the cream and cool over ice. Split the vanilla bean and scrape out the seeds, stirring them into the ice-cream. Chill well before freezing.

MAKES: 6 cups (48 fl oz)

# RICH CUSTARD

*This is the basic mixture for ice-cream. It can also be added to fruit ices to give a little richness and smooth out the sometimes too piquant flavour. The vanilla bean only improves the flavour of whatever fruit it is combined with. If the full quantity of custard is not required, freeze the excess custard and use with other flavours added.*

### INGREDIENTS

4 cups (32 fl oz) cream
•
half a vanilla bean
•
8 egg yolks
•
1 cup (8 oz) sugar
•
2 cups (16 fl oz) milk

Heat the cream and vanilla bean in a heavy-based saucepan to simmering point. Meanwhile, beat the egg yolks, add half the sugar and whisk well. Pour a ladleful of the hot cream onto the yolks, stirring constantly. Add another ladleful, stir well, then pour the yolk mixture into the pan of cream. Add the remaining sugar and stir gently over low heat until the custard thickens and coats the back of a metal spoon. Do not let it approach boiling point or it will curdle.

Remove from heat at once, add the milk and pour the custard into a large bowl to cool. Split the vanilla bean and scrape out the tiny black seeds with a knife. Stir them into the custard. For quick cooling, stir it over a bowl of ice cubes. When well chilled, freeze.

MAKES: 6 cups (48 fl oz)

# RICH PINEAPPLE ICE-CREAM

*While based on the rich ice-cream custard, the addition of fresh pineapple makes it an outstanding dessert which is not too rich. Simmering the fruit with sugar ensures that, when frozen, the fruit is not icy, since sugar inhibits freezing.*

### INGREDIENTS

1 cup (150 g/5 oz) puréed pineapple
•
1 cup (150 g/5 oz) diced pineapple
•
¾ cup (6 oz) sugar
•
1 cup (8 fl oz) cream
•
3 cups (24 fl oz) Rich Custard
(see above)

Prepare pineapple with sugar as described in Fresh Pineapple Yoghurt Freeze on page 220 and after the diced pineapple has been simmered for 10–12 minutes, pour it into a bowl and leave to cool, then chill. Have the cream and custard chilled and turn freezer to its coldest setting. Combine the cream and custard, stir in the pineapple and pour into a stainless steel container.

Freeze until half frozen, then stir thoroughly and return to freezer. Stir once or twice more during freezing. I don't recommend using the food processor for this ice-cream as it will purée the diced pineapple and the dessert will lose some of its texture.

SERVES: 8

# FRESH PEACH ICE-CREAM

*To concentrate the flavour of peach, reduce the pulp by cooking in an open pan, then mixing it with Rich Custard. The addition of a vanilla bean is very important in the custard recipe.*

### INGREDIENTS

6 large, fully ripe peaches
•
1 cup (8 oz) sugar
•
2 cups (16 fl oz) Rich Custard
(see page 219)
•
peach slices for decoration

Pour boiling water over the peaches in a bowl, leave 30–60 seconds then plunge them into cold water. Remove the skins and seeds, and roughly chop. There should be about 750 g (1½ lb) of peaches. Purée in a blender or food processor.

Put the pulp into an enamel saucepan, add sugar and stir over medium heat until reduced by a third. Allow to cool, then chill. Stir gently into the custard, also chilled, and freeze. If not using an electric churn, freeze until firm, then purée until smooth in a food processor. Return to freezer until 15 minutes before serving, transfer to refrigerator to reach right temperature and serve with fresh peach slices.

SERVES: 6–8

# FRESH PINEAPPLE YOGHURT FREEZE

*This recipe uses a whole, medium-sized pineapple and makes a large amount of not-too-rich ice-cream with a tangy flavour. For a party, present it in a pineapple shell.*

### INGREDIENTS

400 g (13 oz) peeled and cored
pineapple
•
1½ cups (12 oz) sugar
•
3 cups (24 fl oz) Rich or Light
Custard (see pages 218, 219)
•
1 cup (8 fl oz) milk
•
1½ cups (12 fl oz) natural yoghurt

Choose a ripe, sweet pineapple, peel it and cut out the core. Discard the core and weigh 400 g (13 oz) of pineapple, finely dice half and purée the rest in a blender or food processor.

Place the pineapple purée in a medium-sized saucepan and add the sugar. Bring to simmering point and cook for 5 minutes. Add diced pineapple and simmer a further 10–12 minutes. Cool and chill the pineapple mixture and add to it the custard, milk and yoghurt.

Freeze to the slushy stage, beat with a hand mixer or electric beater and return to the freezer until firm. Allow to stand at room temperature for a few minutes, then scoop into the pineapple shell and, if liked, decorate with extra diced pineapple simmered in a sugar syrup, and a sprig of fresh basil or mint.

SERVES: 12

FRESH PEACH ICE-CREAM

# RICH COFFEE ICE-CREAM

*There are three ways to make coffee ice-cream; one with instant coffee, one using coffee beans infused in the cream and, for real coffee enthusiasts, finely ground coffee is cooked with the custard and not strained out. Take your choice, depending on how crazy you are about coffee.*

### INGREDIENTS

3 cups (24 fl oz) Rich Custard
(see page 219)
•
3 teaspoons instant coffee granules
or ½ cup (1½ oz) freshly roasted
coffee beans or ground coffee

Cook the rich custard with the coffee beans or ground coffee, cool and chill, then freeze. If whole beans are used, strain the custard before freezing. If using instant coffee granules, dissolve the coffee in a tablespoon of boiling water and stir in after the custard has been cooked. Cool, chill and freeze. Even without a churn a rich mixture like this will be quite smooth.

SERVES: 6–8

# PISTACHIO ICE-CREAM

*The pistachios for ice-cream should not be the toasted variety sold in their shells but raw kernels with a good green colour.*

### INGREDIENTS

2 cups (16 fl oz) Rich or Light
Custard (see pages 218, 219)
•
½ cup (2 oz) pistachios
•
2 tablespoons Amaretto liqueur
•
2 or 3 drops green food colouring

Make and chill the custard. Blanch pistachios for 30 seconds in boiling water, then plunge into cold water. Slip off the skins and chop the nuts finely.

Add the Amaretto and green food colouring to the ice-cream. Freeze until thick, then sprinkle in the pistachios and churn or freeze until ice-cream is firm, or stir nuts in if freezing in a tray.

SERVES: 4

# BANANA ICE-CREAM

### INGREDIENTS

2 cups (16 fl oz) Rich or Light
Custard (see pages 218, 219), chilled
•
2 ripe bananas
•
½ teaspoon vanilla essence (extract)

Put half the custard into an electric blender with the peeled bananas and blend to a purée. Mix with the rest of the custard and stir in the vanilla essence. Churn or freeze in a tray.

SERVES: 4–5

# HAZELNUT PRALINE ICE-CREAM

## INGREDIENTS

¼ cup (2 oz) sugar

•

1 tablespoon water

•

½ cup (2 oz) roasted hazelnuts,
without skins

•

1 teaspoon instant coffee
granules (optional)

•

1 tablespoon boiling water

•

2 cups (16 fl oz) Rich or
Light Custard
(see pages 218, 219)

Place the sugar and water in a small saucepan and bring to the boil, stirring gently. When boiling, cook without stirring until the mixture forms a dark caramel. Add the hazelnuts and pour onto a lightly greased baking tray (pan) to cool. When cool, crush the praline with a rolling pin or in a food processor. Dissolve the coffee in the boiling water and mix through the custard. Freeze until semi-frozen, stir in the praline and freeze again.

SERVES: 6

# PECAN BRITTLE ICE-CREAM

## INGREDIENTS

¼ cup (2 oz) sugar

•

1 tablespoon water

•

½ cup (2 oz) chopped pecans

•

2 cups (16 fl oz) Rich or Light
Custard (see pages 218, 219)

Put sugar and water into a small, heavy-based saucepan and heat without stirring at all until the sugar forms a syrup which bubbles thickly and starts to change colour. When it has turned to a golden brown, remove from the heat and stir in the pecans.

Pour out onto a lightly oiled or non-stick baking tray (pan) and leave until quite cold and brittle. Break into pieces and crush finely in a food processor. Freeze ice-cream and stir in the brittle when it is almost on the point of setting.

SERVES: 4

# OUTDOOR EATING
## IN SPRING

*Mushrooms with Tomato Mousse
and Fresh Coriander*
page 3

*Mushrooms with Guacamole*
page 4

*Fettucine in Creamy Capsicum
(pepper) Sauce*
page 52

*Beans with Walnut Dressing*
page 134

*Green salad
Homemade bread rolls*
page 413

*Hot Strawberry Soufflés*
page 195

# CHOCOLATE FLAKE ICE-CREAM

## INGREDIENTS

185 g (6 oz) dark (semi-sweet)
chocolate

•

2 cups (16 fl oz) Rich or Light
Custard (see pages 218, 219)

Chop the chocolate, place in a dry bowl over a pan of gently simmering water, and stir until melted. Allow to cool. Freeze the custard in a churn and when mixture thickens, pour in the chocolate while the churn is working so the chocolate sets into little flakes.

If not using a churn, freeze the ice-cream until firm, then break into chunks and beat in a food processor or mixer until smooth but not melted. Pour in the melted chocolate and beat vigorously. Return to freezer.

SERVES: 6

# STRAWBERRY YOGHURT SHERBET

*A low-fat dessert that's rich in flavour.*

## INGREDIENTS

400 g (13 oz) strawberries

•

90 g (3 oz) raspberries, fresh or
frozen (optional)

•

1¼ cups (10 oz) sugar

•

¼ cup (2 fl oz) water

•

375 ml (12 fl oz) natural
non-fat yoghurt

•

2 tablespoons Grand Marnier
(optional)

•

1 tablespoon lemon juice

•

10 Fragole Fabbri—glacé
strawberries in syrup (optional)

Wash the strawberries, drain and hull them. Put into electric blender with the raspberries, sugar and water. Blend to a purée, then strain through a nylon sieve and discard the seeds. Return 1 cup (8 fl oz) of purée to blender with the yoghurt and blend. Stir into the rest of the purée, adding Grand Marnier and lemon juice.

If freezing in a machine, stir in the glacé strawberries cut in quarters when mixture is almost firm. If using freezer method, purée the frozen mixture until smooth in a food processor and fold in the quartered glacé strawberries before returning to the freezer.

NOTE: Fabbri glacé strawberries are sold at food specialty stores and Italian delicatessens.

SERVES: 8–10

# GRAND MARNIER ICE-CREAM

### INGREDIENTS

4 egg yolks

•

¾ cup (6 oz) sugar

•

2 cups (16 fl oz) milk

•

300 ml (10 fl oz) thick cream

•

185 g (6 oz) chopped chocolate

•

2 tablespoons Grand Marnier

Whisk the egg yolks with half the sugar until thick and light. Heat milk with remaining sugar, stirring, until it boils. Pour milk on to the yolks, whisking constantly. Return to pan over very low heat and stir briskly until custard thickens. Remove from heat, stir in cream and stand pan in cold water. Chill the custard.

Melt chocolate in a small pan with 3 tablespoons water, stirring until smooth. Add the Grand Marnier. Stir the warm chocolate mixture into the chilled custard, which makes some of the chocolate solidify into flakes. Freeze in an electric churn or in the freezer. If not churning the mixture, stir once or twice during freezing. It is very rich, so make the servings small.

SERVES: 10

# BROWN BREAD ICE-CREAM

*Until you try this, you won't believe that brown bread makes such crisp "praline". An economical ice-cream recipe.*

### INGREDIENTS

5 slices wholemeal
(whole wheat) bread,
crusts removed

•

¼ cup (2 oz) sugar

•

2 tablespoons water

•

1 × 375 ml (12 fl oz) can evaporated
milk, well chilled

•

4 tablespoons dark brown sugar

Crumb the bread. Make a caramel with sugar and water, taking care not to stir once it comes to the boil. When golden brown, stir in the crumbs and spread on a greased baking tray (pan) to cool. When cold, crush with a rolling pin. Whip the chilled evaporated milk until frothy, add brown sugar and continue to beat until it is almost triple in volume. Stir in the brown bread "praline", pour into a loaf tin and freeze.

NOTE: You will find the bread easier to crumb if it is a couple of days old.

SERVES: 6–8

227

# EASTERN
## INFLUENCE

# SNACKS & APPETISERS

Here are some of the more popular 'walkabout' snacks one sees in Eastern countries, when half the population seem to be eating at all hours of the day and night, and the other half seem to be cooking at street stalls to satisfy the demand.
Of course, you don't have to eat on the run. Make these the introduction to your Oriental meals and serve them at the table.

## FRESH SPRING ROLL — LUMPIA

*This is a favourite snack in the Philippines where it contains such exotic ingredients as hearts of coconut palm. You may add canned hearts of palm if the mood is extravagant.*

### INGREDIENTS

FILLING
3 tablespoons vegetable oil
•
1 tablespoon annatto seeds (achuete)
•
1 medium onion, finely chopped
•
1 teaspoon finely chopped garlic
•
1 cup (5 oz) peeled, diced sweet potato
•
1 cup (6 oz) peeled, diced potato
•
2 squares pressed bean curd, diced
•
1 cup (5 oz) green beans, finely sliced
•
1 cup cooked, drained chick peas (3 oz dried)
•
3 cups (6 oz) shredded cabbage
•
200 g (6½ oz) bean sprouts, washed and drained
•
2 tablespoons light soy sauce
•
½ cup (1 oz) roughly chopped fresh coriander
•
salt to taste
•
20 cos (romaine) or mignonette leaves

Begin by making the wrappers. Beat eggs until well mixed, then add water. Sift flour and salt, add to liquid and whisk until smooth. If necessary, strain out any little lumps.

Stir in oil and let batter rest for at least 30 minutes. The batter may be made in an electric blender but needs to be left for longer. If any froth remains on the surface, spoon it off before cooking the wrappers.

Heat a small, heavy-based crêpe pan or frying pan and wipe the base with a piece of paper towel dipped in oil. dipped in oil. Pour a couple of tablespoons of batter into the pan, swirl to coat base thinly and cook until firm but not brown. Turn over gently and give the wrapper a few seconds cooking on the other side. Turn onto a plate. Continue until all the batter has been used. These may be made a day ahead.

To make the filling, heat the oil in a wok, add the annatto seeds and put a lid on immediately as the seeds will pop, jump and spatter—absolute death to any garment you are wearing unless it happens to be bright orange, in which case the spots probably will not show. After 2 minutes of gentle cooking, turn off the heat and allow to cool, then strain out the seeds or lift them out on a slotted spoon.

Gently reheat the same oil, which is now coloured bright orange, and cook the onion and garlic until soft. Add the sweet potato, potato and bean curd and fry, stirring, for a few minutes. Add the green beans, toss, pour in ½ cup (4 fl oz) water, cover and cook gently for 5 minutes or until potatoes and beans are half cooked.

LUMPIA WRAPPERS
5 large eggs

1½ cups (12 fl oz) cold water

1 cup (4 oz) plain (all-purpose) flour

½ teaspoon salt

2 tablespoons oil

SAUCE
3 tablespoons sugar

¼ cup (2 fl oz) light soy sauce

1 cup (8 fl oz) clear stock or water

1 tablespoon cornflour (cornstarch)

1 clove garlic, crushed

Add the chick peas, cabbage and bean sprouts, toss together with the other vegetables, sprinkle soy sauce over and cook covered for 10 minutes. Stir in coriander for the last couple of minutes and season to taste with salt. Place a colander over a bowl, transfer the cooked mixture to colander and allow to cool, letting the liquid drain into the bowl.

Meanwhile to make the sauce, combine sugar, soy sauce and stock or water in a small pan and bring to the boil. Stir in cornflour mixed smoothly with a little cold water and stir until mixture thickens and becomes clear. Stir in garlic crushed with a pinch of salt or sugar.

Place a lumpia wrapper on a board, then spread a washed and dried lettuce leaf over, first tearing off the bottom portion of the leaf with its thick rib. If the leaf is very crisp, press the centre rib with the flat of a knife to make it pliable. Put a couple of spoonfuls of filling on the leaf and roll up the lumpia, tucking in one end and letting the leaf show at the other end. Serve with the dipping sauce.

MAKES: 20

# WHITE MARROW FRIED IN BATTER

*This is a favourite snack in Burma. Serve as finger food, hot and crisp.*

INGREDIENTS

2–3 cups (12–16 oz) sliced marrow (summer squash)

oil for deep-frying

BATTER
½ cup (2 oz) chick pea flour (besan)

½ cup (2 oz) self-raising flour

1 teaspoon salt

1 clove garlic, crushed

½ teaspoon finely grated fresh ginger

¼ teaspoon ground turmeric

½ cup (4 fl oz) water

To make the batter, mix all ingredients together to form a coating batter.

Peel marrow and remove seeds. Cut into finger-size strips.

Heat oil in a large frying pan or wok and when a faint haze begins to rise, dip marrow slices in batter and drop, one at a time, into the oil. Do not try to fry more than 6–8 pieces at a time. When batter is golden, remove from oil, drain on absorbent paper and serve immediately.

SERVES: 6–8

231

# SUSHI RICE WITH VINEGAR AND SUGAR

*Sushi is the Japanese equivalent of the open sandwich. Rice flavoured with a vinegar and sugar dressing takes the place of bread, and is rolled around fillings of pickles, mushrooms or other vegetables and in some cases enclosed in omelettes or bean curd.*
*A selection of sushi can make a complete lunch. Among the most popular types of sushi are* norimaki-zushi *(rice rolled in seaweed),* inari-zushi *(rice in fried bean curd) and* chirashi-zushi *(rice with vegetables.)*

### INGREDIENTS

2½ cups (1 lb) short or
medium grain white rice
•
2½ cups (20 fl oz) cold water
•
5 cm (2 in) piece kombu
(dried kelp), (optional)

### DRESSING

4 tablespoons rice vinegar
or mild white vinegar
•
3 tablespoons sugar
•
2½ teaspoons salt
•
2 tablespoons mirin
or dry sherry

Wash rice several times in cold water and allow to drain for 30 minutes, then put into a saucepan with measured water. If dried kelp is used, wash it well in cold water and add it to the pan. Bring to the boil quickly, cover pan, turn heat down very low and steam for 15 minutes without lifting lid. Remove from heat and let it stand, still covered, for a further 10 minutes. Discard kelp and turn rice into a large bowl. Have ready the dressing ingredients, mixed together until the sugar has completely dissolved. Pour over the rice. Mix gently but thoroughly and cool quickly to room temperature.

SERVES: 6

# SUSHI ROLLED IN SEAWEED (NORIMAKI ZUSHI)

*Vinegared rice with a filling of simmered mushrooms, pickled radish, cucumber, egg, singly or in combination, is rolled neatly in a sheet of seaweed (nori) and cut into small slices.*

## INGREDIENTS

1 quantity Sushi (see page 232)

•

4 dried mushrooms

•

2 tablespoons Japanese soy sauce

•

1 tablespoon sugar

•

2 eggs

•

¼ teaspoon salt

•

few drops vegetable oil

•

1 green cucumber

•

1 small piece takuan (pickled radish)

•

3 tablespoons beni shoga
(red pickled ginger)

•

6 sheets nori (dried laver seaweed)

•

1 teaspoon prepared wasabi
(green horseradish)

While sushi cools, soak mushrooms in hot water for 20 minutes. Cut off and discard stems, shred the caps into very thin slices and simmer in half cup of the soaking liquid, mixed with soy and sugar, until liquid has almost evaporated.

Beat eggs with salt and cook in lightly oiled pan like a flat omelette. Cool, then cut into thin strips. Peel cucumber thinly, leaving a trace of green. Cut lengthways in strips the size of a pencil. Drain the takuan and beni shoga and cut in similar sized strips.

Toast sheets of nori by passing them back and forth over a gas flame or electric hotplate a few times. Put a sheet of nori on a bamboo mat or a clean linen napkin. Divide the rice into six equal portions and spread one portion evenly over two-thirds of the sheet of nori, starting at the nearest end. Smear sparingly with prepared wasabi. In a row down the middle of the rice, put one or a combination of the ingredients.

Roll up sushi in the mat, keeping firm pressure on the rice so that a neatly packed cylinder results. Let the rolls rest for 10 minutes before cutting into six pieces. Arrange on a tray, decorate with tiny leaves or green paper cut into fancy shapes. Serve cold.

NOTE: The bamboo mats are available in most Japanese stores.

MAKES: about 36

# BEAN SPROUT FRITTERS

*Every Asian country has its own version of fritters which are eaten at any time of the day as a snack. They also make a good pre-dinner appetiser.*

### INGREDIENTS

250 g (8 oz) fresh bean sprouts
•
batter (see White Marrow, page 231)
•
oil for deep-frying

Wash bean sprouts, drain well and pinch off tails. Make batter, then fold in bean sprouts. Heat oil and when very hot fry spoonfuls of mixture until golden brown and crisp. Drain on absorbent paper, serve hot.

SERVES: 6–8

# KOREAN PANCAKES

*Shredded omelettes, stir-fried shredded gluten, and various stir-fried vegetables surround a pile of small pancakes. Fillings are rolled in the pancake, dipped in sauce and eaten.*

### INGREDIENTS

PANCAKES
1½ cups (6 oz) plain (all-purpose) flour
•
¼ teaspoon salt
•
2 eggs, beaten
•
1 cup (8 fl oz) milk
•
1 cup (8 fl oz) water
•
vegetable oil for frying
•
few pinenuts and parsley sprigs (optional)

FILLINGS
10 dried Chinese mushrooms
•
3 eggs, separated
•
vegetable or sesame oil for frying
•
2 cups shredded Gluten
(see page 437)
•
2 tablespoons soy sauce
•
ground black pepper to taste
•

To make the pancakes, sift the flour and salt into a bowl. Mix beaten eggs with milk and water. Make a well in the centre of the flour and add liquid, stirring rapidly with a wooden spoon. Beat until smooth and let the batter stand while preparing fillings.

Soak the dried mushrooms in hot water for 30 minutes.

Beat the egg yolks and egg whites separately and cook separately in a lightly greased frying pan to make large, flat omelettes. Do not allow to brown. Turn out on a plate or board and allow to cool, then shred into very fine strips.

Heat about a tablespoon of oil in a pan and stir-fry the gluten, adding 1 tablespoon soy sauce and ground black pepper to taste. Add mushroom liquid, cover and cook for 5–10 minutes, stirring occasionally until liquid has been absorbed.

Peel the carrots, cut into very thin slices, then cut slices into thin shreds, finer than matchsticks. Stir-fry in very little oil, adding salt and pepper to taste. Cut spring onions into similar size lengths and stir-fry briefly. Peel and shred radish and stir-fry until wilted. Season with salt. The aim is to keep the natural colour of the vegetables, so only cook for a short time and do not allow anything to brown. Do not peel zucchini—the green skin adds to the appearance of the dish. Slice finely, then cut into fine strips and stir-fry for a few minutes. Season with salt.

¼ cup (2 fl oz) mushroom soaking
liquid

•

3 tender carrots

•

salt to taste

•

12 spring onions (scallions)

•

1 giant white radish (daikon)

•

250 g (8 oz) zucchini (courgettes)

•

sprinkle of sugar

---

DIPPING SAUCE

¾ cup (6 fl oz) soy sauce

•

3 tablespoons mild vinegar

•

3 tablespoons crushed,
toasted sesame seeds

•

2 tablespoons finely chopped
spring onions (scallions)

Squeeze out water from the mushrooms, cut off and discard tough stalks, then shred the caps into thin slices. Heat very little oil and stir-fry, then add remaining 1 tablespoon soy sauce and pepper, a sprinkling of sugar and ½ cup (4 fl oz) of the water the mushrooms soaked in. Cover and cook for 15–20 minutes or until mushrooms are tender and liquid has been absorbed.

Meanwhile, cook the pancakes. Heat a large frying pan and grease very lightly with oil. Pour in a ladle of the batter, sufficient to make a fairly thin pancake. Cook on medium-low heat so the pancake does not brown. Turn and cook other side, then turn on to a large board. When all the pancakes have been made, cut into small circles with a 7.5 cm (3 in) round pastry or cookie cutter and pile pancakes in centre of tray or dish. Decorate with a few pine nuts and sprig of parsley if desired.

Arrange all the filling ingredients in separate piles around the edge of a plate or in a compartmented tray.

Make the dipping sauce by blending together all ingredients and pouring into individual sauce bowls.

SERVES: 4–6

# FRESH RICE NOODLE SNACK

INGREDIENTS

---

500 g (1 lb) fresh rice noodles

•

1 tablespoon Chinese barbecue
sauce (or hoisin)

•

1 tablespoon light soy sauce

•

1 tablespoon dark soy sauce

•

1 tablespoon sweet chilli sauce

•

2 teaspoons sesame oil

•

2 tablespoons toasted sesame seeds

•

watercress sprigs (optional)

•

chopped fresh coriander (optional)

Cut the rolls of noodles into thin strips and cover them with boiling water in a bowl. Leave to soak for 5 minutes, then drain thoroughly. Put the noodles into a large bowl, add all the other ingredients except the watercress and coriander, and toss lightly until well mixed. Serve as is, or add a few sprigs of watercress or a little chopped coriander and garnish with a tomato butterfly.

NOTE: Soft, fresh rice noodles are sold widely in the refrigerator section of suburban Asian stores. They are the basis for many a tasty snack. The type used here comes in two thin rolls.

If you like your flavours hot, consider substituting chilli oil for sesame oil, but go easy—a few drops will be sufficient.

SERVES: 4

# SUSHI IN FRIED BEAN CURD (INARI-ZUSHI)

*In Japanese groceries you can buy aburage, sheets of fried bean curd. These form "bags" which are filled with sushi and are a favourite snack in Japan. Ideal for taking on picnics.*

Use half as many sheets of aburage as the number of inari-zushi you want, because each sheet makes two. Put aburage into a colander and pour 3 or 4 cups (24–32 fl oz) of boiling water over to remove excess oil. Press out most of the water by rolling in paper towels and sprinkle aburage with a few drops of soy and mirin or dry sherry to give it flavour. Alternatively, simmer the aburage in vegetable stock with 2 tablespoons soy, 1 tablespoon mirin or dry sherry and 1 tablespoon sugar until liquid has been absorbed by the bean curd. Press out excess moisture by rolling in kitchen paper, cut the aburage sheets in half across the centre and pull the cut edges apart to form a pocket.

Fill each pocket three-quarters full with rice mixture, then fold the cut ends over to enclose the filling. Put folded end down on serving tray.

The sushi can have additions as in Chirashi-zushi (see page 237), or be flavoured simply with toasted sesame seeds or a sprinkling of gomasio, a seasoning made from black sesame seeds and sea salt.

# BEAN CURD OMELETTES

## INGREDIENTS

3 squares fresh bean curd
•
3 eggs, beaten
•
½ teaspoon salt
•
¼ teaspoon ground black pepper
•
6 spring onions (scallions), finely chopped
•
peanut oil for frying

## SAUCE

1 tablespoon oil
•
1 small onion, very finely chopped
•
2 cloves garlic, finely chopped
•
1 firm ripe tomato, finely chopped
•
2 tablespoons dark soy sauce
•
2 tablespoons water
•
1 tablespoon sugar

To make the sauce, heat the oil in a small saucepan and fry onion and garlic on a low heat, stirring frequently for 5 minutes or until onion is soft. Add tomato and fry, stirring, for 3–4 minutes, or until tomato is cooked to a pulp. Add soy sauce, water and sugar and bring to the boil. If made ahead, reheat before using.

Chop bean curd into small pieces or mash roughly with a fork. Stir into the eggs, season with salt and pepper, and add spring onions. Heat a large flat frying pan, grease the base lightly with oil and fry the egg mixture in small round omelettes, no larger than a saucer. Make several and keep warm on a hot plate until all the mixture is cooked. Pour the sauce over (which can be made well ahead) and serve immediately. Garnish, if liked, with thin diagonal slices of spring onion leaves.

SERVES: 4

# COLD RICE WITH VEGETABLES (CHIRASHI-ZUSHI)

*I suppose we may call this the Japanese version of a rice salad—different and delicious, lovely for summer.*

### INGREDIENTS

1 quantity Sushi (see page 232)
•
8 dried shiitake mushrooms
•
1 tablespoon Japanese soy sauce
•
1 teaspoon sugar
•
2 eggs
•
pinch of salt
•
vegetable oil
•
½ cup (4 oz) finely shredded bamboo shoot
•
½ cup (3 oz) shelled peas
•
1 piece canned lotus root, sliced
•
1 tablespoon pickled kombu (kelp), thinly sliced
•
1 tablespoon takuan (pickled radish), thinly sliced
•
few shreds beni shoga (pickled ginger root), for garnish

Prepare sushi and cool. Soak mushrooms in boiling water for 30 minutes, remove and discard stems. Slice caps thinly, then simmer for 10 minutes in half a cup of the soaking water with soy sauce and sugar.

Beat eggs slightly, season with salt and cook in a lightly oiled pan to make a thin omelette, taking care not to let it brown. Cool, then cut in thin shreds.

Toss rice gently with all the ingredients, reserving a few of the most colourful for garnish. Serve cold.

SERVES: 6

# STEAMED RICE CAKES

*Glutinous rice cakes—and there are many of them in Asian countries—
are little frivolities which help fill the gaps between meals. Most often they
are rolled in fresh coconut before eating.*

### INGREDIENTS

1 cup (7 oz) glutinous rice
•
1 cup (8 fl oz) water
•
1 tablespoon cooked rice
•
¹/₃ cup (3 fl oz) canned unsweetened
coconut milk
•
3 teaspoons baking powder
•
¾ cup (6 oz) sugar
•
3 tablespoons grated
cheese (optional)
•
fresh grated coconut

Soak glutinous rice in 1 cup water overnight, or for at least 2 hours. Put the rice and measured water into the container of an electric blender, and blend on top speed until smooth. Add the cooked rice, coconut milk, baking powder and sugar, and blend again. If using the grated cheese, stir it in.

Pour mixture into small cups (Chinese wine cups are ideal) and steam over fast boiling water for 20–25 minutes. Each cup should hold only a couple of spoonfuls.

Turn off heat and leave the cakes in the steamer to cool for 10 minutes, then take them out and let them cool completely. Gently loosen from side of cup using a table knife, and if they are difficult to remove, run cold water into the cup and let it flow between the rice cake and the cup. Turn out onto freshly grated coconut, roll in the coconut and serve at room temperature.

MAKES: about 24

# POTATO AND PEA CURRY PUFFS

### INGREDIENTS

500 g (1 lb) potatoes
•
¾ cup (3 oz) shelled peas
•
1 teaspoon salt
•
1 teaspoon ground cumin
•
½ teaspoon chilli powder (optional)
•
½ teaspoon Panch Phora
(see page 456)
•
2 tablespoons lemon juice
•
oil, for deep-frying

Begin by making the pastry. Sift flour and salt into a bowl, lightly rub in butter or oil, add water and mix until ingredients are combined and the dough comes away from sides of the bowl. Add a little more water if necessary, or a sprinkling of flour if the mixture seems too moist. Knead firmly for 10 minutes or until dough is smooth and elastic. Cover with plastic wrap and set aside for at least 30 minutes before rolling out.

Boil the potatoes, peel and dice fairly small. If using fresh peas, cook them until tender. Frozen peas need only to be thawed. Combine potatoes and peas with the salt, cumin, chilli powder, panch phora and lemon juice.

Make small balls of dough and roll out each one on a lightly floured board to the size of a saucer. Cut each circle in half. Put a teaspoon of filling on one side of each

PASTRY

1½ cups (6 oz) plain (all-purpose)
flour

•

½ teaspoon salt

•

1 tablespoon butter or oil

•

½ cup (4 fl oz) lukewarm water

half circle, brush edges with water, fold dough over and press edges together firmly to seal. The shape should be triangular. Cover with a cloth until all are ready and deep fry in hot oil until golden. Drain on absorbent paper.

NOTE: The puffs can also be made using 12 large spring roll sheets. Cut each sheet of spring roll pastry into three equal strips and keep them covered while working, or they will dry out and not be pliable enough to fold.

Put 1 teaspoon of filling at one end and fold the strip of pastry over diagonally to cover it, then pick up the filling in the pastry and fold again and again, making sure there is a perfect triangle every time—not difficult if you line up the straight edges of the pastry. Moisten the end of the strip with water or a mixture of beaten egg and flour to seal. When all the pastries are made, deep-fry in hot oil. Drain on absorbent paper. The pastries also freeze well and may be fried just before required.

NOTE: Serve with Fresh Mint Chutney or Tamarind Chutney (see pages 356 and 362) as a dip.

MAKES: about 36

# PARSI OMELETTE

INGREDIENTS

1 medium potato, diced
(about 1 cup)

•

2 tablespoons ghee (clarified butter)
or oil

•

4 eggs

•

¾ teaspoon salt

•

¼ teaspoon pepper

•

½ teaspoon ground cumin

•

2 tablespoons finely chopped
fresh coriander

•

1 small onion, finely chopped

•

2 fresh red or green chillies,
seeded and chopped

Parboil potato in lightly salted, boiling water for 1–2 minutes, then drain well in a colander. Heat ghee or oil in a frying pan and fry the potato until lightly browned. Lift out on a slotted spoon and set aside.

Separate eggs and beat the whites until frothy, then beat in the yolks, salt, pepper and cumin. Fold in coriander, onion and chillies. Heat omelette pan or clean frying pan with ghee left from frying potatoes, and if necessary, add a little extra ghee. Pour in the egg mixture and when it starts to set, add the fried potato, distributing it evenly over the omelette. Cook on low heat until golden brown on bottom, turn omelette over and cook until brown on other side. Serve hot with chapatis or bread.

SERVES: 2

# VEGETARIAN DUMPLINGS

*This recipe illustrates how any recipe can be adapted using vegetarian ingredients. When you taste these you'll realise they are the equivalent of the little dumplings served at Yum Cha.*

### INGREDIENTS

2 cups  cooked and
minced Gluten (see page 437)
•
4 dried Chinese mushrooms
•
2 tablespoons peanut oil
•
4 spring onions (scallions),
finely chopped
•
1 teaspoon crushed garlic
•
1 teaspoon finely grated ginger
•
2 cups finely chopped
Chinese cabbage (wongah bak)
•
10 water chestnuts, chopped
•
2 tablespoons light soy sauce
•
2 teaspoons sesame oil
•
1 teaspoon salt, or to taste
•
1 large egg, beaten
•
1 tablespoon cornflour (cornstarch)
•
125 g (4 oz) wonton wrappers

Prepare the gluten and when cool, squeeze out excess water and mince in food processor or chop finely.

Soak the mushrooms in hot water for 30 minutes, then discard the mushroom stems and finely chop the caps.

Heat a wok, add the peanut oil and when the oil is hot, fry the spring onions, garlic and ginger, stirring, for a few seconds until fragrant. Add the cabbage and toss until soft. Add water chestnuts, mushrooms and gluten, and toss for 1–2 minutes, then transfer the mixture to a large bowl.

Mix together the soy sauce, sesame oil, salt, beaten egg and cornflour. Pour over the gluten mixture and mix well with your hands to distribute the seasonings and bind together.

Place a tablespoon of the mixture in the centre of each wonton wrapper, gather the wrapper to enclose the filling and squeeze the dumpling firmly to make the dough adhere to the filling. Press the corners of the pastry down with the back of a teaspoon.

Place the dumplings in an oiled steamer and steam for 10 minutes. Serve warm, or refrigerate until needed and reheat by steaming for a couple of minutes.

MAKES: about 24

VEGETARIAN DUMPLINGS

# PEANUT WAFERS

*An accompaniment to rice and curries on festive occasions, these crisp and crunchy wafers are also delicious served by themselves, as a snack or as an accompaniment to drinks. In this case, make them rather small.*

## INGREDIENTS

½ cup (2 oz) rice flour

•

2 tablespoons ground rice
or plain flour

•

1 teaspoon ground coriander

•

½ teaspoon ground cumin

•

¼ teaspoon ground turmeric

•

¾ teaspoon salt

•

1 cup (8 fl oz) coconut milk

•

1 clove garlic, crushed

•

1 small onion, finely chopped

•

125 g (4 oz) roasted, unsalted peanuts

•

oil for frying

Sift all the dry ingredients into a bowl. Add the coconut milk and beat to a smooth thin batter. Crush garlic to a paste then stir to distribute it well through the batter. Stir in onion and peanuts.

Heat enough oil in a frying pan to cover base to a depth of 12 mm (½ in). Oil must be hot, but not to the point of smoking. Drop tablespoons of the batter into the oil. The batter should be thin enough to spread into a lacy wafer. If it holds together and has to be spread with the spoon, it is too thick, and must be thinned by adding a spoonful of coconut milk at a time until the correct consistency is obtained.

Fry until golden brown on the underside, then turn and fry until golden on other side. Drain on absorbent paper over a wire rack to allow air to circulate. This will help wafers retain their crispness for a few hours. Cool and store in an airtight container.

SERVES: 6

# RICE BALLS

*In Japan, rice takes the place of sandwich bread, hamburger buns and hot dog rolls. Rice balls are usually taken on picnics and are sometimes filled with pieces of salted or pickled radish or ginger. They may also be very simply flavoured with sesame seeds or seaweed.*

## INGREDIENTS

3 cups hot cooked rice
(7 oz uncooked)

•

1 tablespoon salted or
pickled radish or ginger

•

2 tablespoons goma sio (black sesame seeds and salt) or powdered
nori (seaweed)

Cook rice and when cool enough to handle, take about half a cup and, with wet hands, roll into firm balls about 7.5 cm (3 in) in diameter. Put a strip of pickled radish or ginger into the centre of the rice ball, moulding the rice around it. Roll the rice balls lightly in goma sio or powdered nori.

MAKES: 6

# EGGS ON SPINACH

*This is the Eastern version of Eggs Florentine—instead of a creamy sauce,*
*there is the special flavour of mild spices.*

### INGREDIENTS

1 bunch spinach

•

1 tablespoon ghee (clarified butter)
or butter

•

1 small onion, finely chopped

•

1 teaspoon finely chopped garlic

•

1 teaspoon finely grated ginger

•

½ teaspoon cumin seeds

•

⅛ teaspoon chilli powder (optional)

•

salt and ground black pepper to taste

•

6 eggs

Wash the spinach very thoroughly, discarding any tough stems, and cook the leaves in a little water in a covered pan for 10–12 minutes or until soft. Drain and chop the spinach.

In a frying pan, heat the ghee or butter and fry the onion, garlic, ginger and cumin until the onion is soft and turning a gold colour. Mix in the chopped spinach. Add the chilli powder (if used) and salt and pepper to taste.

Beat the eggs in a bowl and season to taste with salt and pepper. Pour over the spinach mixture in the pan, cover pan and cook on low heat until the eggs are set. Serve hot.

SERVES: 4

# SPLIT PEA FRITTERS

*This is one of the tastiest fried snacks, and high in protein too.*

### INGREDIENTS

1 cup (6 oz) split peas

•

2 medium onions, finely chopped

•

2 fresh red chillies, finely chopped,
or ¼ teaspoon chilli powder

•

½ teaspoon ground turmeric

•

½ teaspoon salt

•

oil, for deep-frying

•

sliced onion and lemon wedges
to garnish

Soak split peas overnight, or for at least 6 hours, in water to cover. Drain, grind to a paste in a blender, or put it through the fine screen of a mincer twice. Mix in all other ingredients except oil and garnish. Mould paste into small balls and flatten to 12 mm (½ in) thickness. Heat oil in a wok or deep frying pan, and add the fritters one at a time. Fry until golden brown. Drain on absorbent paper. Serve garnished with sliced raw onion and lemon wedges.

MAKES: about 30

# MARBLED TEA EGGS

## INGREDIENTS

6 eggs

•

4 cups (32 fl oz) water

•

3 tablespoons tea leaves

•

1 tablespoon salt

•

1 tablespoon five spice powder

Put eggs into a saucepan, cover with cold water and bring slowly to the boil, stirring gently. Stirring helps to centre the yolks. Simmer gently for 7 minutes. Cool eggs thoroughly under cold running water for 5 minutes. Lightly crack each egg shell by rolling on a hard surface. Shell should be cracked all over, but do not remove.

Bring 4 cups of water to the boil, add tea leaves, salt and five spice powder. Add cracked eggs. Simmer, covered, for approximately 30 minutes longer (overnight if possible). Drain, cool and shell. The whites of eggs will have a marbled pattern on them. Cut into quarters and serve with a dipping sauce.

SERVES: 12–18 as part of a selection of hors d'oeuvres

# SPRING ROLLS

*These crisp fried rolls are popular as snacks or part of a meal.*

## INGREDIENTS

12 water chestnuts

•

6 spring onions (scallions)

•

125 g (4 oz) fresh bean sprouts

•

1 small Chinese cabbage
(wongah bak)

•

2 tablespoons peanut oil

•

½ teaspoon crushed garlic

•

½ teaspoon grated fresh ginger

•

3 cups minced Gluten
(see page 437)

•

1 tablespoon light soy sauce

•

1 teaspoon salt

•

3 teaspoons cornflour (cornstarch)

Chop the water chestnuts and spring onions. Pinch the tails from the bean sprouts. Shred crisp leaf ribs of the cabbage to give 2 cups (8 oz).

Heat a wok, add 1 tablespoon of peanut oil and fry the garlic and ginger over low heat until fragrant but do not brown. Add the minced gluten, increase the heat and stir fry for 2 minutes. Remove from the wok to a large mixing bowl.

Heat the remaining tablespoon of peanut oil in the wok and fry the vegetables for 2 minutes. Add the soy sauce and salt. Make a space in the centre and stir in cornflour mixed with 1 tablespoon of cold water. Stir until the sauce boils and thickens. Transfer from the wok to the gluten mixture. Add the sesame oil and mix well. Allow to cool.

Put 2 tablespoons of the filling at one end of each spring roll wrapper and roll it up, turning in the ends so that the filling is completely enclosed. Dampen the edges with water and press to seal.

Heat plenty of oil in a wok and fry the spring rolls a

1 teaspoon sesame oil

•

1 packet frozen spring roll pastry,
thawed in wrapping

•

peanut oil for deep-frying

few at a time until golden. Drain on absorbent paper and
serve immediately with chilli sauce.

MAKES: 20

# SAVOURY PANCAKE ROLL

### INGREDIENTS

#### PANCAKES

2 egg yolks

•

1 cup (8 fl oz) milk

•

1 cup (8 fl oz) water

•

1½ cups (6 oz) plain (all-purpose) flour

•

oil, for frying

•

egg white and breadcrumbs for coating

#### FILLING

500 g (1 lb) carrots

•

500 g (1 lb) green beans

•

1 cup (5 oz) chopped onions

•

1 cup (5 oz) diced celery

•

1 cup (8 fl oz) milk

•

250 g (8 oz) canned nutmeat (or nutloaf made from nuts and soya beans, available at specialty health food stores)

•

salt

•

soy sauce

•

nutmeg and pepper to taste

•

2 teaspoons plain (all-purpose) flour

•

2 teaspoons soft butter

•

3 hard-boiled eggs, diced

To make the pancakes, beat the egg yolks, add milk and water, then gradually add the flour, beating until the batter is smooth. Rub a non-stick 20 cm (8 in) frying pan lightly with oil, and cook pancakes on fairly low heat. Stack them as they are cooked, then prepare filling.

Dice the carrots and slice the beans. Heat a little oil in a saucepan and fry the onions until golden brown. Add the carrots, beans, celery, milk and canned nutmeat. Season to taste with salt, soy sauce, nutmeg and pepper. Cook until the vegetables are just tender, then add flour and butter mixed together to thicken the liquid. Cool and add the hard-boiled eggs.

Put a spoonful of filling on each pancake, roll and turn in the edges to enclose the filling. Dip in beaten egg white, then in breadcrumbs, and shallow-fry in hot oil until golden brown. Serve hot.

NOTE: The pancake rolls may be prepared ahead and fried just before serving.

SERVES: 6

# CORN FRITTERS

## INGREDIENTS

375 g (12 oz) fresh whole kernel corn
(frozen or canned)

•

½ cup (2 oz) plain (all-purpose) flour

•

½ cup (2 oz) ground rice (see Note)

•

¼ teaspoon baking powder

•

½ teaspoon salt

•

1 teaspoon ground coriander

•

½ teaspoon ground cumin

•

¼ teaspoon laos powder (optional)

•

½ teaspoon chilli powder (optional)

•

1 medium onion

•

1 clove garlic

•

pinch of salt

•

1 stalk celery

•

scant ½ cup water

•

1 egg, beaten

•

squeeze of lemon juice

•

oil for frying

Cut corn from cobs with a sharp knife, drain canned corn, or thaw frozen corn. Sift the flour, ground rice, baking powder, salt, coriander, cumin, laos and chilli powder into a bowl.

Quarter the onion and cut into very thin slices. Crush the garlic to a smooth paste with a little salt. Dice celery finely. Mix together the water, beaten egg and lemon juice, and add to the flour mixture, beating until smooth. Stir in the corn, onion, garlic and celery.

Heat vegetable oil in a frying pan to a depth of 12 mm (½ in). When oil is hot, drop large tablespoons of mixture into the oil, spreading it with the back of the spoon to make a circle about 7.5 cm (3 in) across. Fry until the underside of fritter is golden brown, then turn with tongs and fry other side. Lift out and drain on absorbent paper placed on a wire rack. This keeps the fritters crisp.

NOTE:  Without the chilli powder the fritters are milder in flavour, but if you like a little excitement in the flavouring, add it. If ground rice is difficult to obtain use plain flour, but ground rice adds crispness.

MAKES: 12–14

# POT STICKERS

### INGREDIENTS

4 dried mushrooms

•

4 spring onions (scallions)

•

1 cup minced Gluten
(see page 437)

•

2 tablespoons finely chopped
bamboo shoot

•

½ teaspoon finely grated fresh ginger

•

½ teaspoon salt

•

2 teaspoons light soy sauce

•

2 teaspoons sesame oil

•

2 teaspoons cornflour (cornstarch)

•

8 tablespoons peanut oil
for cooking

### DOUGH

2 cups (8 oz) plain (all-purpose) flour

•

1 cup (8 fl oz) boiling water

Place the mushrooms in hot water and let them soak for 30 minutes. Discard the mushroom stems and chop the caps finely. Finely chop the spring onions, add to the minced gluten and mix in the mushrooms, bamboo shoot, ginger, salt, soy sauce and sesame oil. Blend the cornflour with 2 tablespoons of cold water and add it to gluten mixture, mixing together well.

To prepare the dough, measure the flour into a large bowl. Pour in the boiling water, stirring with chopsticks or the handle of a wooden spoon for a few minutes. As soon as it is cool enough, knead the dough well until it is soft and smooth, dusting with flour if necessary.

Shape dough into a log, then roll it out on a smooth surface into a sausage shape 2.5 cm (1 in) in diameter. Slice evenly into 30 pieces. Cover with a damp cloth to prevent it from drying out.

On a lightly floured board, roll each piece of dough into a circle 8 cm (3¼ in) in diameter. Make overlapping pleats around one side of the circle, then place a teaspoon of the filling in the centre. Dampen the edges of the dough with water and pinch them together to seal. Keep dumplings under a damp cloth but not touching each other, to prevent sticking.

Heat a large heavy, flat-bottomed frying pan over medium heat. Add 2 tablespoons of the peanut oil and when hot, tilt the pan to coat its entire base and a little way up the sides. Add half the dumplings, pleated side up. (It is easier to cook them in two batches). Lift the dumplings with a flat spatula to prevent them sticking and cook until they are golden underneath.

In a saucepan, bring 1 cup of water and 2 tablespoons of the oil to the boil, then pour this over the dumplings. Loosen any that are sticking. Bring the liquid to the boil again, cover the frying pan and cook for 5 minutes, then reduce the heat and cook for a further 5 minutes. Remove the frying pan lid and cook until the liquid evaporates and dumplings are brown and crusty underneath. Transfer the dumplings to a platter. Cook the remaining dumplings in the same way, using the remaining 4 tablespoons of oil and an extra cup of water. Serve with chilli sauce, soy sauce or red vinegar for dipping.

MAKES: 30

# PARSI SCRAMBLED EGGS

*Among India's many races and religions, it is the Parsi community who make the most use of eggs. A touch of Parsi genius with scrambled eggs turns a simple dish into a feast.*

### INGREDIENTS

6–8 eggs
•
4 tablespoons milk
•
¾ teaspoon salt
•
¼ teaspoon ground black pepper
•
2 tablespoons ghee
(clarified butter) or butter
•
6 spring onions (scallions) or
2 small white onions, finely chopped
•
2–3 fresh red or green chillies,
seeded or chopped
•
1 teaspoon finely grated fresh ginger
•
⅛ teaspoon ground turmeric
•
2 tablespoons chopped fresh
coriander leaves
•
1 ripe tomato, peeled and diced
(optional)
•
½ teaspoon ground cumin

### GARNISH
tomato wedges
•
sprig of fresh coriander leaves

Beat eggs until well mixed. Add the milk, salt and pepper. Heat ghee or butter in a large, heavy-based frying pan and cook the onions, chillies and ginger until soft. Add turmeric, coriander leaves and tomato, if used, and fry for 1–2 minutes longer. Stir in the egg mixture and the ground cumin. Cook over low heat, stirring and lifting the eggs as they begin to set on the base of the pan. Mix and cook until the eggs are of a creamy consistency—they should not be cooked until dry. Turn on to a serving plate and garnish with tomato and coriander. Serve with chapatis, parathas or toasted bread.

SERVES: 4–6

# SOUPS

In Eastern meals, soup is not served as a first course. It can be a whole light meal or it can be served alongside the main dish and sipped throughout the meal, or used to moisten a bowl of rice.

## SHANGHAI EGG POUCH SOUP

*In the original version from China there is minced pork in the egg pouches, but high-protein tempeh or gluten takes its place.*

### INGREDIENTS

125 g (4 oz) bean thread or cellophane noodles
•
6 dried Chinese mushrooms
•
half a Chinese cabbage (wongah bak)
•
8 cups (64 fl oz) Vegetable Stock (see page 448)

### EGG POUCHES

½ cup chopped tempeh or cooked and minced Gluten (see page 437)
•
1 clove garlic, crushed
•
1 spring onion (scallion), finely chopped
•
¼ teaspoon finely grated fresh ginger
•
½ teaspoon salt
•
1 teaspoon cornflour (cornstarch)
•
3 eggs
•
pinch of salt

Soak the noodles in hot water for 20 minutes and drain. Soak the mushrooms in hot water for 30 minutes, then drain. Discard the stems and cut the caps into quarters. Wash the cabbage and cut it into thick slices.

To make the pouches, combine the tempeh or gluten with the garlic, spring onion, ginger, salt, cornflour and mix well. In a separate bowl, beat the eggs with 1 tablespoon of cold water and a pinch of salt. Add a little beaten egg to moisten.

Lightly oil a ladle and hold it over a low gas flame. Pour in about ¼ cup (4 tablespoons) of the beaten egg and swirl to give an even, thick coating of egg, pouring the excess egg back into the bowl. Put a teaspoon of the filling mixture on one side of the egg and fold the other side over, sealing the edge if necessary with a little of the uncooked egg. The pouches can also be cooked in a heavy-based frying pan instead of a ladle but the shape will not be as good. Place on a plate when made.

To cook the soup, heat the stock in a clay pot or flameproof casserole and season with salt if necessary. Add noodles, return to the boil and simmer for 5 minutes. Arrange the egg pouches in the pot and simmer for a further 5 minutes. In the centre, place the sliced cabbage and the mushrooms and simmer the soup for 5 minutes more.

NOTE: This dish can be prepared ahead to the stage where the noodles have been cooked in the soup. Have the egg pouches, cabbage and mushrooms ready in the refrigerator. About 20 minutes before serving, reheat the soup and continue with the recipe.

SERVES: 6–8

# CHINESE VEGETARIAN COMBINATION SOUP

*This is the kind of soup that makes a light meal in itself.*

## INGREDIENTS

8 dried Chinese mushrooms
•
2 tablespoons dried wood
(cloud ear) fungus
•
1 square pressed bean curd
•
2 tablespoons light soy sauce
•
2 teaspoons sesame oil
•
1 teaspoon sugar
•
2 small carrots
•
12 green beans
•
125 g (4 oz) snow peas (mangetout)
•
8 leaves Chinese cabbage
(wongah bak)
•
250 g (8 oz) broccoli
•
375 g (12 oz) fine egg noodles
•
2 tablespoons peanut oil
•
12 spring onions (scallions), chopped
•
2 teaspoons finely chopped garlic
•
3 tablespoons cornflour (cornstarch)
•
3 eggs, beaten

### SEASONINGS
2 tablespoons light soy sauce
•
3 tablespoons Chinese wine or
dry sherry
•
2 teaspoons sesame oil
•
1 teaspoon salt
•
¼ teaspoon ground white pepper

Soak the dried mushrooms in hot water for 30 minutes. Discard the mushroom stems and cut the caps into fine strips. Reserve the soaking water to use as part of the liquid. Soak the wood fungus in cold water for 10 minutes, then cut into small pieces, trimming off any gritty portions.

Cut the bean curd into small dice or strips. Combine the light soy sauce, sesame oil and sugar, and toss the bean curd in this mixture.

Wash the carrots and cut wedge-shaped sections out of them, lengthways, then slice across to give flower shapes. String and slice the beans very thinly. String the snow peas. Cut leaf ribs of the cabbage into bite-size pieces. Finely shred the leaves, keeping leaf ribs separate from the shredded leaves. Slice broccoli stems and divide head into florets.

Cook the noodles until just tender, drain and divide among six soup bowls.

Heat a wok, add the peanut oil and when hot, fry the chopped spring onions and garlic for a few seconds, stirring. Do not let them brown. Add the mushrooms, the sliced leaf ribs of Chinese cabbage and the broccoli stems, and fry for 1 minute longer. Add 6 cups (48 fl oz) of water including the mushroom soaking water, and the seasoning Bring to the boil and simmer, covered, for 5 minutes. Add the carrots and beans and cook for a further 3 minutes, then add the snow peas, wood fungus, shredded cabbage leaves and broccoli florets and cook 1 minute longer.

Dissolve the cornflour in 3 tablespoons of cold water and stir it into the soup until it boils and thickens. Drizzle in the beaten egg and stir gently so that it sets in fine shreds. Add the bean curd and heat through. Ladle the soup mixture over the noodles and serve hot.

SERVES: 6

# SOUTH EAST ASIAN MENUS

*Asian food is particularly suitable for buffet style meals since the dishes are all served at once, not divided into courses. For another menu see Festive Yellow Rice on page 263 which, with the suggested accompaniments, makes a very special meal. The flavours in these menus are representative of Indonesian, Malaysia, Singapore, Burma and Sri Lanka.*

Gado Gado *page 340*

Fragrant Rice *page 269*

Egg and Coconut Curry *page 306*

Bean Sayur *page 311*

Fresh pineapple


Split Pea Fritters *page 243*

Steamed Rice *page 270*

Eggs in Chilli Sauce *page 299*

Mixed Vegetables with Coconut *page 334*

Savoury Potatoes and Peas *page 333*

Cucumber Sambal *page 351*

Rice Vermicelli with Eggs and Almonds
*page 276*

Vegetable Curry *page 308*

Eggplant Pickle *page 350*

*or*

Eggplant Yoghurt Relish *page 314*

Spicy Coconut Custard *page 372*

Burmese Style Sour Soup *page 254*

Chilli Fried Rice *page 264*

Savoury Tempeh *page 436*

Bean Sayur *page 311*

Fresh fruit

# LENTIL SOUP

### INGREDIENTS

1 cup (6 oz) dried red lentils

•

2 medium onions

•

1 teaspoon sliced garlic

•

1 small stick cinnamon

•

¼ teaspoon whole black peppercorns

•

2 bay leaves

•

6 cups (48 fl oz) water

•

1 tablespoon ghee (clarified butter)
or oil

•

6 or 8 curry leaves

•

1 teaspoon salt or to taste

•

½ teaspoon Garam Masala
(see page 456)

•

1 cup (8 fl oz) coconut milk
(optional)

The common red lentil, available in every supermarket, is probably the quickest and easiest to cook and makes the base for this spicy soup.

Pick over the lentils, discarding any discoloured ones or small stones. Wash lentils well, pouring off any that float. Drain and put into a saucepan with 1 onion and ½ teaspoon garlic, the cinnamon, peppercorns and bay leaves. Add water and bring to the boil. Cover and simmer until lentils and onion are soft. Strain through a sieve, to purée the lentils and discard the spices.

Slice remaining onion very thinly. Heat ghee or oil in a saucepan and fry the onion and curry leaves until onion is very brown. Add the lentils, salt and garam masala and simmer for a minute or two. If a richer soup is preferred, add the coconut milk at the end and stir until heated through.

NOTE: Coconut milk may be purchased, in some countries, in cans or in powdered form that is reconstituted by stirring into water. (See page 443 for information on coconut milk, if unavailable.)

SERVES: 4

# SOUR SOUP, BURMESE STYLE

### INGREDIENTS

2 teaspoons sesame oil or corn oil

•

1 onion, finely sliced lengthways

•

2 cloves garlic, crushed

•

¼ teaspoon ground turmeric

•

2 or 3 green tomatoes, chopped

•

1 cup (1½ oz) torn spinach or
other greens

•

4–6 cups (32–48 fl oz) rhubarb stock
or boiling water (see Note)

•

salt to taste

Heat oil in a saucepan and when very hot, fry the onion, garlic and turmeric, stirring, for 30 seconds. Add the tomatoes and spinach, stir well, then add the stock or water and bring to the boil. Cover and simmer until vegetables are tender. Taste and add salt as necessary. Serve with rice.

NOTE: Sour greens, such as sorrel, rosella or tamarind leaves are used to make the stock for this soup (or substitute green tomatoes or rhubarb stalks). If rhubarb stalks are used, cut them into short lengths and boil, then strain and use the liquid combined with spinach or other green leaves. **Do not use rhubarb leaves as they are poisonous.**

SERVES: 4–6

# MILD SOUP, BURMESE STYLE

## INGREDIENTS

4–6 cups (32–48 fl oz) Vegetable
Stock (see page 448) or water

•

2 medium onions, peeled
and sliced finely

•

3 peppercorns

•

2–3 cups (about 12–16 oz) prepared
vegetables

Bring stock or water to the boil. Add onions and peppercorns and boil for a further 5 minutes. Last of all, add half a cup of the vegetables chosen to each cup of stock or water. Pumpkin and cauliflower may take about 5 minutes to cook sufficiently but the other vegetables should be done in about 3 minutes. Add salt if necessary.

NOTE:   Any of the following vegetables may be used in this recipe: marrow (summer squash), peeled and cut in thin strips; zucchini (courgettes), cut thinly in discs; pumpkin, diced; okra, topped and tailed and sliced diagonally; cauliflower, each floret sliced lengthways; cabbage, shredded finely; Chinese cabbage or other leaves, shredded crossways.

SERVES: 4–6

# COCONUT MILK SOUP

*A favourite in Sri Lanka, Malaysia and Indonesia, this is not a first course soup but is served as an accompaniment to be spooned over rice or to be sipped between mouthfuls of rice and curry. If a less rich soup is required, substitute skimmed milk for part of the coconut milk.*

## INGREDIENTS

1 tablespoon fenugreek seeds

•

1 large onion, finely chopped

•

12 curry leaves

•

1 small stick cinnamon

•

2 fresh green chillies, slit and seeded

•

¼ teaspoon ground turmeric

•

½ teaspoon salt

•

2½ cups (20 fl oz) thin coconut milk
(see page 443)

•

2 cups (16 fl oz) thick coconut milk
(see page 443)

•

lemon juice to taste

Wash the fenugreek seeds and soak in cold water for at least 30 minutes. Put into a saucepan with all the ingredients except the thick coconut milk and lemon juice. Simmer on very low heat until onions have reduced to a pulp and the milk has been thickened by the fenugreek seeds. Stir well, add thick coconut milk and heat without boiling, then stir in lemon juice and add more salt if required

NOTE:   If a thicker soup is preferred, add a few slices of potato at the start

SERVES: 6

# SZECHWAN SOUP

*There is a good amount of protein in this soup from the bean curd and eggs.*

## INGREDIENTS

125 g (4 oz) bean starch noodles
•
15 dried Chinese mushrooms
•
1 tablespoon dried wood (cloud ear) fungus
•
1 tablespoon oil
•
1 tablespoon dark soy sauce
•
2 teaspoons sugar
•
¼ cup (2 fl oz) hot water
•
½ cup (4 oz) fresh bean curd, diced small
•
6 cups (48 fl oz) Vegetable Stock (see page 448)
•

Cook the noodles in boiling water for 15 minutes, drain then cut into short lengths. Soak mushrooms in hot water for 30 minutes. Cut off and discard stems, then slice caps finely. Soak wood fungus in water for 10 minutes to soften, trim off any gritty portions and cut remaining fungus into small pieces. Set aside.

Heat oil in a saucepan and fry mushrooms, stirring constantly, until they start to brown. Add dark soy sauce, sugar and ¼ cup (2 fl oz) water and simmer, covered, until mushrooms have absorbed almost all the liquid. Add bean curd and stir fry for 1 minute. Add stock and noodles, bring to the boil, then reduce heat and simmer for 3 minutes. Add light soy, vinegar, wine and chilli oil.

Dribble beaten eggs into simmering soup, stirring constantly so that the egg separates into fine shreds. Mix cornflour smoothly with cold water, then add to soup away from heat. Return to heat and stir constantly until soup

1 tablespoon light soy sauce

•

1 tablespoon Chinese sweet vinegar
or other mild vinegar

•

1 tablespoon Chinese wine or
dry sherry

•

1 teaspoon chilli oil

•

2 eggs, beaten

•

1½ tablespoons cornflour
(cornstarch)

•

6 tablespoons cold water

•

salt and pepper to taste

has thickened. Season to taste with pepper and salt. Put a spoonful of wood fungus in the bottom of each soup bowl and pour a ladle of the boiling soup over. Serve immediately.

SERVES: 6–8

# TWELVE VARIETIES SOUP

INGREDIENTS

2 tablespoons oil

•

2 onions, sliced

•

2 cloves garlic, sliced

•

1 small choko (chayote)

•

¼ cup (1 oz) bean sprouts

•

¼ cup (1 oz) shredded cabbage

•

¼ cup (1 oz) chopped cauliflower

•

¼ cup (1 oz) sliced green beans

•

¼ cup (1 oz) dried mushrooms,
soaked

•

¼ cup (1 oz) dried wood
(cloud ear) fungus, soaked

•

1 sprig tender celery leaves

•

2 spring onions (scallions)

•

1 tablespoon soy sauce

•

2 eggs

•

salt and pepper to taste

Heat oil in wok and fry onions and garlic. Add all the vegetables together with soy sauce and cook briefly with lid on. When vegetables are slightly wilted, transfer contents to a large saucepan. Add 4 cups (32 fl oz) water and bring to boil rapidly. Just before serving, add unbeaten eggs to the rapidly boiling soup and stir. Add salt and pepper to taste just before serving.

SERVES: 4–6

# SOUR SOUP

*In Asia, this kind of soup is served as a digestive. It is wonderfully effective but I wouldn't suggest you try it as a first course—it's not that kind of soup.*

### INGREDIENTS

2 tablespoons ground coriander

•

1 tablespoon ground cumin

•

1 dried chilli (optional)

•

¼ teaspoon whole black peppercorns

•

8 curry leaves

•

5 cups (40 fl oz) hot water

•

1 tablespoon tamarind pulp

•

1 medium onion, finely sliced

•

4 cloves garlic

Put coriander, cumin, chilli, peppercorns and curry leaves into a saucepan and dry roast over medium heat, shaking the pan or stirring constantly, until the spices smell aromatic. Add the water, tamarind, onion and garlic, and bring to the boil. Simmer for 20 minutes or until onions and garlic are soft. Serve for sipping between mouthfuls of rice.

SERVES: 4

# MILD SOUP WITH CELLOPHANE NOODLES, THAI STYLE

### INGREDIENTS

small bundle cellophane noodles (see note)

•

5 cups (40 fl oz) Vegetable Stock (see page 448)

•

1 onion, finely sliced

•

2 cloves garlic, finely sliced

•

6 button mushrooms, sliced

•

1 tablespoon light soy sauce

•

1 medium zucchini (courgette)

•

salt and pepper to taste

Soak noodles in hot water and when softened, cut into short lengths. Bring stock to the boil, then add onion and garlic. Add the drained noodles and cook until they are swollen and soft. Stir in the mushrooms, soy sauce and zucchini and cook just until tender. Taste and add salt and pepper as required. Serve hot.

NOTE: It is possible to buy small bundles of mung bean thread or cellophane noodles, approximately 50 g (1½ oz), and this is much easier than trying to cut off some from a big bundle.

SERVES: 4

# ASIAN STAPLE DISHES

Asian meals don't have main courses because all the food is served at once, but some dishes can be classified as main dishes.

Some of the dishes in this section include a high protein food such as lentils, milk products, nuts or seeds.

The all-important rice, staple food of Asia, is the background against which complementary dishes are savoured. It would be unthinkable to serve an Asian meal, no matter how many different dishes it comprised, without the central dish of rice. (see To Cook Rice, page 438)

Whether eating Chinese, Indian, South-East Asian or Thai food, rice is always the main item and is eaten in greater quantity than any of the accompanying dishes. In this context, rice is a main dish. In some countries noodles supplement the rice, and at some meals take the place of rice. They may be wheat noodles, rice noodles or bean starch noodles, and in Japanese cuisine, buckwheat noodles. While this makes for variety, nothing ever supplants rice as the basic food. This chapter offers the important rice and noodle dishes on which Asian meals are based.

## MUSHROOM PILAF

*Spicy Indian flavours combined with mushrooms and rice.*

### INGREDIENTS

250 g (8 oz) mushrooms
•
2 cups (14 oz) long grain rice
•
2 tablespoons oil or ghee
(clarified butter)
•
2 teaspoons black mustard seeds
•
½ teaspoon cumin seeds
•
¼ teaspoon black cumin
(kalonji) seeds
•
small piece cinnamon stick
•
5 cardamom pods
•
1 onion, finely chopped
•
1 or 2 cloves garlic, finely chopped
•
3 cups (24 fl oz) hot water
•
1½ teaspoons salt or to taste

Wipe over the mushrooms if necessary (don't wash or peel) and cut them in thick slices. Wash the rice well and leave to drain in a colander. In a heavy-based saucepan, heat the oil and add the different seeds, cinnamon and cardamom. Fry until the mustard seeds begin to pop, then add the onion and garlic and fry, stirring occasionally, until onion is soft.

Add mushrooms and rice and fry, stirring, for 1 minute. Pour in the hot water, add salt and stir, then bring to the boil over high heat. Cover pan with a well fitting lid, turn heat as low as possible, and cook for 20 minutes. Remove from heat and allow to stand, uncovered, for a few minutes before forking the mushrooms through the rice, as they will have risen to the top.

Transfer to serving dish with a metal spoon and serve hot, accompanied by curries, or as a light main dish with an omelette or fried egg.

SERVES: 4–6

# SEMOLINA PILAF

*The Indian flavours in this dish are guaranteed to tempt appetites even of non-vegetarians.*

## INGREDIENTS

4 tablespoons vegetable oil
•
2 cups (10 oz) coarse semolina
•
1 teaspoon black mustard seeds
•
10 curry leaves
•
2 tablespoons split mung dhal
or other split lentils
•
2 dried red chillies (optional)
•
1 large onion, finely chopped
•
1 red or green chilli, sliced
•
1 tablespoon grated fresh ginger
•
2 cups (about 8–16 oz) diced
vegetables
(broccoli, carrots, capsicum/pepper)
•
2 cups (16 fl oz) hot water
•
1½ teaspoons salt
•
2 teaspoons butter
•
lemon wedges for serving

Heat 1 tablespoon oil in a heavy-based saucepan and fry the semolina, stirring constantly, until pale golden. Turn the semolina into a bowl and wipe out the pan with absorbent paper.

Heat remaining oil in the pan and fry the mustard seeds, curry leaves, dhal and dried chillies, broken into pieces.

When dhal is golden, add onion and fry, stirring, until soft and starting to colour. Add fresh chilli, ginger and vegetables, stir and cook for 2 minutes. Add water and salt and bring to the boil.

Add semolina and stir constantly until it boils. Keep stirring until quite dry. Cover pan tightly and cook on very low heat until semolina is cooked through, about 8 minutes. Stir the butter through and serve warm with a wedge of lemon for squeezing over each serving.

SERVES: 4

SEMOLINA PILAF

# FRIED RICE

*An Indonesian version of the ubiquitous fried rice found throughout Asia.*

### INGREDIENTS

3 eggs

salt and pepper to taste

oil for frying

2 medium onions

2 cloves garlic

4 cups cold cooked rice
(9 oz uncooked)

6 spring onions (scallions),
thinly sliced

2 tablespoons light soy sauce

3 tablespoons onion flakes

1 green cucumber, thinly sliced

dried tempeh crisps

oil for deep frying

Beat eggs with salt and pepper to taste. Heat very little oil in a frying pan and make an omelette with half the beaten eggs. Turn on to a plate to cool. Do not fold omelette. Repeat process with remaining beaten eggs. When cool, put one omelette on top of the other, roll up and cut into thin strips.

Chop onions roughly, put into a blender container with the garlic and blend to a paste. If blender is not available, finely chop onions and crush garlic, then mix together.

Heat 3 tablespoons of oil in a large frying pan or wok and fry the blended ingredients until cooked. Add 2 tablespoons more oil and when hot, stir in the rice and spring onions, tossing and mixing thoroughly until very hot. Sprinkle with soy sauce and mix evenly.

Serve the fried rice garnished with strips of omelette, fried onion flakes and cucumber. Surround with deep-fried tempeh crisps.

NOTE: Most Asian grocery stores sell tempeh crisps.

SERVES: 6–8

# GHEE RICE

### INGREDIENTS

2 cups (14 oz) Basmati or other long
grain rice

2½ tablespoons ghee
(clarified butter)

1 large onion, finely sliced

4 whole cloves

6 cardamom pods, bruised

1 cinnamon stick

3½ cups (28 fl oz) Vegetable Stock
(see page 448) or water

2½ teaspoons salt

Wash rice well and drain for at least 30 minutes. Heat ghee in a saucepan and fry onion until golden, add spices and drained rice. Fry, stirring with slotted metal spoon, for 5 minutes over moderate heat. Add hot vegetable stock and salt, and bring to the boil.

Reduce heat to very low, cover pan tightly with lid and cook for 15–20 minutes without lifting lid. At end of cooking time, uncover and allow steam to escape for 5 minutes. Gently fluff up rice with a fork, removing whole spices.

When transferring rice to a serving dish, again use a slotted metal spoon to avoid crushing grains of rice. Serve hot, accompanied by curries, pickles and sambals.

SERVES: 4–5

# FESTIVE YELLOW RICE

*This is a special occasion dish in Indonesia and other Asian countries—
rice cooked in coconut milk, coloured and flavoured with turmeric. It is shaped
into a cone, surrounded by garnishes and served with complementary dishes.*

### INGREDIENTS

1 kg (2 lb) long grain rice

•

4 tablespoons oil

•

2 large onions, finely sliced

•

3 cloves garlic, finely chopped

•

8 cups (64 fl oz) coconut milk

•

4 teaspoons salt

•

2 teaspoons ground turmeric

•

3 daun salam or 6 curry leaves

•

2 strips pandanus leaf (optional)

•

banana leaves or bamboo leaves
for serving

### ACCOMPANIMENTS

Almond-Crusted Tempeh
Croquettes (see page 119)

•

Fried Beancurd with Peanuts
(see page 295)

•

Chilli Fried Cauliflower
(see page 316)

•

Green Bean Sambal (see page 356)

### GARNISH

Marbled Tea Eggs (see page 244)

•

2 green cucumbers

•

3 fresh red chillies

•

3 fresh green chillies

If rice needs washing, wash well beforehand and allow to drain at least 1 hour.

Heat oil in a large saucepan with a well fitting lid. Fry onions and garlic until onions are soft and golden, stirring frequently to prevent burning. Add rice and fry for 1–2 minutes, then add coconut milk, salt, turmeric and leaves for flavouring. Bring to the boil, stirring with a long spoon. As soon as liquid comes to the boil, turn heat very low, cover tightly with lid and allow to cook for 20 minutes. Uncover and quickly stir in with a fork, any coconut milk that remains unabsorbed around edge of pan. Replace lid and leave on low heat for a further 3 minutes.

Turn off heat, uncover and allow steam to escape and rice to cool slightly. Remove leaves used for flavouring and gently fork rice on to a large platter or a tray lined with well washed banana leaves or bamboo leaves. Shape into a cone, pressing firmly. Use pieces of greased banana leaf or foil to do this. Surround rice with all the accompaniments, which should be made beforehand, then garnish.

To make the garnish, shell the marbled eggs and cut each in two lengthways. Score the skin of the cucumbers with a fork and slice very thinly. Cut chillies into thin diagonal slices. Flip out seeds with point of small knife. Scatter the sliced chillies over the cone, and put sliced cucumbers and marbled eggs around base of cone. Garnish top with a chilli flower made by slitting a chilli and soaking in iced water for some hours.

SERVES: 8–10

# RICE WITH LENTILS

*In India this is a main dish and is accompanied by curries, chutneys, pappadams and invariably a portion of fresh yoghurt, either by itself or mixed with sliced cucumbers or bananas.*

### INGREDIENTS

1 cup (6 oz) dried red lentils

•

2½ tablespoons oil or ghee
(clarified butter)

•

2 large onions, sliced thinly

•

1 cup (7 oz) long grain rice

•

3½ cups (28 fl oz) hot water

•

2½ teaspoons salt

•

¼ teaspoon each ground black
pepper, cloves, cardamom,
cinnamon and nutmeg

Wash the lentils well, removing any that float. Drain thoroughly until dry.

Heat oil or ghee in a medium-size saucepan with a well fitting lid. Fry the onions over medium heat, stirring occasionally until golden brown. Remove half the fried onion and set aside. Add lentils and rice to pan and fry, stirring, for 3 minutes. Add hot water, salt and spices. Stir well and bring to the boil quickly.

Turn heat very low, cover tightly and cook without lifting lid for 20 minutes or until the liquid has been absorbed and rice and lentils are cooked. Serve on a dish with the reserved onions scattered over the top.

SERVES: 4

# CHILLI FRIED RICE

### INGREDIENTS

4 cups cold cooked rice
(9 oz uncooked)

•

3 tablespoons peanut oil

•

1 large onion, finely chopped

•

1 fresh red chilli and 1 fresh
green chilli, seeded and sliced

•

1 tablespoon Thai style
Red Curry Paste (see page 452)

•

2 eggs, beaten

•

pepper and salt to taste

•

3 tablespoons light soy sauce

•

1 cup (2 oz) chopped spring onions
(scallions), including green tops

•

chilli flowers and ½ cup (1 oz)
chopped fresh coriander leaves for
garnish

Heat oil in a wok and fry onion and sliced chillies until soft. Stir in the curry paste and fry until the oil separates from the mixture. Add rice and toss thoroughly until coated with the curry mixture and heated through. Push rice to side of wok and pour the beaten eggs, seasoned with salt and pepper, into the centre. Stir until eggs start to set, then mix through the rice, tossing on high heat until eggs are cooked. Sprinkle light soy sauce evenly over the rice and mix well, then remove from heat. Stir the spring onions through. Garnish with coriander leaves and chilli flowers and serve.

SERVES: 4

# SPICY RICE WITH CASHEWS

### INGREDIENTS

3 cups (21 oz) long grain rice

•

3 tablespoons ghee (clarified butter)

•

3 tablespoons oil

•

3 large onions, finely sliced

•

5 cardamom pods, bruised

•

2 small sticks cinnamon

•

6 whole cloves

•

20 whole black peppercorns

•

½ teaspoon ground turmeric

•

5 cups (40 fl oz) hot water

•

3 teaspoons salt

•

1 cup (5 oz) raw cashew nuts

•

2 sprigs fresh curry leaves or
20 dried curry leaves

•

3 fresh green chillies,
seeded and sliced

•

2 teaspoons black mustard seeds

### GARNISH
2 tablespoons chopped
fresh coriander

•

½ cup (2 oz) freshly grated coconut

Wash rice well and leave to drain for at least 30 minutes. In a large, heavy-based saucepan, heat half the ghee and oil and fry the onions and whole spices until onions are golden brown, stirring frequently. Remove half the onions and set aside for garnish. Add turmeric and rice to pan and fry, stirring with slotted metal spoon, until all the grains are coated with the ghee. Add the hot water and salt, stir well and bring to the boil. Cover with a tight-fitting lid and turn heat very low. Cook for 20–25 minutes without lifting lid.

Heat remaining ghee and oil in a small pan and fry the cashew nuts until golden. Remove with slotted spoon. Fry the curry leaves, green chillies and mustard seeds until the seeds pop. Pour over the rice and lightly fork through. Dish up rice and garnish with the fried cashews, chopped coriander leaves and grated fresh coconut.

SERVES: 6

# COMBINATION FRIED RICE

INGREDIENTS

INGREDIENTS

2 cups (14 oz) short grain rice

2½ cups (20 fl oz) water

12 dried Chinese mushrooms

2 leeks

4 stalks celery

250 g (8 oz) green beans

125 g (4 oz) bean sprouts (optional)

3 tablespoons peanut oil

1 tablespoon sesame oil

1 teaspoon finely grated fresh ginger

2 cloves garlic, finely grated

1 cup (2 oz) coarsely grated carrot

1 cup sliced bamboo shoots
(optional)

1 cup (2 oz) chopped spring onions
(scallions)

½ cup (4 fl oz) mushroom liquid

2 tablespoons light soy sauce

salt to taste

Cook rice in the 2½ cups (20 fl oz) of water the day before required, or cook some hours ahead and allow to cool. With the fingers, separate grains and spread out rice so grains dry. Refrigerate.

Soak mushrooms in hot water for 30 minutes, then squeeze out as much liquid as possible and reserve liquid. With a sharp knife, cut off and discard stems, cut mushroom caps into thin slices. Wash leeks very well in cold water, making sure all grit is washed away, then cut into thin slices. Use the white portion and only a little of the green leaves. String celery and green beans and cut into very thin diagonal slices. Wash and drain bean sprouts and pick off any brown tails.

Heat peanut oil and sesame oil in a large wok or very large frying pan, add ginger and garlic and fry, stirring well, for 30 seconds. Add mushrooms, leeks, celery, beans and carrots and stir-fry over high heat for 3 minutes. Stir in bean sprouts and bamboo shoot and fry 1 minute longer. Add rice, toss and fry over high heat until heated through, then mix in spring onions. Mix mushroom liquid and soy sauce together, and sprinkle evenly over the rice. Continue tossing until well mixed and season to taste with salt. Serve hot.

SERVES: 6

# SIMPLE FRIED RICE

INGREDIENTS

2 tablespoons peanut oil

3–4 cups cold cooked rice
(7–9 oz uncooked)

2 tablespoons light soy sauce

6 spring onions (scallions),
sliced diagonally

Heat oil in wok until very hot. Add rice and stir-fry until grains are all separate and lightly coloured. Sprinkle with sauce and toss to mix evenly. Add sliced spring onions and toss over heat for 1 minute longer. Serve hot.

SERVES: 3–4

# OIL RICE

## INGREDIENTS

2 cups (14 oz) glutinous rice

•

3 large onions

•

1½ teaspoons turmeric

•

6 tablespoons oil

•

4 cups (32 fl oz) hot water

•

2 teaspoons salt

•

4 tablespoons toasted sesame seeds

Wash rice well and leave to drain and dry. Slice onions thinly, keeping them uniform in thickness. Sprinkle turmeric over onions and mix lightly. Heat oil in a medium-size saucepan and fry onions until brown. Remove two-thirds of the onions and set aside for garnish. Add rice to pan and stir until it is well mixed with the oil. Add water and salt, stir well and bring to the boil. Turn heat very low, cover tightly and cook for 20 minutes by which time the rice should be cooked and the water completely absorbed.

Some people like a crust on the rice. To encourage a crust to form, leave the rice on low heat for 5–10 minutes longer until a slight crackling sound is heard. Serve hot, garnished with fried onion and accompanied by the sesame seeds lightly bruised and mixed with a little salt. This is generally served as a dish by itself, not with curries.

SERVES: 4–6

# RICE WITH LENTILS AND TAMARIND

## INGREDIENTS

½ cup (3 oz) toor dhal

•

1 cup (7 oz) long grain rice

•

2¾ cups (22 fl oz) water

•

¼ teaspoon ground turmeric

•

1½ teaspoons salt

•

3 tablespoons oil

•

½ teaspoon asafoetida (optional)

•

2 tablespoons coriander seeds

•

4 dried red chillies,
stalks and seeds removed

•

small piece cinnamon stick

Wash the dhal and rice, drain well, then put into a saucepan with water, turmeric and salt. Bring to the boil, cover and cook until water is absorbed, about 20 minutes.

Meanwhile, heat 3 teaspoons oil and fry the asafoetida (if used) for about 3 minutes. Remove the asafoetida and fry the coriander and chillies for 3–4 minutes. Put asafoetida, coriander, chillies, cinnamon, cloves and coconut into an electric blender, add just enough water to facilitate blending, and blend until spices form a paste.

Top and tail beans and cut into small pieces. Cook in lightly salted boiling water until almost tender. Drain, reserving liquid. Soak the tamarind pulp in ½ cup (4 fl oz) of this liquid, and squeeze to dissolve the pulp, then strain and discard seeds and fibres. If using instant tamarind, dissolve in the hot liquid.

Heat remaining oil in a saucepan and fry the mustard seeds and curry leaves until the seeds pop. Add beans,

20 cloves

•

3 tablespoons freshly grated or
desiccated coconut

•

500 g (1 lb) green beans

•

¼ cup tamarind pulp or
2 teaspoons instant tamarind

•

1½ tablespoons mustard seeds

•

12 curry leaves

•

2 tablespoons ghee (clarified butter)

•

¼ cup (1½ oz) raw cashews

tamarind liquid, turmeric, salt and spice paste, and bring to the boil. Cover and simmer for 5 minutes. Add the cooked dhal and rice, and stir well, taking care not to mash the grains. Heat the ghee in a small pan and fry the cashew nuts until golden. Drain. Pour the ghee over the rice and mix. Serve hot, garnished with the fried cashews.

NOTE: Slices of fried eggplant and potato are sometimes added to this dish.

SERVES: 4–5

# RICE VERMICELLI WITH DRIED MUSHROOMS

### INGREDIENTS

250 g (8 oz) rice vermicelli

6 leaves mustard cabbage
(gai choy)

•

2 medium potatoes

•

12 dried Chinese mushrooms

•

1 tablespoon dark soy sauce

•

2 teaspoons sugar

•

1 teaspoon sesame oil

•

1 clove garlic, crushed

•

1 teaspoon finely grated
fresh ginger

•

1 tablespoon Chinese wine
or dry sherry

•

1 tablespoon light soy sauce

•

salt to taste

•

3 tablespoons peanut oil

Soak the vermicelli for 10 minutes in hot water and drain in a colander. Wash the mustard cabbage, trim off the leaves and cut the leaf ribs into thin strips. Peel and dice the potatoes. Pour 1 cup (8 fl oz) boiling water over the mushrooms, and leave to soak for 30 minutes. Squeeze out and reserve the liquid, discard stems and cut the mushroom caps into thin slices. Put into a small saucepan with the dark soy sauce, sugar, sesame oil and half the soaking liquid, and cook for 5 minutes or until the liquid is almost absorbed.

Mix together the garlic, ginger, wine, light soy and remaining mushroom liquid.

Heat a wok, add the peanut oil and swirl to coat the sides of the wok. Add the potatoes and deep fry until they are golden brown. Re-heat the oil in the wok or add a little more if necessary and stir-fry the sliced cabbage for 1 minute, then add the mixed liquids and cook for a further 2 minutes. Add the vermicelli and toss until heated through. Add fried potatoes and the mushrooms, and toss to mix well. Serve quickly.

SERVES: 4

# FRAGRANT RICE

### INGREDIENTS

4½ cups (36 fl oz) coconut milk

•

½ teaspoon ground black pepper

•

1 teaspoon finely grated lemon rind
or 1 stalk fresh lemon grass

•

½ teaspoon ground nutmeg or mace

•

½ teaspoon ground cloves

•

1 daun salam or 3 curry leaves

•

2½ teaspoons salt

•

500 g (1 lb) long grain rice

Put the coconut milk with all the flavourings, spices and salt into a large saucepan with a well fitting lid. Bring slowly to the boil, uncovered. Stir in the rice and return to the boil, then turn heat very low, cover and steam for 20 minutes. Uncover, fork the rice lightly from around sides of pan, mixing in any coconut milk that has not been absorbed, then replace lid for 5 minutes. Serve hot with curries and hot sambals.

Serves: 6

# STEAMED RICE IN COCONUT MILK

## INGREDIENTS

500 g (1 lb) medium or
long grain rice

•

1¼ cups (10 fl oz) coconut milk

•

2½ teaspoons salt

Soak rice in cold water overnight. Drain rice, spread in top part of a steamer and steam over rapidly boiling water for 30 minutes. Halfway through steaming, stir rice and turn it so that the rice on the bottom comes to the top and vice versa.

Gently heat the coconut milk with the salt in a large saucepan, stirring. Do not boil. Add the steamed rice, stir well, cover tightly and let stand for a further 30 minutes, by which time the milk should be completely absorbed. Once more spread the rice in top part of steamer, bring water back to the boil and steam for 30 minutes, starting on high heat and gradually turning heat lower until in the end the water merely simmers. Serve hot with vegetable dishes, both mild and hot.

SERVES: 4–5

# RICE WITH MIXED LENTILS

## INGREDIENTS

1 cup (6 oz) mung dhal

•

½ cup (3 oz) dried red lentils

•

1½ cups (10 oz) Basmati or other
long grain rice

•

500 g (1 lb) fresh peas

•

1 tablespoon ghee (clarified butter)

•

3 tablespoons vegetable oil

•

6 cardamom pods, bruised

•

1 small stick cinnamon

•

4 small bay leaves

•

4 whole cloves

•

4 large onions, finely sliced

In a dry pan, roast the mung dhal, stirring constantly, until an even gold brown. Turn into a bowl and wash well, then leave to drain. Wash red lentils separately and leave to drain. If using Basmati rice or other rice that needs washing, wash well and leave to drain for at least 30 minutes. Meanwhile, shell the peas. There should be about ¾ cup (3½ oz) of shelled peas.

Heat the ghee and oil in a heavy-based saucepan. Add the cardamom pods, cinnamon, bay leaves and cloves, and the sliced onions. Fry over medium heat, stirring frequently, until the onions are golden brown. Transfer to a plate with a slotted spoon. To the oil left in the pan, add the ginger, chilli and cumin seeds. Fry, stirring, until ginger is golden. Stir in the rice and red lentils and fry, stirring, for 3 minutes. Add the turmeric and ground cumin, and fry for a further 2 minutes. Add fresh peas, mung dhal, water and salt, stir and bring to the boil. Return the cardamom, cinnamon, bay leaves and cloves to the pan. Turn heat very low, cover and cook for 30–35 minutes or until liquid is absorbed and

1 tablespoon finely grated
fresh ginger

•

1 fresh green chilli, seeded and sliced

•

1 teaspoon cumin seeds

•

½ teaspoon ground turmeric

•

1 teaspoon ground cumin

•

4 cups (32 fl oz) hot water

•

3 teaspoons salt or to taste

GARNISH
2 tablespoons chopped fresh
coriander (optional)

peas are tender. Transfer to serving dish with a metal spoon and garnish with the fried onions and the chopped fresh coriander, if used.

Serve with an accompaniment of peeled, diced tomatoes dressed with a pinch of chilli powder and salt to taste. Pickles or chutneys and a bowl of yoghurt complete the meal.

SERVES: 4–5

# RICE WITH YOGHURT, SOUTH INDIAN STYLE

*In southern India, this dish is often served as the finale to a festive meal, but it may also be presented as the main dish, accompanied by curries and pickles.*

## INGREDIENTS

2½ cups (1 lb) long grain rice

•

4 cups (32 fl oz) water

•

2½ teaspoons salt

•

2 tablespoons ghee (clarified butter)
or oil

•

1 teaspoon black cumin
(kalonji) seeds

•

1 teaspoon black mustard seeds

•

1 teaspoon urad dhal

•

¼ teaspoon asafoetida (optional)

•

3 fresh red or green chillies,
seeded and sliced

•

3 cups (24 fl oz) natural yoghurt

•

salt to taste

Put well washed and drained rice into a saucepan with the water and salt. Bring quickly to the boil, then cover tightly, turn heat very low and cook for 20 minutes without lifting lid.

In another pan, heat the ghee and fry the black cumin, mustard, dhal, asafoetida (if used) and chillies until the mustard seeds pop and the dhal is golden brown. Remove from heat, stir into the yoghurt and add a little salt to taste. Pour the yoghurt over the rice and mix gently but thoroughly.

SERVES: 4–6

# Rice with Fresh Cheese, Nuts and Vegetables, Moghul Style

## Ingredients

2½ cups (1 lb) Basmati rice or other long grain rice

•

250 g (8 oz) Panir (see page 437) or ricotta cheese

•

3 tablespoons flour

•

1 teaspoon ground turmeric

•

oil for deep-frying

•

2 tablespoons ghee (clarified butter)

•

¼ cup (1 oz) slivered blanched almonds

•

2 medium onions, thinly sliced

•

1 teaspoon finely chopped garlic

•

2 teaspoons finely shredded fresh ginger

•

5 cardamom pods, bruised

•

1 small stick cinnamon

•

3 whole cloves

•

10 whole peppercorns

•

1 cup (2½ oz) small cauliflower sprigs

•

½ cup (2 oz) shelled peas

•

4 cups (32 fl oz) water

•

3 teaspoons salt

•

2 tablespoons pistachio kernels, blanched

•

¼ cup (1½ oz) sultanas (golden raisins)

Wash rice well and leave to drain for at least 30 minutes. Cut panir or ricotta cheese into small cubes and leave on absorbent paper to drain if there is any excess moisture. Rub over with flour and turmeric mixed together. In a heavy-based pan, heat enough oil to deep fry the cheese, and add to it 1 tablespoon of the ghee for flavour. Deep fry the cubes of cheese, a few at a time, until golden. Remove from oil with slotted spoon and place on paper towels to drain.

In the same oil, fry the almonds until golden, remove and drain. Pour off all but about 2 tablespoons oil, add the remaining tablespoon of ghee and fry the sliced onions, garlic, ginger, cardamom, cinnamon, cloves and peppercorns. When the onions are golden, add the cauliflower and peas and fry, stirring, for 2 minutes. Add the rice and fry, stirring, for a further 3 minutes. Add water and salt, bring to the boil, then turn heat very low and cook, tightly covered, for 20 minutes without lifting the lid. Remove from heat and pick out whole spices which will have come to the top. Fork the fried cheese, half the almonds, pistachios and sultanas through the rice. Dish up and garnish with remaining nuts and sultanas and small red tomatoes. Serve with two or more accompaniments.

Serves: 6

RICE WITH FRESH CHEESE, NUTS AND VEGETABLES, MOGHUL STYLE

# ROTIS WITH SAVOURY FILLING

*This recipe is Indian in origin, but has come to be associated with Singapore's open-air eating places.*

## INGREDIENTS

3 cups (12 oz) roti flour or plain white (all-purpose) flour
•
1 teaspoon salt
•
1 tablespoon ghee (clarified butter) or oil
•
1 cup (8 fl oz) lukewarm water
•
½ cup (4 fl oz) oil

### FILLING
2 beaten eggs
•
pepper and salt to taste

Put flour and salt into a large bowl, rub in ghee or oil, then add the water all at once and mix to a fairly soft dough. Knead dough for at least 10 minutes. Divide into balls of equal size and put them into a small bowl containing the oil. If there is not quite enough oil to cover the dough, add a little more. Leave for at least 1 hour.

Have the filling ready. Season the eggs well with salt and pepper, and beat slightly.

On a very smooth surface, spread a little oil from the bowl and flatten one of the dough balls with a rolling pin or with the hand. Gently press with fingers, spreading the dough until it is almost as thin as strudel pastry. Have a griddle preheated and lightly greased with ghee or oil.

Drape the roti over a rolling pin and carry it to the griddle, placing it on the hot surface, as you would put the top on a pie. It will cook very quickly, so spoon on some beaten egg and spread it over the middle portion of the roti with the underside of the spoon. Fold over the sides of the roti, envelope fashion, to completely enclose the filling, then turn with a frying slice (spatula) and cook the other side, spreading a little more ghee or oil on the griddle before you put it down. It is ready when crisp and golden on both sides. Serve hot.

Sometimes the rotis are cooked without any filling and served with a curry. It is broken, dipped and eaten in the same way as chapati or paratha.

MAKES: 10–12

# RICE WITH SESAME SEEDS

## INGREDIENTS

2½ cups (1 lb) long grain rice
•
4 cups (32 fl oz) water

Put rice, water and salt into a heavy-based saucepan, bring to the boil. Cover with a well fitting lid, turn heat very low and cook for 20 minutes. Turn off heat and leave while preparing seasoning.

2½ teaspoons salt

•

2 tablespoons light sesame oil

•

1 teaspoon mustard seeds

•

12 curry leaves

•

1 cup (4 oz) sesame seeds

•

lemon juice to taste

Heat sesame oil in a small saucepan and fry the mustard seeds and curry leaves until the leaves are brown and mustard seeds pop. Add the sesame seeds and keep stirring over medium heat until the seeds are an even golden brown. Mix this seasoning together with the hot cooked rice and add a little lemon juice to taste. Serve with curried vegetables, fresh chutney and fried pappadams.

SERVES: 4–6

# RICE NOODLES WITH CURRIED EGGS

## INGREDIENTS

6–8 eggs

•

1½ cups (12 fl oz) thick coconut milk
(see page 443)

•

½ cup (4 fl oz) Burmese Curry Paste
(see page 451)

•

½ cup (2 oz) besan (chick pea flour)

•

2 cups (16 fl oz) thin coconut milk

•

500 g (1 lb) rice noodles,
dried or 1 kg (2 lb) fresh
rice noodles, cooked

•

2 teaspoons chilli oil

•

½ cup (1 oz) finely chopped
coriander

Simmer the eggs gently for 10 minutes to hard-boil them. Cook thick coconut milk in a saucepan, stirring constantly, until it becomes thick and the oil rises to the top. Keep cooking until it is very oily, then add the curry paste and stir for 2 minutes.

Mix besan with cold water to form a thin cream. Add thin coconut milk to the pan and when it comes to a boil, stir in the besan mixture. Cook and stir constantly until it thickens, taking care it does not become lumpy or stick to the base of the pan.

Add the cooked noodles, bring the combination to simmering point, stir in chilli oil, and remove from the heat. Add eggs and fresh coriander. Serve in a large bowl.

NOTE: If dried rice noodles are used, they will have to be boiled in a large amount of water until cooked through. Do not overcook. Drain well.

If fresh rice noodles are bought as large sheets (sa hor fun, available at Chinese grocers), cut into narrow strips and pour boiling water over them in a colander or steam gently for a few minutes to heat through.

SERVES: 6–8

# RICE VERMICELLI WITH EGGS AND ALMONDS

## INGREDIENTS

500 g (1 lb) rice vermicelli

•

4 tablespoons ghee (clarified butter)
or oil

•

3 large onions, finely sliced

•

10 curry leaves

•

1 packet powdered saffron or
½ teaspoon saffron strands

•

1 teaspoon ground turmeric

•

1 teaspoon ground cardamom
or Garam Masala (see page 456)

•

salt and pepper to taste

•

6 hard-boiled eggs

•

2 cups shelled peas,
cooked and drained

•

½ cup (2 oz) slivered almonds,
toasted or fried

Soak rice vermicelli in very hot water for 10 minutes or drop into a large pan of boiling water for 2 minutes. Drain in a colander. Heat ghee or oil in a large saucepan and fry onions with curry leaves until golden brown.

Add saffron dissolved in a tablespoon of hot water, turmeric, cardamom, salt and pepper. Add rice vermicelli and toss ingredients together until well mixed and evenly coloured. Taste, and correct seasoning if necessary. Serve hot, with eggs, peas and almonds arranged on top.

SERVES: 6

# CELLOPHANE NOODLES

*These noodles are an example of how Eastern people make a satisfying and very flavoursome meal based on a pure starch ingredient. The cellophane or spring rain noodles as they are called, are made from mung bean starch and are transparent when cooked. They have no flavour, but the texture is highly regarded. Serve with a Burmese or Thai curry.*

For 6 people, use a large packet (500 g/1 lb) of bean starch noodles.

Bring a large saucepan of salted water to the boil, drop in noodles and cook for 20 minutes. Drain. Serve in a large bowl. Serving is easier if the noodles are cut into shorter lengths with a sharp knife. They are not difficult to divide once cooked. Each person puts some noodles in a bowl, ladles curry or soup over the noodles and adds their own accompaniments. Everything is mixed together and a lemon wedge squeezed over to add piquancy. The crisp fried chillies are held by the stalk and bitten into (with caution) when a hot mouthful is desired.

ACCOMPANIMENTS: These include the following, each one served separately in a bowl:
finely sliced spring onions (scallions)
chopped fresh coriander leaves
finely sliced white onion
roasted chick peas, finely ground in a blender or crushed with a mortar and pestle
crisp fried noodles, broken into small pieces
fried onion flakes
thin slices garlic, fried in oil until golden
lemon wedges

dried chillies, fried in oil until puffed and crisp
chilli powder

NOTE: If cooking for fewer than 6 people, I suggest you buy these noodles in smaller bundles—they also come in 50 g (1½ oz) and 100 g (3½ oz) sizes. It is exceedingly difficult to divide up the large skeins, as these noodles in their uncooked state are very tough. If you have to do it, use sharp scissors.

Roasted chick peas are sold in Greek delicatessen shops.

# COMPLEMENTARY DISHES

All the dishes in this chapter are meant to be served with rice or flat bread (see Chapatis, Parathas, etc in the chapter on Bread, page 396). Because it is so easy to cook in a wok and much less oil is needed, I have suggested cooking many of the dishes in this marvellous all-purpose utensil. But a frying pan or saucepan will handle the recipes quite satisfactorily, as long as you are aware that more oil or other cooking medium will be required in a flat pan. And don't get too enthusiastic with the stir-frying, because without the high, flaring sides of the wok you could end up with most of the ingredients scattered around the stove!

## YOGHURT WITH SPINACH

### INGREDIENTS

1 large bunch spinach

•

2 teaspoons ghee (clarified butter) or oil

•

1 teaspoon black mustard seeds

•

1 teaspoon cumin seeds

•

1 teaspoon ground cumin

•

⅛ teaspoon chilli powder (optional)

•

¾ teaspoon salt or to taste

•

1½ cups (12 fl oz) yoghurt

Wash spinach thoroughly in several changes of water. Remove any tough stems and put the leaves into a saucepan with very little water. Cover and steam over low heat until spinach is tender. Drain and chop finely.

In a small pan, heat ghee or oil and fry the mustard seeds until they start to pop. Add cumin seeds and ground cumin and fry, stirring, until seeds are brown. Do not allow to burn. Remove from heat, stir in chilli powder and salt and allow to cool. Mix in the yoghurt, then stir this mixture into the spinach. Serve cold or at room temperature as a side dish with rice and curry, or with one of the Indian breads.

SERVES: 4–6

## BRAISED GLUTEN WITH VEGETABLES

### INGREDIENTS

250 g (8 oz) prepared Gluten (see page 437)

•

6 dried Chinese mushrooms

•

2 tablespoons dried wood (cloud ear) fungus

•

1 carrot

Prepare the gluten and after it has been boiled and cooled, cut it into thin slices.

Soak the mushrooms in 1½ cups (12 fl oz) hot water for 30 minutes. Drain, reserving the water. Discard the mushroom stems and slice the caps. Soak the wood fungus in cold water for 10 minutes, drain and discard any hard bits, then cut into bite-size pieces.

Cut the carrot into matchstick strips and beans into

12 green beans

•

3 spring onions (scallions)

•

1 teaspoon finely grated ginger

•

2 tablespoons peanut oil

•

1 tablespoon light soy sauce

•

1 tablespoon dark soy sauce

•

2 teaspoons sugar

•

1 tablespoon sesame oil

diagonal slices. Chop the spring onions and put them on a saucer with the grated ginger.

Heat a wok, add the peanut oil and swirl to coat the sides. Fry the spring onions and ginger for a few seconds, then add the sliced gluten and mushrooms, and fry for 1–2 minutes. Add 1 cup (8 fl oz) of the mushroom soaking water and stir in the soy sauces, sugar and 2 teaspoons of the sesame oil. Cover and simmer on low heat for 8 minutes. Add the carrots and beans, cover the wok and simmer for a further 8 minutes.

Finally, stir the wood fungus through and cook for 2 minutes longer. The liquid in the wok should now be reduced to about ¼ cup (2 fl oz). Sprinkle with the remaining teaspoon of sesame oil and serve at once with hot steamed rice.

SERVES: 4

# FRIED OKRA

*Okra (bhendi) is a type of bean that has been known in Asia for a long time. It originated in Africa from whence it made its way to America and is widely used in Creole cookery. You can recognise okra by the slightly furry, striated pods shaped like a furled umbrella.*

## INGREDIENTS

500 g (1 lb) small, tender okra

•

2 tablespoons ghee (clarified butter) or oil

•

½ teaspoon Panch Phora (see page 456)

•

1 large onion, finely chopped

•

1 teaspoon ground coriander

•

½ teaspoon ground turmeric

•

½ teaspoon chilli powder

•

½ teaspoon salt, or to taste

•

1 tablespoon lemon juice

•

½ teaspoon Garam Masala (see page 456)

Wash the okra, cut off and discard stem ends and slice into bite-size pieces.

Heat ghee or oil and fry the panch phora for a minute. Add onion and fry, stirring, until soft. Mix in coriander, turmeric, chilli and salt. Add okra, stir, cover and cook on low heat, stirring now and then, until okra is tender. Sprinkle with lemon juice and the garam masala. Toss to mix and serve with rice or Chapatis (see page 398).

SERVES: 4

# BRAISED CHINESE MUSHROOMS AND BEAN CURD

*The flavour of Chinese mushrooms is wonderful when cooked in this way and, served with steamed rice, makes a satisfying meal.*

## INGREDIENTS

12–16 dried Chinese mushrooms
•
250 g (8 oz) fried bean curd or
pressed bean curd
•
2 tablespoons peanut oil
•
2 spring onions (scallions),
cut into 5 cm (2 in) lengths
•
¾ cup (6 fl oz) Vegetable Stock
(see page 448)
•
2 tablespoons dark soy sauce
•
½ teaspoon sugar
•
1 teaspoon cornflour (cornstarch)
•
1 teaspoon sesame oil

There are two types of bean curd suitable for this dish— pressed bean curd and squares of fried bean curd. Both are available from Chinese stores. The pressed bean curd will require deep frying before adding to the sauce.

Soak the mushrooms in water for 30 minutes. Drain, discard the mushroom stems and cut the caps in half.

Split squares of the fried bean curd into two—then cut each square diagonally in half. If using the pressed bean curd, cut in the same way, then deep fry in hot oil until golden brown. Drain.

Heat a wok, add the peanut oil and swirl it around the wok. When hot, add the spring onions and mushrooms, and stir on medium-high heat for about 30 seconds. Add the stock, soy sauce and sugar and simmer, covered, for 20 minutes. Add bean curd slices. Bring to the boil, cover the wok and simmer for 5 minutes.

Blend the cornflour with 1 tablespoon of water and stir it into the sauce until it boils and thickens. Add sesame oil, toss the mixture lightly and serve with rice.

NOTE: The soft white bean curd (tofu) available in packets can be used for this dish but take care to avoid mashing it. Cook the spring onions and mushrooms, add the liquids and seasonings, then simmer and thicken as described. At this stage, open the container, slide the bean curd on to a plate and drain off its liquid. Cut it into squares and carefully slide it into the sauce over a low heat. Do not stir, but spoon some of the sauce over the bean curd to heat it through. Slide the mixture out of the wok on to a serving dish.

SERVES: 4

BRAISED CHINESE MUSHROOMS AND BEAN CURD

# STIR-FRIED EGGS WITH MIXED VEGETABLES

*Serve as part of a meal with other dishes or as a light main dish on its own.*

## INGREDIENTS

4 eggs

•

½ teaspoon salt

•

15 g (½ oz) dried wood (cloud ear) fungus (wan yee)

•

250 g (8 oz) Chinese cabbage (wongah bak)

•

1 carrot

•

4 spring onions (scallions)

•

2 tablespoons peanut oil

•

½ teaspoon finely grated fresh ginger

•

1 tablespoon light soy sauce

•

½ teaspoon sugar

•

1 teaspoon sesame oil

Beat the eggs with salt until yolks and whites are well mixed. Soak the wood fungus in a large bowl of water for 15 minutes, then rinse well and trim off any gritty portions. Cut large pieces in half.

Cut cabbage leaves in half lengthways (or thirds if they are large), then shred finely crossways. This keeps the shreds from being long and stringy. Cut the carrot into matchstick strips. Cut the spring onions into short lengths.

Heat a wok, add 1 tablespoon of the peanut oil and stir-fry the eggs until they set. Transfer to a plate. Wipe out the wok. Add the remaining tablespoon of peanut oil and when hot, fry the ginger for a few seconds. Add the cabbage and carrot, and stir-fry for 1 minute, then cover the wok and cook until half tender, about 2 minutes. Add the spring onions, wood fungus, soy sauce, sugar and sesame oil. Stir to mix, cover the wok and cook on low heat for 1 minute. Add the cooked eggs, toss well together and serve immediately.

SERVES: 4–6

# BRAISED VEGETABLE COMBINATION

*In Chinese cuisine this is also known as "Buddha's delight".*

## INGREDIENTS

125 g (4 oz) dried bean curd or Gluten steak (see page 437) or dried soy bean protein

•

12 dried Chinese mushrooms

•

30 dried lily buds

•

2 tablespoons dried wood (cloud ear) fungus

Break dried bean curd into bite-size pieces and soak in cold water for 20 minutes. Drain, pour boiling water over and allow to stand for a further 20 minutes. Drain well. Wash mushrooms and soak in 2 cups (16 fl oz) hot water for 30 minutes. Drain, reserving the water. Remove stems and squeeze out excess moisture from caps. If large, cut caps in half. Soak lily buds in hot water for 30 minutes, drain, pinch off tough stem ends and either tie a knot in each one or cut in half.

1 canned bamboo shoot
•
1 canned lotus root
•
1 small can sliced water chestnuts
•
3 tablespoons peanut oil
•
2 tablespoons light soy sauce
•
2 tablespoons hoisin sauce
•
1½ cups (12 fl oz) mushroom soaking
liquid
•
3 sections star anise
•
2 teaspoons sesame oil
•
2 teaspoons sugar
•
2 teaspoons cornflour (cornstarch)
•
2 tablespoons cold water

Soak wood fungus in cold water for 10 minutes, drain and cut in bite-size pieces. Cut bamboo shoot and lotus root into thin slices, then into bite-size pieces. Drain water chestnuts.

Heat a wok, pour in peanut oil and swirl to coat sides. When very hot, add bean curd, mushrooms and lily buds, and stir-fry for a few minutes over medium high heat. Add the soy and hoisin sauces stirred into the mushroom liquid. Add star anise. Bring to the boil, turn heat low, cover and simmer for 15 minutes. Add bamboo shoot, lotus root, water chestnuts, sesame oil and sugar, stir well. Cover and simmer for 10 minutes longer. If liquid evaporates too rapidly, add more mushroom liquid or hot water.

Mix cornflour smoothly with cold water and stir into liquid. Cook until it becomes clear and thickens. Add wood fungus and push other vegetables to side of pan, allowing fungus to heat through. Serve hot with rice.

NOTE: Prepare Gluten steaks as described on page 437, or dried soy bean protein according to directions on packet.

SERVES: 6

# BRAISED CABBAGE, CHINESE STYLE

INGREDIENTS

1 small Chinese cabbage
(wongah bak)
•
2 tablespoons peanut oil
•
1 tablespoon sesame oil
•
2 cloves garlic, crushed
•
2 teaspoons finely grated
fresh ginger
•
¼ cup (2 fl oz) soy sauce
•
¼ cup (2 fl oz) water
•
2 teaspoons sugar
•
pepper and salt to taste

There are so many kinds of Chinese cabbage and more than one variety may be used in this method of cooking. The type used in this recipe is the pale green, tightly packed cabbage also known as *Tientsin* or celery cabbage, or by its Chinese name, *wongah bak*.

Quarter cabbage lengthways, then across into 2.5 cm (1 in) slices.

Heat the oil in a wok and fry garlic and ginger over low heat, stirring. Add the cabbage and toss until all the cabbage is lightly coated with oil. Add the remaining ingredients, cover the wok and cook on very low heat for 6–8 minutes or until cabbage is tender but still crisp. Serve with rice or noodles.

SERVES: 4

# FAR EASTERN MENUS

*With a complex soup one needs only steamed rice and a simple dish. Though most Oriental meals do not feature dessert, the Almond Bean Curd is very suitable for those who like a sweet ending.*

Shanghai Egg Pouch Soup *page 250*

Steamed Rice *page 438*

Braised Chinese Mushrooms and Bean Curd *page 280*

Almond Bean Curd *page 372*

*Serve the Marbled Tea Eggs as a hors d'oeuvre if you like. The eggplant has robust flavours, the corn and snowpeas delicate. Add another dish if there are more than 4–6 people being served.*

Marbled Tea Eggs *page 244*

Steamed Rice *page 438*

Eggplant, Chinese Style *page 291*

Mini Corn, Snow Peas and Cucumber *page 288*

*Korean Pancakes, or Guchulpan, are ideal for breaking the ice because everyone has to choose the filling for their pancakes, and roll them up themselves . . . which can be hilarious if you are not too practised with chopsticks!*

Korean Pancakes *page 234*

Steamed Rice *page 438*

Stir Fried Asparagus *page 293*

*An ideal selection for hot weather.*

Vegetable Platter with Sesame Sauce
*page 294*

Chilled Noodles *page 290*

*or*

Chirashi-Zushi *page 248*

Radish & Apple Salad *page 179*

Kimizu Dressing *page 182*

# MIDDLE EASTERN MENUS

*The light, fresh flavours of Middle Eastern food make it very suitable for temperate climates. Do not overlook the crisp, lightly-pickled vegetables and olives bought ready to serve and placed on the table as appetisers, together with home-made dips such as Baba Ghannouj and Hummus bi Tahini.*

Baba Ghannouj *page 40*
with flat bread

Felafel *page 2*

Fattoush *page 162*

Zucchinis with Tomatoes and Garlic

*page 132*

Guava Pie *page 206*

Cucumber and Yoghurt Soup *page 69*

Crisp Spicy Toast *page 15*

Tabbouli *page 172*

Riz bi Sharieh *page 135*

Braised Endive, Lebanese style *page 147*

Rich Coffee Ice-cream *page 222*

# STIR-FRIED LONG BEANS AND MINCED GLUTEN

*When long beans, or snake beans as they are sometimes called, are in season this is a good dish to add to the menu. Make sure the beans are firm, very slender and a deep green colour. Even if thicker, paler beans are being sold more cheaply, they are past their prime and will be tough.*

### INGREDIENTS

500 g (1 lb) long beans
•
3 tablespoons peanut oil
•
3 teaspoons finely grated
fresh ginger
•
2 cups minced Gluten
(see page 437)
•
3 tablespoons roughly chopped
spring onions (scallions)

### SAUCE
1 cup (8 fl oz) Vegetable Stock
(see page 448) or water
•
1 tablespoon light soy sauce
•
1 tablespoon dark soy sauce
•
1 teaspoon cornflour (cornstarch)

Top and tail the long beans, then wash and pat dry on paper towels. Cut into 5 cm (2 in) lengths and set aside. Mix the sauce ingredients except for the cornflour and set aside. Separately, mix the cornflour with 1 tablespoon of cold water to make a smooth paste.

Heat a wok, add 2 tablespoons of the oil and swirl. Fry 1 teaspoon of the ginger for 10 seconds, then add the beans and stir-fry for 1 minute. Remove beans to a plate. Return the wok to the heat, add the remaining tablespoon of oil and when hot, add the remaining 2 teaspoons of ginger. Fry for a few seconds, then add the minced gluten and stir-fry on high heat for 2–3 minutes.

Add the sauce ingredients, cover and simmer for 5 minutes. Then add the beans, stir, cover and cook for a further 3 minutes. Add spring onions and toss over high heat. Stir in the cornflour paste until the sauce thickens. Serve immediately.

SERVES: 4–6

# STIR-FRIED WATERCRESS WITH BEAN CURD

*This is an ideal light luncheon dish for hot weather, since it is served cold, yet has palate-tempting flavours which help the blandness of the bean curd.*

### INGREDIENTS

500 g (1 lb) watercress
•
1 teaspoon salt
•
2 tablespoons peanut oil
•
1 large dried red chilli

Wash the watercress well and shake dry. Finely chop the leaves and stems, place in a bowl, sprinkle with salt and toss well. Cover the bowl and chill for 30 minutes or longer. Drain and squeeze out liquid.

Heat a wok over a medium heat, add the peanut oil and when hot, add the whole chilli and fry until it is dark in colour. On high heat, fry the garlic for just 3–4 seconds,

½ teaspoon crushed garlic

•

2 teaspoons sesame oil

•

250 g (8 oz) fresh bean curd

---

SAUCE

1 tablespoon light soy sauce

•

1 tablespoon Chinese wine
or dry sherry

•

½ teaspoon sesame oil

•

1 teaspoon chopped fresh
coriander leaves

add the watercress and stir-fry, turning constantly for 30 seconds. Turn off the heat, mix in the sesame oil and turn the mixture into a serving dish. Allow to cool, then chill.

Have the bean curd well chilled. Combine the ingredients for the sauce in a small serving bowl. Drain the bean curd, cut it into squares and carefully place them on the chilled watercress. Sprinkle the sauce over the dish.

SERVES: 4

# SHREDDED GLUTEN WITH CASHEWS

*Gluten, with its spongy texture, absorbs the flavour of ingredients it is cooked with. It is made from the protein part of wheat and is sold in powder form in most health food stores.*

INGREDIENTS

250 g (8 oz) vegetables

•

250 g (8 oz) prepared Gluten slices
(see page 437)

•

3 tablespoons peanut oil

•

½ teaspoon grated fresh ginger

•

½ teaspoon crushed garlic

•

1 tablespoon ground bean sauce
(mor sze jeung)

•

½ teaspoon chilli sauce
(or spicy ketchup) (optional)

•

1 tablespoon light soy sauce

•

½ cup (4 fl oz) water

•

2 teaspoons cornflour (cornstarch)

•

125 g (4 oz) deep fried cashew nuts

Choose a combination of two vegetables for this dish, such as broccoli stems, red or green capsicum (sweet peppers), green beans, water chestnuts, bamboo shoots or spring onions (scallions).

Prepare the gluten and after it has been boiled and cooled, cut it into shreds. Cut the vegetables the same size as the gluten. Heat a wok, add 2 tablespoons of peanut oil and swirl to coat the inside of the wok. Cook the ginger and garlic over low heat for a few seconds, then increase the heat, add the vegetables and stir-fry for a minute or two. Remove.

Add the remaining oil to the wok and stir-fry the gluten for 2 minutes. Mix the bean sauce, chilli and soy sauce with the water and stir it into the mixture. Cover the wok and simmer for 15 minutes.

Return the vegetables and cook for just 1 minute longer. Blend cornflour with a little water, add and stir until the sauce boils and thickens. Add the cashews. Serve immediately with hot rice.

SERVES: 4

# CAULIFLOWER WITH PECANS

*Like all Chinese-style vegetables, cook just until tender, but still crisp to bite.*

## INGREDIENTS

1 small or ½ large cauliflower

•

¼ cup (2 fl oz) oil

•

½ cup (2 oz) pecan halves

•

3 spring onions (scallions), cut into bite-size lengths

•

½ teaspoon salt

•

1 tablespoon light soy sauce

•

½ cup (4 fl oz) water or Vegetable Stock (see page 437)

•

1 teaspoon sesame oil

Cut off thick stems and divide cauliflower into bite-size florets. Heat a wok, add 2 tablespoons oil and toss the pecan halves over medium heat until they are golden brown. Lift onto absorbent paper and leave until cool and crisp. Wipe out wok with paper towels.

Heat the remaining 2 tablespoons oil, add the spring onions and cauliflower, and toss to coat with the oil. Stir salt and soy sauce into the water and pour over the vegetables, then bring rapidly to the boil, cover and cook for 4–5 minutes. Turn off heat. Sprinkle with the sesame oil and toss well to distribute flavours. Mix in the fried pecans and serve at once.

SERVES: 4–6

# MINI-CORN, SNOW PEAS AND CUCUMBER

## INGREDIENTS

1 × 440 g (15 oz) can young corn cobs (baby corn)

•

250 g (8 oz) snow peas (mangetout)

•

1 cucumber

•

1 tablespoon peanut oil

•

1 teaspoon sesame oil

•

¼ teaspoon crushed garlic

•

¼ teaspoon finely grated fresh ginger

•

salt to taste

Drain liquid from can of corn. Remove stems and strings from snow peas. Peel and cut cucumber into thin slices. Heat peanut oil in a wok, add sesame oil, garlic and ginger and stir once, then add corn and snow peas. Stir-fry for 1 minute over high heat. Add cucumber slices and cook 1 minute longer. Serve at once.

SERVES: 4

CAULIFLOWER WITH PECANS

# BRAISED VEGETABLES WITH BEAN CURD

*Made from soy beans, bean curd is known in China as "the meat without a bone". It is available in many forms—soft, firm pressed, deep-fried. In this recipe I used soft bean curd which has a smooth, custard-like texture.*

### INGREDIENTS

6 squares fresh bean curd
•
12 dried Chinese mushrooms
•
3 tablespoons dried wood (cloud ear)
fungus (optional)
•
1 small can bamboo shoots
or braised bamboo shoots
•
1 can young corn cobs (baby corn)
•
2 tablespoons peanut oil
•
1 tablespoon sesame oil
•
2 tablespoons soy sauce
•
1 tablespoon sugar
•
2 cups (16 fl oz) mushroom liquid
•
1 teaspoon hoisin sauce

Cut squares of bean curd into quarters and place on a double thickness of absorbent paper towels.

Soak mushrooms in 3 cups (24 fl oz) of hot water for 30 minutes. Cut off and discard stems. Squeeze out excess moisture from caps and reserve mushroom water. Soak fungus in hot water for 10 minutes, then wash well, removing any grit. If large, cut into bite-size pieces. If using one large bamboo shoot, slice into smaller strips, but if using the smaller braised bamboo shoots they may be used whole. Drain the corn cobs.

Heat oil in a wok and fry mushrooms on high heat until brown, turning them frequently. Add all the ingredients except bean curd and wood fungus and bring to simmering point. Cover and simmer for 25–30 minutes. Add wood fungus and bean curd and heat through. Do not stir too vigorously after adding bean curd or it will break up. Serve with hot boiled rice.

SERVES: 4

# CHILLED NOODLES

*In hot Japanese summers, ice-cold noodles make a very popular light meal. For something so simple, it is surprisingly flavoursome.*

### INGREDIENTS

200 g (7 oz) soba (buckwheat noodles)
•
1 sheet nori (dried laver seaweed)
•
1 tablespoon finely grated
fresh ginger
•
3 spring onions (scallions),
very finely sliced

Bring a large saucepan of water to the boil and add noodles. When water returns to the boil, add 1 cup (8 oz) cold water. Bring to the boil again and cook until the noodles are just tender. This does not take long, about 2 minutes, so keep testing and stop cooking as soon as they are tender enough to bite. Drain in a colander and hold under running cold water until they are quite cold. Drain well.

To make the Dipping Sauce, put the soy sauce and sherry

DIPPING SAUCE

½ cup (4 fl oz) Japanese soy sauce
•
½ cup (4 fl oz) mirin or dry sherry
•
salt or sugar (optional)

into a small pan and bring to the boil. Remove from heat and cool. Taste and add salt or sugar as desired.

Toast sheet of nori by waving it over a gas flame or electric hot plate or under griller until crisp. It takes just a few seconds, so watch that it doesn't burn. Put noodles on plates and crumble the nori over.

Mix ginger with spring onions and put a small portion on each plate. Pour dipping sauce into individual sauce dishes for each person. The ginger mixture is stirred into the sauce and the noodles are dipped in the sauce before eating.

SERVES: 4

# EGGPLANT, CHINESE STYLE

INGREDIENTS

1 kg (2 lb) eggplants (aubergines)
•
2 cups (16 fl oz) peanut oil
for deep frying
•
¼ cup (2 fl oz) dark soy sauce
•
2 tablespoons vinegar
•
1 tablespoon Chinese wine
or dry sherry
•
2 tablespoons sugar
•
1 teaspoon sesame oil
•
1 teaspoon chilli oil (optional)
•
1–2 teaspoons sweet chilli sauce
•
1 teaspoon finely grated fresh ginger
•
1 teaspoon finely chopped garlic

Slice off and discard stalk end of eggplants but do not peel. Halve lengthways, then cut into wedges lengthways, about 2.5 cm (1 in) thick. Cut wedges into 5 cm (2 in) lengths.

Heat the oil in a wok or frying pan and fry half the eggplants at a time on high heat, turning the pieces so they brown evenly. Let them cook to a dark golden brown, then lift out on a slotted spoon and drain on absorbent paper. When all the eggplant has been fried, set aside to cool.

To make the sauce, combine the soy sauce, vinegar, sherry, sugar, sesame oil, chilli oil and chilli sauce. Stir to dissolve the sugar.

Pour off all but a tablespoon of oil remaining in the pan used for cooking eggplants. Heat, then add the ginger and garlic, and stir quickly over medium heat until they turn golden. Add the sauce mixture, bring to the boil, then return eggplants to the pan and cook over high heat, turning until they have absorbed most of the sauce.

Transfer to a serving dish as soon as cooking is completed. Don't leave in a steel wok or a metallic taste will develop. Serve warm or cold.

SERVES: 4–6

# ORIENTAL-STYLE SPROUTS

*The simplicity of this recipe will leave you unprepared for the superb flavour imparted by the fresh ginger and sesame oil.*

### INGREDIENTS

500 g (1 lb) tender young
Brussels sprouts
•
2 tablespoons light vegetable oil
•
½ teaspoon finely grated fresh ginger
•
2 tablespoons light soy sauce
•
1 teaspoon oriental sesame oil

Wash and trim the sprouts and if they are not small, halve lengthways. Cook in lightly salted boiling water just long enough to make them tender—they must be crisp, not soft. Drain.

In a wok or large frying pan, heat the oil and fry the ginger for a few seconds, stirring. Toss in the vegetables and stir-fry for 1 minute, then sprinkle the soy sauce and sesame oil over and toss again to distribute the seasonings. Serve at once.

SERVES: 4

# BRAISED BROCCOLI, CHINESE STYLE

*When you use broccoli florets for a recipe, don't throw away the stems. This is just one example of how they make good eating.*

### INGREDIENTS

approximately 250 g (8 oz)
broccoli stems
•
2 tablespoons peanut oil
•
1 clove garlic, crushed
•
½ teaspoon grated fresh
ginger (optional)
•
2 tablespoons oyster sauce
or soy sauce
•
1 teaspoon sugar
•
½ teaspoon sesame oil
•
½ cup (4 fl oz) broccoli cooking liquid
•
2 teaspoons cornflour (cornstarch)
•
1 tablespoon cold water

Cut the broccoli stems into bite-size lengths, peel any that seem tough and halve any thick stems.

Bring lightly salted water to the boil in a saucepan, drop in the stems and return to the boil, then cook for 2–3 minutes or until bright green and just tender. If using flowers as well, add them after 2 minutes and boil no more than 1 minute. Drain in colander, saving liquid.

Heat oil in a wok and stir fry the drained broccoli for 1 minute, adding garlic and ginger. Add the sauce, sugar, sesame oil and cooking liquid and let it boil.

Mix the cornflour with the cold water and stir it into the liquid until it thickens slightly. Toss the broccoli in the sauce and serve at once.

SERVES: 4

# STIR-FRIED ASPARAGUS

### INGREDIENTS

500 g (1 lb) fresh asparagus spears
•
2 tablespoons peanut oil
•
½ cup (4 fl oz) water
•
a good grinding of sea salt
•
1 teaspoon oriental sesame oil

Snap off tough ends of asparagus, thinly peel the bottom half of each spear if necessary and wash well. Cut into bite-size pieces, holding the knife at an angle so the cuts are on the diagonal, exposing a much greater cut surface than a straight cut would.

Heat a wok, add the peanut oil and swirl to coat surface. On high heat, stir-fry the asparagus until the pieces are coated with oil and have turned a brighter green. Add the water and salt, cover and cook on high heat for about 4 minutes, just until the asparagus is tender. It should still have the crispness that is typical of oriental vegetables. Uncover and sprinkle with sesame oil, toss to mix and serve right away.

SERVES: 4

# MIXED BRAISED VEGETABLES

*Use a mixture of white Chinese cabbage, mustard cabbage, leeks, cauliflower, spring onions (scallions), and beans in any combination or proportions. Weigh after trimming and slicing.*

### INGREDIENTS

2 tablespoons peanut oil
•
1 teaspoon sesame oil
•
1 large clove garlic, crushed
•
1 teaspoon grated fresh ginger
•
750 g (1½ lb) sliced vegetables
•
½ cup (4 fl oz) hot water or Vegetable Stock (see page 448)
•
2 teaspoons light soy sauce
•
½ teaspoon salt
•
2 teaspoons cornflour (cornstarch)
•
1 tablespoon cold water

Heat oils in a wok with garlic and ginger, add vegetables and stir-fry for 2 minutes. Add hot water or stock, sauce and salt mixed together. Cover and simmer for 4 minutes. Push vegetables to side of wok, add cornflour mixed with cold water and stir until thick. Toss vegetables in sauce and serve immediately with boiled rice.

SERVES: 4–6

# VEGETABLE PLATTER WITH SESAME SAUCE

### INGREDIENTS

30 g (1 oz) dried agar-agar strips
•
250 g (8 oz) button mushrooms
•
2 tablespoons peanut oil
•
salt to taste
•
250 g (8 oz) green beans
•
4 spring onions (scallions)
•
250 g (8 oz) fresh bean curd
•
1 carrot

### SESAME SAUCE
3 tablespoons sesame paste
(or toasted, ground sesame seeds)
•
2 tablespoons light soy sauce
•
2 tablespoons water
•
2 tablespoons sesame oil
•
½ teaspoon chilli oil

Soak the agar-agar in cold water for 10 minutes, then drain and cut into 5 cm (2 in) lengths. Wipe the mushrooms with a damp towel and slice.

Heat a wok, add the peanut oil and heat. Add the mushrooms and stir-fry over moderate heat for 2 minutes. Turn out on to a serving dish and season to taste with salt. Allow to cool.

String the beans, top and tail them and leave whole, or halve if large. Blanch the beans in boiling water for 3 minutes, then drain and cool. Cut the spring onions into bite-size lengths. Slice the bean curd. Peel the carrot and cut it into strips. Blanch briefly—they should still be crisp.

To make the sesame sauce, stir the sesame paste until it is smooth, then blend in the other ingredients. In cold weather it may be necessary to warm the sesame paste before mixing. Arrange the vegetables on a serving platter, with a bowl of the sauce for spooning over them.

NOTE:   Other suitable vegetables to use as they are in season are cooked asparagus, blanched broccoli stems, sliced (canned) water chestnuts and strips of zucchini (courgettes) that have been briefly fried in a little oil.

SERVES: 6

# BEAN CURD AND BEAN SPROUTS

### INGREDIENTS

2 squares pressed yellow bean curd
•
250 g (8 oz) fresh bean sprouts
•
2 cloves garlic, crushed
•
2 tablespoons oil
•
salt and pepper to taste
•
soy sauce to taste

Cut the bean curd in slices. Wash and drain the bean sprouts, pinching off any brown "tails".

Fry garlic in hot oil until turning golden, add bean curd and bean sprouts and stir-fry for 3–4 minutes. Add seasonings to taste and serve immediately.

SERVES: 6

# FRIED BEAN CURD WITH PEANUTS

### INGREDIENTS

4 squares pressed yellow bean curd
•
peanut oil for frying
•
½ cup (3 oz) raw peanuts
•
1 large clove garlic, crushed
•
½ cup (2½ oz) crushed roasted
peanuts or 125 g (4 oz) crunchy
peanut butter
•
2 tablespoons dark soy sauce
•
3 tablespoons tamarind liquid
(see Note)
•
½ teaspoon sambal ulek
or chopped fresh chillies
•
1 teaspoon palm sugar or brown sugar
•
½ cup (4 fl oz) coconut milk
•
1 cup (2 oz) finely shredded cabbage
•
1 cup (2 oz) fresh bean sprouts
•
4 spring onions (scallions),
finely sliced, to garnish

Dry bean curd thoroughly on paper towels, then cut each square into 9 cubes. Heat peanut oil in a wok or frying pan and fry the bean curd, taking care not to stir or break it up, until golden brown on all sides. Drain on absorbent paper. In the same oil, fry peanuts for 3–4 minutes, drain, rub skins off. Set aside.

Make the sauce by pouring off all but a tablespoon of oil and frying the garlic over low heat, stirring constantly. Add crushed peanuts, soy sauce, tamarind liquid, sambal and sugar. Stir until well mixed. Remove from heat. Gradually add the coconut milk until sauce is of a thick pouring consistency. Put bean curd on a dish, cover with the shredded cabbage and then with the bean sprouts. Spoon sauce over and garnish with spring onions and fried peanuts.

NOTE: Make the tamarind liquid by soaking 1 teaspoon dried tamarind in ¼ cup (2 fl oz) hot water. Squeeze firmly to dissolve, then push through nylon strainer, discarding seeds and fibres. Alternatively, mix 1 tablespoon tamarind pulp with 2 tablespoons water.

SERVES: 4

# QUICK-FRIED LONG BEANS

### INGREDIENTS

500 g (1 lb) long beans
•
2 tablespoons peanut oil
•
1 small clove garlic, crushed
•
½ teaspoon finely grated
fresh ginger
•
1 teaspoon sesame oil
•
½ teaspoon salt

Wash and cut beans into 5 cm (2 in) lengths. Heat oil in a wok or frying pan and add garlic, ginger and beans. Fry, stirring constantly over high heat, for 2 minutes. Stir in sesame oil and salt. Serve at once.

SERVES: 4

# HEAVENLY BRAISED VEGETABLES

### INGREDIENTS

12 dried Chinese mushrooms

•

3 tablespoons dried wood (cloud ear)
fungus (wan yee)

•

250 g (8 oz) canned bamboo shoots

•

1 × 425 g (14 oz) can young
corn cobs (baby corn)

•

2 tablespoons peanut oil

•

1 tablespoon sesame oil

•

2 tablespoons soy sauce

•

1 tablespoon sugar

•

2 cups (16 fl oz) mushroom soaking
liquid

Soak mushrooms in 3 cups (24 fl oz) hot water for 30 minutes. Remove and discard stems, then squeeze out excess moisture from caps. Reserve mushroom liquid. Soak fungus in water for 10 minutes, rinse and drain, then halve each piece. Slice bamboo shoots thinly. Drain corn.

Heat oil in a wok and fry mushrooms on high heat, stirring constantly until brown, about 5 minutes. Add remaining ingredients, except wood fungus. Add mushroom liquid, cover and simmer over low heat for 25–30 minutes. Add wood fungus and heat through. Serve with rice.

SERVES: 4

# STIR-FRIED LETTUCE

*In winter, when the thought of salad is not really tempting, it takes hardly
5 minutes to turn a lettuce into a hot dish. Cook just before eating so
it will be very crisp.*

### INGREDIENTS

1 firm lettuce

•

1–2 tablespoons peanut oil

•

½ teaspoon crushed garlic

•

¼ teaspoon finely grated fresh ginger

•

¼ teaspoon salt

•

1 teaspoon sugar

•

2 teaspoons light soy sauce

•

few drops of sesame oil

Wash the lettuce, drain and dry well. Halve lengthways, then cut each half twice lengthways and twice crossways to give chunky, bite-size pieces.

Heat a wok, add the peanut oil and swirl the wok to coat the inside with oil. Add the garlic and ginger, stir-fry for 10 seconds, then add the lettuce and stir-fry on high heat for 30–40 seconds. Turn off heat, add salt, sugar, soy sauce and sesame oil, and toss to distribute the seasonings. The lettuce should retain its crisp texture. Serve at once, by itself or as a base for other dishes.

SERVES: 4–6

HEAVENLY BRAISED VEGETABLES

# FRIED BEAN CURD
# WITH SOY SAUCE

## INGREDIENTS

4 squares pressed yellow bean curd

•

oil, for deep-frying

•

125 g (4 oz) fresh bean sprouts

•

4 spring onions (scallions),
finely sliced

•

¼ cup (2 fl oz) dark soy sauce

•

1 tablespoon palm sugar or
brown sugar

•

1 onion, roughly chopped

•

1 teaspoon sambal ulek or
1 fresh chilli, seeded and chopped

•

1 clove garlic

Dry bean curd thoroughly on paper towels. Cut each cake of bean curd into 9 cubes and deep-fry in hot oil, taking care not to break the curd, until browned on all sides. Drain well on paper, then arrange on dish. Spread washed and drained bean sprouts over, then garnish with the spring onions.

To make the sauce, put the soy sauce, sugar, onion, sambal or chilli and garlic into the container of electric blender. Blend until smooth. Spoon sauce over bean curd and serve.

SERVES: 6

# BEAN CURD IN
# SALTED SOYBEAN PASTE

## INGREDIENTS

3 squares pressed yellow bean curd

•

2 cloves garlic

•

3 fresh red chillies

•

2 teaspoons salted soya bean paste

•

2 tablespoons peanut oil

•

¼ cup (2 fl oz) water

•

1 tablespoon light soy sauce

•

salt to taste

•

2 tablespoons chopped celery leaves

•

2 tablespoons chopped spring
onions (scallions)

Dice bean curd, grate garlic finely, then seed and shred chillies. (Wear gloves when handling chillies.) Mash salted soya bean paste. Heat oil, then fry garlic and chillies until garlic starts to turn brown. Add salted soya beans and stir-fry for 1 minute, then stir in bean curd and fry, stirring. Add water and soy sauce and cook until liquid dries up. Taste and add salt if necessary. Remove from heat, mix in celery and spring onions and serve with rice.

SERVES: 6

# SHREDDED CABBAGE

250 g (8 oz) cabbage
•
1 medium onion, finely chopped
•
2 fresh green chillies, seeded
and chopped
•
¼ teaspoon ground turmeric
•
¼ teaspoon ground black pepper
•
½ teaspoon black mustard seeds
•
1 teaspoon salt
•
½ cup (2 oz) desiccated or
grated fresh coconut

Shred cabbage very finely. Wash well, drain and put into a large saucepan with the water that clings to the cabbage. Add all other ingredients except the coconut. Cover and cook gently until cabbage is tender but not overcooked, stirring from time to time. Uncover and add coconut. Stir well, and when any liquid in the pan has been absorbed by the coconut, it is ready.

SERVES: 6

# EGGS IN CHILLI SAUCE

*This is a very hot Indonesian dish, intended as a sambal or accompaniment,
and therefore half a hard-boiled egg per serving is sufficient.*

3 eggs
•
3 tablespoons peanut oil
•
1 medium onion, finely chopped
•
1 clove garlic, crushed
•
1 tablespoon sambal ulek
or chopped fresh chillies
•
½ teaspoon laos powder (optional)
•
3 kemiri or Brazil nuts, finely grated
•
½ teaspoon salt
•
2 teaspoons palm sugar or
brown sugar
•
½ cup (4 fl oz) coconut milk
•
lemon juice to taste

Hard-boil the eggs, stirring them gently for the first 3–4 minutes of cooking so that the yolks are centred. Heat oil and fry onion and garlic until onion is soft and golden. Add sambal ulek, laos and grated nuts, and fry for a few seconds. Add salt, sugar, coconut milk and lemon juice and simmer gently, stirring constantly, until thick and oily in appearance. Put in the shelled and halved eggs, spooning the sauce over them. Serve hot or at room temperature.

SERVES: 6

# SPICY SQUASH, INDIAN STYLE

*Indians like to eat vegetable dishes which are full of flavour accompanied by Chapatis (see page 398). Here is how to make a bland squash fairly jump with joy.*

## INGREDIENTS

500 g (1 lb) spaghetti or other squash

•

1 tablespooon oil or ghee
(clarified butter)

•

1 teaspoon cumin seeds

•

½ teaspoon black mustard seeds

•

1 or 2 fresh chillies, seeded
and sliced finely

•

1 onion, finely chopped

•

½ teaspoon salt, or to taste

•

½ teaspoon chilli powder (optional)

Cook the squash in boiling salted water, drain well and scoop out flesh with a fork. Heat oil or ghee in a wok or saucepan and fry the cumin and mustard seeds on medium heat until seeds start to pop. Add chillies and onion, stir now and then, and cook until onion is soft. Add squash, salt and chilli powder and cook uncovered for 5 minutes, tossing to distribute flavours. Serve warm.

SERVES: 4

# SPICY FRIED CAULIFLOWER, INDIAN STYLE

## INGREDIENTS

½ cauliflower

•

3 tablespoons peanut oil

•

1 teaspoon black mustard seeds

•

½ teaspoon black cumin
(kalonji) seeds

•

1 clove garlic, crushed

•

½ teaspoon grated fresh ginger

•

½ teaspoon ground turmeric

•

1 teaspoon ground cumin

•

½ teaspoon salt or to taste

Wash cauliflower and divide into small sprigs. Thicker stalks may be sliced thinly. Heat oil in a deep frying pan or wok and fry the whole seeds until they start to pop. Add the garlic, ginger, turmeric and cumin, stir for half a minute, then add cauliflower and toss well to coat with the spice mixture.

Sprinkle with salt, add ½ cup (4 fl oz) water, cover and cook on medium heat for about 8 minutes. Uncover and cook quickly to evaporate any moisture but don't let cauliflower become mushy.

SERVES: 4

# INDIAN PEA POD CURRY

*When peas are young and snapping tender, even the pods are put to good use. But the tough, plastic-like lining must be removed as described below, as it is impossible to chew and swallow.*

## INGREDIENTS

pods from 500 g (1 lb) tender young peas

•

1 tablespoon ghee (clarified butter) or oil

•

1 medium onion, finely chopped

•

1 teaspoon finely grated fresh ginger

•

1 teaspoon ground turmeric

•

1 teaspoon salt

•

1 teaspoon Garam Masala (see page 456) or ground cumin

•

½ teaspoon chilli powder

•

2 ripe tomatoes, diced

•

2 medium potatoes, peeled and diced

Separate halves of the pods. Hold each half with the inner side towards you and bend stalk end inwards so that the fleshy part of the pod cracks. Then pull downwards, peeling off and discarding the tough, transparent inner lining of the pod. Wash the pods and remove any strings from edges.

Heat ghee and fry onion and ginger over low heat until onion is soft and golden. Add turmeric, salt, garam masala or cumin and chilli powder. Stir and fry for 1 minute, then add the tomatoes, potatoes and pea pods.

Stir well, cover and cook until potatoes and pea pods are tender. Keep heat low and if necessary, add a few spoonfuls of water now and then. Stir to ensure curry does not stick to base of pan.

The tomatoes should provide sufficient liquid and the curry should be moist but not with a liquid gravy. Serve with rice or Chapatis (see page 398).

SERVES: 4

# SHREDDED LEAFY GREENS WITH COCONUT

*Fresh green leaves are very much part of the Sri Lankan diet and are served at almost every meal in the form of a quickly cooked dish called* mallung. *It can best be described as a dry accompaniment, very tasty, to be eaten with rice. One or two different mallungs are served with every meal and play an important part in nutrition. This is how the people of Sri Lanka get their vitamins.*

*The leaves of many common plants are used; some of them grow in Western countries too—for instance, the yellow flowered cassia. The flowers are dried to make an infusion for medicinal purposes, and the leaves are stripped from the stems and used for mallung. They have a pleasant sour flavour. Tender passionfruit leaves also make delicious mallung. One of the most popular leaves are gotukolle, which look like violet leaves but are really a type of cress which grows near water; as a substitute, use the common curly parsley so readily available. When the leaves on your bunch of radishes are fresh and green, don't throw them away—use them in this recipe.*

### INGREDIENTS

2 cups (4 oz) finely shredded green
leaves
•
1 medium onion, finely chopped
•
2 green chillies, seeded
and chopped (optional)
•
½ teaspoon ground turmeric
•
2 tablespoons lemon juice
•
1 teaspoon salt
•
2–3 tablespoons grated fresh
or desiccated coconut

Put leaves into a saucepan with all the ingredients except the coconut. If there is not much water clinging to leaves after washing, add a sprinkling of water. Stir well, cover and cook over medium heat for about 6 minutes. Uncover, add coconut and toss over low heat until coconut absorbs all the liquid. Remove from heat. Serve hot or cold as an accompaniment to rice.

SERVES: 6

# STIR-FRIED SALAD SPROUTS

*One of the quickest-cooking dishes, literally less than 5 minutes on the stove—but do the preparation ahead.*

### INGREDIENTS

3 cups salad sprouts (mung bean,
alfalfa, fenugreek, lentil)
•
1 large carrot

Rinse the salad sprouts in a large bowl of cold water. Drain well in a colander and pinch off straggly tails.

Cut the carrot into long diagonal slices no more than 6mm (¼ in) thick, then stack 3–4 slices together and cut into matchstick strips. Either blanch the carrot strips in

2 spring onions (scallions)

•

few stalks of choy sum
(Chinese vegetable) (optional)

•

1 tablespoon peanut oil

•

½ teaspoon finely chopped garlic

•

1 tablespoon light soy sauce

•

few drops of sesame oil

boiling water for 1 minute or if you have a microwave oven, cover with plastic wrap and microwave for 30 seconds.

Cut the lower half of the spring onions into bite-size lengths, and roughly chop the dark green leaves, keeping the two separate. If using choy sum, cut into bite-size lengths.

Place a wok over heat and when hot, pour in the peanut oil and allow to heat, then swirl the wok so that it is coated with oil. Throw in the garlic and spring onion leaves and stir-fry for 30 seconds. Add the choy sum, and stir-fry for 1 minute. Mix in the well-drained sprouts, white portions of spring onion, and carrot and stir-fry for 1 minute. Stir in the soy sauce and mix well. Turn off the heat, sprinkle the sesame oil over, toss to mix, and serve at once, accompanied by steamed rice.

NOTE: If liked, bean curd (cut into strips or diced) may be added with the sprouts.

SERVES: 4

# SPICY CABBAGE IN COCONUT MILK

*Cabbage has never tasted go good as in this rich coconut gravy with exciting hot and sour flavours from Indonesia.*

### INGREDIENTS

500 g (1 lb) cabbage

•

2 onions, chopped

•

2 cloves garlic

•

2 fresh red chillies, seeded and chopped,
or 1 teaspoon chilli powder

•

1 daun salam or 3 curry leaves

•

2 tablespoons peanut oil

•

2 strips lemon rind

•

1½ cups (12 fl oz) thick coconut milk
(see page 443)

•

1 teaspoon salt

•

1 tablespoon dried tamarind pulp

Wash and coarsely shred the cabbage. Put chopped onions, garlic and chillies into the container of an electric blender and blend to a purée. Alternatively, grate onions and garlic, chop chillies finely or use chilli powder and mix well.

In a wok or large saucepan, fry the curry leaves in hot oil for 1 minute, turn in the blended mixture and fry, stirring, until the mixture turns a darker colour. Stir constantly or mixture might stick to base of pan. Add lemon rind, coconut milk and salt, stir well while bringing to simmering point. Add the cabbage and simmer, uncovered, for a few minutes until the cabbage is cooked but still crisp. Stir in the tamarind and serve.

SERVES: 6

# PUMPKIN CURRY

500 g (1 lb) pumpkin

•

1 small onion, finely chopped

•

2 cloves garlic, finely chopped

•

3 fresh green chillies,
seeded and chopped

•

8–10 curry leaves

•

½ teaspoon fenugreek seeds

•

½ teaspoon ground turmeric

•

1½ cups (12 fl oz) thin coconut milk
(see page 443)

•

1 teaspoon salt

•

½ cup (4 fl oz) thick coconut milk
(see page 443)

•

1 teaspoon black mustard seeds

Peel pumpkin and cut into large chunks. Put into a pan with all the ingredients except the thick coconut milk and mustard seeds. Bring slowly to simmering point and cook gently, uncovered, until pumpkin is almost tender. Meanwhile, grind the mustard seeds with a mortar and pestle and mix with the thick coconut milk. Add to the simmering pot and cook for 5 minutes longer on very gentle heat.

SERVES: 6

# STEAMED AND SPICED EGGPLANT

2 large firm eggplants (aubergines)

•

1½ tablespoons peanut oil

•

5 kemiri or Brazil nuts, chopped

•

½ teaspoon laos powder (optional)

•

½ teaspoon sambal ulek or
freshly chopped chilli

•

1 tablespoon tamarind pulp

•

1 tablespoon dark soy sauce

•

1 teaspoon palm sugar or
brown sugar

•

½ cup thick coconut milk
(see page 443)

Peel the eggplants and cut into cubes. Drop into lightly salted boiling water or cook over steam until tender. Drain well. Heat oil in a wok or small frying pan and fry the kemiri nuts over low heat, stirring constantly. Add laos, sambal ulek, tamarind pulp, soy sauce, sugar and coconut milk. Simmer gently, pour over eggplants before serving. Serve with hot cooked rice.

SERVES: 6

PUMPKIN (squash) CURRY

# EGG AND COCONUT CURRY

## INGREDIENTS

6–8 eggs

•

2 tablespoons oil

•

1 medium onion, finely sliced

•

1½ teaspoons crushed garlic

•

1 teaspoon finely grated fresh ginger

•

2 or 3 fresh green chillies,
seeded and sliced

•

6 curry leaves

•

1 teaspoon ground turmeric

•

2 cups (16 fl oz) thin coconut milk
(see page 443)

•

1½ cups (12 fl oz) thick coconut milk
(see page 443)

•

1 teaspoon salt

•

lemon juice to taste

Put the eggs into cold water, bring slowly to the boil, stirring for the first 5 minutes to centre the yolks. Simmer for 10 minutes, then cool quickly under cold running water. Shell the eggs and set aside.

Heat oil in a saucepan and fry the onion, garlic, ginger, chillies and curry leaves on low heat until onions are soft, without letting them brown. Add turmeric and stir, then add the thin coconut milk and simmer uncovered for 10 minutes. Add the thick coconut milk and salt, and stir constantly while letting it come to simmering point. Halve the eggs lengthways and simmer them in the coconut gravy just until heated through. Remove from heat, stir in lemon juice to taste. Serve with white rice.

SERVES: 4–6

# SPICY BEAN SPROUTS

## INGREDIENTS

500 g (1 lb) fresh bean sprouts

•

2 tablespoons ghee
(clarified butter) or oil

•

2 cloves garlic, crushed

•

1 teaspoon finely grated fresh ginger

•

2 medium onions, finely chopped

•

½ teaspoon ground turmeric

•

1 teaspoon ground cumin

•

1 tablespoon desiccated coconut

•

1 teaspoon salt

•

½ cup (4 fl oz) coconut milk

Wash bean sprouts, picking off any straggly tails. Drain in a colander.

Heat ghee or oil in a wok or large frying pan and fry the garlic, ginger and onions, stirring until onions are soft and golden. Stir in turmeric, cumin and coconut. Add bean sprouts, toss and fry for 3 minutes, then sprinkle salt over, add coconut milk, cover and cook for 5 minutes. Serve with rice or Chapatis (see page 398).

SERVES: 4

# BEAN STARCH SHEETS AND BRAISED GLUTEN

## INGREDIENTS

1 cup sliced Gluten (250g/8 oz)
(see page 437)
•
2 tablespoons peanut oil
•
few slices of fresh ginger
•
2 spring onions (scallions)
•
2 tablespoons dark soy sauce
•
¼ cup (2 fl oz) water
•
3 sheets green bean starch
•
250 g (8 oz) French beans
•
1 tablespoon peanut oil

### SAUCE

2 tablespoons Chinese sesame paste
•
1 tablespoon sesame oil
•
2 tablespoons dark soy sauce
•
2 tablespoons Chinese wine
or dry sherry
•
1 tablespoon chilli sauce
•
1 tablespoon Chinese sweetened
vinegar
•
2 teaspoons sugar

Prepare gluten and cut into thin slices. Heat oil and fry the ginger, spring onions and gluten for 2 minutes, then add the soy sauce and the water. Cover and simmer for 5 minutes, then leave to cool.

Soak the sheets of green bean starch in hot water for 20 minutes, then boil them for 5 minutes. Drain and refresh under cold running water. Cut into strips 5 × 1 cm (2 × ½ in). Drain thoroughly and chill.

String the beans and cut them into diagonal strips. Drop them into boiling water to which the peanut oil has been added, and boil rapidly for 2 minutes. Drain and allow to cool.

Combine the sauce ingredients. In cold weather it may be necessary to warm the sesame paste to mix.

Arrange the strips of green bean starch on a platter, top with gluten slices and beans. Spoon the sauce over. Serve on a bed of crisp lettuce leaves. If like, garnish with fresh coriander.

SERVES: 4

# WATER CONVOLVULUS IN SWEET GRAVY

## INGREDIENTS

500 g (1 lb) kangkung or substitute
(see Note)
•
1½ cups (12 fl oz) coconut milk
•
1 large onion, finely chopped
•
1 small clove garlic, crushed
•
1 teaspoon salt
•
1 teaspoon finely grated fresh ginger
•
1 fresh red chilli, seeded and sliced
•
2 tablespoons palm sugar or
brown sugar
•
½ teaspoon laos powder
(optional)

Wash the greens very well in several changes of cold water and drain. Slice coarsely. Put coconut milk and all other ingredients into a large saucepan and bring to the boil, uncovered. Add the green vegetables. Cover and simmer on low heat for 20 minutes or until tender. Serve hot with rice and other dishes.

NOTE: *Kangkung* is the name by which this tasty dark green leafy vegetable is known in South-East Asian countries. It is highly prized for its nutritional value and is now available in most countries. You may find it as *Ong Choy* in Chinese greengrocers. Alternatively you may substitute watercress, spinach or chicory. Although chicory is bitter, this preparation contains sugar and the resulting bitter-sweet combination is fascinating.

SERVES: 6

# VEGETABLE CURRY

*Here is the basic white curry from South-East Asia. In it you can cook
beans, pumpkin, okra, capsicum (sweet peppers), potatoes, zucchini (courgette),
asparagus or other vegetables of your choice.*

## INGREDIENTS

3 cups (24 fl oz) thin coconut milk
(see page 443)
•
1 medium onion, finely sliced
•
2 fresh green chillies, seeded and split
•
½ teaspoon ground turmeric
•
2 cloves garlic, finely sliced
•
½ teaspoon finely grated fresh ginger
•
5 cm (2 in) cinnamon stick
•
4 pieces dried daun pandan
or rampe leaf
•

Put all ingredients, except sliced vegetables, salt and thick coconut milk into a large saucepan and simmer gently, uncovered, for approximately 10 minutes. Add sliced vegetables and salt, and cook gently until vegetables are just tender. Add thick coconut milk and simmer for 5 minutes longer. Serve with boiled rice, other curries and accompaniments.

VARIATION: RAW CASHEW NUT CURRY

A curry of fresh cashew nuts is one of the delights of Sri Lankan cooking. Fresh cashew nuts are unobtainable except in the country in which they are grown but raw cashews, from health food shops and Chinese grocery stores, make a very good substitute if soaked for an hour or two in cold water.

1 sprig lemon grass or
2 strips lemon rind

•

8 curry leaves

•

750 g (1½ lb) vegetables, sliced

•

salt to taste

•

1 cup (8 fl oz) thick coconut milk
(see page 443)

Proceed as for Vegetable Curry but substitute 250 g (8 oz) raw cashew nuts for the sliced vegetables. Simmer for approximately 30 minutes, or until cashews are tender. Serve with boiled rice and other accompaniments.

SERVES: 4–6

# GREEN BANANA CURRY

### INGREDIENTS

4 or 5 unripe bananas

•

1 teaspoon salt

•

1 teaspoon ground turmeric

•

¼ cup (2 fl oz) oil

•

2 cups (16 fl oz) coconut milk

•

1 small onion, finely sliced

•

2 fresh green chillies, sliced

•

¼ teaspoon fenugreek seeds

•

8 curry leaves

•

small stick cinnamon

Rub hands with oil before starting to handle unripe bananas, as this prevents staining. Alternatively, wear rubber gloves. Peel the bananas, halve crossways and then cut into slices or quarter lengthways. Rub them with salt and turmeric.

Heat oil in small frying pan and fry the banana slices a few at a time, until they are golden brown all over. Set aside. Put all the remaining ingredients into a saucepan and simmer, uncovered, until onion is soft. Add fried bananas and simmer until gravy is thick.

NOTE: The green bananas used for this curry must be really unripe, otherwise the texture will not be correct.

SERVES: 6

# VEGETABLES IN COCONUT GRAVY

*Any vegetables in season can be used. French beans, cabbage, cauliflower, broccoli, zucchini (courgette), pumpkin and winter bamboo shoots are an excellent combination in this recipe from Indonesia.*

### INGREDIENTS

500–750 g (1–1½ lb) vegetables

•

2 tablespoons peanut oil

•

1 onion, finely chopped

•

2 cloves garlic, crushed

•

1 teaspoon sambal ulek or
1 fresh red chilli, seeded and chopped

•

1 sprig lemon grass or 2 strips lemon rind

•

1 large ripe tomato

Slice vegetables into small pieces: cauliflower or broccoli should be broken or cut into florets, beans sliced very thinly, cabbage shredded coarsely and the shreds cut across once or twice into bite-size lengths. Zucchini or pumpkin can be sliced thinly or diced. Winter bamboo shoots, more tender than the ordinary variety, are cut into short strips, or can be halved and sliced for a half moon shape.

Heat oil in a medium-size saucepan and fry the onion until soft and starting to colour. Add garlic and chilli and fry over low heat for 2 minutes, stirring the mixture. Mix in lemon grass or substitute and the tomato, which has been peeled, seeded and chopped. Stir and cook to a pulp.

Add stock and coconut milk and bring to simmering

2 cups (16 fl oz) Vegetable Stock
(see page 448)
•
1½ cups (12 fl oz) coconut milk
•
3 teaspoons peanut butter
•
1 teaspoon salt, or to taste

point with lid off. Add vegetables according to the time they take to cook. They should be tender but still crisp. In the selection suggested you would add the beans, simmer for 4 minutes, then add the cauliflower and broccoli, simmer for a further 3 minutes, then add the cabbage, zucchini, pumpkin and bamboo shoots and cook for 3 minutes longer. Stir in the peanut butter and add salt to taste. A squeeze of lemon juice may be added if a sharper flavour is preferred.

SERVES: 6

# BEAN SAYUR

*If you glance down the list of ingredients in this Indonesian dish, and think it's a lot of trouble to take over a few beans, please try it once—I'm sure it won't be the last time.*

### INGREDIENTS

2 tablespoons peanut oil
•
1 onion, finely chopped
•
2 cloves garlic, crushed
•
2 fresh red chillies, seeded
and chopped
•
1 teaspoon finely grated lemon rind
•
2 teaspoons ground coriander
•
1 teaspoon ground cumin
•
½ teaspoon laos powder (optional)
•
1 teaspoon salt
•
2 tablespoons dried tamarind pulp
or lemon juice
•
1 daun salam or 3 curry leaves
•
3 cups (24 fl oz) Vegetable Stock
(see page 448)
•
500 g (1 lb) fresh green beans, sliced
•
1½ cups (12 fl oz) coconut milk

Heat oil, fry onion, garlic and chillies for 5 minutes over medium heat, stirring all the time. Add lemon rind and ground spices, then fry for 1 minute. Add salt, tamarind pulp, daun salam or curry leaves, stock and beans. Bring to the boil, simmer for 8 minutes, then add coconut milk. Simmer for 5 minutes more and serve.

NOTE: When serving this sayur as the main dish, rice vermicelli can be added. Soak 125 g (4 oz) of rice vermicelli in very hot water for 10 minutes, then drain well. Add to sayur and cook for a further 2 minutes.

SERVES: 6

# STEAMED VEGETABLES WITH COCONUT

### INGREDIENTS

250 g (8 oz) fresh green beans

•

4 carrots

•

250 g (8 oz) bean sprouts

•

½ small cabbage

•

1 canned bamboo shoot

•

1 cup (3 oz) fresh grated or
desiccated coconut

•

2 tablespoons hot milk or water
(if using desiccated coconut)

•

1 small onion, finely chopped

•

½ teaspoon sambal ulek
or chilli powder

•

1 teaspoon salt

•

2 tablespoons lemon juice

Prepare beans, carrots, bean sprouts and cabbage as for Gado-Gado (see page 340). Cut bamboo shoot into strips the same size as the beans. Put the coconut into a bowl. If using desiccated coconut, sprinkle hot milk or water over and mix with the fingertips to moisten evenly. Add onion, sambal or chilli powder, salt and lemon juice. Mix thoroughly together.

Sprinkle coconut mixture over vegetables, reserving some to garnish the dish when served. Put vegetables in a steamer and steam for 5–8 minutes. Turn on to serving dish and sprinkle with reserved coconut. Serve on its own or as an accompaniment.

SERVES: 4–6

# SPICED STEAMED CAULIFLOWER

### INGREDIENTS

1 small cauliflower

•

2 tablespoons butter or ghee
(clarified butter)

•

salt and pepper to taste

•

¼ cup (1 oz) finely chopped cashews

•

2 teaspoons chironji nuts or
sunflower seeds

•

½ teaspoon Garam Masala
(see page 456)

Steam the cauliflower until half cooked. Put into an oven dish, spread with half the butter or ghee and season with salt and pepper. Cover and bake in an oven preheated to 180°C (350°F) until tender, then remove lid and brown under griller (broiler). In remaining butter or ghee, lightly fry the cashews until golden, add chironji or sunflower seeds and fry a little longer. Mix in the garam masala and sprinkle over the cauliflower. Serve hot.

SERVES: 4

STEAMED VEGETABLES WITH COCONUT

# EGGPLANT YOGHURT RELISH

*As a palate pleaser, this is hard to beat.*

## INGREDIENTS

4 small or 2 large eggplants
(aubergines)

•

salt

•

turmeric

•

chilli powder

•

oil for deep frying

•

2 onions, sliced finely

•

2 green (hot) chillies,
seeded and sliced

•

6 cloves garlic, crushed with
1 teaspoon salt

•

2 teaspoons finely grated fresh ginger

•

1 heaped teaspoon hot
English mustard

•

¼ cup (2 fl oz) white vinegar

•

1 teaspoon sugar

•

½ cup (4 fl oz) cream or yoghurt

Cut the eggplants into cubes and sprinkle with ½ teaspoon each of salt, turmeric and chilli powder. Heat oil for deep frying and fry the cubes in batches until deep golden brown. Drain on paper towels, then arrange on a serving dish. Place the sliced onions and chillies over the eggplants. Mix the other ingredients into a creamy sauce and just before serving, pour it evenly over the eggplants, onions and chillies, and gently mix with a fork. Serve cold as an accompaniment to rice and curries.

NOTE: In Sri Lanka, where this recipe originated, garlic cloves are very small, so perhaps just one jumbo size garlic clove would do—depends how keen you are on the pungent bulb.

SERVES: 8

# STIR-FRIED BOK CHOY

*There are so many vegetables called Chinese cabbage. This is chard cabbage, one with thick white leaf ribs and dark green leaves. Most often they are long and large leaves but sometimes you come across bunches of tiny ones which you can cook whole, being careful to wash out any sand that collects at the base of the leaves.*

## INGREDIENTS

500 g (1 lb) Chinese chard
cabbage (bok choy)

•

2 tablespoons peanut oil

Prepare the bok choy. Separate the leaves from the heart, wash them well and trim off a small slice at their base. Lay the leaves flat on the chopping board and remove the tough leaf edges, leaving just a little border of green on the white stems. Cut the stems into 5 cm (2 in) lengths.

1 clove garlic, bruised

•

3 slices fresh ginger

•

¼ cup (2 fl oz) water

•

1 teaspoon sugar

•

½ teaspoon salt

•

1 teaspoon sesame oil

Heat a wok, add the peanut oil and swirl to coat the wok. Add the garlic and ginger, and fry for a few seconds just until golden. Add the cabbage and stir-fry for 1 minute. Then add the water, the sugar and salt, cover the wok and simmer for 2 minutes.

Uncover and stir-fry again until most of the liquid evaporates. Turn off the heat, sprinkle the sesame oil over and toss to distribute. Remove and discard the garlic and ginger. Serve at once.

NOTE: If the cabbage is not being served right away or must be reheated, use a slightly different method. After washing and cutting the stems, blanch them in a large pan of lightly salted boiling water with 1 tablespoon of oil added. Once the water returns to the boil, boil the cabbage for only 30 seconds, then drain. Just before serving, stir-fry as above. This way the cabbage doesn't get that tired look if not served immediately.

SERVES: 4–6

# STIR-FRIED VEGETABLES

*Use any kind of vegetable or a mixture of different vegetables: coarsely shredded cabbage; watercress, broken into bite-size lengths; chokos peeled and sliced; beans sliced diagonally; bean sprouts; sliced celery; and so on.*

INGREDIENTS

3 cups prepared
vegetables

•

2 tablespoons oil

•

1 clove garlic, crushed

•

1 small onion, finely chopped

•

2 daun salam or curry leaves

•

½ teaspoon salt, or to taste

•

1 tablespoon light soy sauce,
or to taste

Vegetables should be washed and well drained. Heat oil in a wok or large frying pan and fry the garlic, onion and curry leaves over medium heat, stirring constantly, until onion is soft. Add vegetables and stir-fry until lightly cooked but still crisp.

If using a mixture of vegetables, add those that take longest to cook first. Stir in salt and soy sauce to taste and serve immediately.

SERVES: 4

# OKRA CURRY

*Those who like this delicately flavoured pod with the strange texture will need no persuading, but if you are ambivalent about it, this recipe may convince you that it's rather good.*

## INGREDIENTS

250 g (8 oz) tender okra
•
½ teaspoon ground turmeric
•
oil for deep-frying
•
1 small onion, finely chopped
•
2 fresh green chillies,
seeded and sliced
•
6 curry leaves
•
1 teaspoon roasted ground coriander
•
½ teaspoon roasted ground cumin
•
small piece cinnamon stick
•
½ teaspoon salt
•
¼ teaspoon chilli powder (optional)
•
1½ cups (12 fl oz) coconut milk
(see page 443)

Wash okra, cut off tops, then slice diagonally into bite-size lengths. Rub with ground turmeric. Heat oil in a small frying pan and deep-fry the okra until lightly browned. Drain.

Put all the other ingredients into a saucepan and simmer, uncovered for 10 minutes or until onions are cooked. Add the fried okra, simmer 5 minutes and remove from heat. Serve with rice.

SERVES: 4

# CHILLI-FRIED CAULIFLOWER

## INGREDIENTS

3 tablespoons peanut oil
•
4 fresh red chillies, finely chopped,
or 2 teaspoons sambal ulek
•
1 large onion, finely chopped
•
2 cloves garlic, finely chopped
•
1 teaspoon salt
•
500 g (1 lb) cauliflower, sliced
•
2 tablespoons hot water

Heat oil in wok or frying pan and fry the chillies, onion and garlic over low heat, stirring frequently, until onion is soft and golden. Add salt, then turn in the cauliflower and toss, stirring constantly until cauliflower is thoroughly mixed with the fried chilli and onion mixture. Sprinkle with the hot water, cover and cook for 10 minutes. Serve hot.

SERVES: 6

# POTATO AND CABBAGE CURRY

### INGREDIENTS

1 onion, finely sliced

•

1 clove garlic, finely chopped

•

2 fresh red or green chillies,
seeded and sliced

•

½ teaspoon ground turmeric

•

1 cup (8 fl oz) thin coconut milk
(see page 443)

•

1 large potato, peeled and diced

•

¼ medium (about 3 cups) coarsely
shredded cabbage

•

1 teaspoon salt

•

1 cup (8 fl oz) thick coconut milk
(see page 443)

•

lemon juice to taste

Put the onion, garlic, chillies, turmeric and thin coconut milk into a saucepan and bring to simmering point. Add potato and cook for 10 minutes or until potato is half cooked. Add cabbage and salt, cook for 3 minutes, then add the thick coconut milk and stir gently until cabbage is cooked. Remove from heat and add lemon juice to taste.

SERVES: 6

# ROJAK

*This is the Malaysian or Indonesian salad that can either be an entrée or,
in larger quantities, makes a meal.*

### INGREDIENTS

1 large or 2 small cucumbers

•

1 small pineapple, not too ripe

•

3 fresh red or green chillies

### DRESSING

3 tablespoons Chinese (rice) vinegar
or other mild vinegar

•

2 tablespoons sugar

•

2 teaspoons sambal ulek or
crushed fresh chillies

•

salt and lemon juice to taste

Peel cucumbers, cut lengthways and remove seeds, then cut into matchstick strips. Cut skin off pineapple and remove all the eyes. Cut pineapple into wedges lengthways, slice off core, then dice flesh. Seed chillies and cut into thin slices. Combine cucumbers, pineapple and chillies in a bowl and sprinkle lightly with salt.

To make the dressing, mix vinegar, sugar, chillies, salt and lemon juice to taste, then toss the dressing with the pineapple mixture. Alternatively, serve the dressing separately.

SERVES: 6

317

# GARLIC CURRY

*In this unusual curry, cloves of garlic are treated as a vegetable. If
250 g (8 oz) garlic sounds terrifying to you, tone down the content by
substituting the garlic with small new potatoes, halved or quartered.*

### INGREDIENTS

250 g (8 oz) large garlic cloves
•
8–10 small onions,
preferably red onions
•
8 large banana capsicums
(large, mild chilli peppers)
•
2 tablespoons coconut oil
(or other vegetable oil)
•
1 teaspoon fenugreek seeds
•
1 teaspoon chilli powder
•
½ teaspoon ground turmeric
•
1½ cups (12 fl oz) coconut milk
•
1 teaspoon salt, or to taste

Peel the garlic and onions. Wash and dry the capsicums.
Heat the oil in a heavy-based saucepan and fry the whole
cloves of garlic and the onions until nicely golden. Add the
capsicums and fry for a minute longer, then add fenugreek
seeds, chilli powder and turmeric, and stir for a few seconds.
Pour in 1 cup (8 fl oz) of hot water and add the salt. Bring
to simmering point, cover and simmer for 15 minutes or
until garlic and onions (and potatoes if they are used) are
tender. Uncover, add the coconut milk and stir while
returning to the simmer. Cook gently, uncovered, for 5
minutes and serve with rice.

SERVES: 4

# STUFFED CHILLIES

*Large, long mild chillies are filled with a potato mixture enlivened
by small, hot chillies.*

### INGREDIENTS

8 banana capsicums (large,
mild chilli peppers)
•
1 large onion, roughly chopped
•
1 ripe tomato, peeled
and roughly chopped
•
1 teaspoon chopped fresh ginger
•
2 fresh red chillies, seeded
•
¼ cup (2 fl oz) oil
•
½ cup (4 fl oz) hot water

Start by making the potato filling. Peel and dice the potatoes
and cook in lightly salted boiling water until soft. Drain
well. Heat the oil in a small pan and add the turmeric.
Add onion and chillies and fry, stirring now and then, until
soft. Remove from heat, add to the potatoes together with
salt and pepper and mix thoroughly. While potatoes should
not be mashed, they should be sufficiently soft to hold
together.

Wash banana capsicums (peppers) and dry them. Slice
off the tops and with pointed knife, remove seeds and pith
from the centre. Stuff with potato filling, using the handle
of a teaspoon to fill them right to the end.

Put onion, tomato, ginger and red chillies into an electric

½ teaspoon Garam Masala
(see page 456)
•
2 tablespoons chopped fresh
coriander (optional) to garnish

---

POTATO FILLING
500 g (1 lb) potatoes
•
2 tablespoons oil
•
½ teaspoon ground turmeric
•
1 medium onion, finely chopped
•
2 small, hot chillies, seeded and
finely chopped
•
¾ teaspoon salt
•
¼ teaspoon ground black pepper

blender and blend to a purée. Heat the oil in a frying pan or saucepan and fry the capsicums, turning them gently, until almost cooked. Transfer to a plate and add the blended mixture to the oil left in the pan. Stir and fry until the mixture smells cooked and oil separates from the mass. Add hot water, cover and cook over low heat for a few more minutes. Stir well, taking care it does not stick to the pan. Lay the capsicums in the mixture, sprinkle with garam masala, cover and cook for a further 5 minutes. Sprinkle with chopped fresh coriander and serve with rice or Chapatis (see page 398).

SERVES: 4

# PINEAPPLE COCONUT CURRY

INGREDIENTS

1 small pineapple, not too ripe
•
1 tablespoon oil
•
1 small onion, finely chopped
•
1 clove garlic, finely chopped
•
small stick cinnamon
•
3 whole cloves
•
3 cardamom pods, bruised
•
3 teaspoons ground coriander
•
1½ teaspoons ground cumin
•
½ teaspoon chilli powder
or 1 fresh chilli
•
1 teaspoon salt
•
1 cup (8 fl oz) thick coconut milk
(see page 443)
•
1 teaspoon palm sugar or brown sugar

Peel pineapple with a sharp knife and remove the eyes with a series of slanting cuts. Cut into 8 wedges lengthways and trim off the hard core. Now cut each wedge into thick slices crossways.

Heat oil in a saucepan and fry onion, garlic and whole spices over medium heat, stirring frequently, until onion is soft. Add coriander, cumin, chilli and salt, and stir for a few minutes until spices are browned. Add pineapple and stir well to coat with the spice mixture. Add coconut milk and sugar, and bring to simmering point, stirring constantly. Do not cover pan. Simmer for 3–4 minutes or until pineapple is just tender. Fruit should not be too soft.

SERVES: 6

# BEAN CURD WITH HOT SAUCE

### INGREDIENTS

4 squares pressed bean curd

•

1 teaspoon finely chopped ginger

•

1 teaspoon finely chopped garlic

•

1 tablespoon finely chopped
spring onion (scallion)

•

1 tablespoon peanut oil

•

½ cup (4 fl oz) Vegetable Stock
(see page 448) or water

•

1 teaspoon ground bean sauce
(mor sze jeung)

•

1 teaspoon chilli paste

•

1 tablespoon tomato sauce

•

½ teaspoon salt

•

½ teaspoon sugar

•

1 teaspoon dark soy sauce

•

1 teaspoon cornflour (cornstarch)

•

few drops of sesame oil

Cut the bean curd into small dice. Have the chopped ginger, garlic and spring onion ready on a plate. Bring 4 cups (32 fl oz) of water to a rolling boil in a wok, add the diced bean curd and bring the water back to the boil for a few minutes until the bean curd is heated through. Pour into a sieve and allow to drain.

Dry the wok, add the peanut oil and when hot, stir-fry the ginger, garlic and spring onion. Add the stock or water, bean sauce, chilli paste, tomato sauce, salt, sugar and soy sauce and allow it to boil. Blend the cornflour with 1 tablespoon of cold water and stir it into the mixture.

Place the bean curd in the wok and sprinkle the sesame oil over. With a large ladle, scoop the sauce over it, taking care not to mash the bean curd. If liked, serve on a bed of Stir-Fried Lettuce (see page 296) and garnish with a chilli flower.

NOTE:  In most Chinese grocery stores you can buy soft bean curd in plastic boxes, soaking in water. You can also buy pressed or firm bean curd, either white or coloured yellow, in a tray wrapped in plastic film. Buy the firm one for this dish.

SERVES: 4

BEAN CURD WITH HOT SAUCE

# EGGPLANT AND POTATO CURRY

## INGREDIENTS

2 small eggplants (aubergines)

•

2 large potatoes

•

2 large ripe tomatoes

•

1 large onion

•

2 fresh green chillies

•

1 bunch spinach

•

½ cup (4 fl oz) oil

•

1 ½ teaspoons finely chopped ginger

•

½ teaspoon cumin seeds, crushed

•

½ teaspoon ground turmeric

•

1 teaspoon salt

•

1 teaspoon palm sugar or
brown sugar

Wash eggplants and cut in small cubes. Peel and dice the potatoes, then peel and chop the tomatoes. Finely chop the onion. Seed and slice the chillies. Wash the spinach in several changes of water, remove tough stalks and roughly chop the leaves.

Heat oil in a deep frying pan or wok until smoking hot. Fry the potatoes until golden, remove from pan. Fry the eggplants and remove from pan. If necessary, add an extra tablespoon of oil. Add the onion and fry until soft and golden, then stir in ginger, cumin and turmeric, and fry for 1 minute. Add chillies, tomatoes and salt, then add the potatoes, eggplants and spinach. Stir. Cover and cook on low heat until spinach is soft, adding ½ cup (4 fl oz) water if necessary. Add palm sugar, stir and cook uncovered until liquid evaporates. Serve with rice or Chapatis (see page 398).

SERVES: 6

# FRIED BITTER GOURD AND EGGPLANT

*Fresh bitter gourds or* karela *as they are called in India are sold in Chinese greengrocers as bitter melon. Buy these whenever possible but if canned ones are used, add them only during the last few minutes of cooking.*

## INGREDIENTS

1 large or 2 small bitter gourds
(bitter melons)

•

1 medium or 2 small eggplants
(aubergines)

•

3 medium onions

•

2 fresh red or green chillies

•

¼ cup (2 fl oz) oil

Halve the bitter gourds lengthways, and if seeds are large and mature, remove and discard. If the bitter gourds are tender, the seeds may be left in. Slice thickly lengthways, then cut into 5 cm (2 in) lengths. Wash but do not peel eggplants. Cut them into small cubes. Chop the onions and seed and slice the chillies.

Heat oil in a heavy-based saucepan and add the panch phora. Fry for 1 minute, then add onions and chillies. Fry, stirring occasionally, until onions are golden. Add ginger and turmeric, then fry the bitter gourd for 3 minutes, stirring.

½ teaspoon Panch Phora
(see page 456)
•
2 teaspoons finely grated
fresh ginger
•
½ teaspoon ground turmeric
•
1 teaspoon salt
•
approximately ¼ cup (2 fl oz)
hot water

Add eggplant and salt. Stir well, adding about ¼ cup (2 fl oz) hot water or just enough to cover base of pan. Cover and cook on low heat for about 20 minutes or until the vegetables are cooked through. Stir occasionally, being careful not to mash the pieces of bitter gourd and eggplant. If there is much liquid left in pan when vegetables are tender, cook uncovered to evaporate most of the liquid. Serve with rice of Chapatis (see page 398).

SERVES: 4–6

# OKRA FRIED IN BATTER

### INGREDIENTS

250 g (8 oz) small, tender okra
•
1 teaspoon oil
•
2 teaspoons ground coriander
•
2 teaspoons ground rice
•
¼ teaspoon ground turmeric
•
1 teaspoon finely grated fresh ginger
•
2 fresh green chillies, seeded
and finely chopped
•
1 teaspoon salt
•
squeeze of lemon juice to taste

### BATTER
½ cup (2 oz) chick pea flour
•
½ cup (2 oz) self-raising flour
•
approximately ¾ cup (6 fl oz) water
•
½ teaspoon Garam Masala
(see page 456)
•
½ teaspoon chilli powder
•
1 teaspoon crushed garlic
•
1 teaspoon salt
•
oil for deep-frying

Wash okra, wipe dry with paper towels and make a slit on one side of each pod. Heat the oil and fry the coriander, ground rice, turmeric, ginger and chillies, stirring constantly, until the spices are golden brown. Remove from heat, mix in the salt and lemon juice to taste. Spoon a little mixture into each okra pod.

To make the batter, mix the chick pea and self-raising flours smoothly with enough water to make a fairly liquid coating batter. Stir in the garam masala, chilli powder, garlic and salt. Heat enough oil to deep-fry the okra. Dip each one into the batter, then drop into the hot oil. Fry over medium-high heat until golden brown. Drain on absorbent paper and serve as an appetiser or with rice and curry.

NOTE: Do you know how to choose tender young okra? It is important you do, for mature okra is tough and stringy. Look for small, slender, bright green pods and test by bending the pointed tip. If tender it will snap but if old it will merely bend and you will not be able to break it.

SERVES: 4

# SPICY TOMATO PURÉE

### INGREDIENTS

4 large ripe tomatoes

•

2 tablespoons ghee
(clarified butter) or oil

•

1 small onion, finely chopped

•

1 teaspoon finely chopped
fresh ginger

•

1 fresh green chilli, seeded
and chopped

•

2 tablespoons chopped
fresh coriander

•

½ teaspoon ground black pepper

•

½ teaspoon salt, or to taste

Roast whole tomatoes over gas flame or under griller (broiler) until skins wrinkle. Peel and chop. Heat ghee or oil in a saucepan or wok and fry the onion and ginger until golden. Add tomatoes and remaining ingredients. Cover and cook until the tomatoes are a thick pulp and most of the liquid has evaporated. Serve with rice or Chapatis (see page 398).

SERVES: 4

# SAVOURY FRIED BEANS

*A very simple way of giving exotic flavour to beans.*

### INGREDIENTS

500 g (1 lb) green beans or
long beans

•

1 tablespoon oil or ghee
(clarified butter)

•

½ teaspoon black mustard seeds

•

1 medium onion, finely chopped

•

½ teaspoon finely grated fresh ginger

•

1 teaspoon ground turmeric

•

1 teaspoon Garam Masala
(see page 456)

•

1 fresh red or green chilli,
seeded and chopped

•

½ cup (4 fl oz) coconut milk

•

1½ teaspoons salt, or to taste

Top and tail beans, remove strings and cut them into 5 cm (2 in) lengths. Heat the oil or ghee in a wok or saucepan and fry the black mustard seeds until they pop. Add the onion and ginger and fry, stirring, until onion is soft and golden. Add turmeric, garam masala, chilli and the beans, and fry for 2–3 minutes. Add coconut milk and salt, then cook uncovered, stirring now and then, until beans are just tender.

SERVES: 4–6

# CURRIED VEGETABLES IN COCONUT MILK

### INGREDIENTS

2 tablespoons peanut oil

•

2 medium onions, finely chopped

•

2 fresh red chillies, seeded and sliced

•

4 cloves garlic, finely chopped

•

2 teaspoons finely grated fresh ginger

•

2 teaspoons ground coriander

•

1 teaspoon ground cumin

•

1 teaspoon ground turmeric

•

1 teaspoon ground black pepper

•

½ teaspoon laos powder

•

2 sprigs lemon grass or
1 teaspoon finely chopped lemon
rind

•

4 cups (32 fl oz) Vegetable Stock
(see page 448)

•

2 cups (16 fl oz) thick coconut milk
(see page 443)

•

2 teaspoons salt

•

2 daun salam or curry leaves
(optional)

•

2 large potatoes, peeled and diced

•

250 g (8 oz) green beans, finely sliced

•

500 g (1 lb) cabbage,
coarsely shredded

•

125 g (4 oz) rice vermicelli, soaked
in hot water

•

lemon juice to taste

Heat peanut oil in a large saucepan and fry the onions and chillies over medium heat, stirring occasionally until onions are soft and start to colour, about 4–5 minutes. Add the garlic and ginger and fry for 1 minute, stirring, then add all the ground spices and lemon grass. Fry for 1 minute more, stirring constantly. Pour in the vegetable stock and coconut milk, salt and daun salam, and bring slowly to the boil, stirring constantly. Add potatoes and simmer for 10 minutes, uncovered, then add beans and simmer 5 minutes. At no stage must the sayur be covered. Add cabbage, return to the boil, then add soaked and drained vermicelli and simmer 2–3 minutes. Turn off heat, add lemon juice to taste and serve immediately.

SERVES: 6

# EGGS IN SOY SAUCE

*Hard-boiled eggs, flavoured the Indonesian way. Serve with rice and accompaniments to make a complete meal.*

## INGREDIENTS

2 tablespoons peanut oil

•

1 small onion, finely sliced

•

1 fresh red chilli, seeded and sliced

•

1 clove garlic, crushed

•

½ teaspoon finely grated fresh ginger

•

1 large ripe tomato, diced

•

1 tablespoon vinegar

•

½ teaspoon salt

•

1 tablespoon palm sugar or
brown sugar

•

3 tablespoons light soy sauce

•

½ cup (4 fl oz) water

•

4–6 eggs, hard-boiled and shelled

Heat peanut oil in a saucepan over gentle heat and fry the onion, chilli, garlic and ginger until the onion is soft and starts to turn golden. Add tomato and cook, stirring, until it reduces to pulp. Add vinegar, salt, sugar, soy sauce and water. Cover and simmer until sauce is thick and smooth. Put in halved eggs and heat through. Serve with steamed rice.

SERVES: 4–6

# SPICY STEAMED POTATOES

## INGREDIENTS

500 g (1 lb) small new potatoes

•

1 small onion, roughly chopped

•

1 teaspoon chopped garlic

•

1 teaspoon chopped fresh ginger

•

1 tablespoon lemon juice

•

1 tablespoon water

•

1 teaspoon salt

•

1 tablespoon ghee
(clarified butter) or oil

•

1 small cinnamon stick

•

3 cardamom pods, bruised

•

2 whole cloves

•

1 bay leaf, crumbled

•

½ teaspoon ground turmeric

## GARNISH

½ teaspoon cumin seeds

•

½ cup (4 fl oz) yoghurt

•

½ teaspoon Garam Masala
(see page 456)

•

2 tablespoons chopped fresh
coriander or 2 fresh chillies,
seeded and sliced

Scrub potatoes, but do not peel. Put into a saucepan with just enough water to almost cover, bring to a boil and boil for 5 minutes with lid on pan. Drain immediately and with a fine skewer, prick the potatoes lightly all over.

Put onion, garlic, ginger, lemon juice, 1 tablespoon water and salt in an electric blender and blend to a purée. If blender is not available, chop onion finely, crush garlic and finely grate the peeled ginger.

Heat ghee or oil in a saucepan and fry the cinnamon, cardamom, cloves and bay leaf for 2 minutes. Add the turmeric and stir, then add the blended mixture and fry, stirring, until the mixture smells cooked. Rinse out blender container with about 2 tablespoons extra water, add to pan with the potatoes and stir well. Cover pan tightly, turn heat very low and allow to steam for 15 minutes or until potatoes are cooked.

Roast cumin seeds in a dry pan, stirring constantly until dark brown. Combine yoghurt with garam masala, roasted cumin seeds roughly crushed or pounded, and a pinch of salt. Serve potatoes with yoghurt mixture spooned over and sprinkled with fresh coriander or, if preferred, fresh chillies.

SERVES: 4

# PEAS WITH FRESH CHEESE

*In India, much of the protein content in vegetarian dishes comes from milk, yoghurt or fresh cheese called Panir, which is made at home by adding lime or lemon juice to hot milk. It is firmer than ricotta cheese (however ready-made ricotta is simpler to use!). If you wish to try this, see page 437.*

## INGREDIENTS

375 g (12 oz) Panir (see page 437)
or ricotta cheese

•

½ cup (4 fl oz) oil or melted ghee
(clarified butter)

•

2 onions, finely chopped

•

2 cloves garlic, finely chopped

•

2 teaspoons finely chopped
fresh ginger

•

2 teaspoons ground coriander

•

1 teaspoon ground cumin

•

1 teaspoon ground turmeric

•

1 teaspoon chilli powder, or to taste

•

2 ripe tomatoes, peeled and chopped

•

2 cups (8 oz) shelled fresh peas

•

1½ teaspoons salt

•

1 teaspoon Garam Masala
(see page 456)

•

3 tablespoons chopped fresh
coriander or mint

Cut the homemade cheese or ricotta into 1.25 cm (½ in) slices, then into dice. Leave on paper towels for excess moisture to be absorbed. Heat oil or ghee and fry until golden. Remove on a slotted spoon and drain on absorbent paper. Pour off oil from pan, leaving only about a tablespoon. Fry the onions, garlic and ginger, stirring, until they are soft and golden. Add coriander, cumin, turmeric and chilli powder and stir well. Add tomatoes and peas, salt and garam masala. Cover and simmer until peas are almost done. Add cheese and half the fresh herbs and simmer for 10 minutes. Serve with rice or Chapatis (see page 398), with the remaining fresh herbs sprinkled over.

SERVES: 6

Peas with Fresh Cheese

# YAM CURRY

500 g (1 lb) yam or sweet potato
•
oil for deep-frying
•
1 tablespoon ghee (clarified butter)
•
2 medium onions, finely chopped
•
2 teaspoons finely grated ginger
•
2 fresh red or green chillies,
seeded and chopped
•
1 teaspoon ground coriander
•
1 teaspoon ground cumin
•
½ teaspoon ground turmeric
•
½ teaspoon chilli powder (optional)
•
½ teaspoon Garam Masala
(see page 456)
•
1 teaspoon salt
•
1 tablespoon chopped fresh
coriander
•
lemon juice (optional)

Wash, peel and dice the yam or sweet potato and soak in lightly salted water for 30 minutes. Drain well, then dry on absorbent paper. Heat enough oil for deep-frying and add ghee to give it flavour. Fry the yam, not crowding the pan too much, until the pieces are golden brown and tender. Lift from oil on slotted spoon and drain on paper.

When all the yam has been fried, pour off the oil, leaving about 2 tablespoons. Fry the onions, ginger and chillies over medium heat, stirring frequently, until onion is soft and golden. Stir in all the ground spices and fry for another minute, stirring. Add the yam, sprinkle with salt and fresh coriander, and toss over low heat for 5 minutes. If liked, add a squeeze of lemon juice. Serve hot.

SERVES: 3–4

# POTATO AND PEA CURRY

1 large onion
•
1 fresh red chilli
•
2 teaspoons chopped fresh ginger
•
2 tablespoons oil
•
½ teaspoon ground turmeric
•
2 teaspoons ground coriander

Peel and roughly chop the onion. Seed the chilli and discard stalk, put onion, chilli and ginger into an electric blender and blend to a purée, adding a little water if necessary to facilitate blending.

Heat the oil in a heavy-based saucepan and fry the blended mixture, stirring, for 3–4 minutes. Add turmeric and coriander and fry a little longer. Mix in peas, hot water and salt, cover and cook for 10 minutes before adding the potatoes. If the peas are very young and tender they may be put in together with the potatoes. When peas and potatoes

1 cup (4 oz) shelled peas

•

1 cup (8 fl oz) hot water

•

1 teaspoon salt

•

500 g (1 lb) potatoes, peeled
and cubed

•

2 large ripe tomatoes,
peeled and chopped

•

3 tablespoons yoghurt

•

1 teaspoon Garam Masala
(see page 456)

•

2 tablespoons chopped fresh
coriander to garnish

are half cooked, add tomatoes and continue cooking for a few minutes longer, then mix in the yoghurt, stirred until smooth with a little water. Simmer until liquid is thick. Sprinkle with garam masala and stir gently to mix. Serve garnished with fresh coriander.

SERVES: 6

# GUJERATI POTATOES

*Piquant and spicy, nobody could ever accuse the spud of being bland when it comes in a recipe from India.*

## INGREDIENTS

500 g (1 lb) old potatoes

•

1 tablespoon dried tamarind pulp

•

½ cup (4 fl oz) hot water

•

2 teaspoons brown sugar

•

1½ tablespoons ghee
(clarified butter) or oil

•

½ teaspoon black mustard seeds

•

½ teaspoon turmeric

•

½ teaspoon chilli powder

•

1 teaspoon ground cumin

•

1 teaspoon ground coriander

•

1 teaspoon salt

•

2 fresh green chillies,
seeded and sliced

•

2 tablespoons grated fresh coconut

Peel and dice the potatoes. Soak tamarind in hot water for 5 minutes, squeeze firmly to dissolve the pulp in the water, then strain through a fine nylon strainer to exclude seeds and fibres. Dissolve sugar in the tamarind liquid.

Heat ghee or oil and fry the mustard seeds until they pop. Add turmeric, chilli, cumin and coriander, and fry on low heat for 1 minute. Add potatoes and toss for a minute longer. Sprinkle with salt and ¼ cup (2 fl oz) water, cover with well fitting lid and cook on very low heat for 15 minutes. Add tamarind liquid, chillies and coconut, and stir. Cover and cook for 10 minutes longer or until potatoes are done. Serve hot with rice or Chapatis (see page 398).

SERVES: 6

# GREENS COOKED KASHMIRI STYLE

## INGREDIENTS

500 g (1 lb) washed and cleaned
green leaves (see Note)

•

2 tablespoons mustard oil

•

⅛ teaspoon powdered asafoetida
(optional)

•

½ teaspoon cumin seeds

•

1 teaspoon dried fenugreek leaves
(optional)

•

1 teaspoon grated fresh ginger

•

½ teaspoon ground turmeric

•

½ teaspoon ground fennel

•

2 fresh green chillies, seeded and
sliced

•

1 cup (6 oz) diced potato (optional)

•

1 teaspoon salt or to taste

Put the washed greens into a colander to drain. Heat oil in a wok or saucepan and add asafoetida, cumin seeds, fenugreek leaves and ginger. Fry for 1 minute, stirring. Add the remaining ingredients, including the greens and stir well. Cover and cook for about 10 minutes or until potatoes are soft. Add a little water if necessary. Serve with rice.

NOTE: Use spinach, radish or broccoli leaves or any other leafy greens for this recipe. Some leaves give out a lot of moisture and will not need any water added but those that require longer cooking may need a small amount of water.

SERVES: 4

# SPINACH WITH POTATOES

## INGREDIENTS

500 g (1 lb) new potatoes

•

1 bunch spinach

•

2 tablespoons ghee
(clarified butter) or oil

•

1 teaspoon black mustard seeds

•

1 teaspoon cumin seeds

Scrub the potatoes well and cut into small cubes. Wash the spinach in several changes of water. Discard tough stems and put into a large saucepan with just the water that clings to the leaves. Cover and steam for 10 minutes or until tender, then chop roughly. Do not discard any liquid in pan.

In a large frying pan or wok, heat the ghee or oil and fry mustard and cumin seeds until mustard seeds pop. Cover pan or they will fly all over the stove. Add turmeric, coriander, cumin and the chillies. Add potatoes, stir and

½ teaspoon ground turmeric
•
½ teaspoon ground coriander
•
½ teaspoon ground cumin
•
2 fresh green chillies, slit
and seeds removed
•
1 teaspoon salt or to taste
•
approximately ½ cup (4 fl oz) water
•
½ teaspoon grated nutmeg

fry for a few minutes, then add salt and about ½ cup (4 fl oz) water, cover and cook for 10 minutes. Add spinach, stir, cover and cook for 5–10 minutes longer. Sprinkle nutmeg over and serve with rice or Chapatis (see page 398).

SERVES: 4

# SAVOURY POTATOES AND PEAS

*A spicy vegetable to eat with rice or to use as a filling for samoosas—
little fried pastries.*

### INGREDIENTS

500 g ( 1 lb) potatoes
•
250 g (8 oz) fresh peas in the pod
or 1 cup (6 oz) frozen peas
•
2 tablespoons ghee
(clarified butter) or oil
•
2 medium onions, finely chopped
•
1 teaspoon finely grated fresh ginger
•
1 teaspoon black mustard seeds
•
½ teaspoon black cumin
(kalonji) seeds
•
½ teaspoon ground turmeric
•
½ teaspoon chilli powder
•
1½ teaspoons salt
•
¾ cup (6 fl oz) hot water

Peel and dice potatoes, shell peas. Heat ghee or oil in a heavy-based saucepan and fry the onions and ginger, mustard and cumin seeds. When onions are soft and golden, add the ground turmeric, chilli powder and salt. Toss potatoes and peas in this mixture for 5 minutes, then add hot water, cover tightly and cook on low heat for 30 minutes.

SERVES: 4

# MIXED VEGETABLES WITH COCONUT

*This is one of the most popular ways of serving vegetables in South India. The predominant flavouring is from coconut, for coconut palms grow in abundance along the coastline.*

### INGREDIENTS

about 6 cups mixed
vegetables cut into strips—carrots,
French beans, zucchini (courgettes),
pumpkin, capsicum (pepper),
eggplant (aubergine), choko
(chayote), cucumber
•
½ cup (2 oz) fresh green peas
•
½ cup grated fresh coconut
or 3 tablespoons desiccated coconut
•
1 cup (8 fl oz) water
•
1 teaspoon cumin seeds
•
1 teaspoon chopped garlic
•
2 fresh green chillies, seeded
•
½ cup (4 fl oz) thick coconut milk
(see page 443)
•
1½ teaspoons salt
•
6 curry leaves

Boil each vegetable separately in a little salted water, just long enough to make it tender but not soft and mushy. Take out vegetables on slotted spoon and put them into a bowl. Use the same water for all the vegetables, adding a little water at a time as it boils away, but keeping the quantity small. Save the cooking liquid.

In a blender, put the coconut, water, cumin seeds, garlic and chillies. Blend on high speed until the coconut is very finely ground. Put this into the saucepan with the vegetable stock, add the coconut milk, salt and curry leaves and bring to the boil. Add the vegetables, simmer uncovered for 5 minutes. Serve hot with rice.

SERVES: 6–8

# EGGPLANT PURÉE

*Eggplants cooked to a spicy purée are popular throughout India, but perhaps nowhere more so than in the Punjab. In this recipe the eggplants are roasted first, which adds a certain smoky flavour.*

### INGREDIENTS

2 medium eggplants (aubergines)
•
2 tablespoons oil
•
2 medium onions, chopped

Roast eggplants over gas flame, hot coals, or under a griller (broiler) until the skin is thoroughly blackened all over and the eggplant itself is soft to the touch. When cool enough to handle, remove all skin under running cold water. Mash eggplants or chop roughly.

In a heavy-based saucepan, heat oil and fry the onions

1 teaspoon ground coriander

•

1 teaspoon ground cumin

•

½ teaspoon chilli powder (optional)

•

1 large ripe tomato, chopped

•

3 tablespoons finely chopped
fresh coriander

•

3 spring onions (scallions),
finely chopped

•

1 teaspoon salt, or to taste

•

½ teaspoon Garam Masala
(see page 456)

until lightly browned. Add ground spices and stir for a few seconds, then add tomato, eggplants, fresh coriander, spring onions and salt. Cover and cook on low heat until liquid evaporates and it becomes a purée thick enough to scoop up with pieces of chapati. Add garam masala and simmer, uncovered, for a few minutes longer. Serve hot or cold as an accompaniment to Parathas, Chapatis, (see pages 396, 398) or rice.

SERVES: 6

# MIXED VEGETABLES, SINDHI STYLE

### INGREDIENTS

2 large carrots

•

2 large potatoes

•

2 medium onions

•

2 fresh red or green chillies

•

1 tablespoon ground coriander

•

1½ teaspoons ground turmeric

•

2 tablespoons ghee (clarified butter)

•

2 tablespoons oil

•

1½ teaspoons finely grated
fresh ginger

•

½ cup (1 oz) chopped fresh coriander

•

2 firm ripe tomatoes, peeled
and diced

•

1 cup (8 fl oz) yoghurt

•

1½ teaspoons salt

•

lemon wedges or lemon juice to taste

Peel carrots and potatoes and cut both in julienne strips. Finely chop the onions, then seed and finely slice the chillies. Combine all in a bowl, sprinkle the coriander and turmeric over and toss well. Leave for half an hour.

In a large saucepan, heat the ghee and oil and fry the ginger, stirring, until golden. Add the mixed vegetables and fry for a few minutes. Stir in half the fresh coriander and the tomatoes, yoghurt and salt. Cover and cook for 10–15 minutes or until vegetables are tender. Serve hot with the remaining fresh coriander sprinkled over and accompanied by wedges of lemon or, if preferred, add lemon juice to taste. Serve with plain rice or Rice With Lentils (Kitchri) (see page 264), Chapatis (see page 398) or Puris (see page 400).

SERVES: 4

# SUMMER ALFRESCO LUNCHEON

*Creamy Cucumber Moulds* page 3

•

*White and Green Bean Salad* page 40

*"Cheese and Crackers" Loaf* page 129

*Fattoush—Lebanese Bread Salad*
page 162

*Roasted Capsicums (peppers)* page 147

•

*Homemade bread including Challah
and Cracked Wheat Rolls with
Rosemary* pages 402 and 414

•

*Fresh Peach Ice-cream* page 220

# SPINACH WITH MIXED VEGETABLES

### INGREDIENTS

1 bunch spinach

500 g (1 lb) pumpkin

250 g (8 oz) okra or French beans

2 tablespoons oil

1 teaspoon black mustard seeds

1 medium onion, finely chopped

1 teaspoon finely grated fresh ginger

½ teaspoon ground turmeric

1 cup (8 fl oz) hot water

½ cup (3 oz) raw cashews

½ cup (2 oz) fresh peas

Wash the spinach well, discard any tough stems and roughly chop the leaves. Cut pumpkin into small cubes. String beans, if used, and cut into short lengths.

Heat the oil in a wok or saucepan and fry the mustard seeds until they begin to pop. Add the onion and ginger and fry, stirring now and then, until onion is soft. Add turmeric and fry for 1 minute longer.

Add hot water, cashews and all the vegetables, cover and simmer until they are tender, then remove lid and cook, stirring frequently, until liquid has reduced. Serve with rice or Chapatis (see page 398). If serving with rice, leave somewhat more liquid; if serving with chapatis, allow it to reach a drier consistency.

SERVES: 4–6

# SPICY FRIED POTATOES

### INGREDIENTS

500 g (1 lb) potatoes

3 tablespoons oil

1 teaspoon black mustard seeds

½ teaspoon ground turmeric

1 large onion, finely sliced

1 or 2 fresh green chillies,
seeded and sliced

1½ teaspoons salt

¼ cup (2 fl oz) hot water

1 tablespoon lemon juice

Boil potatoes in their skins until just tender, then peel and dice. Heat the oil in a saucepan and fry the mustard seeds until they pop. Add the turmeric, sliced onion and chillies, and fry until onions are soft and golden. Add the salt and water, bring to the boil, then add potatoes, cover and cook until liquid has been absorbed. Remove from heat. Sprinkle with lemon juice and stir well.

SERVES: 4

# LENTIL PURÉE

### INGREDIENTS

1 cup (6 oz) dried red lentils
•
1½ tablespoons ghee
(clarified butter) or oil
•
1 large onion, finely sliced
•
1 teaspoon finely chopped garlic
•
1 teaspoon finely grated fresh ginger
•
½ teaspoon ground turmeric
•
3 cups (24 fl oz) hot water
•
1 teaspoon salt, or to taste
•
½ teaspoon Garam Masala
(see page 456)

Wash lentils thoroughly, removing those that float on the surface. Drain well. Heat ghee or oil in a saucepan and fry onion, garlic and ginger until onion is golden brown. Add turmeric and stir well. Mix in drained lentils and fry for 1–2 minutes. Add hot water, bring to the boil, then reduce heat to simmer.

Cover and cook for 15–20 minutes or until lentils are half cooked. Add salt and garam masala, mix well and continue cooking until lentils are soft and the consistency is similar to porridge. If there is too much liquid, leave the lid off the pan to speed evaporation. Serve dhal plain or garnished with sliced onions, fried until deep golden brown. Eat with boiled rice, Indian breads, or as a light meal by itself.

SERVES: 4–6

# SPICED PUMPKIN

### INGREDIENTS

500 g (1 lb) pumpkin
•
2 tablespoons oil
•
3 tablespoons toor dhal or split peas
•
1 teaspoon black mustard seeds
•
10 curry leaves
•
1 teaspoon finely chopped garlic
•
2 teaspoons ground coriander
•
1 teaspoon ground cumin
•
½ teaspoon ground turmeric
•
1 teaspoon salt or to taste
•
3 tablespoons fresh grated
coconut or desiccated coconut

Peel and seed the pumpkin, then cut into cubes. Heat the oil in a saucepan and gently fry the dhal, mustard seeds and curry leaves until dhal is golden and the mustard seeds pop. Add the garlic, fry for a minute longer, then add the ground spices and stir well. Put in the pumpkin and just enough water to almost cover the vegetable. Add salt. Cover and simmer until pumpkin is half cooked, then sprinkle in the coconut and continue cooking until pumpkin is soft.

SERVES: 4

# GADO-GADO

*This is one of the most popular dishes in Asia, combining lightly cooked vegetables with a richly flavoured peanut sauce. Vary the vegetables according to what is available.*

## INGREDIENTS

2 large squares pressed bean curd

•

oil for deep-frying

•

3 eggs, hard-boiled

•

boiled potatoes

•

lightly boiled green beans

•

carrots

•

cabbage

•

zucchini (courgettes)

•

1 green cucumber, sliced

•

watercress or other salad greens

### PEANUT SAUCE

7 tablespoons peanut oil

•

1 teaspoon dried garlic flakes

•

2 tablespoons dried onion flakes

•

2 large dried chillies

•

375 g (12 oz) jar crunchy peanut butter

•

1 tablespoon lemon juice

•

1 tablespoon dark soy sauce

•

2 tablespoons raw sugar

•

1 teaspoon chilli sambal (optional)

Cut the bean curd into large slices and deep-fry in hot oil until golden brown. Lift out on a slotted spoon and drain on absorbent paper. Shell the eggs and cut in quarters. Have the vegetables freshly cooked so they may be served warm or at room temperature.

To make the peanut sauce, heat oil in a small frying pan and over low heat, fry the garlic flakes for just a few seconds. The easiest way is to lower them into the oil in a fine metal strainer, and lift them out as soon as they are pale gold. They burn easily, so make sure the oil is not too hot. Drain on absorbent paper. Fry the onion flakes in the same way, leave to drain and cool. Fry the chillies, drain, remove stalks and seeds, then chop finely.

In the same pan, mix together the peanut butter, lemon juice and soy sauce. Cool completely before mixing in the garlic and onion flakes, chillies and sugar. For a more spicy sauce, add the chilli sambal as well.

Arrange the bean curd, the quartered eggs and the vegetables on a platter and spoon over just enough sauce to flavour.

NOTE: This sauce may be made in advance and kept in a screw-top jar in the refrigerator for months. To use, heat the required amount in a small saucepan and mix in enough coconut milk or water to make a thick pouring consistency.

SERVES: 6

GADO-GADO

# DRY POTATO CURRY

## INGREDIENTS

500 g (1 lb) potatoes
•
1½ tablespoons ghee
(clarified butter) or oil
•
1 teaspoon Panch Phora
(see page 456)
•
1 medium onion, finely chopped
•
2 tablespoons chopped
fresh mint or coriander
•
1 teaspoon ground turmeric
•
1½ teaspoons salt
•
½ teaspoon chilli powder (optional)
•
¼ cup (2 fl oz) hot water
•
1 teaspoon Garam Masala
(see page 456)
•
1 tablespoon lemon juice

Peel potatoes, cut into quarters or, if very large, into cubes. In a heavy-based saucepan with lid, heat ghee or oil and add the panch phora. When mustard seeds in the panch phora begin to pop, add the onion and fry, stirring, until soft. Add chopped herbs, turmeric, salt and chilli powder (if used). Add potatoes, stir well, sprinkle with hot water and cover pan tightly.

Cook over very low heat for 20 minutes, shaking pan occasionally to prevent potatoes sticking. Sprinkle with garam masala and lemon juice, replace lid and cook for a further 10 minutes or until potatoes are tender. Serve with Parathas, Chapatis (see pages 396, 398) or rice.

SERVES: 4

# LENTIL CAKES IN YOGHURT

## INGREDIENTS

1½ cups (9 oz) urad dhal
•
1½ teaspoons salt
•
½ teaspoon finely grated
fresh ginger (optional)
•
pinch asafoetida (optional)
•
oil or ghee (clarified butter),
for deep-frying
•
1 cup (8 fl oz) yoghurt
•
1 cup (8 fl oz) buttermilk

Wash urad dhal thoroughly in several changes of water, then soak in cold water overnight. Drain well, put into an electric blender and blend at high speed, adding only as much water as is necessary to facilitate blending. It should form a thick, smooth paste. Add 1 teaspoon salt. Add finely grated fresh ginger and a pinch of asafoetida to the dhal if liked.

With wet hands, form mixture into flat patties about 5 cm (2 in) across, and as each one is made, drop it into hot oil or ghee. Fry, turning with slotted spoon, until pale gold—do not allow the lentil cakes to brown. Drain on absorbent paper and when cool, immerse in cold water for about 10 minutes. Press out excess moisture gently between palms, taking care not to break them.

1 teaspoon cumin seeds

•

½ teaspoon chilli powder

•

2 tablespoons chopped fresh
coriander

•

1 fresh green chilli, seeded
and chopped

Combine yoghurt, buttermilk and ½ teaspoon salt. Immerse the lentil cakes in this mixture and chill thoroughly. Roast the cumin seeds in a dry pan, stirring constantly until dark brown. Crush and sprinkle over the dish together with chilli powder, chopped coriander and fresh chilli. Serve cold as an accompaniment to rice or Parathas (see page 396).

SERVES: 6

# SPICY DICED VEGETABLES

INGREDIENTS

3 medium carrots

•

2 medium potatoes

•

12 tender green beans

•

2 firm ripe tomatoes

•

2 tablespoons mustard oil
or other vegetable oil

•

2 teaspoons black mustard seeds

•

2 dried red chillies (optional)

•

2 onions, finely chopped

•

1 teaspoon finely chopped garlic

•

1 teaspoon finely chopped
fresh ginger

•

1 teaspoon ground coriander

•

1 teaspoon ground cumin

•

½ teaspoon chilli powder (optional)

•

1 teaspoon salt

•

2–3 tablespoons water

•

½ teaspoon Garam Masala
(see page 456), (optional)

Peel and dice the carrots and potatoes. Top and tail the beans and cut them into short lengths, the same size as the diced vegetables. Peel and dice the tomatoes.

Heat oil in a saucepan or wok and fry the mustard seeds and chillies until the seeds pop. Add onions, garlic and ginger, and fry, stirring, until golden. Add coriander, cumin and chilli powder (if used) and fry for a few seconds, then add vegetables and salt and toss until coated with the spices and oil. Add water, cover and cook for 15 minutes or until the vegetables are tender, stirring gently every 5 minutes and adding a little extra water if necessary. Sprinkle with garam masala, if used, towards end of cooking. Serve with rice or Chapatis (see page 398).

SERVES: 4

# SAVOURY CHICK PEAS

1 cup (6 oz) dried chick peas

•

2 teaspoons salt

•

2 tablespoons ghee
(clarified butter) or oil

•

2 onions, finely chopped

•

2 cloves garlic, finely chopped

•

2 teaspoons finely chopped
fresh ginger

•

½ teaspoon ground turmeric

•

¼ teaspoon ground cinnamon

•

¼ teaspoon ground cardamom

•

¼ teaspoon ground black pepper

•

2 large ripe tomatoes, peeled
and chopped

•

1 fresh green chilli, seeded and sliced

•

4 tablespoons chopped fresh mint

•

squeeze of lemon juice

Soak chick peas in plenty of cold water overnight. Drain, rinse and put chick peas with just enough water to cover, in a pressure cooker or heavy-based saucepan. Add salt and cook until just tender, not mushy; about 20 minutes under pressure should be enough. Drain and reserve liquid.

In a large saucepan, heat the ghee or oil and fry the onions, garlic and ginger until golden brown. Add ground spices, tomatoes, chilli and the mint. Add chick peas and stir well, then add reserved liquid and lemon juice. Cover and simmer on low heat until tender and tomatoes have cooked to a pulp. Serve with rice or Indian breads.

SERVES: 4

SAVOURY CHICK PEAS

# SAVOURY BLACK-EYED BEANS

### INGREDIENTS

1 cup (6 oz) dried black-eyed
beans (peas)

•

3 bay leaves

•

2 cardamom pods, bruised

•

2 teaspoons chopped garlic

•

½ teaspoon ground turmeric

•

1 teaspoon salt

•

2 medium onions, roughly chopped

•

2 teaspoons chopped fresh ginger

•

2 dried red chillies, seeded

•

2 tablespoons oil or ghee
(clarified butter)

•

1 teaspoon ground cumin

•

½ cup (4 fl oz) yoghurt

•

½ teaspoon Garam Masala
(see page 456)

•

2 tablespoons chopped fresh
coriander to garnish

Wash beans well and soak overnight in cold water to cover. Drain, cover with fresh water and bring to the boil with the bay leaves, cardamom, 1 teaspoon chopped garlic, turmeric and salt. Cover and simmer until tender, or pressure-cook for about 15 minutes. Drain, reserving liquid.

Put the onions, remaining teaspoon garlic, ginger and chillies into blender and blend to a purée. Heat oil or ghee and fry the blended mixture, stirring. When it begins to brown, add the cumin and fry, stirring, for a few seconds longer. Add the drained beans and the yoghurt blended with ½ cup (4 fl oz) of the liquid in which the beans cooked. Cook for a further 5 minutes or until the gravy thickens. Sprinkle with garam masala and coriander and serve with Chapatis (see page 398) or rice.

SERVES: 4

# SPINACH WITH FRESH CHEESE

### INGREDIENTS

250 g (8 oz) fresh spinach leaves
or other greens

•

1 tablespoon dried fenugreek
leaves (optional)

•

250 g (8 oz) Panir (see page 437)
or ricotta cheese

•

oil, for deep-frying

•

1 tablespoon ghee (clarified butter)

•

½ teaspoon ground turmeric

•

1½ cups (12 fl oz) hot water

•

¼ teaspoon black cumin
(kalonji) seeds

•

small pinch asafoetida (optional)

•

1 tablespoon ground coriander

•

½ teaspoon chilli powder

•

½ teaspoon finely grated fresh ginger

•

1 teaspoon salt

•

½ teaspoon sugar

•

1 cup (8 fl oz) yoghurt

Put the well-washed spinach leaves into a pan with the water that clings to them, add the fenugreek leaves (if used), cover and steam until spinach is soft. Drain well and chop finely. Cut the Panir or ricotta into cubes and spread on absorbent paper for a few minutes so that surface moisture is absorbed. In a small, deep frying pan or wok, heat enough oil to deep fry the cheese cubes. Add a tablespoon of ghee to flavour the oil. When oil is very hot, fry a handful of cheese cubes at a time. Have ready the turmeric stirred into 1 cup (8 fl oz) of hot water and when the cheese is pale gold, lift out on a slotted spoon and drop the cubes into the turmeric water. Repeat until all the cubes are cooked, leave in the water for about 5 minutes, then drain.

Heat about 2 tablespoons of the oil in a saucepan and add the black cumin seeds, asafoetida, coriander, chilli powder and ginger. Stir and fry briefly, taking care not to burn the spices. Add the spinach and salt, and stir for 1–2 minutes, then add about ½ cup (4 fl oz) hot water and the sugar. Simmer for 5 minutes. Stir the yoghurt until it is smooth, add it to the spinach and stir well. Add cheese cubes and simmer for 10 minutes longer. Serve hot with rice or Chapatis (see page 398).

SERVES: 4–5

# FRESH CHEESE IN TOMATO SAUCE

## INGREDIENTS

375 g (12 oz) baked ricotta cheese
(see Note) or Panir (see page 437)

2 tablespoons ghee (clarified butter)

2 tablespoons oil

500 g (1 lb) ripe tomatoes

1 medium onion, finely chopped

1 teaspoon ground turmeric

1 teaspoon chilli powder

3 whole cloves

3 cardamom pods, bruised

¾ teaspoon salt

1 tablespoon sugar or to taste

pinch of saffron strands

2 tablespoons hot water

Cut the cheese in slices about 1 cm (½ in) thick and fry in ghee and oil until golden. Put on a plate and set aside. Add peeled and chopped tomatoes, onion, spices, salt and sugar, and cook until gravy is thick. Add the slices of cheese and simmer in the gravy for 10 minutes. Dissolve saffron in hot water and add about 5 minutes before end of cooking. Serve with rice or Chapatis (see page 398).

NOTE:    In some Italian food stores one can buy baked ricotta, which is firmer and drier in consistency than the soft white ricotta. It is particularly good in this recipe.

# ACCOMPANIMENTS

Here are those tiny, titillating, taste-teasers which are served with many Asian meals. They must be served in small amounts, and I usually put a teaspoon in as a serving spoon, because there could be dire results if somebody ate a large mouthful of some of the spicier combinations! These highly flavoured dishes are wonderful for making a plate of boiled rice interesting, and are a case in point to illustrate that just because a little is good, a lot is not necessarily better.

Where pickles make a large quantity that can be stored for long periods, the number of servings has not been included.

## ONION SAMBAL

### INGREDIENTS

2 medium onions, preferably red onions
•
½ teaspoon chilli powder
•
½ teaspoon salt, or to taste
•
lime or lemon juice to taste

Peel and finely slice the onions. Sprinkle with chilli powder, salt and lemon juice. Toss lightly until well mixed and serve as an accompaniment to rice and curries. Make this sambal just before serving.

SERVES: 6

## BEAN SPROUT SAMBAL

### INGREDIENTS

125 g (4 oz) fresh bean sprouts
•
3 fresh green chillies, seeded and sliced
•
1 small onion, finely sliced
•
3 tablespoons grated fresh coconut or desiccated coconut
•
1 teaspoon salt
•
1 tablespoon lemon juice, or to taste

Wash bean sprouts thoroughly, removing as many of the green skins as possible. Drain well. Mix all ingredients together well and serve as an accompaniment to rice and curries.

SERVES: 6

# EGGPLANT PICKLE

## INGREDIENTS

1 kg (2 lb) eggplants (aubergines)

•

12 dried red chillies

•

4 teaspoons chopped garlic

•

3 teaspoons chopped fresh ginger

•

2 tablespoons black mustard seeds

•

1½ teaspoons ground turmeric

•

1½ cups (12 fl oz) oil

•

3 teaspoons salt

•

½ cup (3 oz) brown sugar
or palm sugar

•

¾ cup (6 fl oz) vinegar

•

2 teaspoons Garam Masala
(see page 456)

Wash eggplants and cut crossways into slices. If eggplants are very large, cut into cubes. Soak chillies in hot water for 5 minutes. In electric blender, combine chillies, garlic, ginger, mustard seeds and some of the water in which the chillies soaked. Blend on high speed until puréed. If a blender is not available, pound with a mortar and pestle. Combine with turmeric.

Heat the oil and fry the blended mixture for a few minutes, then add eggplant, cover and cook on low heat until eggplant is soft, stirring now and then. Add salt, sugar and vinegar, and simmer until thick, stirring to prevent burning. Stir in garam masala, remove from heat. Cool and bottle.

# PICKLED CABBAGE (KIM CHI)

*Kim chi is one of Korea's national dishes, with as many versions as there are cooks. This is one that would appeal to most people.*

## INGREDIENTS

1 large white Chinese cabbage
(wongah bak)

•

common salt (not iodised)

•

cayenne pepper

•

6 spring onions (scallions),
finely chopped

•

6 cloves garlic, finely chopped

•

3 fresh red chillies, finely chopped

Cut base off cabbage and slice lengthways into 6 segments. Dry in the sun for half a day, then halve each segment crossways. Put into an unglazed earthenware pot, scattering good handfuls of salt and a sprinkling of cayenne pepper in between layers. Cover with a wooden lid just small enough to fit inside the pot so that it rests directly on the cabbage.

Weight it down with a heavy stone and leave for a week, then rinse the cabbage thoroughly under cold running water. Squeeze out as much moisture as possible. Slice into 2.5 cm (1 in) sections, or chop more finely if preferred, and put into the rinsed-out jar, this time layering with the onions, garlic, chillies and ginger. Fill jar with the water

3 teaspoons finely chopped
fresh ginger

•

2 cups (16 fl oz) water

•

¼ cup (2 fl oz) light soy sauce

mixed with the soy. Cover with wax paper, put lid back on top and refrigerate. After 4–5 days the kim chi is ready for eating. Serve with hot white rice and a dash of soy sauce.

NOTE: In cold weather kim chi does not require refrigeration, but when weather is warm, it can be stored in the refrigerator for up to 3 weeks.

# GROUND ONION AND CHILLI SAMBAL

*This simple sambal is as basic to the food of Sri Lanka as salt and pepper are to Western food. Very hot, very acid and distinctly salty, it is often the only accompaniment to serve with rice, boiled yams, manioc or sweet potato, or any of the starches that are the staple of the native diet.*

### INGREDIENTS

10 dried chillies

•

1 small onion, chopped

•

lemon juice and salt to taste

Remove stalks from chillies and, if a less hot result is preferred, shake out the seeds. Pound all ingredients together with a mortar and pestle. In Sri Lanka this would be either pounded or ground on the grinding stone. It can be done in a blender, but a wet result is not desirable—it should be a paste. Serve with rice or Steamed Rice Flour and Coconut Cakes (see page 395).

SERVES: 6–8

# CUCUMBER SAMBAL

### INGREDIENTS

1 large or 2 small green cucumbers

•

2 teaspoons salt

•

½ cup (4 fl oz) thick coconut milk
(see page 443)

•

1 fresh red chilli, seeded and sliced

•

1 fresh green chilli, seeded and sliced

•

1 small onion, cut in paper-thin slices

•

2 tablespoons lemon juice

Peel cucumbers and slice very thinly. Put in a bowl, sprinkle with salt and let stand for at least 30 minutes. Press out all liquid and if too salty, rinse with cold water. Drain well. Mix with remaining ingredients and serve as an accompaniment to a curry meal.

SERVES: 6

# CHILLI PICKLE

*Please remember to wear gloves when handling chillies.*

## INGREDIENTS

1 kg (2 lb) long green chillies

2 tablespoons salt

1 tablespoon ground turmeric

1½ tablespoons black mustard seeds

¼ cup (2 fl oz) vinegar

2 tablespoons chopped garlic

2 cups mustard oil
or salad oil

1 teaspoon fenugreek seeds

2 teaspoons black cumin
(kalonji) seeds

2 teaspoons crushed asafoetida

Wash chillies well and rub dry in tea towel. Cut off and discard stalks, slice chillies crossways into 1 cm (½ in) slices. Sprinkle with salt and turmeric, toss well to mix, cover and leave for 2 days, preferably in the sun for a few hours each day. Soak the mustard seeds in the vinegar overnight and next day, grind in electric blender together with the garlic, to form a purée.

Heat oil in a large pan and add the fenugreek seeds and black cumin seeds. Stir and fry until fenugreek is golden brown, then add the asafoetida, stir once, and add the blended mixture and the chillies, together with liquid that comes from them. Cook and stir occasionally until oil rises and chillies are cooked. They should not be too soft. Cool and put into sterilised bottle.

# CUCUMBER ACHAR

*This very spicy pickle is made in the style of the Indian settlers in Malaysia and Singapore, and while it need not be pungent with chillies, the flavour is fantastic.*

## INGREDIENTS

500 g (1 lb) cucumbers

500 g (1 lb) carrots

125 g (4 oz) ginger

15–20 fresh chillies

250 g (8 oz) shallots* or
small pickling onions

2 cups (16 fl oz) white vinegar

125 g (4 oz) sesame seeds

125 g (4 oz) raw peanuts

6 tablespoons peanut oil

Halve the cucumbers lengthways and scoop out the seeds, then cut into finger-size strips. Cut the carrots into thin strips. Peel the ginger and cut into fine shreds. Slit the chillies lengthways and remove seeds. Peel the shallots or pickling onions (*the shallots referred to here are the small purple bulbs similar to garlic, not the bunches of green and white spring onions sometimes called shallots).

In an enamel or stainless steel saucepan, bring vinegar to the boil with an equal amount of water. Add one type of vegetable at a time, bring to the boil and boil for 1 minute, then remove at once and spread out to cool. Allow vegetables to get quite cold so they will stay crunchy.

Toast the sesame seeds in a dry pan until golden brown. Pound or grind the seeds. Roast and pound the peanuts similarly.

1 tablespoon black mustard seeds

•

10–20 dried red chillies,
(optional)

•

1 tablespoon ground turmeric

•

¼ cup (2 oz) sugar, or more to taste

•

salt as required

•

½ cup vinegar, extra

Heat the peanut oil in a wok and fry the shredded ginger until golden. Add the mustard seeds, dried chillies and turmeric and fry for a few minutes. Add sugar and salt and vinegar and stir until mixture thickens, remove from heat and stir in the vegetables, sesame seeds and peanuts. When quite cold, bottle and refrigerate. Serve as an accompaniment to rice and curries.

# FRIED EGGPLANT SALAD

### INGREDIENTS

2 eggplants (aubergines)

•

2 teaspoons salt

•

2 teaspoons ground turmeric

•

oil for frying

•

3 fresh red or green chillies

•

2 small onions

•

lemon juice to taste

•

3 tablespoons thick coconut milk
(see page 443)

Prepare eggplant slices as for Eggplant Pickle (see page 361). Fry in hot oil and drain on absorbent paper. Mix with seeded and chopped chillies, finely sliced onions, lemon juice to taste and thick coconut milk.

SERVES: 6

353

# CUCUMBER PICKLE

*This is a light pickle made in the Burmese style—not overly acid in flavour,
and with the unusual addition of crisply fried garlic and onion, and
toasted sesame seeds.*

### INGREDIENTS

2 large green cucumbers

½ cup (4 fl oz) malt vinegar

2 cups (16 fl oz) water

1 teaspoon salt

¼ cup (2 fl oz) peanut oil

2 tablespoons sesame oil

8 cloves garlic, sliced, or 1
tablespoon dried garlic flakes

1 medium onion, finely sliced, or
2 tablespoons dried onion flakes

2 tablespoons sesame seeds

Peel cucumbers, halve lengthways and scoop out seeds. Cut into strips of finger thickness, then cut into 5 cm (2 in) strips. Bring vinegar, water and salt to the boil, drop in cucumbers and boil just until they look transparent. Do not overcook. Drain immediately and leave to cool.

Heat both oils together and fry the garlic until pale gold. Drain. Fry the onion until golden brown. Toast the sesame seeds in a dry frying pan, stirring constantly, until they are an even gold brown. Transfer to a plate to cool. When the oil is cold, coat the cucumbers with 3 tablespoons of the oil, mixing well with the fingers. Put into a small serving dish, add the fried onion, garlic and sesame seeds, and toss lightly.

SERVES: 6

# CHILLI SAMBAL

*One of the favourite accompaniments to an Asian meal—pungent with chillies,
lightly sweetened to balance the heat.*

### INGREDIENTS

½ cup (4 fl oz) oil

4 medium onions, finely sliced

2 teaspoons chilli powder

2 tablespoons vinegar

salt to taste

2 teaspoons sugar

Heat oil in a large frying pan and fry onions very slowly, stirring occasionally until soft and transparent. It is important to fry onions slowly—all the liquid in the onion must evaporate if the sambal is to have good keeping qualities.

When the onion is golden brown, add chilli powder and vinegar. Stir thoroughly, cover and simmer for 10 minutes. Uncover pan and continue simmering, stirring occasionally, until liquid evaporates and oil starts to separate from other ingredients. Season to taste with salt. Remove from heat, stir in sugar and allow to cool before putting in a clean dry jar. Use in small quantities.

NOTE: If a hotter sambal is preferred, increase quantity of chilli powder.

# MIXED PICKLE

### INGREDIENTS

2 carrots
•
185 g (6 oz) green beans
•
10 fresh red and green chillies
•
1 green cucumber
•
2 tablespoons peanut oil
•
2 cloves garlic, finely grated
•
2 teaspoons finely grated fresh ginger
•
3 candlenuts or Brazil nuts, grated
•
1 teaspoon ground turmeric
•
½ cup (4 fl oz) white vinegar
•
½ cup (4 fl oz) water
•
2 teaspoons sugar
•
1 teaspoon salt
•
1 cup (2 oz) cauliflower florets

Cut carrots into julienne strips. Cut beans into pieces of the same length, then halve each piece lengthways. If beans are very young and slender it will not be necessary to slice them. Leave the chillies whole but remove stems. Peel cucumber and halve lengthways, remove seeds and slice into pieces the same size as the carrots and beans.

Heat oil in a saucepan and fry garlic and ginger on low heat for 1 minute, then add grated nuts and turmeric and fry for a few seconds longer. Add vinegar, water, sugar and salt and bring to the boil. Add carrots and beans, chillies and cauliflower, return to the boil and boil for 3 minutes. Add cucumber and boil for 1 minute longer.

Turn into an earthenware or glass bowl and allow to cool. Use immediately or bottle and store in the refrigerator for a week or two.

# COCONUT SAMBAL

*A quickly made accompaniment to add zip to a meal of rice and curries—*
*no cooking, plenty of flavour.*

### INGREDIENTS

1 cup (3 oz) desiccated coconut
•
1 teaspoon salt
•
1 teaspoon chilli powder, or to taste
•
2 teaspoons paprika
•
2 tablespoons lemon juice
•
1 medium onion, finely chopped
•
2–3 tablespoons hot water

Combine coconut, salt, chilli powder and paprika in a bowl. Sprinkle with lemon juice, onion and water. Mix well with the hands, rubbing ingredients together so that the coconut is evenly moistened. Pile into small bowl.

NOTE: If liked, add 1–2 fresh red or green chillies, seeded and finely chopped.

SERVES: 8

# GREEN BEAN SAMBAL

*This Indonesian dish is quite hot and spicy. Serve with rice.*

## INGREDIENTS

250 g (8 oz) fresh green beans
•
1 tablespoon peanut oil
•
½ teaspoon crushed garlic
•
½ teaspoon sambal ulek or
freshly chopped chillies
•
½ teaspoon salt, or to taste
•
1 small onion, finely sliced

String beans and cut in very fine diagonal slices. Heat oil in a wok or frying pan and toss beans on high heat for 2 minutes, add garlic and fry 1 minute more. Add sambal and salt and fry 1 minute longer. Beans should be tender but still crunchy crisp. Remove from heat, mix in the onion slices and serve as an accompaniment or side dish to a rice and curry meal.

SERVES: 6

# FRESH MINT CHUTNEY

*This is an example of a fresh chutney—a piquant purée of fresh herbs and spices, not even distantly related to Major Grey.*

## INGREDIENTS

1 cup (2 oz) firmly packed mint leaves
•
6 spring onions (scallions),
including green leaves
•
2 fresh green chillies,
roughly chopped
•
½ teaspoon chopped garlic (optional)
•
1 teaspoon salt
•
2 teaspoons sugar
•
1 teaspoon Garam Masala
(see page 456)
•
1/3 cup (3 fl oz) lemon juice
•
2 tablespoons water

In the absence of the grinding stones which are used in India for reducing grains to flour and others which make "wet" masalas and fresh chutneys, a powerful electric blender is the Western cook's best friend when preparing Indian food.

Put mint into blender together with onions cut into short lengths and all other ingredients. Blend on high speed to a smooth purée. If blender is not available, finely chop mint, onions and chillies and pound a little at a time with a mortar and pestle, then mix in remaining ingredients.

Pack the chutney into a small dish, smooth the surface, cover and chill. Serve as an accompaniment with rice, curries, and Chapatis (see page 398).

SERVES: 8

GREEN BEAN SAMBAL

# BITTER GOURD SAMBAL

*Bitter gourds, or bitter melon as the Chinese call them, may be an acquired taste but they are addictive when you get to like them.*

### INGREDIENTS

3 bitter gourds

•

½ teaspoon ground turmeric

•

½ teaspoon salt

•

oil for shallow frying

•

1 medium onion, sliced very thinly

•

2 fresh green chillies,
seeded and sliced

•

lemon juice to taste

Wash bitter gourds and cut crossways into fairly thin 6 mm (¼ in) slices. Rub with turmeric and salt, and fry in oil until golden brown on both sides. Drain on paper, then mix with the onion and chillies, and season with lemon juice and more salt if necessary.

SERVES: 4–6

# ONION, TOMATO AND CHILLI SALAD

*The fruity, sour taste of tamarind pulp enhances the other ingredients.*

### INGREDIENTS

2 medium onions

•

salt

•

1 tablespoon tamarind pulp

•

¼ cup (2 fl oz) hot water

•

2 tablespoons brown sugar or
palm sugar

•

2 firm ripe tomatoes

•

1 tablespoon finely shredded
fresh ginger

•

2 or 3 fresh red or green chillies,
seeded and sliced

•

2 tablespoons chopped fresh
coriander

Peel the onions, halve them lengthways, then cut across into fine slices. Sprinkle generously with salt and leave for 1 hour. Press out all the liquid and rinse once in cold water. Drain well. Soak tamarind pulp in hot water for a few minutes, then squeeze to dissolve pulp and strain, discarding the seeds. If using tamarind concentrate, dissolve in the hot water. Add brown sugar or palm sugar to the tamarind liquid. Scald tomatoes, peel and slice. Combine all the ingredients, add salt to taste, chill and serve.

Salads of this type are not served on their own, but as accompaniments to rice, curries or main dishes.

SERVES: 6

# COCONUT CHUTNEY

½ fresh coconut, grated,
or 1 cup (3 oz) desiccated coconut

•

1 lemon or lime

•

2 or 3 fresh red or green chillies

•

1 teaspoon salt

•

2 teaspoons ghee (clarified butter)
or oil

•

⅛ teaspoon ground asafoetida
(optional)

•

1 teaspoon black mustard seeds

•

1 teaspoon black cumin
(kalonji) seeds

•

10 curry leaves

•

½ teaspoon urad dhal

If using desiccated coconut, sprinkle with about ¼ cup (2 fl oz) water and toss to moisten evenly. Peel the lemon or lime so that no white pith remains. Cut in pieces and remove the seeds. Put into electric blender with the seeded and roughly chopped chillies and blend until smooth. Add the coconut and continue blending to a smooth paste, scraping down sides of blender and adding a little more liquid if necessary. Add the salt and mix.

Heat ghee or oil in a small pan and fry the remaining ingredients, stirring frequently, until mustard seeds pop and dhal is golden. Mix with the blended mixture, pat into a flat cake and serve or as an accompaniment to rice or Chapatis (see page 398).

SERVES: 6–8

# ROASTED COCONUT SAMBAL

*In Sri Lanka, this is made with fresh coconut, roasted in the ashes of the fire until dark brown, then ground on a large stone, but this adaptation is a lot easier to make.*

1 cup (3 oz) desiccated coconut

•

2 medium onions, finely chopped

•

1 teaspoon salt

•

approximately ¼ cup (2 fl oz) lemon
juice

Heat desiccated coconut in a heavy-based frying pan and stir constantly until evenly browned. It should be a fairly deep brown, but be careful not to burn it. Spread coconut on a large plate to cool.

Combine all ingredients in an electric blender, cover and blend on high speed to a smooth paste. It may be necessary to add a little more chopped onion or lemon juice if there is not sufficient liquid.

Shape into a round flat cake and mark the top in a criss-cross pattern with a fork or the back of a knife. Serve with rice and curry.

SERVES: 8

# FRIED ONION SAMBAL

### INGREDIENTS

½ cup (4 fl oz) oil

•

2 large onions, finely sliced

•

6 dried chillies, broken into pieces

•

1 teaspoon salt or to taste

•

2 tablespoons lemon juice

Heat oil in a frying pan and fry onions slowly until soft and transparent. Add chillies, cover and cook for 10–15 minutes, or until oil separates from other ingredients. Stir occasionally while cooking. Add salt and lemon juice and cook a few minutes longer. Serve with boiled rice and curries.

SERVES: 6–8

# GREEN MANGO CHUTNEY

### INGREDIENTS

1 large green mango

•

½ teaspoon salt

•

½ teaspoon chilli powder or to taste

Peel and thinly slice the mango, then cut it into fine slivers. Toss with the salt and chilli powder and serve as an accompaniment to a curry meal, or as an appetiser at the start of a meal.

NOTE: Tart green cooking apples may be used instead of mango.

SERVES: 4–6

# PAPPADAMS WITH GARNISH

*These dried lentil wafers come in many varieties and are sold in packets, ready for deep-frying. They may be served simply fried or, as here, presented with a flourish as I remember from a meal at the Taj Mahal Hotel in Bombay.*

### INGREDIENTS

6 large pappadams

•

oil for deep-frying

•

½ cup (2 oz) grated fresh coconut

•

2 tablespoons finely chopped fresh coriander

•

chilli powder to taste

Heat oil in wok or deep-frying pan and fry the pappadams one at a time for just a few seconds, until they swell and turn golden. Drain on absorbent paper. Sprinkle each one with the coconut, coriander and chilli powder, and serve at once as an accompaniment to rice and curries.

SERVES: 6

# EGGPLANT PICKLE, SRI LANKAN STYLE

*Keeps for weeks in the refrigerator and makes a great flavour accent with rice and curries.*

## INGREDIENTS

1 kg (2 lb) eggplants (aubergines)
•
1 tablespoon salt
•
2 teaspoons ground turmeric
•
oil for deep-frying
•
3 tablespoons black mustard seeds or whole grain mustard
•
½ cup (4 fl oz) vinegar
•
2 onions, finely chopped
•
4 cloves garlic, sliced
•
1 tablespoon finely chopped fresh ginger
•
1 tablespoon ground coriander
•
2 teaspoons ground cumin
•
1 teaspoon ground fennel
•
3 tablespoons tamarind pulp
•
¾ cup (6 fl oz) hot water
•
3 fresh green chillies, seeded and sliced
•
1 stick cinnamon
•
1 teaspoon chilli powder
•
2 teaspoons sugar
•
salt to taste

Wash and thinly slice unpeeled eggplants, rub with salt and turmeric and leave for at least an hour. Drain off liquid and dry slices on paper towels. Heat oil for deep-frying and fry the eggplants in batches over medium heat until deep brown on both sides. Lift out with a slotted spoon and put into a dry bowl. Reserve the oil.

In a blender container, put the mustard, vinegar, onions, garlic and ginger. Cover and blend to a smooth paste.

Toast coriander, cumin and fennel in a dry pan over gentle heat until brown and fragrant. Soak tamarind in hot water and squeeze to dissolve pulp, straining out seeds and fibre.

Heat ½ cup (4 fl oz) reserved oil and fry the blended mixture for 5 minutes. Add the toasted ground spices, chillies, cinnamon, chilli powder and tamarind liquid. Add fried eggplants and any oil that has collected in the bowl. Stir well, cover and simmer for 15 minutes. Remove from heat, stir in sugar. Add salt to taste if necessary, cool completely and store in clean, dry jars.

# TAMARIND CHUTNEY

## INGREDIENTS

3 tablespoons dried tamarind pulp

•

1 cup (8 fl oz) hot water

•

1 teaspoon salt

•

2 teaspoons palm sugar or
brown sugar

•

1 teaspoon ground cumin

•

½ teaspoon ground fennel

•

2 teaspoons finely grated fresh ginger

•

lemon juice to taste

•

pinch chilli powder (optional)

Put tamarind pulp into a bowl with hot water and soak until water is cool. Knead and squeeze pulp away from the seeds until it has dissolved in the water, then strain through a fine nylon sieve, pushing all the pulp through. If necessary, add a little more water to help remove all pulp from the seeds. Add salt, sugar and other ingredients to the tamarind and stir to mix well. Taste and add more salt if necessary, lemon juice to sharpen the flavour and if liked, a small pinch of chilli powder.

SERVES: 8

# CRISP SPICED COCONUT WITH PEANUTS

*This is one of those spicy and crisp accompaniments, so much a part of
a meal of rice and curry.*

## INGREDIENTS

1 cup (3 oz) desiccated coconut

•

1 small onion, very finely chopped

•

1 clove garlic, crushed

•

1 teaspoon finely grated fresh ginger

•

2 tablespoons peanut oil

•

1 teaspoon ground coriander

•

1 teaspoon ground cumin

•

1 teaspoon salt

•

1 tablespoon tamarind liquid or
lemon juice

•

1 cup (5 oz) roasted unsalted peanuts

In a bowl, mix the coconut, onion, garlic and ginger. Heat peanut oil in a wok or frying pan, add the coconut mixture and fry on medium low heat, stirring constantly, until coconut is golden brown. Add coriander, cumin, salt, tamarind liquid or lemon juice and continue stirring and frying on very low heat until coconut is dry and crisp. This takes quite a while and cannot be hurried by raising the heat. Allow to cool, then mix in peanuts. Serve as an accompaniment to a rice meal, or use as a garnish to sprinkle over dishes.

SERVES: 6

# BANANA AND YOGHURT RAITA

*Salty and sweet, and only slightly spicy, raita is a good*
*accompaniment to curry.*

### INGREDIENTS

2 cups (16 fl oz) yoghurt
•
½ teaspoon salt
•
2 tablespoons desiccated coconut
•
2 teaspoons sugar
•
2 teaspoons ghee (clarified butter)
or oil
•
½ teaspoon cumin seeds
•
½ teaspoon black cumin
(kalonji) seeds
•
½ teaspoon black mustard seeds
•
½ teaspoon ground cumin
•
½ teaspoon chilli powder (optional)
•
3 large ripe bananas, sliced
into rounds

In a bowl combine the yoghurt, salt, coconut and sugar. In a small saucepan, heat the ghee or oil and fry the seeds until they crackle. Remove from heat and add the ground cumin and chilli powder, then pour over the yoghurt and mix well. Stir the bananas through the mixture, cover and chill before serving.

SERVES: 4

# YOGHURT WITH CUCUMBERS

*This type of salad is known as a raita, a cooling accompaniment to an Indian meal. Cucumber is probably the most popular, but cooked diced beetroot (beets) or sliced ripe bananas may be used instead.*

### INGREDIENTS

2 green cucumbers
•
2 teaspoons salt
•
2 tablespoons finely chopped spring onion (scallion)
•
1½ cups (12 fl oz) yoghurt
•
lemon juice to taste
•
1½ teaspoons cumin seeds
•
1 tablespoon chopped fresh coriander or mint

Peel the cucumbers, halve them lengthways and remove the seeds. Cut the cucumbers into small dice, sprinkle with salt and leave for 15 minutes, then drain away liquid and rinse the cucumbers quickly in cold water. Drain well. Combine with onion, yoghurt, lemon juice and taste to see if more salt is required. Roast the cumin seeds in a dry pan, shaking pan or stirring constantly until brown. Bruise or crush seeds and sprinkle over yoghurt. Serve chilled, garnished with coriander or mint.

SERVES: 6

# LEEKS FRIED WITH CHILLI

*Try this once and you'll never again throw out the green portion of leeks. In fact, save the white part for Vichyssoise (see page 80) and use just the leaves, and you'll have two dishes from one bunch of leeks. Tasty and terrific!*

### INGREDIENTS

4 medium leeks
•
¼ cup (2 fl oz) oil
•
½ teaspoon ground turmeric
•
1 teaspoon chilli powder, or to taste
•
1 teaspoon salt

Wash leeks very well, taking care to remove all sand and grit. Discard any tough or withered leaves but use the green portions as well. With a sharp knife, slice very thinly. When slicing the leaves make a tight bundle and hold firmly.

Heat oil in a large saucepan and add the leeks. Fry, stirring, for 5 minutes, then add the remaining ingredients and stir well. Cover and cook over low heat for 30 minutes, stirring occasionally. The leeks will reduce considerably in volume. Uncover and cook until liquid evaporates and leeks have an oily appearance. Serve as an accompaniment to a rice meal.

SERVES: 6

# SAFFRON AND CREAM SAUCE

## INGREDIENTS

⅛ teaspoon saffron strands
•
2 tablespoons boiling water
•
2 tablespoons blanched pistachios
•
¼ cup (1 oz) blanched almonds
•
1 tablespoon ghee (clarified butter)
or butter
•
¾ cup (6 fl oz) cream
•
½ cup (4 fl oz) milk
•
¼ teaspoon ground cardamom
•
½ teaspoon salt, or to taste
•
½ teaspoon white pepper

Pound saffron with a mortar and pestle, then dissolve in the boiling water. Put pistachios and almonds into an electric blender and grind finely, or pound with a mortar and pestle. Heat the ghee or butter in a small pan and fry the ground nuts, stirring constantly. Add the saffron, cream, milk, cardamom, salt and pepper and simmer, stirring constantly, until sauce is thick. Serve with Parathas (see page 396) and Dry Potato Curry (see page 342).

SERVES: 6

# FRESH CORIANDER AND COCONUT CHUTNEY

## INGREDIENTS

1 cup (2 oz) fresh coriander
•
2 tablespoons desiccated coconut
•
3 tablespoons water
•
1 teaspoon chopped garlic
•
1 fresh green chilli, seeded
•
1 teaspoon Garam Masala
(see page 456)
•
1 teaspoon salt
•
2 tablespoons lemon juice

Put the well washed coriander into an electric blender with all other ingredients and blend on high speed until smooth. If necessary, add a little water to facilitate blending but do not make the mixture too wet.

SERVES: 6

# WEDDING PICKLE

*This fruit pickle is traditionally served at Parsi weddings. Parsis are descendants of Persians who fled to India in the 13th century and stayed to become prominent citizens. I was honoured when talented Parsi cooks invited me to dine on some of their most celebrated dishes and generously furnished me with recipes.*

## INGREDIENTS

½ cup (3 oz) chopped dates
•
½ cup (3 oz) raisins
•
½ cup (3 oz) chopped dried apricots

½ cup (3 oz) chopped dried figs
•
1 cup (8 fl oz) water

500 g (1 lb) carrots
•
1 teaspoon cumin seeds
•
2 small cinnamon sticks
•
1 teaspoon ground cardamom
•
¼ teaspoon ground cloves
•
2 cups (16 fl oz) vinegar
•
2 cups palm or brown sugar
•
3 teaspoons salt
•
2 teaspoons chilli powder
•
2 teaspoons ground black
mustard seeds
•
1 teaspoon crushed garlic
•
1 teaspoon grated fresh ginger

Soak dried fruits in water for 1 hour. Wash and scrape the carrots and grate on fine grater. Put all the ingredients into a stainless steel or enamel pan and bring slowly to the boil, stirring. Simmer until the fruit is very soft and the liquid syrupy. Cook and store in sterilised bottles. Remove cinnamon sticks before serving.

# DESSERTS

Desserts are not a feature of Oriental meals. In addition, most of the recipes are closely guarded secrets and so most people buy them from specialty sweetmakers rather than attempt to make them at home.

Sweets are eaten between meals rather than as dessert at the end of a meal. Even those liquid sweets which are served with bowl and spoon are eaten as refreshers or energy boosters at any hour of the day.

However, especially to the Western palate, ending a meal with a sweet dish provides a nice finish. Here are some of the more popular and easily made sweets of the East.

## MANGO, MOGHUL STYLE

*This is sheer, unadulterated extravagance but the exotic flavours will evoke thoughts of the Moghul Emperors in their summer palaces of white marble, feasting on similar delicacies.*

### INGREDIENTS

2 or 3 firm ripe mangoes
•
1/3 cup (3 oz) sugar
•
½ cup (4 fl oz) water
•
4 green cardamom pods
•
pinch of saffron strands
•
2 tablespoons unsalted pistachio kernels

With a sharp knife, peel the mangoes thinly and slice or cube the flesh. Put sugar and water into a saucepan and set over medium heat. Crush the cardamom pods with a mortar and pestle and add to the pan. Pound the saffron with a mortar and pestle, then pour a tablespoon of boiling water into the mortar and dissolve the saffron before adding it to the simmering syrup.

When sugar has dissolved, continue to cook the syrup for 5 minutes before adding the mango. Bring to the boil, then lower heat and simmer gently for about 10 minutes. Blanch pistachio kernels for 1 minute in boiling water, drop into cold water and slip off the skins. Put the mangoes into a shallow glass dish, displaying some of the deep green pistachios on the surface where they look wonderful against the bright yellow fruit.

Serve with pouring (light) cream or, to be totally authentic, with a rich reduced cream made Indian-style by simmering 3 cups (24 fl oz) of milk and ½ cup (4 fl oz) cream in a heavy, wide-based pan, stirring frequently, until it has reduced to less than half its original volume. Scrape the thickened milk from the pan, allow to cool, then add a teaspoon of sugar and whisk until smooth.

Serve in a small jug to pour over individual servings of mango. If left in the refrigerator overnight, it will be thick enough to spoon like clotted cream.

SERVES: 4–5

# INDIAN MENUS

*Some of these menus have many items, some just a few, but each one is a well balanced meal. The flavours come from all over the vast sub continent, representing the rich foods of the north as well as the simple flavours of the south.*

Potato and Pea Curry Puffs *page 238*

Fresh Mint Chutney *page 356*

Rice with Mixed Lentils *page 270*

Mixed Vegetables, Sindhi Style *page 335*

Eggplant Puree *page 334*

Banana and Yoghurt Raita *page 363*

Creamy Vermicelli Pudding *page 375*

Ghee Rice *page 262*

Spicy Fried Cauliflower *page 300*

Spinach with Potatoes *page 332*

Carrot Sweetmeat *page 374*

Chapatis *page 398*

or

Parathas *page 396*

Peas with Fresh Cheese *page 328*

Eggplant Puree *page 334*

Dry Potato Curry *page 342*

Saffron and Cream Sauce *page 365*

Toast of the Shah *page 371*

Rice with Fresh Cheese, Nuts and
Vegetables *page 272*

Lentil Cakes in Yoghurt *page 342*

Almond Cream Sweetmeat *page 371*

Kashmiri Tea *page 434*

# SAGO PUDDING

*This is the famous pudding served at the end of "curry tiffins" as the extended lunches were called in Colonial times. For those with fond memories of such occasions, here is Gula Malacca, to give it the familiar local name.*

### INGREDIENTS

2 cups (8 oz) sago or minute tapioca

•

8–10 cups (64–80 fl oz) water

•

1 small stick cinnamon (optional)

•

2 tablespoons coconut milk

•

pinch of salt

### FOR SERVING

250 g (8 oz) palm sugar or brown sugar

•

½ cup (4 fl oz) water

•

2 strips pandan leaves, fresh or dried

•

1¼ cups (12 fl oz) coconut milk

•

pinch salt

Slowly dribble the sago into the water which you have brought to a fast boil in a large saucepan with the cinnamon stick if used. Let it boil for 5–7 minutes. Turn off heat, cover the pan with a well fitting lid and leave for 10 minutes. The sago will finish cooking in the stored heat and the grains will be clear. Run cold water into the pan, stir, then drain in a sieve, shaking the sieve so the water runs off. Discard the cinnamon.

Turn the sago into a bowl, stir in the 2 tablespoons of coconut milk and pinch of salt. This quantity of milk is just enough to give it a pearly white appearance instead of that unattractive grey look. Divide between individual dessert dishes or moulds, or pour into one large mould. Chill until set.

To make the syrup, chop the palm sugar into small pieces or shave with a sharp knife. Put into a small saucepan with the water and pandan leaves and heat gently until the sugar has melted. Strain through a fine sieve to remove any small impurities. Cool and chill.

Unmould and serve the sago chilled, accompanied by syrup and coconut milk. A little syrup may be poured around the mould when it is turned out on the serving dish, but it is more usual to serve the syrup and coconut milk in small jugs or bowls with spoons so people may help themselves.

SERVES: 6–8

# TOAST OF THE SHAH

## INGREDIENTS

6 slices of bread, cut thick
as for toasting

•

4–6 tablespoons ghee
(clarified butter) or butter

•

1½ cups (12 fl oz) milk

•

1 cup (8 fl oz) cream

•

1 cup (8 oz) sugar

•

¼ teaspoon saffron strands

•

¼ teaspoon ground cardamom

•

1 tablespoon rosewater

•

1 tablespoon each slivered blanched
pistachios and almonds

Trim crusts off the bread and if slices are large, cut in half. Heat the ghee in a large, heavy-based frying pan and fry the bread until golden on both sides. It may be necessary to add more ghee. Remove slices of fried bread to a plate.

Add milk and cream to the pan in which the bread was fried. Bring to the boil and add the sugar. In the meantime, toast saffron strands in a dry pan, crush with a mortar and pestle, add 2 tablespoons of hot milk and dissolve the saffron in it. Return to the pan and boil hard, stirring constantly, for 10 minutes. Put in the slices of fried bread in one layer and simmer over low heat until milk has been absorbed, carefully turning slices of bread over once.

Transfer bread to a heated serving dish, sprinkle with cardamom and rosewater and decorate with slivered nuts. Serve hot.

SERVES: 6

# ALMOND CREAM SWEETMEAT

## INGREDIENTS

4 cups (32 fl oz) milk

•

¾ cup (6 oz) sugar

•

125 g (4 oz) blanched almonds,
pulverised in blender,
or 1 cup ground almonds

•

pinch of ground cardamom

•

2 tablespoons blanched
pistachio nuts

•

edible silver leaf (varak) (optional)

In a heavy-based saucepan or large frying pan, boil the milk over fairly high heat, stirring all the time, until it has reduced and is very thick. This is called *khoa* or condensed milk. Add sugar and stir for 10 minutes on low heat. Add the ground almonds and continue to cook and stir until the mixture comes away from the sides and base of pan in one mass. Remove from heat, sprinkle cardamom over and mix well.

Turn mixture on to a greased plate and smooth top with the back of a buttered spoon. Cool slightly, mark in diamond shapes with a knife and decorate with halved pistachio nuts and silver leaf. Before it is quite firm, cut with a sharp knife along the markings, then leave to get cold before separating into pieces.

MAKES: about 16 pieces

# ALMOND BEAN CURD

*Nice to serve at the end of a Chinese meal.*

## INGREDIENTS

4 cups (32 fl oz) water
•
4 teaspoons powdered agar-agar or
1 cup soaked and drained agar-agar
strands
•
1 can (13 oz/400 g) sweetened
condensed milk
•
2 teaspoons almond essence (extract)

Put water into a saucepan, sprinkle agar-agar over and bring to the boil. Boil and stir until agar-agar has dissolved. Powdered agar takes only a couple of minutes to dissolve, strands take longer. Add condensed milk and almond essence and stir well. Pour into a large shallow dish or a large cake tin. Allow to cool and set, then chill. Cut into cubes or diamond shapes and serve by itself or with canned fruits or melon balls.

SERVES: 6–8

# SPICY COCONUT CUSTARD

*This rich custard is very popular throughout Asia.*

## INGREDIENTS

4 eggs
•
175 g (5 oz) palm sugar
(see Note)
•
½ cup (4 fl oz) water
•
1½ cups (12 fl oz) thick coconut milk
(made with milk instead of water, see
page 443)
•
¾ cup (6 fl oz) evaporated milk
•
½ teaspoon ground cardamom
•
¼ teaspoon ground mace
•
pinch ground cloves
•
1 tablespoon rosewater

Beat eggs slightly (they should not be frothy). Dissolve palm sugar in water over a low heat, cool slightly. Add palm sugar syrup, or black (or dark brown) sugar and maple syrup, to beaten eggs, add the coconut milk and stir to dissolve sugar.

Strain through a fine strainer into a large jug, add evaporated milk, spices and rosewater. Pour into individual custard cups. Put custard cups in a baking dish with water to come halfway up sides of cups and bake in an oven preheated to 160°C (325°F) for approximately 1¼ hours or until set.

Alternatively put the same depth of water into an electric frypan. Set temperature at 120°C (260°F), put custard cups in, cover and cook until set, approximately 1¼ hours. Cool and chill custards before serving.

NOTE: If palm sugar is not available, substitute half cup firmly packed black (or dark brown) sugar and half cup maple syrup.

SERVES: 4–6

ALMOND BEAN CURD

# CARROT SWEETMEAT

## INGREDIENTS

500 g (1 lb) carrots

•

60 g (2 oz) ghee (clarified butter)

•

¼ teaspoon ground cardamom

•

1¼ cups (10 oz) sugar

•

½ cup (4 fl oz) hot water

•

1 cup (8 fl oz) cream

•

¼ cup (1 oz) dried milk powder
(or khoa/condensed milk,
see Almond Cream Sweetmeat
page 371)

•

2 tablespoons blanched slivered
almonds or pistachios

•

edible silver leaf (varak)
to garnish (optional)

Wash and peel carrots, then grate them finely. Heat ghee and cardamom in a heavy-based saucepan and add the carrots. Cook uncovered over medium heat, stirring. Cover and turn heat very low, allowing carrots to cook in steam until soft and the liquid has nearly evaporated. Make a syrup by boiling the sugar and water. Add syrup to carrots and stir in the cream and milk powder or khoa, blending all the ingredients well. Cook, stirring constantly, until the mixture is thick enough to come away from sides of the pan in one lump. Turn onto a greased dish, smooth top with buttered aluminium foil if necessary, and allow to cool. Decorate with almonds or pistachios and, if liked, with silver leaf. Cut into small diamond shapes or squares.

MAKES: about 20 pieces

# CREAMY RICE BLANCMANGE

## INGREDIENTS

3 cups (24 fl oz) milk

•

3 tablespoons ground rice

•

3 tablespoons sugar

•

3 cardamom pods, bruised

•

1 tablespoon rosewater or
2–3 drops rose essence

•

2 tablespoons blanched pistachios
or almonds

•

red food colouring (optional)

•

edible silver leaf (varak) (optional)

Mix a little of the milk with the ground rice to form a smooth cream. Bring the rest of the milk to the boil with the sugar and cardamom pods, stirring with a wooden spoon. Remove from heat and stir in the ground rice, then return the pan to the heat and stir constantly until the mixture boils and thickens. Boil, stirring, for 3–5 minutes. Remove from heat, add rose flavouring and half the nuts, finely chopped. Pour into individual dessert dishes and decorate tops with the remaining nuts, chopped or slivered. For special occasions, tint the mixture a pale rose pink. Chill for a few hours before serving. In winter, this sweet may be served warm.

SERVES: 4

# FRIED MILK BALLS IN ROSE SYRUP

*Anyone addicted to Indian sweets will recognise this popular dish of gulab jamun.*

### INGREDIENTS

¾ cup (3½ oz) full cream (whole milk) milk powder

•

3 tablespoons self-raising flour

•

pinch of bicarbonate of soda (baking soda)

•

¼ teaspoon ground cardamom

•

1 tablespoon soft butter or ghee (clarified butter)

•

approximately 3 tablespoons water

•

ghee or oil for deep-frying

### SYRUP

2 cups (1 lb) sugar

•

4 cups (32 fl oz) water

•

5 cardamom pods, bruised

•

2 tablespoons rosewater or few drops rose essence

Sift milk powder, flour, bicarbonate of soda and ground cardamom into a large bowl. Rub in butter or ghee, then add enough water to give a firm but pliable dough which can be moulded into balls the size of large marbles, or into small sausage shapes.

Before frying the shapes, make the syrup by combining the sugar, water and cardamom pods and heating until sugar has dissolved.

Heat ghee (or oil flavoured with a little ghee) and fry the shapes over low heat until they slowly turn golden brown. Lift out on a slotted spoon and drain on absorbent paper.

Put the fried milk balls into the warm syrup and add rosewater when they have cooled somewhat. Leave for at least 4 hours, or overnight. The milk balls will swell and become spongy. Serve at room temperature or chilled.

MAKES: about 18

# CREAMY VERMICELLI PUDDING

### INGREDIENTS

5 cups (40 fl oz) milk

•

½ cup (2½ oz) broken vermicelli

•

6 tablespoons sugar

•

2 tablespoons sultanas (golden raisins)

•

¼ cup (1 oz) blanched, slivered almonds

•

2 drops kewra essence (optional)

•

1 tablespoon chopped pistachios

Bring milk to the boil, stirring constantly. Add the vermicelli and cook until soft. Add the sugar, sultanas and almonds. Stir over medium heat until the mixture is like a thick custard. Remove from heat, add the flavouring essence and spoon into a dessert dish or individual bowls. Decorate with pistachios. Serve warm or chilled.

SERVES: 4

# EAST
# MEETS WEST

# BREAKFAST & BRUNCH

Breakfast is such a personal meal. Lunch, dinner, afternoon tea and supper are all much easier to offer recipes for than breakfast.

Some folks just aren't ready for anything solid until well into the day. Fruit or fruit juice is the preferred breakfast for many people, while others feel cheated if they cannot fortify themselves with a cooked meal before starting on the day's work.

Then again, there are those who need nourishment but cannot find time on most mornings to do any serious cooking. In the recipes that follow I have tried to offer suggestions for all the foregoing situations as well as those lovely leisurely weekends or holidays when one stays in bed late, then enjoys preparing a late breakfast that doubles as lunch. That's how the idea of brunch came about, and a very civilised one it is, too.

Even the cereal eaters are catered for, because we don't want anyone resorting to those over-sweetened, empty calories that are sold in cardboard boxes. Food should not only be nutritious, it should also be delicious. My muesli recipes, may I say, are most "munchable".

Browse and choose what the occasion and your preferences dictate. There are also choices in the chapter on breads and baking, for some great breakfast loaves or rolls.

## READY-TO-EAT CEREALS
## HAZELNUT MUESLI

*This is a natural muesli, not a toasted one. Only the hazelnuts and sunflower seeds are toasted to bring out their flavour.*

### INGREDIENTS

100 g (3½ oz) hazelnuts

½ cup (2 oz) sunflower seeds

½ cup (4 oz) raw sugar or unrefined black (dark brown) sugar

1½ cups (6 oz) oat bran

3 cups (9 oz) rolled oats

1 cup (3 oz) wheatgerm

½ cup (3 oz) sultanas (golden raisins)

10 dried apricot halves, chopped

10 dried apple rings, chopped

Toast hazelnuts in an oven preheated to 180°C (350°F) for 15 minutes to intensify the flavour. Rub in a dry tea towel and most of the skins will come off. Crush or chop roughly. Toast sunflower seeds in a dry frying pan, tossing and stirring constantly. Turn out on a plate to cool.

In an electric blender, put raw sugar and bran, and blend on high speed until finely ground. Empty into a large bowl. Blend remaining bran—it's easier to eat if finely ground. Process half the oats to a coarse, mealy consistency (leave remainder as is). Add all ingredients to bowl and mix well. Store in an airtight container for 3 weeks in summer and 6 weeks in winter.

For a breakfast serving, combine 4 spoonfuls with milk and a freshly grated apple or sliced ripe banana.

MAKES: about 16 servings

# ALMOND GRANOLA

*This is a beautifully crisp, crunchy breakfast food which I find practical to make in large quantities so there is at least a week's supply for a family. It is more than a breakfast cereal; we sometimes nibble it by the handful while watching television.*

### INGREDIENTS

250 g (8 oz) unblanched almonds
•
125 g (4 oz) sunflower seeds
•
5 cups (15 oz) rolled oats
•
1 cup (3 oz) wheat germ
•
¾ cup (3 oz) oat bran
•
¹/₃ cup (3 fl oz) maize (corn)
or sunflower oil
•
¾ cup (6 fl oz) honey
•
1 teaspoon almond extract
(optional)

Place the almonds on a baking tray in an oven preheated to 180°C (350°F) for 8–10 minutes, remove and cool. Toast the sunflower seeds in the same way, for about 5 minutes. Crush the almonds coarsely. In a large bowl, combine almonds and sunflower seeds, oats, wheat germ and bran.

In a small saucepan, heat the oil and honey gently just until the honey is liquid. Remove from heat, stir in almond essence if using it, then pour over the ingredients in the bowl. With both hands, mix thoroughly to evenly distribute the sweetness.

Oil a large roasting dish and put half the mixture into it. Bake in the oven at the same temperature for 15 minutes, stirring mixture well every 5 minutes to prevent it browning too much around the edges and on top. Turn into a large bowl and leave to cool. Roast the remaining half of the mixture in the same way. When both lots are quite cold, store in an airtight container. To make it even better, stir through a handful of sultanas (golden raisins) or currants. Cool, then store in an airtight container for 4 weeks.

Serve ½ cup portions with milk for breakfast, or serve it dry for snacking.

MAKES: 7 cups, about 14 servings

# SWISS-STYLE MUESLI

*While on holiday in Switzerland, the delights of muesli (a rather more decadent version than that served in sanatoriums) were discovered and this has been a favourite ever since.*

### INGREDIENTS

4 tablespoons rolled oats

•

4 tablespoons cold water

•

sugar to taste

•

ripe peach or other stone fruit

•

pouring (light) cream

Soak the oats in water overnight. Add sugar and diced peach and mix gently with enough cream to make it a nice spoonable consistency.

This can also be made with ripe berries in season, but the original version is simply soaked oats and grated apple.

SERVES: 2

# COOKED CEREALS

# WHOLE WHEAT AND DRIED FRUIT COMPOTE

*This Armenian specialty called Anooshabour (try saying it—it has a nice sound) will give you a new perspective on whole wheat. Chewy and not too sweet, I find it is a good breakfast dish as well as a dessert.*

### INGREDIENTS

½ cup (2 oz) whole kernel wheat

•

2 cups (16 fl oz) water

•

2 tablespoons honey

•

½ cup (3 oz) sultanas
(golden raisins)

•

16 dried apricot halves

•

8 large prunes

•

2 teaspoons rosewater (optional)

Wash the wheat, drain, then put into a saucepan with the measured water and bring to the boil. Pour into a vacuum flask, cover tightly and leave overnight. This little trick cuts the cooking time dramatically. If no flask is available, leave in the covered pan. Next day bring to the boil again and simmer until tender. Add the honey and fruit and simmer until liquid is thick and wheat is soft but still holding its shape. If necessary, add more hot water while cooking. When slightly cool, stir in rosewater. Serve warm or cold.

SERVES: 8

SWISS-STYLE MUESLI

# CREAMY OATMEAL PORRIDGE

*Not traditional, but very nice and creamy smooth, and especially suitable
for those always-in-a-hurry people.*

### INGREDIENTS

2 cups (16 fl oz) milk or milk
and water
•
½ cup (1½ oz) quick-cooking oats
•
pinch of salt
•
brown sugar to taste
•
nut (pat) of butter

Bring the milk and water to the boil, stir in the oats and salt and cook, stirring, for 1 minute. Serve with brown sugar for sprinkling over, and a small nut of butter for those whose conscience and cholesterol levels permit such an indulgence.

SERVES: 2

# SCOTS-STYLE OATMEAL PORRIDGE

### INGREDIENTS

½ cup (1½ oz) rolled oats or oatmeal
•
2½ cups (20 fl oz) water
•
salt to taste
•
cold milk for serving

Soak the oats or oatmeal in water overnight. Add salt and bring to the boil over medium heat, stirring constantly. Simmer for 15–20 minutes. Coarser oatmeal will take longer. Serve with a separate bowl of cold milk in which each spoonful is dipped before being eaten.

VARIATION: Some recipes don't require the overnight soaking but stipulate whisking the oats into fast boiling water. Continue whisking until mixture returns to the boil, then cover the pan and cook on very low heat for 10 minutes. Stir in the salt, cover and cook for a further 15 minutes.

SERVES: 2

# THE LIQUID BREAKFAST

Surely we all know those days when there is simply no time to sit down to breakfast—that's when these delicious and nutritionally sound drinks make a lot of sense. They take just a couple of minutes and sustain the student or worker until lunch time.

# BANANA FLIP

*Even kids who say they don't have time for breakfast will willingly gulp
this down.*

### INGREDIENTS

1 egg

•

1 ripe banana

•

1 cup (8 fl oz) cold milk

•

1 teaspoon honey or to taste

•

few drops vanilla (optional)

Break the egg into the jar of an electric blender, add the
rest of the ingredients and buzz on high speed for 20 seconds
or until smooth and frothy. Pour over ice cubes in a glass
in hot weather, or serve at room temperature if preferred.

SERVES: 1

# VANILLA FLIP

*Ice-cream in the morning? If it makes nourishment more acceptable to children
who would otherwise miss breakfast altogether, I'm all for it—especially when
the ice-cream is home-made.*

### INGREDIENTS

1 egg

•

1 cup (8 fl oz) cold milk

•

1 teaspoon sugar

•

½ teaspoon pure vanilla

•

1 small scoop vanilla ice-cream

Put the egg, milk, sugar and vanilla into an electric blender
and blend on high speed until smooth and frothy. Pour into
a glass, add a scoop of vanilla ice-cream (or any favourite
flavour) and serve with a straw.

SERVES: 1

# MALTED MILKSHAKE

*A hot drink when the weather is cool is another sensible breakfast offering.*

### INGREDIENTS

1 tablespoon malted milk powder

•

hot water

•

2 teaspoons drinking chocolate
(optional)

•

¾ cup hot milk

Dissolve the malted milk powder in hot water, stir in the
drinking chocolate until dissolved, then add the hot milk
and mix.

SERVES: 1

# COFFEE AND RUM FLIP

*I don't know that this should be a breakfast drink, but I daresay there are occasions when one is staying home with a cold and needs something to warm the cockles of the heart. Without the alcohol it is also delicious and definitely the preferred version if you are venturing out.*

### INGREDIENTS

1 egg

•

1–2 teaspoons rum or brandy

•

½ cup (4 fl oz) very hot coffee

•

½ cup (4 fl oz) hot milk

•

1 teaspoon sugar or to taste

•

grating of nutmeg

Whisk the egg until light and frothy. Add the rum, whisk in the hot coffee and milk, and stir in sugar to taste. Sprinkle nutmeg on foamy top and sip while very hot.

SERVES: 1

# FRUIT FEASTS

Even if all you want is fruit, it is nicer when presented with flair. Pawpaw (papaya) or melon wedges should be de-seeded and served with a wedge of lime for squeezing over. Pineapple should have not only the skin but also the core removed for greater enjoyment.

Fruit salads of sliced banana, chopped apple or pear, and a few grapes are light and satisfying. Toss in lemon, lime or orange juice to help prevent the fruit going brown. A spoonful of cottage cheese served alongside with a few nuts sprinkled over provides protein content.

# GRILLED GRAPEFRUIT

Halve a grapefruit and use a curved grapefruit knife to loosen the segments. Drizzle a little honey over each half and place under a preheated griller (broiler) until warm and glazed. Centre with a glacé cherry or sprig of mint and serve right away.

# WAFFLES, MUFFINS, CROISSANTS AND SUCH

## DATE AND PECAN MUFFINS

### INGREDIENTS

1 cup (4 oz) wholemeal
(whole wheat) flour

2 teaspoons baking powder

½ cup (2 oz) self-raising flour

pinch of salt

60 g (2 oz) butter

½ cup (4 fl oz) buttermilk or milk

2 tablespoons raw sugar

1 egg, beaten

½ teaspoon vanilla essence (extract)

1 cup (3 oz) bran cereal

½ cup (2½ oz) chopped dates

½ cup (2 oz) roughly broken pecans

Sift first four ingredients into a bowl. Melt butter over gentle heat, add milk and sugar, and stir until sugar has dissolved. Add egg and vanilla and pour over the bran cereal. When the bran has softened, stir in the flour, dates and pecans quickly and lightly, using a fork, taking care not to overmix. The mixture will be lumpy. Put large tablespoons of mixture into greased muffin pans so they are three-quarters full. Bake in an oven preheated to 200°C (400°F) for 20–25 minutes or until risen and golden. Serve warm with butter.

MAKES: 12 muffins

# MUSHROOM MUFFINS

## INGREDIENTS

1¾ cups (7 oz) self-raising flour, white, or wholemeal (whole wheat)

•

1 teaspoon baking powder

•

1 teaspoon salt

•

90 g (3 oz) butter

•

1 small onion, finely chopped

•

1½ cups (6 oz) finely chopped mushrooms

•

¾ cup (6 fl oz) milk

•

1 egg, beaten

•

1 tablespoon finely chopped parsley

•

¼ teaspoon freshly ground black pepper

Sift the dry ingredients into a large bowl. Heat two-thirds of the butter in a small pan and gently cook the onion until soft, not allowing it to brown. Add the mushrooms and sauté for just 1–2 minutes, stirring. Allow to cool.

Mix together the milk, egg and chopped parsley, the onion and mushroom and the pepper. Stir into the flour mixture with a fork, just until mixed. Add the remaining butter, melted. Fill 18 greased muffin cups three-quarters full and bake in an oven preheated to 210°C (425°F) for 20 minutes or until well risen and golden brown. Serve hot with butter.

MAKES: 18

# BLUEBERRY MUFFINS

## INGREDIENTS

1 cup fresh blueberries

•

1 cup (4 oz) fine wholemeal (whole wheat) flour

•

1 cup (4 oz) plain (all-purpose) flour

•

4 teaspoons baking powder

•

60 g (2 oz) butter, melted

•

2 eggs, beaten

•

¾ cup (6 fl oz) milk

•

¼ cup (2 oz) sugar

•

1 teaspoon vanilla

Rinse the blueberries and leave on absorbent paper towels to dry. Sift flours and baking powder into a bowl. Combine the melted butter, beaten eggs, milk, sugar and vanilla. Stir until sugar has dissolved. Pour over the flour and mix lightly with a fork, just enough to moisten—do not beat or overmix. Fold in the blueberries, taking care not to crush them.

Put large spoonfuls of the mixture into non-stick or well greased muffin pans to three-quarters full and bake in an oven preheated to 210°C (425°F) for 10 minutes. Reduce temperature to 200°C (400°F) and continue baking for a further 10–12 minutes or until well risen and golden. Run a spatula around each muffin and place on a wire rack. Serve warm.

MAKES: 12 muffins

# CHOCOLATE CROISSANTS

*My children (and us grown-ups too) love croissants with a centre of dark chocolate just on the point of melting. Easy to do—not easy to stop eating.*

Split croissants lengthways, put on a baking sheet and place in an oven preheated to 180°C (3550°F) for 8–10 minutes. Have ready a row of dark chocolate squares—about 3 squares for each croissant. Remove from oven and quickly pop the chocolate into the hot croissants. Leave at room temperature for a few minutes until the heat of the croissants softens the chocolate—if you can stave off the marauders that long. Enjoy!

# THE BORN AGAIN CROISSANT

*What to do with stale croissants? This simple trick turns them into the kind of delicious pastry you would go miles out of your way to buy. Fresh croissants will be too soft and soggy. It's worth leaving some to go stale just to enjoy these Almond Croissants. Wonderful for a brunch party.*

### INGREDIENTS

8 stale croissants

•

1½ cups (12 oz) sugar

•

1½ cups (12 fl oz) water

•

1 cup (8 fl oz) milk

•

1 tablespoon fine semolina

•

60 g (2 oz) unsalted butter

•

60 g (2 oz) caster (superfine) sugar

•

1 egg , beaten

•

60 g (2 oz) ground almonds

•

1 teaspoon vanilla

•

60 g (2 oz) flaked almonds

Halve the croissants lengthways. Make a syrup with the sugar and water, stirring until the sugar dissolves. Bring to the boil, then let it cool. Dunk the croissants briefly in the syrup and drain on a wire rack placed over a tray.

Mix milk and semolina together in a small saucepan and stir constantly over low heat until it boils and thickens. Cook for a couple of minutes longer, stirring. Remove from heat and cool.

Cream the butter and sugar until smooth, add the egg and beat again. Mix in the ground almonds and vanilla. Add cooked semolina and mix well. Sandwich the croissant halves together with no more than a tablespoon of the almond mixture. Spread a little more almond mixture on top and sprinkle with the flaked almonds. Bake in oven preheated to 160°C (325°F) for 15–20 minutes or until golden brown and crisp on top. Serve warm.

MAKES: 8

# WAFFLES

*If you have a waffle iron, it is great fun to have a waffle-baking brunch with family or guests. Steaming cups of hot soup or hot cocoa and good conversation fill the gaps until each waffle is baked. They can be served with savoury or sweet toppings. If no waffle iron is available, cook the same batter in a heavy-based frying pan and call them griddle cakes.*

### INGREDIENTS

2 cups (8 oz) self-raising flour
•
1 teaspoon baking powder
•
½ teaspoon salt
•
3 eggs, separated
•
1½ cups (12 fl oz) milk
•
3 tablespoons melted butter
•
1 tablespoon sugar
•
1 teaspoon vanilla extract
(optional, for sweet waffles)

Sift flour, baking powder and salt together. Beat egg yolks, stir in the milk and melted butter. (If these are to be sweet waffles, add a tablespoon of sugar and teaspoon of vanilla essence.) Add the sifted dry ingredients to the liquid mixture all at once and beat vigorously with a rotary beater or whisk until the batter is smooth. Shortly before cooking whisk the egg whites until stiff and fold into the batter.

Heat the waffle iron and, if necessary, brush with flavourless oil (non-stick waffle irons will not need greasing). Pour about a third to half a cup of batter into the centre of the waffle iron, close the lid and bake until steam stops escaping from around the edge. Waffles should be deep golden brown and crisp. Serve hot.

If cooking the mixture in a frying pan, have the pan very hot, grease lightly and pour the batter in, allowing it to spread of its own accord. When mixture has risen and bubbles form on top, use a frying slice (spatula) to flip over. Cook until second side is golden.

NOTE: For savoury waffles, top with grated cheese, sautéed onions or mushrooms. For sweet waffles, serve drizzled with honey, maple syrup or chocolate sauce, and topped with a scoop of ice-cream.

MAKES: about 8

# CHEESE CROISSANTS

Ready baked croissants are available either at your local French pâtisserie or from the supermarket freezer. They really brighten up breakfast, whether simply served with coffee or dressed up a bit.

For a savoury croissant, split in half lengthways, spread with a little prepared mustard (your choice of favourite blend) and place sliced sharp cheese inside. Sprinkle the top with freshly grated parmesan or romano cheese and a pinch of paprika if liked. Place on a baking sheet and bake in an oven preheated to 180°C (350°F) for 8 minutes or just until the cheese starts to melt.

WAFFLES

# YEAST-RISEN WAFFLES

### INGREDIENTS

15 g (½ oz) fresh compressed yeast
or 1 sachet (envelope) dry yeast

•

¹/₃ cup (3 oz) lukewarm water

•

1 teaspoon sugar

•

½ teaspoon salt

•

1½ cups (12 fl oz) lukewarm milk

•

1 tablespoon wheatgerm

•

1 cup (4 oz) wholemeal
(whole wheat) flour

•

1 cup (4 oz) plain (all-purpose) flour

•

3 eggs, separated

•

3 tablespoons melted butter

Crumble the yeast over warm water in a bowl and leave to soften, then stir until dissolved. Add sugar, salt and 1 cup (8 fl oz) of the milk. Toast wheatgerm lightly in a small dry pan and add with both flours to yeast mixture. Beat well with a wooden spoon until smooth. Cover the bowl and leave in a warm place, protected from draughts, until the mixture has risen and is bubbly.

Beat the egg yolks, stir into the remaining milk, then add the melted butter. Stir into the yeast mixture. Cover and leave to rise once more. Just before baking the waffles, beat the egg whites until stiff and fold into the batter.

Bake in a preheated waffle iron until golden brown and crisp. If no waffle iron is available, cook them as flapjacks or fluffy pancakes in a lightly greased frying pan, using about ½ cup (4 fl oz) batter for each. Serve at once with warm buttered syrup, jam and whipped cream, or with a savoury topping.

MAKES: 8

# FRENCH TOAST

*For extra nutrition make this favourite with wholemeal (whole wheat) or wholegrain bread. Crisp and buttery outside, soft and custardy within— no wonder it is a favourite with people of all ages.*

### INGREDIENTS

2 eggs

•

1 teaspoon sugar

•

½ teaspoon vanilla extract

•

¹/₃ cup (3 fl oz) milk

•

4 thick slices wholemeal
(whole wheat) bread

•

1 tablespoon butter

•

cinnamon sugar, honey or
jam for serving

Beat the eggs with sugar in a large, flat dish. Add vanilla and milk, stir well. Cut the slices of bread in half to form strips or triangles. Dip first one side, then the other in the egg mixture until all has been soaked up.

Heat half the butter in a large, heavy-based frying pan and fry the soaked bread on one side until golden brown. Flip the slices over and fry the second side, adding remaining butter to the pan. Serve hot, sprinkled with cinnamon sugar or with honey or jam.

SERVES: 2

# SPANISH OMELETTE

*When a hearty breakfast is in order, as on a weekend or during holidays, enjoy the combination of potatoes, onions and eggs that make this such a popular dish. It doubles as a light lunch or supper dish too.*

### INGREDIENTS

2 onions
•
2 large potatoes
•
1 small red capsicum (sweet pepper)
•
¼ cup (2 fl oz) olive oil
•
6 eggs
•
salt and pepper to taste

Peel and dice the onions and potatoes making the dice about 1 cm (½ in) in size. Dice the capsicum a little smaller.

Heat the oil in a large, heavy-based frying pan and cook the onions and potatoes over medium-low heat, stirring frequently, until the onions are translucent and the potatoes are tender. Add the capsicum and cook a few minutes longer, stirring until cooked but still crisp.

Beat the eggs in a bowl, season with salt and pepper, then pour the eggs into the pan, lifting the vegetables and allowing the egg to flow underneath. Cook on gentle heat until the underside is firm and golden. Finish cooking the top surface under a preheated grill (broiler) or in the oven on high heat, just until set and golden. Slide onto a heated plate and serve warm, cut into wedges.

SERVES: 4

# SCRAMBLED EGGS

*Even easier than omelettes, and just as savoury. Have ready the toast or rolls with which the eggs will be served because they are best served as soon as they are ready.*

### INGREDIENTS

6 eggs
•
2 tablespoons finely chopped fresh herbs such as dill, parsley, chives, chervil, thyme
•
½ teaspoon salt
•
¼ teaspoon white pepper
•
2 tablespoons butter

Beat eggs until yolks and whites are thoroughly combined but not enough to make them frothy. Stir in most of the chopped herbs, leaving a little for sprinkling over after the eggs are cooked. Stir in salt and pepper.

Heat a pan and melt the butter. Pour in the egg mixture and stir constantly with a wooden spoon over low heat until eggs start to set. Do not cook until dry and firm—the eggs should be moist and creamy. Sprinkle with reserved herbs and serve hot with buttered toast points.

SERVES: 4

# EGGS BENEDICT

*The original recipe calls for a slice of ham under the egg but the combination*
*of toasty muffin, perfectly poached egg and velvety smooth Hollandaise sauce*
*is superb as is.*

### INGREDIENTS

2 English muffins
•
4 eggs
•
Hollandaise Sauce (see page 440)

Split and toast the muffins. Poach the eggs in boiling water with a teaspoon of vinegar added. Drain, trim off any ragged edges of egg white, and place eggs on the warm toasted muffin halves. Spoon Hollandaise sauce over and serve immediately.

SERVES: 4

# FRENCH OMELETTE

### INGREDIENTS

3 eggs
•
3 teaspoons cold water
•
salt and pepper to taste
•
2 teaspoons butter

Break eggs into bowl and beat with a fork just long enough to combine yolks and whites. Add water and season with salt and pepper.

Heat butter in an omelette pan over medium heat. When the butter foams and starts to turn golden, pour in the eggs. Give it a few seconds undisturbed, then with the flat of the fork, start to gently pull the set mixture from the sides of the pan to the centre, tilting the pan so the liquid egg runs out to the sides. This gives the typical shirred look of the classic omelette.

When the omelette is pale gold on the underside and still creamy on top, fold one side over, using a spatula, then fold the other side. If the filling is used it should be hot and well seasoned, and placed down the centre of the omelette before it is folded.

Slide the omelette onto a warm plate. Some people like their omelettes very soft, almost runny in the middle—these take about 1 minute to cook. I prefer them to be set but not dry, so the cooking time is slightly longer, about 3 minutes. Cook to your preference.

VARIATION: Herb omelettes are delicious and are simply made by adding 1–2 tablespoons of your favourite herbs to the beaten eggs. Fresh coriander, dill, oregano, parsley, thyme, marjoram and chives are all suitable, singly or in combination.

SERVES: 2

SPANISH OMELETTE

# FILLINGS FOR OMELETTES

Vegetables left over from a meal are a cook's best friend when it comes to filling omelettes. They're already cooked and only need reheating.

SPINACH: Melt 2 teaspoons butter in a small pan and add ½ cup cooked, drained and chopped spinach (about 6 oz raw). Add 2 tablespoons cream and season to taste with salt, pepper and grated nutmeg. If the spinach already has butter, cream or seasoning added, just heat and use.

VEGETABLE: Finely chop 1 small onion, half a capsicum (pepper) and a peeled, seeded tomato. Cook the mixture in 1 tablespoon heated olive oil or butter in a covered pan for 5 minutes or until the vegetables are just tender.

ASPARAGUS: Lightly cooked asparagus spears (or drained, canned asparagus) may be heated in a little butter or thick white sauce with grated cheese to flavour.

CHEESE: Firm tasty (sharp) cheese may be coarsely grated, or else thinly sliced and placed down the middle of the omelette. Fold over, and leave in the pan an extra few seconds so the cheese is half melted. Delicious.

MUSHROOM: Slice 3–4 fresh mushrooms thinly. Cook in a tablespoon of hot butter or oil until just slightly softened. Season with freshly ground black pepper and salt.

# MILK RICE

*A simple preparation of rice cooked in coconut milk. It is usually served with hot sambals but some prefer it with palm sugar and freshly grated coconut.*

### INGREDIENTS

2 cups (14 oz) short grain white rice
•
3 cups (24 fl oz) water
•
2 cups (16 fl oz) thick coconut milk
(see page 443)
•
2 teaspoons salt, or to taste
•
1 stick cinnamon (optional)

Put rice and water into a pan and bring to the boil. Cover and cook for 15 minutes. Add coconut milk, salt and cinnamon, then stir well with handle of wooden spoon. Cover pan and cook on low heat for a further 10–15 minutes, until all the milk has been absorbed. Remove cinnamon, cool slightly, then turn out on a flat plate. Mark off in diamond shapes and cut when firm.

NOTE: If you find it difficult to buy palm sugar, use unrefined black (dark brown) sugar (from health stores) as a substitute.

SERVES: 4–5

# STEAMED RICE FLOUR AND COCONUT CAKES

*This combination of flour and freshly grated coconut steamed in a bamboo cylinder is a favourite Asian breakfast. The resulting roll, which looks something like a white suet pudding but infinitely lighter in texture, is served with fresh coconut milk, hot sambals and curries.*

## INGREDIENTS

2 cups (8 oz) grated fresh coconut
or 2 cups (6 oz) desiccated coconut
and 1 cup (8 fl oz) water
•
1 cup (4 oz) rice flour
•
1 cup (5 oz) medium fine semolina
•
1½ teaspoons salt
•
coconut milk for serving
(see page 443)

If using desiccated coconut, put it into a large bowl and sprinkle with the water. Work gently with the fingertips until all the coconut is evenly moistened. Fresh coconut does not need water. Add sifted flour, semolina and salt to coconut in bowl and rub gently with the fingertips as for making pastry. The mixture should be like fine crumbs. Fill containers (see Note, below) with the mixture and press down lightly. Steam in a large pot over boiling water for 10–15 minutes. Allow to cool slightly, then unmould.

Serve with coconut milk for moistening, and a hot sambal or curry or with sweet accompaniments such as grated palm sugar or dark brown sugar.

NOTE: To improvise a steamer, take a tall, narrow cylindrical can such as a coffee can, cut away the base, make a dozen or so small holes in the lid and invert the can so the lid is now the base. Fill the can with the coconut mixture. Place in a large pot on a trivet so it is above water level and steam for 10–15 minutes, push out of the can onto a serving plate and cut into slices. If you have a microwave oven, use paper cups for individual cakes and cook for about 3 minutes on medium high.

SERVES: 4–6

# BAKED EGGS

*An advantage to this recipe is that you don't have to stand over a pan—pop them in the oven and forget them for the 10 minutes or so they take to cook.*

Preheat oven to 180°C (350°F). For each person butter a small ovenproof ramekin, break in 1–2 eggs and season with a good grinding of black pepper and salt. Pour a teaspoon of cream or a little melted butter over the egg and cover with a piece of greaseproof paper to prevent top drying out. Bake for 8–10 minutes or until set but not hard. Serve at once with buttered toast.

# BREADS

## UNLEAVENED BREADS

## FLAKY WHOLEMEAL BREAD (PARATHA)

### INGREDIENTS

1½ cups (6 oz) fine wholemeal (whole wheat) flour
•
1½ cups (6 oz) plain (all-purpose) flour or roti flour
•
1½ teaspoons salt
•
6–8 tablespoons ghee (clarified butter)
•
1 cup (8 fl oz) water
•
extra ghee for cooking

Sift wholemeal flour, plain flour and salt into a mixing bowl and rub in 1 tablespoon of the ghee. Add water, mix and knead dough as for Chapatis (see page 398). Cover dough with plastic wrap and set aside for 1 hour.

Divide dough into 12–14 equal portions and roll each into a smooth ball. Melt ghee in a small saucepan over a low heat and cool slightly. Roll each ball of dough on a lightly floured board into a very thin circular shape. Pour 2 teaspoons of the melted ghee into the centre of each and spread lightly with your hand.

With a knife, make a cut from the centre of each circle to the outer edge. Starting at the cut edge, roll the dough closely into a cone shape. Pick it up, press the apex of the cone and the base towards each other and flatten slightly. You will now have a small, roughly circular lump of dough. Lightly flour the board again and roll out the dough very gently, taking care not to press too hard and let the air out at the edges. The parathas should be as round as possible but not as thinly rolled as the first time.

Cook on a hot griddle or in a heavy-based pan, liberally greased with extra ghee. Turn parathas and spread with more ghee until they are golden brown. Serve hot with vegetable curries and chutneys.

NOTE: Parathas can be made using only plain (all-purpose) flour if preferred.

MAKES: 12–14

# CHAPATIS

*The chapatis of India, daily bread of the people, have deservedly gained
popularity in many countries.*

## INGREDIENTS

3 cups (12 oz) fine wholemeal
(whole wheat) flour
or roti flour

•

1 teaspoon salt or to taste

•

1 tablespoon butter or oil (optional)

•

1 cup lukewarm water

Put flour into a mixing bowl, reserving about ½ cup (2 oz) for rolling out chapatis. Mix salt into the flour, then rub in butter or oil, if used. Add water all at once and mix to a firm but not stiff dough. Knead dough for at least 10 minutes—the more it is kneaded, the lighter the bread will be. Form dough into a ball, cover with clear plastic wrap and leave for 1 hour or longer. If left overnight the chapatis will be very light and tender.

Shape dough into balls about the size of a large walnut. Roll out each one on a board lightly floured with reserved flour, to a circular shape as thin as a French crêpe. Heat a griddle plate or heavy-based frying pan until very hot. Cook the chapatis, starting with those that were rolled first, as the resting between rolling and cooking seems to make them lighter. Put chapati on the griddle and leave for about 1 minute, then turn and cook other side for 1 minute, pressing lightly around the edges with a folded tea towel or an egg turner. This encourages bubbles to form and makes the bread lighter. As each one is cooked, place in a pile in a clean tea-towel until all are ready. Serve immediately with butter or dry curries of vegetables or lentils.

MAKES: 20–24

# PUNJABI SOURDOUGH BREAD

*A slightly fermented bread that is traditionally served with a preparation
of Savoury Chick Peas (see page 344).*

## INGREDIENTS

¾ cup (6 fl oz) natural yoghurt

•

2 teaspoons sugar

•

½ teaspoon bicarbonate of soda

•

1 cup (4 oz) plain (all-purpose) flour

•

2½ cups (10 oz) fine wholemeal
(whole wheat) flour

Mix yoghurt, sugar, bicarbonate of soda and plain flour in a bowl, cover with muslin and leave overnight in a warm place to allow natural fermentation to take place. Sift the wholemeal flour and salt into a bowl, rub in the butter. Add the fermented mixture and the lukewarm water. Mix to a dough, adding as much extra plain flour as necessary. Knead hard for 10 minutes. Cover and leave in a warm place for about 2–3 hours, then divide into 12–14 portions.

Roll out each one thinly on a floured board to the size

2 teaspoons salt
•
1 tablespoon butter
•
½ cup (4 fl oz) lukewarm water
•
oil for deep-frying

of a saucer. Fry one at a time in hot, deep oil, spooning oil on top. They will puff and become golden when they are done. Remove with slotted spoon and drain on absorbent paper. Serve warm.

MAKES: 12–14

# SWEET FLAKY BREAD

*This Indian-style bread has a filling of sweetened lentil purée and is quite delightful. Children love it.*

## INGREDIENTS

1 cup (6 oz) toor or channa dhal
•
1 cup (8 oz) sugar
•
2 tablespoons ghee (clarified butter)
•
½ teaspoon ground cardamom
•
1½ cups (6 oz) fine wholemeal
(whole wheat) flour
•
1½ cups (6 oz) roti or plain
(all-purpose) flour
•
1 teaspoon salt
•
1 cup (8 fl oz) lukewarm water
•
extra ghee for cooking

Wash the dhal and soak overnight. Next day cook in plenty of water until very tender. This takes some time and a pressure cooker may be used to good effect. Drain away any excess moisture and mash the dhal to a purée. For a very smooth result, push it through a sieve.

Return the mashed dhal to a heavy-based saucepan, add sugar and 1 tablespoon ghee and cook over medium heat. The sugar will make the mixture wet, but in about 10 minutes the mixture should thicken and become dry. Stir constantly, scraping from side of pan. Remove from heat and turn mixture into a bowl, stir in cardamom and leave to cool.

Make a dough by mixing both kinds of flour and the salt together, rubbing in the remaining ghee and adding water all at once. Knead for 10 minutes until smooth and elastic. Set aside, covered, for at least 30 minutes.

Divide dough into 10 portions. Take portions of dhal filling about the same size as the dough. Flatten the dough to a small circle, place a ball of the filling on it and bring the dough together to completely enclose the filling, pressing edges together to seal. Roll out very gently, on a lightly floured surface, taking care not to break the dough which should be quite thin and about the size of a large saucer. Cook on a hot griddle or in a heavy-based pan, using a little ghee. Drizzle a little melted ghee over the top and turn over to cook second side. Continue turning and cooking, adding more ghee as necessary, until golden on both sides.

NOTE: If preferred, dough may be made with all white flour instead of wholemeal.

MAKES: 10

# DEEP-FRIED WHOLEMEAL BREAD (PURIS)

These are the delicious round loaves called puris in India. Make them small and they will puff better.

Proceed as in the recipe for Chapatis (see page 398). When all the dough is rolled out, heat approximately 2.5 cm (1 in) of oil in a deep frying pan. When a faint haze rises from the oil, fry puris one at a time, over a moderate heat. Spoon hot oil continually over the cooking puri until it puffs and swells. Turn over and fry other side in the same way. When both sides are pale gold in colour, drain on absorbent paper. Serve immediately with curries and savoury vegetable dishes.

# CHICK PEA FLOUR BREAD

*An Indian bread with lots of flavour and the bite of fresh chillies. Exciting!*

## INGREDIENTS

2 cups (8 oz) roti flour or fine wholemeal (whole wheat) flour

•

1 cup (4 oz) besan (chick pea flour)

•

2 teaspoons salt

•

½ teaspoon ground black pepper

•

1 tablespoon butter or oil

•

2 fresh green chillies, seeded and finely chopped,
or 3 tablespoons finely chopped capsicum (sweet pepper)

•

3 tablespoons finely chopped fresh coriander

•

3 tablespoons finely chopped spring onion (scallion)

•

3 tablespoons finely chopped spinach

•

¼ teaspoon crushed ajowan seeds

•

1 cup (8 fl oz) water

•

ghee (clarified butter) or oil for shallow frying

Sift both kinds of flour together with salt and pepper into a bowl. Rub in butter or oil and mix in the chillies, coriander, spring onion, spinach and ajowan seeds. Add water and mix to a dough, kneading firmly until it is smooth and elastic. Cover with plastic wrap and set aside for 1 hour or longer.

Roll balls of the dough out on lightly floured board to the size of a large saucer, and a thickness of about 2.5 mm (1/10 in). Heat a griddle or heavy-based frying pan and cook as for Parathas (see page 396). These tasty loaves need only a little yoghurt or a fresh chutney as accompaniment.

MAKES: about 15

# LAVOSH

*This Armenian crispbread is so delicious you will have to hide it well to test the fact that it keeps crisp for weeks. A food processor and pasta roller make it quick and easy.*

### INGREDIENTS

2½ cups (10 oz) plain (all-purpose)
flour
•
1 teaspoon sugar
•
1 teaspoon salt
•
1 large 60 g ( 2 oz) egg
•
150 ml (¼ pt) water
•
1 tablespoon melted butter
•
1 egg, beaten with
2 tablespoons water
•
2 tablespoons sesame seeds
•
1 tablespoon poppy seeds
•
1 teaspoon caraway seeds, optional
•
coarse salt for sprinkling

Put flour, sugar and salt into a food processor fitted with a steel blade. Beat the egg and mix with water and butter. Start the motor and slowly pour liquid through feed tube. As soon as mixture forms a ball, stop the machine. Alternatively, knead by hand to a smooth, elastic dough. Wrap in plastic and refrigerate for 1 hour.

Preheat oven to 190°C (375°F). On a floured surface, take one-twelfth of the mixture and roll into a thin oval, or pass between the rollers of a pasta machine until very thin. Place on greased baking sheets, brush with beaten egg and water, then sprinkle with seeds and coarse salt. Bake until pale gold in colour and very crisp. If rolled by machine they will need only 8–10 minutes baking but if rolled by hand they may take a little longer. Cool on a wire rack and store in a plastic bag fastened with a twist tie.

MAKES: 12 crispbreads 25 × 15 cm (10 × 6 in)

# ROTI

*A flat bread eaten in Asia. Added moisture and richness are given by mixing grated coconut with the flour. It is popular at breakfast time served with savoury vegetable curries or simply spread with butter.*

### INGREDIENTS

2 cups (8 oz) self-raising flour
or rice flour
•
½ cup (2 oz) grated fresh coconut
or ½ cup (1½ oz) desiccated coconut
•
1 teaspoon salt
•
scant 1 cup (8 fl oz) water
•
ghee (clarified butter) or
oil for cooking

Mix flour, coconut and salt in a mixing bowl. Add enough water to form a soft dough. Knead until it forms a ball and does not stick to sides of the bowl. Rest dough for about 30 minutes. Shape into balls, approximately the size of a golf ball. Pat each one out to a circle the size of a saucer. Cook on a hot griddle or in a heavy-based pan very lightly greased with ghee or oil. Serve hot.

SERVES: 6–8

# FLAT BREAD (ROTI) WITH CHILLIES

*This is a quickly made, very savoury bread to eat by itself or as an accompaniment to vegetable curries.*

### INGREDIENTS

4 cups (1 lb) rice flour, roti flour or plain (all-purpose) flour

•

1 teaspoon baking powder

•

1 cup (4 oz) grated fresh or 1 cup (3 oz) desiccated coconut

•

2 teaspoons salt

•

2 teaspoons butter or margarine

•

1 tablespoon finely chopped onion

•

2 teaspoons finely chopped fresh red or green chilli

•

1 egg, beaten

•

scant 2 cups (16 fl oz) water

•

little ghee (clarified butter) or oil for cooking

Mix flour, baking powder, coconut and salt in a large bowl. Rub in butter until evenly distributed, stir onion and chilli through the flour, then add the egg and sufficient water to bind the mixture to a stiff dough. Knead until it forms a ball and doesn't stick to the bowl. Rest dough for 30 minutes. Take a lemon-size lump of dough and pat between floured hands to a circle the size of a bread-and-butter plate. Cook on a hot griddle or in a heavy-based frying pan, greased very lightly. Serve hot with sambals or curries.

MAKES: about 12

# YEAST RISEN BREADS

Baking bread is therapeutic for the cook and has fringe benefits for everyone else. There's something about the rhythm and effort of kneading that is deeply satisfying, and the fragrance of yeast is just about the nicest thing that can happen to any kitchen.

# CHALLAH

*Pronounced hal-lah, this plaited loaf is the traditional Jewish sabbath bread, slightly sweet, enriched with oil and eggs, and so good that it never has time to get cold. If serving it warm, pull it apart because even a sharp knife can compress the bread.*

### INGREDIENTS

30 g (1 oz) fresh compressed yeast or 1 sachet (envelope) dry yeast

Sprinkle yeast over warm water in a large mixing bowl and stir to dissolve. Leave for 10 minutes until frothy, then stir in the salt, honey, oil and beaten eggs. Take 2½ cups

1 cup (8 fl oz) warm water

•

1 teaspoon salt

•

¼ cup (2 fl oz) honey

•

¹/₃ cup (3 fl oz) oil or melted butter

•

2 eggs, lightly beaten

•

4–5 cups (1–1¼ lb) plain
(all-purpose) flour

•

1 tablespoon gluten flour (optional)

•

beaten egg, for glazing

(10 oz) of the measured flour and sift twice with the gluten flour. The gluten may be omitted, but it does help the braid to hold its shape better.

Add the sifted mixture to the bowl and beat hard with a wooden spoon or electric mixer for 5 minutes or until smooth and elastic. Add 2 more cups (8 oz) of flour, half a cup at a time, or as much as the dough will take and still remain soft. Knead on a floured surface for 10 minutes or until smooth and not sticky. Place dough in a warm, greased bowl, turning it over so top surface is greased. Cover and put in a warm place for 15–20 minutes, by which time the dough should have risen enough to hold an impression when lightly pressed with two fingers.

Punch down dough, divide in two equal portions (weigh them to make sure) and divide each half into 3 or 4 equal pieces. (Three strand plaits are easy to do, but four strand plaits require more concentration, I find.) Squeeze, roll and shape each piece into a strand about 2.5 cm (1 in) thick and 40 cm (16 in) long. Place strands side by side on a greased baking tray, join them at one end and start plaiting.

Here's how to do a four-strand plait. Let's number the strands 1 to 4, going from left to right. Place 1 over 2, under 3, over 4. Repeat until plait is done, then press ends together and tuck under. Make a second plait with remaining dough on another tray. Cover and leave in a warm place until doubled in size. Brush with beaten egg to glaze and if liked, sprinkle with poppy seeds or lightly toasted sesame seeds. Bake challah for 35–40 minutes in oven preheated to 180°C (350°F), or until they are well browned and sound hollow when tapped on the base.

After they have baked for 25 minutes, swap the trays over so that the one on top doesn't get too dark. If necessary, cover lightly with foil to prevent overbrowning. Serve warm. The extra loaf may be left to cool on a wire rack, then packed in foil and frozen. Reheat in a hot oven from frozen state, still wrapped in foil, for 25 minutes.

MAKES: 2 plaits

# OATMEAL COTTAGE LOAF

*A moist golden loaf lightly sweetened with honey that could be the
mainstay of a meal. Butter, a good cheese and a salad are all you need
to serve with it.*

## INGREDIENTS

1¼ cups (10 fl oz) water

•

1 cup (3 oz) rolled oats

•

½ cup (4 fl oz) honey

•

60 g (2 oz) butter, or
3 tablespoons oil

•

3 teaspoons salt

•

2 sachets (envelopes) dry yeast,
or 60 g (2 oz) fresh compressed yeast

•

½ cup (4 fl oz) warm water

•

2 eggs, beaten

•

5–5½ cups (1¼–1¹/₃ lb) plain
(all-purpose) flour

•

1 egg white

•

extra ½ cup (1½ oz) rolled oats

Measure the water into a pan and bring to the boil.
Meanwhile measure oats, honey, butter or oil and salt into
a large bowl. Pour boiling water over, stirring, to dissolve
butter and honey. Cool until lukewarm.

Sprinkle the yeast over warm water, stir until dissolved,
then add to the lukewarm oat mixture with the beaten eggs
and mix well. Add 2 cups (8 oz) of the flour and beat well
with a wooden spoon until smooth, then add enough of
the remaining flour to make a soft dough. On a surface
sprinkled with the flour that remains, knead dough for 10
minutes, or until soft and smooth, flouring hands
occasionally.

Wash, dry and grease the bowl and put dough in, turning
it to grease the top. Cover and leave in a warm place for
1½ hours, or until doubled in volume. Punch down and
divide into two equal portions.

Take a quarter from each piece of dough and make 2
small balls. With the larger amount of dough, make 2 large
balls. Place a large ball of dough on a greased baking tray,
then place the small ball on top and press firmly through
the centre with the floured handle of a wooden spoon, or
two fingers dipped in flour, until you touch the tray. Cover
and leave to rise in a warm place until double in bulk, about
1 hour.

Brush loaves lightly with egg white, which has been beaten
with a tablespoon of cold water, and sprinkle with extra
rolled oats. Bake in an oven preheated to 190°C (375°F)
for 15 minutes, then reduce heat to 180°C (350°F) and bake
for a further 30 minutes, or until well risen and golden.
Test by tapping bottom crust. Cover with foil if becoming
too brown. Cool on a wire rack.

MAKES: 2 loaves

OATMEAL COTTAGE LOAF

# SWEDISH RYE BREAD

*A dark loaf with the fragrance of anise and orange—a typical
Scandinavian-type bread.*

## INGREDIENTS

1 sachet (envelope) dry yeast or
30 g (1 oz) fresh compressed yeast
•
¼ cup (2 fl oz) warm water
•
¼ cup (1½ oz) brown sugar
•
2 tablespoons molasses
•
2 teaspoons salt
•
60 g (2 oz) butter
•
1½ cups (12 fl oz) hot water
•
1½ tablespoons grated orange rind
•
1 teaspoon anise seeds, crushed
•
about 4 cups (1 lb) plain flour
•
2½ cups (10 oz) rye flour
•
milk for glazing

Sprinkle yeast over warm water in a bowl and leave to soften for a few minutes, then stir to dissolve. Put brown sugar, molasses, salt and butter into another bowl, then pour over hot water and stir to dissolve sugar. Add orange rind and crushed anise and stir. Cool until lukewarm, then mix in the yeast. Add 2 cups (8 oz) of the plain flour to the liquid mixture and beat hard. Add rye flour and beat again, then add enough of the remaining plain flour to form a soft dough, setting aside some of the flour for kneading. Knead vigorously for 10 minutes, or until dough becomes smooth and elastic. Form into a ball, put into a clean, dry, greased bowl, turn dough over so top is greased, then cover and leave in a warm place to rise until almost double, about 1½ hours.

Punch down dough, divide into 2 equal portions and form each into a ball. Place on 2 lightly greased baking trays, cover and allow to rise in a warm place for 2 hours, or until almost double. Brush with milk and bake the loaves in an oven preheated to 190°C (375°F) for 25–30 minutes, covering tops if they brown too quickly. Cool on a wire rack.

MAKES: 2 loaves

# PUMPERNICKEL

*A dark, dense bread with lots of flavour.*

## INGREDIENTS

2 sachets (envelopes) dry yeast
•
½ cup (4 fl oz) warm water
•
4 teaspoons salt
•
¼ cup (2 fl oz) molasses
•
1 cup (8 oz) mashed potatoes

Sprinkle yeast over warm water and leave for 5 minutes to soften, then stir to dissolve. Put the salt, molasses and mashed potatoes into a large bowl and pour over the boiling water. Mix well and cool to lukewarm, then stir in the yeast and all the rye flour and cornmeal. Add 1 cup (4 oz) of the whole wheat flour at this stage and mix to a stiff dough. Leave to rest for 10 minutes.

On a floured surface sprinkled with some of the remaining whole wheat flour, knead the dough with floured hands.

2 cups (16 fl oz) boiling water

•

7 cups (2 lb) rye flour

•

½ cup (2 oz) cornmeal

•

2 cups (8 oz) whole wheat flour

•

milk for glazing

Add more of the flour while kneading until the whole amount is taken up, and knead for at least 10 minutes or until it is no longer sticky. Put into a large, greased bowl, turn over, then cover and leave in a warm place to rise until one and a half times its original volume. (A heavy dough like this one will not double in volume.)

Knead again on a floured surface for 5 minutes and leave to rise again for about 45 minutes. Knead gently again, divide in half and shape each portion into a round loaf. Place on greased baking trays, brush tops with cold water and leave to rise for about 30 minutes, or until increased slightly in size. Bake in an oven preheated to 190°C (375°F) for 1¼ hours, or until loaves sound hollow when tapped with knuckles. To glaze the tops, brush bread with milk three times during baking. Cool on a wire rack. Cut into thin slices to serve.

MAKES: 2 loaves

# CHEESE CASSEROLE BREAD

*One of those marvellously easy no-knead loaves, and tasty too.*

### INGREDIENTS

1 sachet (envelope) dry yeast

•

1 cup (8 fl oz) warm water

•

1 tablespoon honey

•

1½ teaspoons salt

•

⅓ cup skim milk powder

•

1 tablespoon vegetable oil

•

2½ cups (10 oz) plain (all-purpose) flour (or use half wholemeal (whole wheat) flour)

•

1 egg

•

1 cup (4 oz) finely grated tasty (sharp) cheese

Sprinkle yeast over warm water in a large bowl and leave to soften, then dissolve. Stir in the honey, salt, milk powder and vegetable oil. Add 1 cup (4 oz) of flour and beat until smooth. Beat in the egg and cheese, then add another cup of flour and beat again for 1 minute. Add remaining ½ cup (2 oz) of flour and mix in thoroughly.

Butter a round or square 2 litre (66 fl oz) casserole dish, put the dough into it, cover with a clean tea towel and leave in a very warm spot for 20 minutes. (A dishwasher on the drying cycle, or a warm, turned-off oven are ideal, and so is a sink half filled with hot water, the bread container resting on an upturned bowl to keep it above water level.) The soft dough will not rise much during this time, but it will when baked.

Put into a cold oven and turn the temperature to 180°C (350°F). Bake for 40 minutes, or until risen and golden brown. Cool slightly on a wire rack and eat while still warm.

MAKES: 1 large loaf

# BREAKFAST & BRUNCH MENUS

*When time is short, have homemade muesli or granola ready to serve in moments. But when there is a leisurely brunch to serve, give yourself the pleasure of freshly baked breads and waffles.*

## COOL WEATHER FARE

Eggs Benedict *page 392*

Nut Bread *page 419*
spread with cream cheese

or

Waffles *page 388*

Mocha Warmer *page 432*

## SUBSTANTIAL

Grilled Grapefruit *page 384*

Spanish Omelette *page 391*

Potato Poppyseed Rolls *page 413*

Mexican Chocolate *page 432*

## INDULGENT

Cheese Croissants *page 388*

or

The Born Again Croissant *page 387*

New York Hot Chocolate *page 431*

## HEALTHY

Fruit and Vegetable Cocktails *page 430*

Swiss-style muesli *page 380*

Bran Bread *page 412*
with honey

# SESAME LOAVES

30 g (1 oz) fresh yeast or
1 sachet (envelope) dried yeast

•

¾ cup (6 fl oz) warm water

•

3 teaspoons sugar

•

½ cup (4 fl oz) natural yoghurt

•

1 egg, beaten

•

¼ cup (2 oz) butter, melted

•

1½ cups (6 oz) fine wholemeal
(whole wheat) flour

•

2½ cups (10 oz) plain
(all-purpose) flour

•

2 teaspoons salt

•

2 tablespoons sesame seeds

Sprinkle yeast over the warm water and stir to dissolve. Add sugar and leave in a warm place for 10 minutes. It should start to froth, showing that the yeast is alive. Stir yoghurt until smooth and set aside ¼ cup (2 oz) for later. Combine the remaining ¼ cup (2 oz) yoghurt with egg, butter and yeast mixture. In a large bowl, dump the wholemeal flour (no need to sift) and salt. Stir in the liquid and beat with a wooden spoon until smooth. Add the plain flour and salt. When mixture gets too stiff to use the spoon, knead by hand on a lightly floured surface for a full 10 minutes, working in as little extra flour as possible. Dough should then be smooth and elastic and not stick to hand or board.

Place in a warm, greased bowl, turning ball of dough over so top is greased. Cover with plastic wrap and set in a warm place to prove. (In winter, use a warm, turned-off oven or set the bowl in the electric dishwasher just after it has finished its drying cycle!)

When dough has doubled in bulk (about 1 hour) punch down and knead lightly, then divide into 8–10 equal portions. Put two ungreased baking trays into an oven preheated to 260°C (500°F). Form dough into balls and pat each one out to an oval shape about 1 cm (½ in) thick. Spread them with the reserved yoghurt and sprinkle with sesame seeds. Put loaves on heated baking trays and bake in very hot oven (260°C/500°F) until well risen and golden brown, about 10 minutes. Serve warm or at room temperature.

NOTE: This recipe is based on the famous Indian leavened bread baked in a tandoor oven and known as *Naan*. For flavoursome garlic loaves, mix remaining ¼ cup (2 fl oz) yoghurt with ½ teaspoon crushed garlic and spread thinly over the loaves. Sprinkle with poppy seeds or black cumin seeds and bake.

MAKES: 2 loaves

# PUNJABI LEAVENED BREAD (NAAN)

*This is the famous very popular bread known as Naan which is baked in a tandoor—a clay oven—at a very high temperature. Here is a recipe which enables you to cook it in a domestic oven.*

## INGREDIENTS

30 g (1 oz) fresh compressed yeast or 1 sachet (envelope) dried yeast

¾ cup (6 fl oz) lukewarm water

3 teaspoons sugar

½ cup (4 fl oz) natural yoghurt

1 egg, beaten

¼ cup (2 oz) melted ghee (clarified butter) or butter

2 teaspoons salt

approximately 3½ cups (14 oz) plain (all-purpose) flour

2 tablespoons poppyseeds or black cumin (kalonji) seeds

Crumble or sprinkle yeast over ¼ cup (2 fl oz) warm water and leave for a few minutes to soften, then stir to dissolve. Add 1 teaspoon of the sugar, stir, then leave in a warm place for 10 minutes or until it starts to froth. This is to test whether the yeast is alive. If it shows no signs of bubbling, start again with a fresh batch of yeast.

Stir yoghurt until smooth, then mix ¼ cup (2 fl oz) yoghurt with the rest of the sugar, the remaining ½ cup (4 fl oz) lukewarm water, egg, melted ghee or butter and salt. Stir in the yeast mixture. Put 2 cups (8 oz) flour into a bowl, make a well in the centre and pour in liquid mixture, beating well with a wooden spoon until it is a smooth batter. Add remaining flour a little at a time and when it gets too stiff to use the spoon, knead with the hands for 10–12 minutes or until dough is smooth and elastic, using as little extra flour as possible. Form dough into a ball, then put it into a clean, dry, greased bowl and turn it over so that the top is greased. Cover with a cloth and leave in a warm place until it doubles in size. Punch down dough and divide into 8 balls, leave to rest for 10 minutes. Put two ungreased baking trays into an oven preheated to 230°C (450°F).

Pat dough into circles keeping them thin in the centre and thicker around the rim, then pull one end outwards, making a teardrop shape. They should be a handspan long and little more than half as wide at the base. Brush with reserved yoghurt and sprinkle with poppy or black cumin seeds. Put 2–3 loaves on each hot baking tray. Bake about 10 minutes or until golden and puffed. If naan is not brown enough, put under a preheated grill (broiler) for 1–2 minutes.

MAKES: about 8 loaves

# BRAN BREAD

1 cup (3 oz) unprocessed bran

•

1 tablespoon golden syrup or honey

•

1 tablespoon butter or margarine

•

½ cup (4 fl oz) boiling water

•

3½ cups (14 oz) self-raising flour

•

1 teaspoon salt

•

1 cup (8 fl oz) milk

Put bran, syrup and shortening into a bowl, pour over boiling water, mix, then cool slightly. Sift the flour and salt, stir in the bran mixture and milk, and knead to a smooth dough. Put into a greased 18 cm (7 in) round, deep cake pan. Take a larger sponge pan, grease it and invert it over the top— the idea is that this loaf should bake and steam at the same time. Put it in an oven preheated to 260°C (500°F) for 40–50 minutes. It should sound hollow when tapped with a knuckle. Delicious served warm from the oven. It also freezes well and toasts beautifully. Particularly good served with cheese.

VARIATION: Substitute ½ cup (2 oz) flour with ½ cup (3 oz) wheatgerm, and use buttermilk in place of milk. Add ½ teaspoon bicarbonate of soda when sifting the flour.

MAKES: 1 loaf

# MALTED RYE BREAD

30 g (1 oz) fresh compressed yeast
or 1 sachet (envelope) active
dry yeast

•

¼ cup (2 fl oz) warm water

•

½ cup (4 oz) unrefined black
(dark brown) sugar

•

2 tablespoons malt extract

•

2 teaspoons salt

•

60 g (2 oz) butter

•

1½ cups (12 fl oz) hot water

•

finely grated rind of 1 orange

Crumble or sprinkle yeast over the measured warm water in a bowl and stir to dissolve. Dissolve the sugar and malt extract, salt and butter in the hot water and stir in the orange rind. Cool until lukewarm. Mix with the yeast, then stir in 3 cups (12 oz) of plain flour and beat well. Add the rye flour and enough of the remaining plain flour to form a soft dough, reserving some of the plain flour for kneading.

Turn onto a lightly floured surface, cover and allow to rest for a little while, then knead until smooth and elastic, about 10 minutes. Use remaining flour to keep dough from sticking. When dough is smooth, place it in a warm greased bowl, turning it once to grease top. Cover and allow to rise in a warm place for 1½ hours or until almost doubled in volume. Punch down and divide into two equal portions, forming each into a ball.

3½–4 cups (14–16 oz) plain
(all-purpose) flour
•
2½ cups (10 oz) rye flour

Lightly grease two baking trays, shape dough into smooth round loaves and place one on each tray. Cover and allow to rise in a warm place until almost double in volume, about 1 hour. Brush tops of loaves lightly with milk or water and bake for 25–30 minutes in an oven preheated to 200°C (400°F).

MAKES: 2 loaves

# ROLLS, STICKS, PRETZELS AND CRISPBREADS

# POTATO POPPYSEED ROLLS

*These are so delicious you could build a meal around them.*

### INGREDIENTS

400 g (13 oz) potatoes
•
45 g (1½ oz) fresh compressed yeast,
or 3 teaspoons dry yeast
•
2 cups (16 fl oz) warm water
•
about 1 kg (2 lb) plain
(all-purpose) flour
•
2 teaspoons salt
•
1 egg yolk
•
1 tablespoon water
•
1½ teaspoons sea salt
•
1 tablespoon poppyseeds

Boil the potatoes, then peel and mash them. Dissolve the yeast in warm water. Put all but 1 cup (4 oz) of the flour and salt into a large bowl and make a well in the centre. Pour the dissolved yeast in the well and sprinkle a little flour over. Leave for 15 minutes and it should start to froth. Add the mashed potatoes and knead the dough well, adding as much extra flour as necessary to make a smooth dough. Cover and prove in a warm place for 30 minutes, or until risen. Punch down and divide into two equal portions.

Make about 20 small balls of equal size from each half, and arrange on a greased baking tray in a circular or hexagonal shape. Cover and prove until well risen. Beat egg yolk with water and brush over the rolls. Sprinkle with sea salt and poppy seeds and bake in an oven preheated to 200°C (400°F) for 30 minutes, or until golden brown. Remove to a wire rack to cool. Serve warm with unsalted butter.

MAKES: about 40

# SALT AND CARAWAY STICKS

*You may prefer the flavour of cumin or sesame seeds to caraway.*

## INGREDIENTS

1 sachet (envelope) dry yeast

•

¾ cup (6 fl oz) warm water

•

1½ teaspoons sugar

•

1 teaspoon salt

•

¼ cup (2 fl oz) olive oil

•

3 cups (12 oz) plain (all-purpose)
flour

•

cornmeal for baking

•

beaten egg for glazing

•

coarse salt and seeds for sprinkling

Dissolve yeast in water, stir in sugar, salt and olive oil. Combine with flour and knead well. If liked, the dough may be made in a food processor, adding the liquid to half the flour with the motor running and using the steel blades. Add remaining flour and process until it forms a ball.

Let dough rest for 15 minutes, then divide into 16 equal pieces and roll each one between palms and work surface to form a rope about 40 cm (15 in) long. As they are made, place them 5 cm (2 in) apart on baking sheets sprinkled with cornmeal and leave them to rise, covered, for 20 minutes. Brush with beaten egg mixed with a tablespoon of water and sprinkle with coarse salt and seeds of your choice. Bake in an oven preheated to 260°C (500°F) for 15 minutes, then cool on a rack.

MAKES: 16

# CRACKED WHEAT ROLLS WITH ROSEMARY

## INGREDIENTS

1 cup (4 oz) cracked wheat
(burghul or bulgur)

•

1½ cups (12 fl oz) boiling water

•

45 g (1½ oz) fresh compressed yeast
or 2 sachets (envelopes) dry yeast

•

½ cup (4 fl oz) warm water

•

1½ cups (12 fl oz) milk

•

1 tablespoon dried rosemary

•

60 g (2 oz) butter or
¼ cup (2 fl oz) oil

•

¼ cup (2 oz) sugar

•

2 teaspoons salt

Put the cracked wheat into a bowl and pour the boiling water over. Cover and leave to soak for an hour.

Sprinkle yeast over warm water in a small bowl and stir to dissolve. Heat the milk in a saucepan until it starts to bubble around the edges of the pan. Add the rosemary, butter, sugar and salt, and stir until the butter and sugar have dissolved. Cool to lukewarm and stir in the beaten egg. Mix with the cracked wheat, add the wholemeal flour and beat vigorously with a wooden spoon to develop the gluten. Add the white flour gradually and when the mixture is too stiff to beat, turn dough onto a floured board and start kneading with lightly floured hands. Knead for 8–10 minutes or until dough is smooth and elastic and does not stick to hands or board. Form dough into a smooth ball.

Wash and dry the bowl and grease it. Place the ball of dough in the bowl, turn it over so the top is greased, cover and leave in a warm place for an hour, or until dough

1 egg, beaten

•

3 cups (12 oz) fine wholemeal
(whole wheat) flour

•

3 cups (12 oz) plain (all-purpose)
flour

has doubled in volume and holds an impression when lightly touched with a fingertip. Punch down and divide dough into 20 balls—more if you prefer smaller rolls. Roll each one to a smooth ball and place on a greased baking tray, cover and allow to rise until doubled in size. Bake in an oven preheated to 200°C (400°F) for 15 minutes or until well risen and brown.

MAKES: 20 rolls

# WHOLEMEAL ROLLS

*The basic dough may be made with wholemeal flour, white flour, or a mixture of the two.*

### INGREDIENTS

1 sachet (envelope)
dry yeast

•

1¼ cups (10 fl oz) warm water

•

2 teaspoons sugar

•

2 cups (8 oz) fine wholemeal
(whole wheat) flour

•

2 cups (8 oz) plain (all-purpose) flour

•

1½ teaspoons salt

•

45 g (1½ oz) butter

Soften yeast in ½ cup (8 fl oz) of the warm water, then stir to dissolve and add sugar. Leave in a warm place until frothy, about 10 minutes. In a large bowl, combine flour and salt. Rub in the butter and add the dissolved yeast and remaining water all at once. Mix to a dough, and knead for 10 minutes on a lightly floured surface. Leave to prove, then punch down and knead lightly to eliminate air bubbles. Shape into rolls.

To make Parkerhouse rolls: roll dough on a floured board to about 12 mm (¼ in) thickness, and cut into circles with a large scone (biscuit) cutter. Brush dough with melted butter, crease across the centre of the circle with the back of a knife and fold over. Place on a greased baking tray, cover with a damp cloth and leave to rise for about half an hour. Brush with melted butter for dull finish and with beaten egg for a glazed look. Bake in an oven preheated to 230°C (450°F) for 20–25 minutes or until golden brown.

To make Cloverleaf rolls: pinch off walnut-sized pieces of dough and roll to form smooth balls. On a greased baking tray, place three balls of dough, just touching. Leave space between one cluster and the next. Cover with a damp cloth, leave to rise, then brush them with lightly beaten egg and sprinkle with poppy seeds. Bake as for Parkerhouse rolls.

MAKES: 24

# POCKET BREAD

## INGREDIENTS

1 teaspoon dry yeast

•

1 cup (8 fl oz) warm water

•

½ teaspoon sugar

•

1 cup (4 oz) plain (all-purpose)
flour

•

1 cup (4 oz) wholemeal
(whole wheat) flour

•

½ teaspoon salt

•

25 g (¾ oz) butter

Dissolve yeast in water, stir in sugar. Put both kinds of flour and salt into a bowl, rub in the butter, add the liquid and knead well until smooth. Cover and prove in a warm place, then punch down and divide into 12 pieces. Roll each one into an oval shape about 3 mm (⅛ in) in thickness. Lay dough on greased baking sheets and leave for 30 minutes. Bake in an oven preheated to 260°C (500°F) for 6–8 minutes or until puffed and golden.

MAKES: 12

# SOFT PRETZELS

## INGREDIENTS

1 sachet (envelope) dry yeast

•

1¼ cups (10 fl oz) warm water

•

½ teaspoon sugar

•

4 cups (1 lb) plain (all-purpose) flour

•

1 egg yolk

•

1 tablespoon water

•

coarse sea salt for sprinkling

Dissolve yeast in warm water, add sugar and set aside for 10 minutes. Mix in the flour, knead until smooth and elastic, then leave to prove in a greased bowl set in a warm place until double in volume. Punch down, knead lightly, then form into even sized pieces, each about 100 g (3½ oz). Roll between hands and work surface to form long pencils about 60 cm (24 in) in length.

On a greased baking sheet, form the pretzel shapes. Arrange dough in a loop, ends towards you. Cross ends over twice and rest both ends on the loop, pointing away from you. Cover and leave to rise for 10–15 minutes or until only slightly increased in volume. Brush with egg yolk beaten with the water, sprinkle with coarse salt and bake in an oven preheated to 260°C (500°F) for 10 minutes. Cool on rack.

MAKES: about 12

# QUICK BREADS
# HERB DAMPER

## INGREDIENTS

4 cups (1 lb) self-raising flour
•
1 teaspoon salt
•
1 small onion, finely chopped
•
1 tablespoon butter
•
2 tablespoons chopped fresh herbs
•
1¼ cups (10 fl oz) milk

Sift flour and salt into a large bowl. Sauté the chopped onion gently in butter until soft and turning golden. Cool, then rub into flour with the herbs.

Add milk and mix lightly to form a dough. On a greased baking tray, shape dough into a round cake and with a sharp knife, cut a slash on one side to make it rise unevenly in true damper fashion. Bake in an oven preheated to 200°C (400°F) until well risen and golden, about 35–45 minutes. It should sound hollow when tapped with a knuckle on the bottom crust.

MAKES: 1 loaf

# CORN MUFFINS

1 cup (4 oz) self-raising flour
•
¼ teaspoon salt
•
1 cup (6 oz) cornmeal
•
1¼ cups (10 fl oz) milk
•
1 egg, lightly beaten
•
3 tablespoons melted butter or oil
•
2 teaspoons honey
•
½ cup (2 oz) corn kernels,
cooked and drained

Preheat oven to 200°C (400°F). Place muffin pan (or gem iron) in oven to heat.

Sift flour and salt into a bowl and stir in cornmeal. Combine milk, egg, butter, honey and corn, and mix into dry ingredients. Remove pan from oven—use oven mitts because it will be very hot—and quickly grease using a pure bristle brush dipped in oil, or a wad of absorbent paper. (A nylon brush will come to grief on the hot pans.) Fill the moulds two-thirds full and bake at 220°C (425°F) for 15–20 minutes or until well risen and golden. Serve warm.

MAKES: 12 muffins

# FIG AND HONEY BREAD

INGREDIENTS

1 cup (6 oz) chopped dried figs
•
1 cup (8 fl oz) water
•
¾ cup (6 fl oz) honey
•
2 tablespoons melted butter
•
1 egg, beaten
•
1 cup (4 oz) chopped pecans
or walnuts
•
1½ cups (6 oz) sifted flour
•
2 teaspoons baking powder

Put the figs and water into a small saucepan and cook on low heat until the figs have absorbed all the water and become soft. Cool until lukewarm, then stir in honey and butter. Add the beaten egg and chopped nuts.

Turn the mixture into a bowl, sift the flour and baking powder together and stir gently but thoroughly into the fruit and nut mixture.

Bake in a greased 20 × 10 cm (8 × 4 in) loaf pan in an oven preheated to 160°C (325°F) for 45–50 minutes, or until cooked through. Allow to cool on wire rack, wrap and keep one day before serving.

MAKES: 1 loaf

# NUT BREAD

### INGREDIENTS

2 cups (8 oz) self-raising flour

•

¾ cup (6 oz) caster (superfine) sugar

•

1 cup (4 oz) chopped pecans, walnuts
or brazil nuts

•

2 eggs

•

1 cup (8 fl oz) milk

•

1 teaspoon vanilla extract

•

3 tablespoons melted butter

Grease a loaf pan 20 × 10 cm (8 × 4 in). Sift flour into a large bowl, then stir the sugar and nuts through. Beat the eggs until frothy, add milk, vanilla and melted butter. Have milk at room temperature, as the butter will solidify if milk is chilled.

Stir the liquid mixture into the flour, sugar and nuts, mixing with a spoon or spatula just until combined and no pockets of flour remain.

Turn into the greased pan and bake in an oven preheated to 180°C (350°F) or until well risen and golden. A fine skewer inserted in the centre should come out clean. Cool in the tin for 10 minutes, then turn out on a wire rack and allow to cool completely before slicing. Serve in thin slices.

MAKES: 1 loaf

# PEAR AND CHOCOLATE LOAF

### INGREDIENTS

125 g (4 oz) dried pears

•

3 cups (12 oz) self-raising flour

•

¾ cup (6 oz) sugar

•

½ cup (3 oz) chopped dark
(semi-sweet) chocolate

•

2 eggs

•

1¼ cups (10 fl oz) milk or buttermilk

•

¹/₃ cup (3 oz) maize (corn)
or sunflower oil

•

dash vanilla extract

With a sharp knife, cut the pears into thin strips, discarding any tough portions near the core. Toss the pear strips in a tablespoon or so of the measured flour.

Sift remaining flour and sugar into a large bowl, stir in the pears and chopped chocolate. Beat the eggs and add the milk or buttermilk, the oil and the vanilla essence. Pour on to the dry ingredients and stir just until mixed.

Divide the dough equally between two buttered loaf pans, 20 × 10 cm (8 × 4 in), and bake in an oven preheated to 180°C (350°F) for 50 minutes or until a fine skewer inserted into the centre of the loaves comes out clean. Turn out on a wire rack to cool, then wrap in plastic or foil and keep overnight before slicing.

MAKES: 2 loaves

# APRICOT NUT BREAD

### INGREDIENTS

200 g (6½ oz) dried apricots
•
2¼ cups (9 oz) self-raising flour
•
¾ cup (6 oz) caster (superfine) sugar
•
1 large egg, beaten
•
1 cup (8 fl oz) milk or buttermilk
•
3 tablespoons melted butter
or salad oil
•
½ cup (2 oz) roughly chopped pecans
or walnuts

Cut the apricots into thin strips, then toss them in a tablespoon of the measured flour.

Sift the flour into a bowl, stir the sugar through. Combine beaten egg, milk and melted butter or oil and add to the dry ingredients, stirring until mixed, then fold in the apricots and nuts.

Turn into a greased 22.5 × 12.5 cm (9 × 5 in) loaf pan and bake in an oven preheated to 180°C (350°F) for 1 hour or until a skewer inserted in the centre comes out clean. Cool in the pan for 10 minutes, then turn out on a wire rack. When cold, wrap and keep overnight before serving in thin slices.

MAKES: 1 loaf

# CARROT LOAF

### INGREDIENTS

¾ cup (6 oz) raw sugar
•
¾ cup (6 fl oz) maize (corn)
or sunflower oil
•
2 teaspoons vanilla essence (extract)
•
3 large eggs
•
2 cups (8 oz) fine wholemeal
(whole wheat) flour
•
4½ teaspoons baking powder
•
1 teaspoon mixed spice (optional)
•
1½ cups (3 oz) coarsely grated
carrots, loosely packed
•
½ cup (2 oz) chopped walnuts or
pecans
•
½ cup (3 oz) sultanas (golden raisins)
or mashed ripe banana (optional)

Preheat oven to 180°C (350°F) and prepare a loaf pan by brushing with oil and lining with greaseproof paper. In a large bowl, stir together the sugar, oil and vanilla. Add eggs one at a time, beating well after each. Sift the dry ingredients together and stir in, then add the carrots, nuts and optional sultanas or banana. Pour the mixture into the prepared pan and bake for 1 hour or until a skewer inserted into the centre of the loaf comes out clean. Cool in pan for 10 minutes, then turn out on a wire rack to cool completely. When cold, wrap in foil and leave for at least one day before slicing and serving.

MAKES: 1 loaf

# BEVERAGES

To complete this book, here are some cool drinks to quench your thirst when the temperature soars, and some warming potions to cheer you when winter winds blow.

Many of the cool fruit drinks are made easily in an electric blender, an appliance to be found in most kitchens these days. If you also own a juice extracting machine, then a whole world of fruit and vegetable cocktails is open to you.

## COLD DRINKS

## FRESH LEMONADE

### INGREDIENTS

4 lemons
•
1 cup (8 oz) sugar, or to taste
•
1 large bottle soda water (club soda)
•
ice cubes

Wash the lemons well and slice thinly, reserving 6 slices. Put the rest into a large pottery bowl and sprinkle with the sugar. Crush with a wooden spoon to make the juices run and to extract all the flavour from the rind.

Dilute to taste with soda water, strain and ladle into glasses. Add 2–3 ice cubes to each glass. Decorate with a reserved lemon slice.

NOTE: A mixture of oranges and lemons may be used if preferred.

SERVES: 6

# MANGO MILKSHAKE

## INGREDIENTS

1 ripe mango
•
2 cups (16 fl oz) chilled milk
•
sugar to taste
•
small scoops ice-cream (optional)

Peel and slice the mango and put the flesh into an electric blender with the milk and about 1 tablespoon of sugar. Blend until smooth, pour into glasses and, if liked, top each with a small scoop of vanilla ice-cream.

SERVES: 2–3

# SPICED TEA

## INGREDIENTS

½ cup (4 oz) sugar
•
1 cup (8 fl oz) water
•
1 stick cinnamon
•
6 whole cloves
•
3 cardamom pods (optional)
•
2 tablespoons tea leaves
•
4 cups (32 fl oz) boiling water
•
juice of 1 large lemon
and 2 oranges
•
ice cubes
•
iced water or soda water (club soda)
to taste
•
orange or lemon slices to decorate

Boil sugar, water and spices for 5 minutes, then remove from heat. Put the tea in a large pot and pour the boiling water over, leave for 5 minutes. Strain into a large bowl, add the strained syrup and leave to cool.

Stir in the strained lemon and orange juice, then add ice cubes and dilute with iced water or soda water to taste. Serve decorated with slices of orange or lemon.

SERVES: 8–10

# LIME RICKEY

This is a non-alcoholic version which is quite delicious. Squeeze the juice of half a lime into a tall glass, add blackcurrant or cherry cordial and fill the glass with chilled soda water. Stir well, add ice cubes if liked and garnish with 1–2 thin slices of lime.

# MANGO COOLER

### INGREDIENTS

1 ripe mango, peeled and sliced

•

½ cup (4 oz) passionfruit pulp

•

sugar to taste

•

chilled soda water (club soda)
and ice cubes

•

slices of green lime

Purée the mango, mix with the passionfruit pulp and sweeten to taste. Pour into two tall glasses, then slowly add the soda water, stirring gently. Add ice and serve garnished with a slice of green lime and a colourful straw. (Use straws that are sufficiently wide to let the passionfruit seeds through.)

SERVES: 2

# MANGO BUTTERMILK SHERBET

### INGREDIENTS

2 ripe mangoes

•

2 cups (16 fl oz) cultured buttermilk

•

2 tablespoons lime or lemon juice

•

½ cup (4 oz) sugar to taste

Peel and purée ripe mangoes and combine in blender container with the rest of the ingredients. Taste and adjust quantity of sugar according to flavour of the fruit. Pour into glasses and add crushed ice.

SERVES: 6

# PEACH FIZZ

### INGREDIENTS

3 ripe peaches

•

sugar to taste

•

chilled champagne or soda water
(club soda)

Peel the peaches and slice into a blender with the sugar—exactly how much will depend on how ripe and sweet the peaches are. Purée until smooth, pour into a jug and stir in the soda. Of course, you could use champagne and add a touch of peach brandy. Delicious, but not a drink to drive on. Pour over crushed ice in tall glasses.

SERVES: 2

# ICED TEA

To make iced tea, use twice the amount of tea leaves you would use for hot tea, because it is going to be diluted with the ice. Make a pot of tea, strain, then pour over ice cubes.

If liked, add a few sprigs of fresh mint to the pot or perhaps the thinly pared rind of a lemon, and when serving, decorate the glass with a fresh mint sprig or slice of lemon. Sweeten to taste. Alternatively, add a dash of lemon cordial to the iced tea and stir.

# STRAWBERRY SODA

*While strawberries are at the height of their season, make a syrup to which
soda or ice-cold milk can be added for a delicious drink.*

### INGREDIENTS

400 g (13 oz) ripe strawberries
•
1 cup (8 oz) sugar
•
½ cup (4 fl oz) water
•
chilled milk and soda water
(club soda) for serving

Wash the strawberries well, drain and hull them. Put the sugar and water into a pan and stir over heat, until sugar dissolves, then boil hard for 3 minutes.

Add the strawberries and crush them with a potato masher. Simmer for 10 minutes. Cool, then blend until smooth in an electric blender.

Transfer to a jar and store in the refrigerator. Put about ¼ cup (2 fl oz) syrup into a large glass and fill with equal quantities of chilled milk and soda water. Stir well.

SERVES: 10

# PAWPAW FRAPPÉ

### INGREDIENTS

250 g (8 oz) ripe pawpaw (papaya),
peeled and seeds removed
•
1 tablespoon sugar
•
½ cup (4 fl oz) orange juice
•
good squeeze lemon or lime juice
•
8 ice cubes

Put all the ingredients into the container of an electric blender and blend on high speed until the ice is crushed. Pour into 2 tall glasses and serve at once.

SERVES: 2

ICED TEA

# VANILLA MALT YOGHURT SHAKE

### INGREDIENTS

1 cup (8 fl oz) vanilla yoghurt
•
1 tablespoon malted milk powder
•
1 tablespoon honey
•
2 cups (16 fl oz) cold milk

Combine all ingredients in an electric blender and blend on high speed for about 1 minute. Pour into glasses and serve with straws.

### VARIATION FOR A BANANA YOGHURT SHAKE

Add 1 ripe banana to the above and blend until smooth.

SERVES: 2

# INDIAN MILK SHERBET

*In the West, a sherbet is a frozen dessert, but in the East it is a drink. In this version a rose-flavoured syrup is mixed with milk, crushed ice and sparkling squares of red and green agar-agar jelly in tall glasses.*

### INGREDIENTS

agar-agar jelly
•
Rose Syrup (see page 430), to taste
•
ice cold milk, as required
•
crushed ice
•
2 teaspoons soaked tulsi seeds (optional)

### JELLY

3 cups (24 fl oz) water
•
4 teaspoons agar-agar powder or 1 cup soaked agar-agar strands
•
6 tablespoons sugar
•
12 drops rose essence or 1 tablespoon rosewater
•
1 teaspoon liquid red food colouring
•
1 teaspoon liquid green food colouring

To make the jelly, put the water into a saucepan and sprinkle agar-agar powder over. (If agar-agar strands are used, soak at least 2 hours in cold water, then drain and measure 1 cup loosely packed.) Bring to the boil and simmer gently, stirring, until the agar-agar dissolves. The powder takes about 10 minutes and the strands take longer, about 25–30 minutes. Add sugar and stir to dissolve, cool slightly, then add rose essence, to taste. Divide mixture between two large shallow dishes and colour one red and the other green. Leave to set. When quite cold and firm, cut with a sharp knife, first into fine strips, then across into small dice.

Put about 2 tablespoons each of diced jelly and rose syrup into tall glasses, fill up with ice-cold milk and crushed ice. If liked, some soaked tulsi seeds can be floated on top.

NOTE: Agar-agar can be bought in powder form by the gram or ounce from chemists, or in packets from Asian grocery stores. It is popular in Asia for making jellies and sweetmeats because it sets without refrigeration. Tulsi seeds are the seeds of a variety of basil, *Ocimum carnum*. They are sold in Asian food shops—if from India they will be labelled Tulsi, and from Thailand they will be called Luk Manglak.

Rose syrup can also be bought from Asian grocery stores.

SERVES: 12

# ALMOND MILK

*Nutrition experts tell us that almonds are rich in protein and are good food value. The people of India seem to have known this instinctively for centuries, and incorporate almonds in sweet and savoury dishes. This refreshing drink is ideal when the weather is so hot that the appetite flags. The goodness of almonds and seed kernels is extracted by grinding them together with milk. Serve as a cool treat.*

### INGREDIENTS

20 almonds

•

2 tablespoons sunflower kernels

•

1½ cups (12 fl oz) water

•

1 cup (8 fl oz) milk

•

sugar to taste

•

few drops rosewater or essence

Blanch the almonds and put into an electric blender with the sunflower kernels and half the water. Blend at high speed until finely ground and strain into a jug through fine, clean muslin. Return the ground mixture left in the cloth to the blender with the remaining water. Blend and strain once more. Mix milk with the almond liquid, add sugar to taste and just enough rosewater or essence to add a subtle flavour. Add crushed ice, or keep refrigerated until served. A pretty touch is to float a few small rose petals on top of the drink.

NOTE: The finely ground almond residue may be used for thickening curries.

SERVES: 2

# BUTTERMILK OR YOGHURT DRINK

*This cooling beverage is known as lassi in India and is very popular in both sweet and salty flavours.*

### INGREDIENTS

2 cups (16 fl oz) cultured buttermilk and 2 cups (16 fl oz) iced water or 1 cup (8 fl oz) yoghurt and 3 cups (24 fl oz) iced water

•

salt and pepper, to taste

•

pinch of cumin, toasted and ground (optional)

Mix equal parts of cultured buttermilk and iced water, or beat yoghurt until smooth and gradually stir in iced water. Season with salt, pepper and a pinch of toasted, ground cumin. Alternatively, sweeten lightly with sugar and serve with ice.

Another yoghurt drink popular with children and adults is 2 tablespoons yoghurt stirred with 2 teaspoons of sugar in a tall glass, with iced soda (club soda) or lemonade added. It froths and looks like a milk shake, so even children who do not like yoghurt will find it acceptable.

SERVES: 4

# STRAWBERRY APPLE FIZZ

*Children and adults alike think this is the best fruit drink there is. Use very ripe berries—small ones will do, they're not expensive and often have better flavour.*

### INGREDIENTS

250 g (8 oz) ripe strawberries
•
2 cups (16 fl oz) pure apple juice
•
chilled soda water (club soda)

Wash and drain the berries. Hull them and put into a blender with the apple juice. Blend until smooth, then strain through a nylon strainer and discard the seeds. Pour into a jug and just before serving, add chilled soda water to taste. Add sugar to taste if necessary.

SERVES: 6

# BABACO FRAPPÉ

*Babaco is a new fruit on the market and while it has curiosity value, the flavour needs some help. I found that a slice of mango or the juice of a lime gives it a tremendous lift.*

### INGREDIENTS

1 ripe babaco
•
1 mango
•
1 tablespoon sugar
•
squeeze of fresh
lime juice (optional)
•
ice cubes or crushed ice

The babaco should be fully ripe, bright yellow and very fragrant. Wash it well, because it is best used skin and all for flavour. Remove stem end and slice into an electric blender jar. Peel and slice the mango and add to the babaco. Add sugar and a squeeze of lime juice if liked, and blend until smooth. Pour over crushed ice or add ice cubes to blender jar and blend together with fruit. Serve right away. If liked, thin the mixture with a little soda water (club soda).

SERVES: 3–4

# WATERMELON COOLER

### INGREDIENTS

3 cups diced watermelon, pink
portion only, seed removed
•
sugar to taste, if necessary
•
juice of 1 lime
•
crushed ice

Put watermelon, sugar and lime juice into a blender and blend until smooth, pour over crushed ice and serve straight away.

SERVES: 2

STRAWBERRY APPLE FIZZ AND BABACO FRAPPÉ

# ROSE SYRUP

### INGREDIENTS

3 cups (1½ lb) white sugar
•
2 cups (16 fl oz) water
•
20 drops rose essence or
1½ tablespoons rosewater
•
1 teaspoon liquid red
food colouring

Put sugar and water into a saucepan and cook over gentle heat until sugar dissolves. Allow to cool, then stir in rose essence and red food colouring. The colour should be quite strong, as it will be mixed with large proportions of water or milk.

Stir 2 tablespoons into a tall glass of iced water, milk or soda water and add crushed ice. The amount of syrup used may be increased or decreased according to taste.

MAKES: 3¾ cups

# FRUIT AND VEGETABLE COCKTAILS

For the best tasting and healthiest drinks, extract the juice just before drinking. Wash the fruit and vegetables thoroughly and cut them into pieces to fit the feed tube of the machine you are using.

I like to put some cubes of ice in the jug into which the juice flows so it is kept cold all the time. Here are some of our favourite combinations. Use proportions which are to your taste. Although oranges and other citrus fruit are normally peeled before juicing, half an orange or 1 small lime seeded and put through the extractor, skin and all, adds a fragrant but sharp accent which is delicious. If preferred, add water to dilute the juice. *Sip* it slowly for the most beneficial effect.

COMBINATIONS:

Celery, apple and carrot
Carrot and celery
Apple, orange, celery and lime
Celery, apple and parsley
Carrot, cucumber and beet

# ICED COFFEE

*This is great for young people's parties—I used to dance the night away on nothing stronger. It is a thirst quenching, cold, sweet, milky coffee with a dash of vanilla added.*

For each serving, use slightly more instant coffee than you normally would for each cup of water—a slightly rounded teaspoonful instead of a level measure. Dissolve in ½ cup (4 fl oz) of hot water, then add 1–2 teaspoons of sweetened condensed milk. Stir to dissolve in the hot liquid before adding ½ cup (4 fl oz) of ice cold milk and a little vanilla to taste. Serve chilled in tall glasses.

# HOT DRINKS
## COCOA

This may seem a simple enough drink not to need a recipe, but have you noticed how many people serve this with lumps of cocoa in it? Not surprising, because cocoa is famous for its ability to form lumps. The solution is quite simple. Put the cocoa and sugar into a dry cup and stir them together—the sugar knocks the lumps out of the cocoa.

For each cup use 1 teaspoon each cocoa and granulated sugar. Add a little boiling water and mix to a smooth cream. Pour on milk which has been brought to boiling point, rising in the pan with froth on top. If you wish the cocoa to have a nice layer of froth, lift the pan and pour the milk so that aeration takes place.

# NEW YORK HOT CHOCOLATE

*I was seduced by this rich, creamy, sinfully delicious brew on a winter's day in New York. The famed Rumpelmayer's Restaurant was where it happened, and it spoilt me for any other hot chocolate. I saw them melting down a huge block of chocolate to make the beverage which was served in little 2-cup pots and served with whipped cream. I was discreet enough to pass up the cream, since the chocolate was rich enough on its own. But would I be as strong if faced with the same temptation again? Who knows. No, I didn't ask them for the finer details of their recipe, but my version isn't bad either!*

### INGREDIENTS

150 g (5 oz) dark (semi-sweet)
chocolate (best quality)
•
1 cup (8 fl oz) cream
•
2 cups (16 fl oz) milk
•
2 teaspoons Dutch cocoa
•
2 teaspoons sugar
•
1 level teaspoon cornflour
(cornstarch)
•
dash vanilla essence (extract)
(optional)
•
whipped cream (optional)

Chop the chocolate and melt it in a bowl over hot water. In another pan, bring cream and milk to scalding point, stir half of it into the melted chocolate and stir until smooth. Return to the saucepan with the rest of the milk and set over low heat. Stir cocoa, sugar and cornflour together so there are no lumps in the cocoa. Then dissolve it in a little boiling water. Stir into the chocolate mixture and whisk or stir constantly until it comes to the boil and thickens slightly. Beat briskly with a wire whisk or rotary beater until foamy, then immediately pour into cups and serve. If whipped cream is used, it should be whipped just until thick, not stiff.

NOTE: Hot chocolate with a dash of Pear William eau de vie in it is quite something . . . more of a dessert than a drink.

MAKES: 4–5 small cups

# MEXICAN CHOCOLATE

### INGREDIENTS

150 g (5 oz) milk chocolate
•
150 g (5 oz) dark
(semi-sweet) chocolate
•
2 cups (16 fl oz) milk
•
1 stick cinnamon
•
ground cinnamon to taste

Chop both kinds of chocolate and melt over hot water. Put the milk and cinnamon stick into a saucepan and heat until bubbling. Add the melted chocolate, stirring briskly. Simmer for a few minutes, then remove the cinnamon stick, taste and add a sprinkling of ground cinnamon if a stronger flavour is required. Whisk with a wire whisk, rotary beater or hand-held electric wand (mixer) until the chocolate is foamy. Pour into cups and serve at once.

SERVES: 6

# MOCHA WARMER

### INGREDIENTS

2 cups (16 fl oz) strong, hot coffee
•
2 cups (16 fl oz) boiling milk
•
1 tablespoon cocoa
•
1 tablespoon sugar

Pour the coffee into 4 cups. Pour a little of the boiling milk onto the cocoa and sugar mixed together, and stir until smooth. Add remaining milk, stirring briskly, then fill up the half cups of coffee with the cocoa mixture. Serve hot.

For a richer mixture, use the New York Hot Chocolate recipe (see page 431) but substitute a cup of strong espresso coffee for a cup of milk. Or stir in 3 teaspoons instant coffee dissolved in 2 tablespoons boiling water.

SERVES: 4

# MULLED WINE

*When guests arrive out of the cold, make them welcome with a steaming
mug of spicy mulled wine.*

Use burgundy or similar red wine. Pour the wine into an enamel or stainless steel saucepan and to each bottle add ½ cup (4 fl oz) liquid honey, 1 small stick cinnamon, 5 whole cloves and 5 cardamom pods. Place over low heat and let it come almost to simmering point, turn off the heat and leave it for at least 30 minutes for the spices to infuse the wine. Heat before serving, but do not boil. For a drink with less alcohol content, the wine may be heated with an equal amount of water. Adjust sweetening to taste.

MEXICAN CHOCOLATE

# KASHMIRI TEA

*Sitting around a bubbling samovar is one of the joys of a Kashmir winter. If you don't have a samovar, try it anyway, using a teapot, but give authenticity to the occasion by serving it in little bowls (like Chinese rice bowls) instead of teacups with handles.*

### INGREDIENTS

1 teaspoon Kashmiri green tea
•
4 cardamom pods, bruised
•
1 small piece cinnamon stick
•
pinch of saffron strands
•
4 cups (32 fl oz) boiling water
•
2 tablespoons finely flaked almonds
•
sugar or honey to taste

Prepare the samovar with coals in its central tube, or warm the teapot by letting it stand for a minute or two with boiling water in it. Rinse out, put in the tea and spices and pour the measured boiling water over. Allow to steep for 5 minutes. Put a teaspoonful of almonds in each bowl. Pour the tea over the almonds, sweeten to taste and drink hot.

SERVES: 4

# CAFFÈ LATTE

Start with strong black coffee made the Italian way—either espresso or one of the other ingenious ways they have of getting the most flavour out of the ground beans. Pour equal quantities of coffee and boiling milk into a large cup. Sweeten or not, as desired.

# HOT CHOCOLATE MALTED

Dissolve 2 teaspoons malted milk powder in a cup of hot milk and stir in a teaspoon of drinking chocolate. For a stronger chocolate flavour use cocoa, dissolving it in a little boiling water first, then add the hot milk and malted milk powder and stir well.

# THE BASICS

## PROTEIN SOURCES

What most new vegetarians worry about is not getting enough protein in their diet. If milk, cheese, yoghurt and eggs are included in the diet this is not a problem, and there are other sources.

### LENTILS AND MILK PRODUCTS

Dried beans, peas, lentils, collectively called "pulses" are popular vegetarian foods of India. So too are milk products such as a fresh home made cheese. Yoghurt appears often as an accompaniment or a dipping sauce, either on its own or spiced, or as a dessert at the end of a meal.

### BEAN CURD

Bean curd, called "the meat without a bone" is the mainstay of Chinese and Japanese cuisines, even for non-vegetarians, since few people can afford to get all their protein from animal sources.

FRESH BEAN CURD is sold from refrigerator sections in Asian grocery stores and there are three main forms.

*Soft bean curd* immersed in water, with a consistency like firm custard: this is also available in long-life vacuum packs, either waxed cardboard boxes or plastic tubes. It is sometimes labelled "Silken Tofu".
*Pressed bean curd* is available in packs of about 400 g (13 oz) and is much firmer in texture.
*Fried bean curd*, usually large cubes in plastic bags, but in Japanese shops this is in the form of flat sheets (aburage).

DRIED BEAN CURD is sold in packets in the form of a fine "skin" which is used for wrapping savoury mixtures and steaming or deep frying. It also comes in sticks, which are formed by gathering the bean curd skin together. These need soaking before cooking, and stand up to longer cooking than the softer forms.

### TEMPEH

Tempeh or fermented soy bean cakes are another good protein source. I have used a savoury tempeh as the basis of quite a few recipes and no doubt you will think of other ways to use this versatile mixture, the recipe for which is on page 436.

### GLUTEN

Another protein ingredient is gluten, the protein part of wheat. Gluten "steaks" often stand in for meat and poultry. Buy gluten flour from a health food store and make the gluten yourself—it is fascinating to work with.

Since these items appear frequently in recipes throughout the book, to avoid repetition I have dealt with basic methods of preparing them in this chapter.

### DRIED PEAS, BEANS AND LENTILS (*points to watch*)

While there are other foods besides pulses which give the average person flatulence or wind, undoubtedly beans have a well-earned reputation as the surest way to a rumbling tum.

The flatulence is caused by sugars, called *oligosaccharides*, present in the beans. These need to be broken down by soaking and cooking, or bacteria attack them in the small intestine, producing "gas". But there are ways in which this unfortunate side effect can be lessened or eliminated.

The first rule is that dried beans or lentils must

be very well cooked, for a partially cooked bean is a potential trouble maker. One test for whether a bean is cooked is to lift it from the cooking liquid and blow on it. In a fully cooked bean the skin should peel away. Another method is to bite through the bean or press it between finger and thumb. There should be no firm centre. A pressure cooker is invaluable for making sure they are thoroughly cooked in the shortest possible time.

Lengthy soaking could also cause fermentation, especially in warm weather. It is best to soak them in plenty of water to cover, in the refrigerator. Or bring to the boil, leave to soak in the covered pan for 2 hours, then drain and cover with fresh water before continuing with the recipe.

Salt added to the soaking water also helps prevent fermentation—add 2 teaspoons salt to each 2 cups beans with sufficient water to cover. Drain and replace with fresh water for cooking.

A preliminary short cooking with a pinch of bicarbonate of soda (no more than half teaspoon soda to 2.5 litre/74 fl oz water) followed by a thorough rinsing, is another way to tenderise beans. Cover with fresh water and continue cooking, but salt is not added until the beans or lentils are almost cooked or they will take even longer to become tender. When using a pressure cooker, salt may be added at the start of cooking.

Adding certain spices such as cumin and fennel, or garlic is advocated in India. They also use asafoetida (an incredibly pungent resin) in tiny amounts—about the size of a peppercorn. In Mexico it is recommended that a couple of avocado leaves toasted, crumbled and added to the dish will prevent flatulence. Oregano and fresh coriander are used in bean dishes for the same reason.

# SAVOURY TEMPEH

*This would have to be one of our most popular recipes. It is based on the fermented soy-bean cakes called tempeh, which are available in the freezer section of most Asian food stores, since tempeh is used in Indonesian cooking. It is too good to be confined to just one recipe, so you will find it in a few different dishes.*

### INGREDIENTS

100 g (3½ oz) tempeh
•
2 tablespoons oil
•
1 medium onion, finely chopped
•
2 cloves garlic, very finely chopped
•
1 or 2 green or red chillies, seeded and finely chopped
•
½ teaspoon salt, or to taste
•
½ teaspoon black pepper
•
250 g (8 oz) potatoes, cooked and mashed

Cut the tempeh into thin slices, then stack the slices and cut first one way and then at right angles so the tempeh is diced finely.

Heat the oil in a small pan and fry the tempeh until golden brown and crisp. Remove from pan, add remaining tablespoon oil and on low heat, fry the onion, garlic and chillies until golden brown and the liquid has almost all evaporated. Remove from heat, stir in salt, pepper, tempeh and mashed potatoes. Serve with vegetables or salad.

There are many variations on this theme, all delicious. Baked Capsicums (see page 122) and Almond-Crusted Potato Croquettes (see page 119), or just the basic mixture shaped into patties, crumbed and shallow-fried, baked or barbecued.

SERVES: 4

436

# PANIR OR FRESH CHEESE

Bring 4 cups (32 fl oz) milk to the boil, stirring occasionally to prevent a skin forming on the surface. As it rises up in the pan turn off the heat and stir in 3–4 tablespoons of lemon juice. Let it stand for 5 minutes and when firm curds have formed, strain through a fine muslin and let it hang for an hour or so, then press to remove as much moisture as possible. Weight it down and leave in a cool place for an hour or more. Cut into cubes.

# GLUTEN "STEAKS" AND MINCED GLUTEN

*Gluten is the protein part of wheat and may be purchased in the form of a fine flour from most health food stores. When prepared as described below the result is a vegetarian "meat" or "poultry" which is popularly used in Chinese cuisine. The absorbent texture enables the gluten to absorb the flavours it is cooked with, and it provides a chewy-textured protein addition to vegetarian meals.*

### INGREDIENTS

½ cup (2 oz) gluten flour
•
½ cup (4 fl oz) water

Put the gluten flour and water into a bowl and mix with a wooden spoon. It may be necessary to add a little more water, because the absorbency varies (as it does with plain flour). It will form a rubbery dough. With wet hands, shape the dough into a ball, place it in a bowl, cover and leave for 30 minutes.

Bring a large saucepan of water to the boil. On a wet board, cut the dough with a wet knife into slices 2 cm (¾ in) thick. Drop the slices into the boiling water, cover the saucepan and cook for 30 minutes. They will swell to about three times their size, so put in only as many as there will be room for. Drain in a colander and allow to cool. When cool enough to handle, squeeze gently to remove excess water. Refrigerate, covered with plastic wrap. They will keep for up to a week.

The gluten may be cut into cubes and simmered in casseroles, sliced thinly and used in stir-fried dishes, minced or shredded.

For Minced Gluten: Drain and cool, then squeeze out excess water and mince finely in a food processor.

YIELDS: about 300 g (10 oz) prepared gluten

# TO COOK RICE

Many cooks find it diffiuclt to cook rice successfully. For practical and nutritional reasons, I use the absorption method rather than the water-bath method.

There should be no problem with the following table of proportions of rice and water. Measure carefully, and when the rice comes to the boil cover with a well fitting lid, turn the heat down very low and start timing. There should never be any problem in cooking rice perfectly with each grain separate and firm.

Short or medium grain rice absorbs less liquid than long grain rice. Natural or unpolished rice does not require more water, but does take about twice as long to cook, as the bran covering of the grains slows absorption.

If rice needs washing, leave to drain in a large colander for at least 30 minutes, especially if cooking by the pilaf method, where the rice grains are fried in oil or butter before the liquid is added. If cooking in liquid there is no need for the long draining and drying time, but reduce the amount of liquid by ¼ cup (2 fl oz) for each 2 cups (16 fl oz) liquid.

Use a pan which is not too wide for a small amount of rice and not too narrow and deep for a large amount. Don't lift the lid or stir once the rice comes to the boil, the pan is covered and the timing starts. It is the steam which cooks the rice, and in lifting the lid you are letting it escape.

## WHITE LONG GRAIN RICE

Allow 2 cups (16 fl oz) water for the first cup (7 oz) or rice, plus 1½ cups (12 fl oz) water for each additional cup of rice. Use the same cup for measuring rice and water, preferably a standard measuring cup.

1 cup (7 oz) rice . . . 2 cups (16 fl oz) water
2 cups (14 oz) rice . . . 3½ cups (28 fl oz) water
3 cups (21 oz) rice . . . 5 cups (40 fl oz) water

Bring to the boil, cover and cook on very low heat for 18–20 minutes.

## WHITE SHORT OR MEDIUM GRAIN RICE

Allow 1½ cups (12 fl oz) water for the first cup (7 oz) of rice and 1 cup (8 fl oz) water for each additional cup of rice.

1 cup (7 oz) rice . . . 1½ cups (12 fl oz) water
2 cups (14 oz) rice . . . 2½ cups (20 fl oz) water
3 cups (21 oz) rice . . . 3½ cups (28 fl oz) water
Bring to the boil, cover and cook on very low heat for 12–15 minutes.

## NATURAL OR UNPOLISHED OR BROWN RICE

The grain has been husked but not polished. It retains the bran coating and is more nutritious than polished rice. With the new thoughtful approach to eating, more people are using and enjoying natural rice. Allow the same proportions of water as for long grain white rice, but increase cooking time to 35 minutes.

# TO COOK WHEAT

Whole wheat kernels, or wheat berries as they are sometimes called, take a long time to cook but there is a way to shorten the cooking time.

Put 1 cup (8 oz) of wheat into a saucepan with water to cover, bring to the boil and pour into a wide-mouth vacuum flask with boiling water up to the top. Cover tightly and leave overnight. The grains swell and soften, and from this stage they take no longer to cook than rice. Here is a delicious Rice and Wheat Pilaf which illustrates how to combine different grains to good effect and makes a sustaining accompaniment to any vegetable.

# RICE AND WHEAT PILAF

## INGREDIENTS

½ cup (4 oz) whole grain wheat

•

2 cups (14 oz) basmati or other
long grain rice

•

1 tablespoon oil

•

1 tablespoon butter

•

1 onion, finely sliced

•

3¾ cups (30 fl oz) water

•

1½ teaspoons salt or to taste

•

1 stick cinnamon (optional)

•

3 cardamom pods (optional)

Wash the wheat, bring to the boil and soak in a vacuum flask overnight. Wash the rice and leave to drain for at least 30 minutes in a wide colander.

In a heavy-based saucepan with a well fitting lid, heat the oil and butter and fry the onion on medium heat, stirring frequently, until soft and translucent and starting to turn golden brown. Add the rice and fry for about 3–4 minutes, stirring with a metal spoon, then add the drained wheat and toss together. Add water and salt and bring to the boil, then turn heat down very low, cover tightly and cook without lifting the lid or stirring for 20 minutes. Uncover and allow steam to escape for a few minutes before fluffing the pilaf with a long-pronged fork. Serve hot.

NOTE:  If you wish to serve the pilaf with an Indian-style dish, add a small stick of cinnamon and 3 cardamom pods when frying the onions. For yellow rice, add a half teaspoon of turmeric just before frying the rice.

SERVES: 6

# CHILLI AND PEANUT SAUCE

*Serve this hot sauce with boiled vegetables, Savoury Pancake Rolls (see page 246), Rice Steamed in Coconut Milk (see page 270), or as a spicy accent with a meal of rice and curries. For novices, reduce the number of chillies to 3 or 4.*

## INGREDIENTS

oil for deep-frying

•

1 cup (5 oz) raw peanuts

•

10 large dried red chillies

•

1 medium onion, roughly chopped

•

6 cloves garlic, peeled

•

3 tablespoons coconut or peanut oil

•

Heat oil in a wok or frying pan and fry the raw peanuts over medium heat, stirring constantly. Lift them out as soon as they show signs of turning gold. They will continue to cook in their own heat, so don't leave them in the oil until they are brown or they will be overdone and bitter. Drain on absorbent paper and allow to cool, then rub off skins and pound, crush or work in blender until they are coarsely ground. They should be crisp and have lots of crunchy bits, not worked to a smooth paste. Put dried chillies into a bowl and pour very hot water over them to cover. Soak for 20 minutes at least.

1 tablespoon tamarind pulp

•

1 teaspoon salt

•

1 cup (8 fl oz) thick coconut milk
(see page 443)

•

1 tablespoon palm sugar
or brown sugar

In the container of an electric blender, put the soaked chillies and about 2 tablespoons of the soaking water, the onion and garlic, and blend to a smooth paste. Heat 3 tablespoons oil in a wok or frying pan and fry the blended mixture over medium heat, stirring constantly, until it darkens in colour and the onions and garlic smell cooked. Remove from heat. Stir in the tamarind pulp, salt, coconut milk and sugar, and transfer to a bowl to cool. When sauce has cooled, stir in the peanuts so they retain their crunchiness.

# HOLLANDAISE SAUCE

*Lovely to serve with vegetables, but undoubtedly rich. The classic Hollandaise is simply egg yolks, lemon juice and butter whisked together over simmering water until it thickens. Lighten the sauce and get more servings by folding in the whipped egg whites.*

### INGREDIENTS

185 g (6 oz) unsalted butter

•

3 egg yolks

•

2 tablespoons water

•

2 teaspoons lemon juice

•

salt and white pepper to taste

Start by clarifying the butter. Melt the butter in a small pan, remove from heat and skim off any foam, then gently pour the clear butter off, discarding the milky liquid at the bottom.

Carefully remove all traces of egg white and the specks from yolks, then combine yolks and water in a non-metal bowl. Place it over a pan of gently simmering water, making sure the bowl does not touch the water.

Whisk the yolks until they thicken like a custard. Add the butter, drop by drop at first and then in a fine stream, beating all the while. (An electric or cordless whisk is ideal for this). When all the butter has been incorporated and the sauce is thick, add the lemon juice and salt to taste, and a pinch of white pepper. Keep the sauce warm until serving time by standing it in a bowl of lukewarm water.

To lighten the sauce, fold in two of the egg whites beaten until they hold soft peaks, and/or ½ cup (4 fl oz) whipped cream.

VARIATION: For Sauce Noisette, add ¼ cup (1 oz) toasted ground hazelnuts or almonds, which does even more for vegetables than the basic Hollandaise.

# PIZZAIOLA SAUCE
# (FRESH TOMATO SAUCE)

*This Italian style sauce is one of the most useful items to have in the freezer. It goes on pasta, pizza, almost anything that needs a flavour boost. When tomatoes are cheap, buy up big and make more than one batch, then freeze in 1 or 2 cup (8–16 fl oz) quantities.*

### INGREDIENTS

2 kg (4 lb) firm ripe tomatoes

•

¹/₃ cup (3 fl oz) olive oil or sunflower oil

•

3 medium onions, finely chopped

•

3 teaspoons finely chopped garlic

•

2 bay leaves

•

2 teaspoons dried oregano, or 2 tablespoons fresh oregano

•

2 tablespoons fresh basil, chopped

•

1 scant tablespoon sugar

•

2 teaspoons salt, or to taste

•

½ teaspoon black pepper, or to taste

•

4 tablespoons tomato paste stirred into 1 cup (8 fl oz) water

Scald and peel the tomatoes, chop them roughly and discard seeds where possible, but you don't have to be too particular about this.

Heat the oil in a large stainless steel saucepan and on low heat, fry the onions, garlic and bay leaves until the onions are soft and golden.

Add the tomatoes, herbs and seasonings and tomato paste. Simmer, uncovered, until tomatoes are pulpy and the sauce is thick and reduced. Remove bay leaves. Cool and store in refrigerator in a covered container.

MAKES: 4 cups (32 fl oz)

# GARLIC CUSTARD FOR
# VEGETABLE TARTS

*Garlic custard may sound strange, mostly because we're conditioned to think of custard as a sweet. But I remember savoury custards made by my aunt— an adventurous, inventive cook—and poured over and around stuffed capsicums (peppers) which were then baked and served as a main dish. Delicious! Here is a formula which may be used with many vegetables in savoury tarts, blending flavours, bonding the vegetables to the pastry base, and increasing the appeal of the dish. Don't be alarmed at the quantity of garlic—the pre-cooking ensures it ends up sweet and surprisingly gentle.*

### INGREDIENTS

8 large cloves of garlic, unpeeled

•

Put the cloves of garlic into a small pan with water to cover and bring to a boil. Cover the pan and simmer gently for 20–25 minutes or until they are quite soft when tested.

441

¾ cup (6 fl oz) cream

•

2 teaspoons finely chopped
fresh herbs such as marjoram,
thyme, tarragon, or
½ teaspoon dried herbs

•

2 eggs

•

salt and pepper to taste

Infuse the cream with the herbs in another small pan. Bring gently to simmering point, turn off the heat and leave, covered, until required.

When garlic is done, drain away the water, lay them on a flat plate and mash until smooth, discarding the skins. Stir in a little of the cream, then return the garlic purée to the rest of the cream.

Beat the eggs to combine yolks and whites, add the garlic cream and season to taste. Pour over and around partly cooked vegetables in prepared tart shell and bake in an oven preheated to 180°C (350°F) for about 40 minutes or until the custard is set and golden. Serve warm or cold. Cut into squares or tiny wedges, this makes a good party hors d'oeuvre, or in larger servings, a delicious entrée or main course.

Makes: sufficient for 1 × 25 cm (10 in) tart

# PESTO SAUCE

*A wonderfully versatile sauce of fresh basil, garlic, olive oil and pinenuts
which is served on pasta, in minestrone, or used to add flavour to dips.*

### INGREDIENTS

2 cups (3–4 oz) fresh basil leaves,
packed

•

4–6 large cloves garlic

•

¼ cup (1 oz) pinenuts

•

1 teaspoon salt or to taste

•

1 cup (8 fl oz) best olive oil

•

freshly ground black pepper to taste

•

¼ cup (1 oz) freshly grated
parmesan cheese

Wash and dry the basil and put into a blender with the garlic, pinenuts, salt and most of the olive oil. Blend until smooth and add the rest of the oil if necessary. Add pepper to taste, then stir in the cheese. When serving as a sauce with pasta, toss until each strand is coated with the sauce.

Note: This keeps well in the refrigerator for 4–6 weeks, provided the surface is covered by the oil.

# COCONUT MILK

Coconut milk is not the clear liquid in the nut. This is a mistaken idea held by many people in countries where the coconut is not an everyday item of food. Coconut milk is extracted from freshly grated white meat of the mature coconut and it is very rich in fats and therefore useful for smoothing and enriching dishes.

It is possible to buy, though you may need to try specialty stores, very good quality coconut milk in cans, waxed or plasticised cardboard cartons and vacuum-sealed plastic packets. These are usually quite concentrated and should be diluted with water—the exact amount depending on the thickness of the canned product. An equal amount of water is generally adequate, unless a very rich result is required, in which case, use the coconut milk undiluted. Dilute only the amount required immediately, pour the rest into ice cube trays and freeze. When firm, turn them into a freezer bag or container and use as required. Coconut milk is very perishable and unless frozen as described, it must be stored in the refrigerator and used within 2 days.

Coconut milk can be extracted from grated fresh coconut (see page below) or use a good brand of canned coconut milk. Canned coconut milk will need diluting with water. Stir in a good pinch of salt to accentuate the flavour. Coconut milk should be freshly made and served at room temperature, as chilling solidifies the fat.

Even more convenient is the recently available instant coconut milk in powdered form. Add to warm water and stir until dissolved, just as with powdered dairy milk. Because you make up only as much as you need at the time, it is more economical.

**USING FRESH COCONUT** Sometimes it is possible to buy grated fresh coconut, frozen. Or if you have an implement such as those used in Asia and the South Pacific for grating the nut from the shell, you may grate the fresh coconut yourself. Pour 2 cups (16 fl oz) hot water over the grated flesh of one coconut and knead hard, then strain through a fine sieve or muslin bag, pressing out as much moisture as possible. This is the first extract or thick coconut milk.

Pour about 1½ cups more hot water over the grated coconut and knead again to extract more milk. Strain into a separate bowl. This is thin coconut milk. Repeat once more and add to the second extract or thin milk. Unless thick coconut milk or thin coconut milk is specified in a recipe, use a combination of thick and thin coconut milk.

**USING DESICCATED COCONUT** shredded, unsweetened Put 2 cups (6 oz) desiccated coconut into a large bowl and pour over 2½ cups (20 fl oz) hot water, for a richer result use milk instead of water. Cool until lukewarm, then knead firmly with the hand or whiz in a blender. Strain through a fine strainer, squeezing out as much liquid as possible. This should give about 1½ cups (12 fl oz) of thick coconut milk.

Repeat the process, using the same coconut and 2½ cups (20 fl oz) more hot water. This extract will yield approximately 2 cups (16 fl oz) thin coconut milk because of the moisture retained in the coconut.

# HEARTY AUTUMN FARE

Corn Chowder  page 78

•

Golden Nuggets with Vegetable
Ragoût  page 37

Almond Crusted Potato Croquettes
page 119

Braised Fennel with Onion  page 139

Broccoli in Garlic Butter  page 136

•

Lavosh Crisp Bread  page 401

•

Caramel Apple Dumplings  page 211

# PIZZA OR TART DOUGH

1½ cups (6 oz) flour—white,
wholemeal (whole wheat), or half
and half

•

½ teaspoon salt

•

1 sachet (envelope) active
dry yeast

•

½ cup (4 fl oz) lukewarm water

•

1 teaspoon sugar

•

2 tablespoons oil or melted butter

Put flour and salt in a large bowl. Sprinkle yeast over the water in a small bowl and leave for a few minutes to soften, then add the sugar and stir to dissolve. Sprinkle a teaspoon of flour over the top and leave it in a warm place for 10 minutes until it froths.

Pour yeast mixture over the flour and add the oil or butter. Beat with a wooden spoon until flour is dampened. Turn it onto a floured board and knead the dough for 10 minutes or until smooth and elastic. Form into a ball and place in a greased bowl, turning it so the top surface is greased. Cover and put in a warm place until doubled in bulk, about 1 hour.

Punch down and knead lightly. Roll to a 25 cm (10 in) circle and line a greased pizza tray or flan pan, making a rim around the edge.

NOTE: This dough is sufficient for two smaller pizzas, if rolled more thinly. Divide in two equal portions. Roll each to a 22 cm (8½ in) circle, lift onto two greased baking sheets and make a slight rim around the edges. Leave in a warm place to prove while making the filling. Spread with filling and bake in a pre-heated hot oven 200°C (400°F) for 20 minutes or until golden brown.

# RICH YEAST DOUGH

For a richer pizza or tart crust, reduce the water by half and add 1 beaten egg and 60 g (2 oz) soft butter. Use all white flour or a mixture of wholemeal (whole wheat) and white.

# QUICK SHORTCRUST PASTRY

## INGREDIENTS

1 cup (4 oz) plain (all-purpose) flour

•

pinch of salt

•

60 g (2 oz) cold butter

•

2 tablespoons water

Put all the pastry ingredients into a food processor fitted with steel chopping blades and process for the few seconds it takes to form a ball. Wrap in greaseproof paper or plastic and refrigerate for 20 minutes while making the filling.

Roll out between sheets of greaseproof paper and rest it for 5 minutes, then line a 20–22.5 cm (8–9 in) lightly greased pie plate. The pastry should be as thin as possible on the base but build it up on the sides and crimp the edges to give a decorative effect. Prick base well, and bake in a preheated hot oven 200°C (400°F) for 12–15 minutes or until golden.

# NO ROLL DOUGH

*In hot weather, when pastry is difficult to roll, this is ideal. Just pat it into the pie plate. It is not suitable for decorative effects, but deliciously crisp and short.*

## INGREDIENTS

90 g (3 oz) butter

•

2½ tablespoons milk

•

pinch of salt

•

1 cup (4 oz) self-raising flour, sifted

Put the butter and milk in a pan over gentle heat until the butter melts. (If a sweet pastry is required, add 2 teaspoons sugar and dissolve.) Add the sifted flour and stir to form a ball. Pat into a lightly buttered pie plate, keeping it as even as possible and building up the sides. Fill and bake in a moderately hot oven 190°C (375°F) 25–30 minutes or until filling is firm and pastry is golden.

MAKES: 1 × 22.5 cm (9 in) pie shell

# VEGETABLE STOCK

*If you cook vegetables in a minimum amount of water (which is all you should ever use), add no salt to the water and after draining the vegetables, taste the cooking liquid. Most vegetables impart a delicious, sweet and natural flavour. In addition, the liquid contains many nutrients. Save it for stock. Also, if vegetables used for cooking are washed well before being peeled, the peelings are useful for the stock pot. But if making a stock that does not rely on by-products from other cooking, here is a good basic stock with flavours that blend with most other dishes.*

### INGREDIENTS

1 tablespoon olive oil or butter
•
20 whole black peppercorns
•
2 medium onions, sliced
•
2 medium carrots, sliced
•
1 stalk celery, sliced
•
handful of parsley sprigs
•
few celery leaves
•
½ bay leaf (optional)
•
8 cups (64 fl oz) cold water
•
1 teaspoon salt

In a large saucepan, heat the oil or butter and toss the peppercorns, onions, carrots and celery over medium heat until coated. Cover with lid, turn heat very low and sweat the vegetables for about 10 minutes to bring out their flavour. Add the parsley sprigs and celery leaves, bay leaf, water, and salt. Bring to the boil, cover and simmer about 40 minutes. Strain.

MAKES: about 6 cups (48 fl oz)

# JAPANESE TEMPURA-STYLE BATTER

### INGREDIENTS

1 egg
•
1 cup (8 fl oz) iced water
•
pinch bicarbonate of soda
•
¾ cup (3 oz) unsifted plain
(all-purpose) flour or tempura flour

Break the egg into a bowl containing the iced water and whisk until frothy. Add bicarbonate of soda and flour. Beat just until the flour is mixed in. Do not overbeat. Batter should be thin so that the merest wisp clings to the vegetables dipped in it, and it should be made just before using. If it seems too thick, add a few drops of iced water. Stand the bowl in a larger bowl containing ice cubes and water to keep it cold.

# INDIAN-STYLE BATTER
# FOR VEGETABLE FRITTERS

*Almost any vegetable can be turned into crisp, hot fritters. Try onions sliced thinly with a bit of the root end left on to hold the slices together, or slices of zucchini (courgette), potato, carrot, capsicum (pepper), eggplant (aubergine), cauliflower or broccoli. If preferred, use a mixture of chopped or diced vegetables, mix into the batter and fry in teaspoonfuls.*

### INGREDIENTS

½ cup (2 oz) chick pea flour
•
½ cup (2 oz) self-raising flour
•
approximately ¾ cup (6 fl oz) water
•
½ teaspoon Garam Masala
(see page 456)
•
½ teaspoon chilli powder
•
1 teaspoon crushed garlic
•
1 teaspoon salt
•
oil for deep-frying

Mix the chick pea and self-raising flours smoothly with the water to make a fairly liquid coating batter. Stir in the garam masala, chilli powder, garlic and salt. Have the vegetables washed and dried, and if necessary cut into bite-size pieces. Dip large pieces in the batter and deep-fry in hot oil for 1–2 minutes. Drain on absorbent paper.

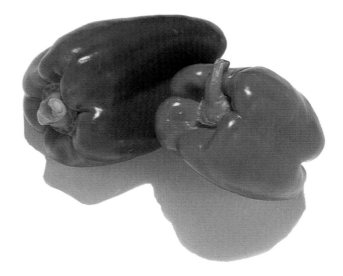

# BASIC CRÊPE BATTER

*Crêpes are very useful for containing mixtures of vegetables, whether they are used as layers, rolled around the filling, or formed into envelope-style pockets. This batter is my favourite, as it makes particularly fine, tender and delicate crêpes. Add salt if the crêpes are to be used for a savoury mixture, a little sugar and vanilla or brandy if they are intended for desserts. To make a sturdier crêpe needed for a wrapping, which is then going to be crumbed and fried, use only 2 eggs and add an extra ½ cup (2 oz) flour.*

### INGREDIENTS

4 eggs
•
1 cup (8 fl oz) water
•
1 cup (8 fl oz) milk
•
1 cup (4 oz) plain (all-purpose) flour
•
pinch salt
•
1 tablespoon melted butter

Whisk eggs with water, milk, flour and salt until smooth. Stir in melted butter. Strain the batter into a bowl, cover and set aside for at least 30 minutes, longer if possible. The batter may be made in a food processor or blender.

Heat a heavy-based crêpe pan and grease very lightly with butter. Using a ladle that holds just enough batter to coat the pan thinly, pour batter into pan and swirl to coat. Quickly pour any excess batter back into the bowl. Cook on medium heat until golden on the underside. Turn the crêpe and cook for about half a minute on second side, then flip onto a plate.

NOTE: For a sweet batter add ½ teaspoon vanilla and 2 teaspoons caster (superfine) sugar. Sugar will help crêpes brown more quickly.

MAKES: about 20

# MUSHROOM BUTTER

### INGREDIENTS

30 g (1 oz) butter
•
1 cup (4 oz) finely chopped mushrooms
•
½ teaspoon salt
•
¼ teaspoon pepper
•
2 tablespoons softened butter

Heat the first amount of butter in a small pan and cook the chopped mushrooms, stirring, for 4–5 minutes. Add salt and pepper and mix, allow to cool. Stir into the softened butter, and chill until firm. Use to flavour sauces or soups.

# CURRY PASTES AND SPICE BLENDS

Since Indian and other Asian food is well represented in this book, here is a collection of recipes you will find useful. I find these invaluable in adding sparkle to many dishes and always have a stock of them.

It would be too much like hard work to make the spice blends each time you need them, so I have given recipes which make enough for several

dishes, since it takes about the same time to make a large quantity as a small one.

All the pastes will keep well in the refrigerator in screw top glass jars for about 4 weeks, and if frozen, will keep for months. I have found small plastic containers ideal for portioning the pastes for the freezer. Usually 3 tablespoons will be sufficient for a dish for 4–6 people.

# BURMESE CURRY PASTE

*Burmese curries are surprising because they do not contain all the ground spices that are used in most other countries. Instead, they are based on onion, garlic and ginger. Chilli and turmeric are the only spices added, and the chilli can be used sparingly or even omitted if hot curries are not to your liking. It is the long, slow cooking of the ingredients in sesame oil that gives the very distinctive aroma and flavour. This takes time, so you may as well cook enough curry paste for more than one meal and freeze it.*

### INGREDIENTS

3 large onions
•
10 cloves garlic
•
1 tablespoon finely grated
fresh ginger
•
2 teaspoons ground turmeric
•
1 teaspoon chilli powder
•
½ cup (4 fl oz) light vegetable oil
•
3 tablespoons oriental sesame oil

Peel and roughly chop the onions and garlic. Put into a food processor or electric blender with the ginger and grind to a smooth puree. Mix in turmeric and chilli powder.

Heat the oil in a fairly large saucepan and, when smoking hot, add the ground ingredients. Take care, it sputters violently. Reduce heat and stir with a long-handled spoon to combine ingredients with oil. Cover and simmer on low heat, stirring frequently all over base of pan. This should take at least 25 minutes for the quantity given here. If mixture starts to stick before the aroma has mellowed and the onions become transparent, add a couple of tablespoons of water, and stir well. When the water content of the onions has evaporated and the mixture turns a rich reddish brown with oil showing around the edge of the mass, the most important stage of cooking is complete. Divide the mixture into 3 equal portions when cool, and freeze what you are not using at once. Each portion is sufficient to cook a curry for 4–5 people using about 750 g (1 lb) vegetables. Add 1 cup (8 fl oz) of water or coconut milk to make a sauce, and season with salt to taste.

SUFFICIENT: for 3 curries

# INDIAN CURRY PASTE

*Any vegetable may be curried and served with rice, chapatis or bought
Middle Eastern loaves.*

## INGREDIENTS

1 cup (3 oz) ground coriander

•

½ cup (1½ oz) ground cumin

•

1 tablespoon ground black pepper

•

1 tablespoon ground turmeric

•

1 tablespoon black mustard seeds

•

2 teaspoons or more chilli powder

•

2 teaspoons salt

•

2 tablespoons crushed garlic

•

2 tablespoons finely grated ginger

•

vinegar for mixing

•

¾ cup (6 fl oz) oil

Combine all the ground spices in a bowl with the garlic and ginger. Gradually stir in just enough vinegar to mix to a thick, smooth paste.

In a heavy-based pan, heat the oil until a faint haze rises from the surface. Stand back and add the paste. Reduce heat and stir with a long-handled spoon until spices are cooked and the oil separates and shows around the edge of the spice mixture. Cool and store in a bottle.

Use about 1 tablespoon for each 500 g (1 lb) of prepared vegetables. Bring curry paste to the boil with about 1½ cups (12 fl oz) Vegetable Stock (see page 448), water or coconut milk, add vegetables and simmer until cooked.

# THAI-STYLE RED CURRY PASTE

*Commercial Thai curry pastes which are becoming so popular usually contain
shrimp paste or ground shrimps. Here is a recipe without the shrimp paste.*

## INGREDIENTS

10 dried red chillies

•

2 large onions, roughly chopped

•

1 teaspoon ground black pepper

•

1 tablespoon ground cumin

•

2 tablespoons ground coriander

•

2 teaspoons ground turmeric

•

1 tablespoon paprika

•

Remove stems from chillies, and if you do not want the curry paste too hot, shake out the seeds. Break the chillies into pieces and pour about ½ cup (4 fl oz) boiling water over. Leave to soak for 15 minutes. Put all the ingredients into an electric blender, with some of the soaking water from the chillies. Blend on high speed until a smooth purée forms, adding more of the soaking water if necessary. Bottle and store in the refrigerator for about 4 weeks, or freeze in small amounts and store for months.

2 teaspoons salt

•

4 tablespoons chopped fresh
coriander, including root

•

4 tablespoons very finely sliced
lemon grass (tender white base only),
or 1 tablespoon chopped lemon rind

•

2 tablespoons chopped frozen
or bottled galangal
or 2 teaspoons galangal powder

•

2 tablespoons chopped garlic

•

3 tablespoons oil

NOTE: To use, heat ½ cup (4 fl oz) coconut cream in a wok, stirring constantly, until oily. Add 1 or 2 tablespoons of the paste and fry over medium heat, stirring, until mixture is fragrant. Add 2 cups (16 fl oz) thin coconut milk or water and 2 cups sliced gluten, cubed potatoes or mixed diced vegetables. Simmer until vegetables are tender. Serve with plain steamed rice or freshly cooked rice noodles.

# THAI GREEN CURRY PASTE

*This is intended to be a rather hot paste, so the seeds are not removed from the chillies. However, if your chilli tolerance is not high, do remove the seeds, slitting the chillies and scraping them out with the point of a knife. Please wear plastic gloves when handling hot chillies.*

### INGREDIENTS

10 fresh green chillies

•

2 cups (4 oz) chopped fresh coriander, including root

•

1 teaspoon black peppercorns

•

2 onions, roughly chopped

•

1 tablespoon chopped garlic

•

2 stems lemon grass, very finely sliced or finely peeled rind of 2 limes or lemons

•

2 teaspoons salt

•

1 tablespoon ground coriander

•

2 teaspoons ground cumin

•

1 tablespoon chopped frozen or bottled galangal

•

1 teaspoon ground turmeric

•

2 tablespoons peanut oil

Remove stems of chillies and roughly chop into pieces. Wash the coriander thoroughly and scrub the roots well. Chop roughly. Put into the container of an electric blender with all the other ingredients. Blend to a smooth paste, adding a little extra oil or water if necessary.

NOTE: To make a delicious vegetable curry, add 2 tablespoons green curry paste to 2 cups (16 fl oz) coconut milk and mix well. Add diced potato, pumpkin, eggplant or sweet potato and simmer, uncovered, until tender, stirring occasionally. Other vegetables such as broccoli, sliced zucchini (courgettes) or green beans should be added last. Be careful not to overcook them, as they are nicest if still slightly crunchy. Serve with rice.

# INDIAN GREEN MASALA PASTE

*A deliciously fresh-tasting spice mixture based on fresh coriander and mint, garlic and ginger. Stir a spoonful into a pot of rice. Use as a flavouring for simmered or stir-fried vegetables, or add to any curry for extra zest.*

### INGREDIENTS

1 teaspoon fenugreek seeds

•

1 tablespoon finely chopped garlic

•

Soak fenugreek seeds in water overnight. They will swell and develop a jelly-like coating. Put into the container of an electric blender with the garlic, ginger, mint, coriander and vinegar. Blend on high speed until very smooth. Mix

2 tablespoons finely chopped
fresh ginger
•
1 cup (2 oz) firmly packed fresh mint
leaves
•
1 cup (2 oz) firmly packed fresh
coriander leaves
•
½ cup (4 fl oz) vinegar
•
3 teaspoons salt
•
2 teaspoons ground turmeric
•
½ teaspoon ground cloves
•
1 teaspoon ground cardamom
•
½ cup (4 fl oz) vegetable oil
•
¼ cup (2 fl oz) sesame oil

in salt and ground spices. Heat vegetable oil and, when very hot, add blended mixture, bring to the boil, and turn off heat. When cool, stir in the sesame oil. Store in a bottle, making sure oil covers the herb mixture. If necessary, heat a little more oil and add it to the bottle.

# MALAYSIAN CURRY PASTE

### INGREDIENTS

½ cup (2 oz) coriander seeds
•
1 tablespoon cumin seeds
•
2 teaspoons fennel seeds
•
6 large dried red chillies
•
6 candlenuts or 4 Brazil
nuts, chopped
•
3 sprigs fresh lemon grass,
finely sliced, or rind
of 1 lemon
•
1 tablespoon chopped garlic
•
1 tablespoon chopped fresh ginger
•
2 teaspoons galangal powder
•
3 teaspoons salt

Lightly roast the seeds in a dry pan, putting each one in the container of an electric blender as they are done. They will require only 2–3 minutes over medium heat. Grind them to a powder.

Discard stems and seeds of chillies and soak the chillies in a little boiling water for 10 minutes. Add to the spices in the blender. Add the rest of the ingredients and just enough water to make a smooth paste. Store in a jar in the refrigerator and use 1–2 tablespoons, simmered in 2 cups (16 fl oz) of coconut milk, to cook 500 g (1 lb) vegetables.

# GARAM MASALA
# (FRAGRANT GROUND SPICE BLEND)

*This is the essential finishing touch to many an Indian dish. It contains mainly sweet, fragrant spices and is added a few minutes before the end of cooking. Again, to save time and trouble making it frequently, make enough to flavour many dishes and store it in a cool place in a tightly capped bottle. If you use it very slowly, put it in the freezer or it could deteriorate in hot weather.*

### INGREDIENTS

4 tablespoons coriander seeds
•
2 tablespoons cumin seeds
•
1 tablespoon whole
black peppercorns
•
2 teaspoons cardamom seeds
(measure after removing pods)
•
4 small cinnamon sticks
•
1 teaspoon whole cloves
•
1 whole nutmeg

In a small pan roast *separately* the coriander, cumin, peppercorns, cardamom, cinnamon (broken into pieces) and cloves. As each one starts to smell fragrant, turn on to a plate to cool. Put all into an electric blender and blend to a fine powder. Finely grate the nutmeg and mix in. Store in a glass jar with an airtight lid.

# PANCH PHORA
# (FRAGRANT SEED MIX)

*In Indian cooking, this mixture of whole seeds is called Panch Phora. "Panch" means five in Hindi, and five aromatic seeds are used to impart spicy flavour without any hotness. Use when stir-frying vegetables.*

### INGREDIENTS

2 tablespoons black mustard seeds
•
2 tablespoons cumin seed
•
2 tablespoons black cumin
seed (kalonji)
•
1 tablespoon fenugreek seed
•
1 tablespoon fennel seed

Combine the seed mixture in a small airtight jar and store in a dark cupboard or in the refrigerator. Shake before using to ensure even distribution. Fry 1 level teaspoon in a tablespoon of oil before adding 500 g (1 lb) vegetables and cook, covered, until just tender, adding a little water if necessary.

# GLOSSARY

**Aburage**: Fried bean curd, Japanese style. Prepared in thin sheets and sold frozen.

**Agar-agar**: This setting agent is derived from seaweed and is available in powder and strands. Used in sweets, it doesn't need refrigeration to set, even on hot days. Available from Asian food stores, health food shops and pharmacies.

For those who prefer to use this as a setting agent in place of gelatine, the rule is to use half as much agar-agar powder as powdered gelatine. It is also important to dissolve the agar-agar completely by boiling in the whole amount of liquid in the recipe. Quickly stir into the remaining ingredients as it will set at 27°C (80°F).

Agar-agar can be used in some recipes, but not all. It does not have the melting quality of gelatine, nor does it give you time allowed by the low setting temperature of gelatine to fold in whipped cream or egg whites. This means it cannot be substituted in Raspberry Mousse or Coconut Chiffon Pie.

**Ajowan seeds** (*Carum ajowan*): These seeds look like celery or parsley seeds but have the flavour of thyme. Used sparingly as a flavouring mainly in crisp fried nibbles and lentil dishes. Available in Asian food stores.

**Annatto seeds, achuete**: Small red seeds used for colouring and flavouring. If not available substitute ¼ teaspoon paprika and ⅛ teaspoon turmeric for each teaspoon of annatto seeds.

**Asafoetida** (*Ferula asafoetida*): Obtained from the resinous gum of a plant growing in Afghanistan and Iran, asafoetida has quite an unpleasant smell by itself. Used mainly in Indian cooking and in very small amounts, its main purpose is to prevent flatulence, a useful quality particularly when dried beans and lentils are the main source of protein. Available from Asian food stores.

**Babaco**: A delicately flavoured, pale yellow, five-sided fruit, which is a good thirst quencher.

**Bean curd, pressed**: A yellow or white bean curd sold in square cakes. It is much firmer than tofu, with a more distinctive flavour.

**Bean curd, tofu** (*Japan*), **dow foo** (*China*): Very perishable. After opening the packet, keep any unused bean curd immersed in lightly salted water in the refrigerator, changing the water daily. It is also available in long-life packs. Tofu has a sweeter and more delicate flavour than dow foo.

**Bean sauce (mor sze jeung), Chinese bean sauce**: Thicker than pouring consistency, this is a smooth sauce made from fermented soy beans.

**Beni shoga**: A Japanese type of pickled ginger used for flavouring and garnishing and coloured red.

**Besan**: Chick pea flour available from most Asian food stores. Pea flour or pea meal from health food stores may be substituted if it is finely sifted.

**Bitter melon, bitter gourd**: About the size of a medium cucumber, with a pebbly textured, glossy skin. When ripe it is a pretty golden colour with bright red seeds, but it should be used when still green in colour and only half mature. The flavour is bitter, but pleasantly so. Popular in Asia, and said to be good for the health, particularly for diabetics.

**Black cummin, Kalonji,** (*Nigella sativa*): The flavour is aromatic and peppery. The Indian name kala zeera translates as black cummin but it is not true cummin. Available from most Asian food stores.

**Black-eyed beans, black-eyed peas, cowpeas** (US): A small creamy coloured kidney shaped bean with a black spot on the skin.

**Borlotti beans** (*Phaseolus vulgaris*), **saligia, Roman or cranberry beans** (US): Creamy coloured beans with red-brown speckles.

**Burghul, bulgur, cracked wheat**: Wheat that has been steamed, dried and cracked. Available in fine, medium or coarse grades.

**Capsicum, bell pepper, sweet pepper**: Sweet and mild-flavoured relative of the fiery chilli pepper. They come in red, green, yellow and even black. Banana capsicums (named for their shape) are also mild and ideal for stuffing.

**Cellophane noodles, Bean thread vermicelli**: These fine noodles are made from the starch of green mung beans. May be soaked in hot water before use, deep fried straight from the packet to make a crisp garnish, or boiled according to the recipe.

**Chick peas,** (*Cicer arietinum*) **Garbanzo beans** (US): These creamy coloured, tasty, highly nutritious legumes are known by their Spanish name, Garbanzo, in the United States. In Italy they are Ceci and in France, Pois Chiche. The Indian name for them is Bengal gram or Channa. They are popular in India, the Middle East and the Mediterranean area.

**Chinese cabbage, Wongah bak, Tientsin cabbage, Peking cabbage, Celery cabbage** (US): It has a firmly packed, elongated form with pale green crinkly leaves. In England Pe-tsai may be used as a substitute.

**Chinese chard, Bok choy, Chinese cabbage** (US): Crisp white stems and large dark green leaves.

**Chinese mushrooms** (*Lentinus edodes*), **Shiitake**: Most readily available dried at Asian food stores but seasonally available as fresh mushrooms. A small quantity imparts an unmistakable flavour. Do not substitute continental mushrooms.

**Chinese wine, Shao hsing**: This is a rice wine which is not always easily obtained, but dry sherry makes an acceptable substitute.

**Chironji nuts, charoli**: A distinctive flavoured, small round nut. Substitute sunflower seeds or pistachio kernels.

**Chokos, chayotes**: Green, pear shaped vegetable.

**Choy sum**: A mild-flavoured vegetable in which the stems, leaves and flowers are all edible. It has jade green leaves, long stems and yellow flowers.

**Clarified butter, ghee**: Pure butter-fat without any milk solids. It can be heated to higher temperatures than butter without burning and imparts a distinctive flavour.

**Coriander (coriandrum sativum), Chinese parsley, cilantro (US):** A fresh herb used mainly in Asian cooking. The leaves are soft and feathery, about the same size as flat-leafed Italian parsley, and have a distinctive, pungent aroma. The t-stems and roots may also be used, depending on the recipe.

**Cornflour, cornstarch (US):** Finely ground maize flour used as a thickening agent.

**Cos lettuce, Romaine (US):** A crisp lettuce with tightly packed elongated leaves.

**Cultured buttermilk:** Once the by-product of butter production but is made these days from skim milk with culture added.

**Curry leaves:** The flavour from curry leaves is much sought after in South Indian, Sri Lankan and Malaysian cooking. These compound leaves, which are composed of a number of smaller shiny leaflets, are used fresh in the tropical countries in which they grow, but outside these regions are mostly available dried. They are added to the oil at the start of cooking and give a good flavour. Never substitute bay leaves or other herbs. The only substitute is daun salam, but if neither is available, it is better to omit them. Curry leaves may not be substituted with curry powder, which is a blend of various ground spices.

**Daikon:** Giant white raddish about 30-40cm (12-15″) long, with a mild flavour.

**Daul salam:** A leaf larger than the curry leaf, used in Indonesian and Malaysian cooking. Very aromatic and similar in flavour to curry leaves.

**Daun Pandan (Pandanus latifolia), rampe leaf:** Long flat green leaves used as a flavouring in curries and rice. In Indonesia, Malaysia and Thailand they are used to flavour and colour sweet snacks.

**Dhal, dals:** Dried beans, peas and lentils
Brown lentils, Malka masoor—Whole lentils with a greeny-brown seed coat. They may be soaked before cooking, but can be cooked in a reasonable time without soaking.
Channa dhal, Bengal gram—Chick peas skinned and split.
Mung dhal, green gram—Green mung beans, skinned and split.
Red lentils, Masoor dhal—skinned and split. Not necessary to soak before cooking.
Toor Dhal, red gram, pigeon peas—Yellow lentils skinned and split.
**Urad, black gram**—A small bean with a dull black coat. Once the skin is removed it is very white and is then known as urad dhal. When soaked, ground and set aside for a few hours, it ferments and is included in batters for South Indian pancakes and other snacks to give a light, spongy texture.

**Eggplant, aubergine:** There are many types of eggplant—oval or nearly round, some slender and long, some the size and shape of eggs. The skins may be deep purple, pale mauve, white, pale green, or purple and white streaked, but the flesh is always white. It discolours quickly when cut, and a stainless steel knife is recommended. Choose fruit which are firm to the touch and with smooth, glossy skin.

**Endive, chicory (US):** Curly leafed with a slightly bitter taste, this vegetable is used mainly as a salad ingredient.

**Fenugreek seeds:** Small brown seeds that are used in small quantities in curries. Because they impart a bitter taste they must be used in the stated amounts. Available from shops specialising in Indian ingredients.

**Galangal**
**Greater galangal (Alpinia galanga), Lengkuas (Malaysian), Laos (Indonesian), Kha (Thai):** It is a distinctively flavoured rhizome with creamy white flesh. Sometimes available fresh from Asian food stores, but also satisfactory when bottled, dried or frozen.
**Lesser Galangal (Alpinia officinarum), kencur (Malaysian and Indonesian), krachai (Thai):** Has a stronger, more aromatic flavour than greater galangal, and is not as widely used. It cannot be substituted for the greater galangal.

**Garbanzo beans:** see Chick peas.

**Gluten:** The protein component of grain found primarily in wheat. When isolated from the grain, it is a fine textured flour. Usually sold in health food stores.

**Granny Smith apples:** Green skinned eating and cooking apple. Golden Delicious makes a good substitute.

**Green bean starch/flour:** Mung bean flour, similar to arrowroot, being clear and thick when cooked. Used for cakes and desserts.

**Hoisin sauce:** A thick, red-brown sauce, made from soy beans, spices and garlic. Keeps indefinitely in a covered jar.

**Jaggery:** See Palm sugar.

**Kangkung, ong choy (Chinese):** It is a dark green, leafy vegetable, high in nutritional value. Substitute watercress, spinach or chicory.

**Kemiri, candlenut:** A hard, oily nut used to flavour and thicken Indonesian and Malaysian curries. Substitute Brazil or Macadamia nuts.

**Kewra essence (Pandanus odoratissimus):** Essence of the screwpine flower, very concentrated, and only the smallest amount is needed to give flavour. Available from Indian specialty food stores.

**Kiwi fruit (Actinidia sinensis):** Chinese gooseberry—An oval fruit with sweet-sour green flesh and tiny black seeds. Remove hairy brown skin before use.

**Kombu:** Japanese kelp seaweed, available dried in broad, greyish ribbons.

**Kumara, sweet potato, yam (US):** A tuberous root with red brown skin and orange coloured, sweet flesh, which can be cooked like a potato.

**Laos powder:** Dried form of greater galangal, very delicate in flavour.

**Mirin:** Japanese rice wine. Substitute dry sherry.

**Miso paste:** Made from cooked fermented soy beans. A number of varieties are available, white, red, dark brown and beige, and there are varying degrees of saltiness.

**Nori:** Dried laver is an edible seaweed and is one of the most popular flavourings in Japanese cooking. Sold in paper-thin purple-black sheets, it must be warmed and crisped before use. Also sold as small flakes, to be sprinkled over food as a flavouring.

**Palm sugar, jaggery, Gula Malacca**: This strong flavoured, dark sugar is made from the sap of the coconut, kitul and palmyrah palm trees. It is available from Asian food stores. Substitute black sugar (unrefined sugar containing a proportion of molasses) or dark brown sugar from supermarkets or health food stores.

**Panch phora**: This is a combination of five aromatic seeds. They are used whole and when added to the cooking oil impart a typically Indian flavour.

**Pawpaw, papaya** (US): Yellow-orange coloured tropical fruit that is said to be good for the digestion. When allowed to ripen on the tree, they are delightfully sweet.

**Pumpkin, squash** (US): There are many varieties of pumpkin including such favourites as butternut and golden nugget.

**Rice vermicelli**: These are very fine rice flour noodles, sold in dried form in Asian grocery stores.

**Rosewater**: This is the diluted essence extracted from rose petals. If you are using rose essence be careful not to over flavour. Two or three drops of rose essence will be equal to a tablespoon of rosewater. Available from pharmacies and shops specialising in Asian ingredients.

**Saffron** (*Crocus sativus*): The world's most expensive spice is obtained by drying the stamens of the saffron crocus. There are only three fragile strands in each flower and they have to be separated from the petals by hand. It is estimated that around 250 000 of the stamens make a kilo of saffron so it is not difficult to see why saffron is so costly. There are cheap imitations, but while safflower or marigold will provide colour, the flavour of saffron is so distinctive that there is no substitute. It takes only a tiny amount to flavour a dish and if a small quantity of good saffron is purchased and kept in an airtight container in the freezer, it will keep its flavour for years.

**Sago**: Small round granules of starch obtained from the sago palm. Very small, roughly pinhead sized granules, as distinct from the larger granules of tapioca. Substitute minute tapioca, the very small variety.

**Sambal ulek**: The Indonesian name for a condiment made of ground fresh chillies and salt. Substitute finely chopped fresh red chillies.

**Sambol, sambal**: These are spicy accompaniments used with rice and noodle dishes.

**Scallions, shallots, spring onions**: A true shallot (*Allium ascalonicum*) is a cluster of small bulbs, reddish brown in colour and with a mild garlic flavour. Spring onions (UK) or scallions (US) (*Allium cepa*) are slender green and white onions which look like miniature leeks. The white root end is sometimes bulbous, sometimes not. These are mistakenly referred to as a shallot in some parts of Australia. However, we intend to persist in calling these quite separate members of the Allium family by their correct names and hope that one day greengrocers and consumers will get it right.

**Semolina, farina** (US): Breakfast Delight (Australia)— Comes in coarse, medium and fine grades and is made from wheat.

**Snowpeas, sugar peas, Chinese peas**: Bright green, small, flat pods containing embryonic peas. They only need to be cooked for a minute or two and are eaten whole.

**Soba**: Japanese buckwheat noodles.

**Spaghetti squash, vegetable spaghetti**: A type of squash in which the flesh, when steamed or boiled, separates into long spaghetti-like strands.

**Tahini, tahina paste**: Sesame seeds crushed into a paste and used in Middle Eastern cooking.

**Takuan**: Pickled daikon, the giant white raddish, used in Japanese food.

**Tamarind**: A tropical tree which bears large beans with brittle brown shells. Inside are hard seeds surrounded by a sweet-sour brown pulp which gives a distinctive acid flavour different to lemon juice or vinegar. Tamarind is mainly sold in dried form with or without the seeds, the shell having been removed. Soak a tablespoonful in ½ cup (4 fl oz) of hot water for a few minutes. Knead and rub with the fingers until the pulp dissolves in the water, then strain out and discard the seeds and fibres. Use the tamarind liquid in the stated quantities.

It is also possible to purchase jars of convenient, ready-to-use tamarind pulp. I use one which is about the consistency of plum sauce. Two tablespoons of this tamarind pulp concentrate is equal to 1 rounded tablespoon of dried tamarind soaked and strained as described. There is another type of instant tamarind which is so firm that it takes ages to dissolve in hot water. Whichever form is used, taste for acidity and add a little at a time to give a pleasantly piquant flavour.

**Tapioca**: Large round pellets made from starch extracted from cassava (manioc) root. It cooks to a clear, gluey consistency. Minute tapioca is a variety that is more the size of sago.

**Telegraph cucumber, continental cucumber**: Slim, long with tender dark green skin and few seeds. Substitute seedless cucumber.

**Tempeh**: Fermented soy-bean cakes.

**Vegetable stock**: Nutritious and flavoursome, it is best to make your own vegetable stock. (See The Basics for recipe.) When time is short one may use vegetable stock cubes, but read the labels and choose one without 'flavour enhancer' or monosodium glutamate.

**Wasabi, wasabe**: Used in Japanese cooking, a very pungent green horseradish. It is available in a dried powdered form in tins, and is reconstituted by the addition of a little cold water.

**Wood fungus, cloud ear fungus, jelly mushrooms**: When dried it looks like black paper, but when soaked it swells to a billowing cloud shape. It is a texture ingredient, adding no flavour of its own, but taking on flavours from the foods that it is cooked with.

**Yeast**: The leavening ingredient in breads and yeast doughs. Available as fresh compressed yeast or dried granules.

**Yoghurt, yogurt, yoghourt**: Semi-solid fermented milk product.

**Zucchini, courgette, Italian squash**: Small marrow that does not require peeling prior to eating. It may be used in hot dishes or as a salad vegetable.

# INDEX

## A

aburage 236
achar, cucumber 352
agar-agar
  almond bean curd 372, *373*
  Indian milk sherbet 426
  vegetable platter with sesame sauce 294
aioli 183
almonds
  almond bean curd 372, *373*
  almond cream sweetmeat 371
  almond-crusted potato croquettes 119
  baklava 210
  barbecued tempeh patties 102
  born again croissant 387
  braised celery with 144, *145*
  and bread soup 68
  camembert in port with green peppercorns 34
  caramel apple dumplings 211
  carrot sweetmeat 374
  cassata alla Siciliana 210
  chick pea and nut burgers 110
  creamy rice blancmange 374
  creamy vermicelli pudding 375
  custard-filled pastries 207
  frangipane fig tart 198
  granola 379
  grilled mushrooms with garlic crumbs 31
  Kashmiri tea 434
  milk 427
  millet pilaf with nuts 123
  rice, capsicum cups with toasted 38
  rice vermicelli with eggs and 276
  rice with fresh cheese, nuts and vegetables, Moghul style 272, *273*
  saffron and cream sauce 365
  tempeh stuffed grilled mushrooms 38
  toast of the Shah 371
anooshabour 380
apple
  baked 195
  cake, Danish 194
  charlotte 202
  dumplings, caramel 211
  hazelnut muesli 378
  omelette Normandy 205
  papaya salad 166
  pie 194
  and radish salad 179
  red cabbage with 132, *133*
  strawberry fizz 428, *429*
  strawberry freeze 214
  tarte aux pommes *189*, 190
  watercress soup 58
apricots
  hazelnut muesli 378
  nut bread 420
  wedding pickle 366
  whole wheat and dried fruit compote 380

arborio rice
  mushroom risotto 100, *101*
  risotta alla Milanese 100
  spring vegetable risotto 131
Armenian potatoes 148, *149*
artichoke
  boiled 19
  cheese fondue with green peppercorns 47
  and onion pizza 155
  and potato salad 166
  strudel 32, *33*
  stuffed 34
asparagus
  filling for omelettes 391
  golden nuggets with vegetable ragoût 37, *37*
  with pasta 84, 85
  with polonaise sauce 24, *25*
  soup 78
  spring vegetable soup 60, *61*
  stir-fried 293
aubergine, *see* eggplant
autumn menus 104, 337, 444
avocado
  fool 188
  guacamole soup 64, 65
  and marinated mushroom salad 160
  mushrooms with guacamole 4
  raspberry and watercress platter 176, *177*
  toasted mushroom sandwiches 24

## B

baba ghannouj 40, *41*
babaco frappé 428, *429*
baklava 210
balsamic vinegar dressing 186
bamboo shoot
  braised vegetable combination 282
  braised vegetables with bean curd 290
  cold rice with vegetables 248
  combination fried rice 266
  steamed vegetables with coconut 312, *313*
banana
  curry, green 310
  flip 383
  ice-cream 222
  and yoghurt raita 363
  yoghurt shake 426
basil
  fettucine in creamy capsicum sauce 52, 53
  pesto sauce 442
  and tomato salad 179
Basmati rice
  with fresh cheese, nuts and vegetables, Moghul style 272, *273*
  ghee rice 262
  how to cook 438
  rice and wheat pilaf 439
  rice with mixed lentils 270
  riz bi sh'arieh 135

batter
  basic crêpe 450
  for vegetable fritters, Indian-style 449
  Japanese tempura-style 449
  okra fried in 323
  white marrow fried in 231
bean curd 435
  almond 372, *373*
  and bean sprouts 294
  braised Chinese mushroom and 280, *281*
  braised vegetable combination 282
  braised vegetables with 290
  Chinese vegetarian combination soup 251
  fresh spring roll 230
  fried 236
  fried, with peanuts 295
  fried, with soy sauce 298
  gado-gado 340, *341*
  with hot sauce 320, *321*
  omelettes 236
  in salted soybean paste 298
  stir-fried watercress with 286
  sushi in fried 236
  Szechwan soup 256
  vegetable platter with sesame sauce 294
bean sayur 311
bean sprouts
  and bean curd 294
  combination fried rice 266
  fresh spring roll 230
  fried bean curd with peanuts 295
  fried bean curd with soy sauce 298
  fritters 234
  and mushroom salad 161
  salad 163
  sambal 349
  spicy 306
  spring rolls 244, *245*
  steamed vegetables with coconut 312, *313*
  stir-fried salad 302
  stir-fried vegetables 315
  twelve varieties soup 257
  and water chestnut salad 167
bean starch noodles, *see* noodles
bean starch sheets and braised gluten 307
beans (dried) 435
  with chilli, Mexican 108, *109*
  chilli con tempeh 121
  hot baked potato variety 42
  minestrone 76
  pasta and pecan salad 164
  red bean salad 169
  salad, white and green 40
  savoury black-eyed 346
  soup 70
  *see also* green beans
beetroot
  bean soup 70
  carrot and cauliflower timbales 27, *29*
  cold jellied borsch 63

Mischa's borsch 59
  and orange soup 72
  pasta 86
  raw salad 162
  Russian salad 174
beets, *see* beetroot
berries
  shortcake with 200, *201*
  summer berry soup 56, *57*
  summer pudding 208
besan, *see* chick pea flour
bitter gourd
  and eggplant fried 322
  sambal 358
bitter melon, *see* bitter gourd
black-eyed beans, savoury 346
blancmange, creamy rice 374
blintzes, orange 202
blue cheese log with walnuts 14
blueberries
  muffins 386
  summer berry soup 56, *57*
  wine soup 75
bok choy, *see* Chinese cabbage
borlotti beans, *see* beans (dried)
borsch
  cold jellied 63
  Mischa's 59
bran bread 412
Brazil nuts
  coconut chiffon pie 203
  eggs in chilli sauce 299
  mixed pickle 355
  nut bread 419
  ravioli with nut filling 99
  steamed and spiced eggplant 304
bread
  aioli 183
  and almond soup 68
  apple charlotte 202
  apricot nut 420
  bran 412
  brown bread ice-cream 227
  carrot loaf 420
  cheese casserole 407
  cheese croûtons 67
  cheese fondue with green peppercorns 47
  cheese puffs 11
  chick pea flour 400
  creamy onion soup 74
  crisp spicy toast 15
  deep-fried wholemeal 400
  fig and honey 418
  flaky wholemeal 396
  French onion soup 62
  French toast 390
  garlic croûtons 156
  gazpacho Andaluz 70
  lavosh 401
  malted rye 412
  mushroom puffs 20
  mushroom soup with miso 69
  naan 411
  oatmeal cottage loaf 404, *405*
  pear and chocolate loaf 419
  pocket 416
  pumpernickel 406

Punjabi leavened 411
Punjabi sourdough 398
quick 417-20
sesame loaves 410
skorthalia 12, *13*
summer pudding 208
Swedish rye 406
sweet flaky 399
toast of the Shah 371
toasted mushroom
    sandwiches 24
unleavened 396-402
yeast-risen 402-20
breakfast menu 408-9
broccoli
    braised, Chinese style 292
    and capsicum soufflés 51
    and cauliflower salad 164,
    *165*
    "cheese and crackers" loaf
    129
    cheese fondue with green
    peppercorns 47
    chick pea and cauliflower
    fricassée 110
    Chinese vegetarian
    combination soup 251
    in garlic butter 136
    and leek flan 91
    semolina pilaf 260, *261*
    soup, cream of 59
brunch menu 408-9
Brussels sprouts
    Oriental-style 292
    and pecan flan with crumble
    topping 103
    timbale 94
buckwheat
    crêpes with creamed leeks 35
    kasha with peas 130
    *see also* noodles
buckwheat noodles, chilled
    290
bulgur, *see* cracked wheat
burgers
    chick pea and nut 110
    lentil, sesame and sunflower
    115
burghul, *see* cracked wheat
Burmese curry paste 451
Burmese style mild soup 255
Burmese style sour soup 254
butter, mushroom 450
buttermilk
    apricot nut bread 420
    drink 427
    lentil cakes in yoghurt 342
    mango sherbet 423
    moulds 206
    pear and chocolate loaf 419
butternut pumpkin
    baked 139
    soup 72, *73*
    *see also* pumpkin

C
cabbage
    basic coleslaw 158
    in coconut milk, spicy 303
    curried vegetables in coconut
    milk 325, *325*
    fresh spring roll 230
    fried bean curd with peanuts
    295
    gado-gado 340, *341*

and Japanese radish salad 167
and potato curry 317
rolls, stuffed 120
shredded 299
stir-fried vegetables 315
twelve varieties soup 257
*see also* Chinese cabbage
caffe latte 432
cake
    chocolate mousse 191
    Danish apple 194
    steamed rice 238
    steamed rice flour and
    coconut 395
camembert
    cheeseboard pizza 49
    in port with green
    peppercorns 34
canapés, mushroom 7
cantaloupe, *see* rockmelon
caponata 48
capsicum
    artichoke strudel 32, *33*
    baked, with rice, pinenuts
    and olives 122
    basic coleslaw 158
    and broccoli soufflés 51
    cheeseboard pizza 49
    chilli con tempeh 121
    cups with toasted almond rice
    38
    fattoush 162
    garlic curry 318
    gazpacho Andaluz 70
    Greek country style salad 158
    guacamole soup 64, *65*
    Lebanese bread salad 162
    lima bean and vegetable stew
    122
    lima bean salad 159
    Mexican beans with chilli
    108, *109*
    mixed vegetables with
    coconut 334
    pasta salad with peas 163
    purée, for spinach and leek
    timbales 29, 30
    rainbow layer crêpes 26
    ratatouille 96-7, 98
    rice salad 171
    roasted 147
    sauce, fettucine in creamy 52,
    53
    semolina pilaf 260, *261*
    stuffed chillies 318
    vegetable mosaic terrine 46
caramel
    apple dumplings 211
    moulds, pumpkin 199
    oranges in 196
caraway sticks, salt and 414
carrot
    bean soup 70
    braised gluten with
    vegetables 278
    and cauliflower timbales 27,
    29
    "cheese and crackers" loaf
    129
    cheese fondue with green
    pepper corns 47
    Chinese vegetarian
    combination soup 251
    and coconut salad 172, *173*
    combination fried rice 266
    confetti vegetable mould 127

corn chowder 78
cream of tomato soup 55
cucumber achar 352
gado-gado 340, *341*
green and gold soup 67
Japanese radish and cabbage
    salad 167
julienne 140
Korean pancakes 234
lentil, sesame and sunflower
    burgers 115
lentil salad 159
loaf 420
minestrone 76
mixed pickle 355
mixed vegetables with
    coconut 334
    and mushrooms 154
    and orange soup 79
    rice and vegetable patties 106
    ring with peas 155
    Russian salad 174
    and saffron soup 63
    savoury pancake roll 246
    savoury pecan loaf 95
    semolina pilaf 260, *261*
    sherry-glazed 151
Sindhi style mixed vegetables
    335
    soup, creamy 71
    spicy diced vegetables 343
    spirali with julienne of
    vegetables 130
    spring vegetable risotto 131
    spring vegetable soup 60, *61*
    squash medley 88, *89*
    steamed vegetables with
    coconut 312, *313*
    stir-fried eggs with mixed
    vegetables 282
    stir-fried salad sprouts 302
    stuffed cabbage rolls 120
    summer salad 178
    sweetmeat 374
    vegetable mosaic terrine 46
    vegetable platter with sesame
    sauce 294
    vegetable stock 448
    vegetarian couscous 116, *117*
    walnut and rice loaf 112
    wedding pickle 366
cashews
    millet pilaf with nuts 123
    nutty nibbles 11
    ravioli with nut filling 99
    rice with lentils and tamarind
    267
    shredded gluten with 287
    spiced steamed cauliflower
    312
    spicy rice with 265
    spinach with mixed
    vegetables 338
cassata à la Siciliana 210
cauliflower
    and broccoli salad 164, *165*
    and carrot timbales 27, *29*
    cheese 106
    "cheese and crackers" loaf
    129
    and chick pea fricassée 110
    chilli-fried 316
    confetti vegetable mould 127
    in green sauce 20, *21*
    Indian style, spicy fried 300
    mixed braised vegetables 293

mixed pickle 355
    with pecans 288, *289*
    rice with fresh cheese, nuts
    and vegetables, Moghul
    style 272, *273*
    spiced steamed 312
    twelve varieties soup 257
caviar, poor man's 148
celery
    asparagus soup 78
    braised, with almonds 144,
    *145*
    caponata 48
    "cheese and crackers" loaf
    129
    cheese fondue with green
    peppercorns 47
    chick pea and cauliflower
    fricassée 110
    chilli con tempeh 121
    combination fried rice 266
    corn chowder 78
    cream of broccoli soup 59
    dieter's eggplant salad, Italian
    style 175
    lima bean and vegetable stew
    122
    minestrone 76
    savoury pancake roll 246
    savoury pecan loaf 95
    Spanish eggplant salad 170
    spicy parsnip soup 74
    spring vegetable soup 60, *61*
    stir-fried vegetables 315
    vegetable stock 448
cellophane noodles 276
    *see also* noodles
cereals
    almond granola 379
    creamy oatmeal porridge 382
    hazelnut muesli 378
    nutty nibbles 11
    Scots-style oatmeal porridge
    382
    Swiss-style muesli 380, *381*
challah 402
champagne
    glazed fruit 197
    peach fizz 423
channa dhal, *see* lentils
chapatis 398
charlotte, apple 202
chayote, *see* choko
cheese
    baked capsicums with rice,
    pinenuts and olives 122
    biscuits, savoury 50
    broccoli and capsicum soufflé
    51
    brown rice baked with 107
    casserole bread 407
    cauliflower 106
    "cheese and crackers" loaf
    129
    cheeseboard pizza 49
    croissants 388
    croûtons 67
    dip, savoury 14
    eggplant and garlic tart 128
    filling for omelettes 391
    fondue with green
    peppercorns 46
    French onion soup 62
    fresh 437
    fresh, in tomato sauce 348
    hot baked potato variety 42

leek and broccoli flan 91
Mexican beans with chilli
  108, *109*
mushroom lasagne 90
and mushroom ramekins 15
peas with fresh 328, *329*
puffs 11
rice and vegetable patties 106
rice with nuts, vegetables and
  fresh, Moghul style 272,
  *273*
sauce, for eggplant lasagne 87
soufflés 92, *93*
spicy filling for baked
  potatoes 126
spinach with fresh 347
spinatspatzle 23
stuffing, eggplant with 119
sweet potato puffs 150
toasted mushroom
  sandwiches 24
tomato and mushroom mini
  quiches 7
tomatoes Provencale 154
triangles 6
vegetable spaghetti 22
walnut and rice loaf 112
wholemeal gougère 54
*see also* cottage cheese; cream
  cheese; Parmesan cheese;
  Pecorino cheese; ricotta
  cheese; Romano cheese
cherry clafouti 200
chick pea flour
  bread 400
  Indian-style batter for
    vegetable fritters 449
  okra fried in batter 323
  rice noodles with curried eggs
    275
  white marrow fried in batter
    231
chick peas
  and brown rice pilaf 111
  and cauliflower fricassée 110
  and coriander pâté 54
  felafel 2, *41*
  fresh spring roll 230
  hummus bi tahini 4, *5*
  and nut burgers 110
  nutty nibbles 11
  savoury 344, *345*
  vegetarian couscous 116, *117*
  vine leaves with rice, currants
    and 8
chicory
  leek and potato custard 43
  *see also* endive
chilli
  bean sprout sambal 349
  bitter gourd sambal 358
  coconut chutney 359
  con tempeh 121
  cucumber achar 352
  cucumber sambal 351
  devilled mushrooms 143
  eggplant pickle, Sri Lankan
    style 361
  flat bread with 402
  fresh mint chutney 356, *357*
  fried eggplant salad 353, *353*
  fried onion sambal 360
  fried rice 264
  harissa 118
  hot baked potato variety 42
  kim chi 350
  leeks fried with 364

Malaysian curry paste 455
Mexican beans with 108, *109*
mixed pickle 355
onion and tomato salad 358
and peanut sauce 439
pickle 352
pickled cabbage 350
rojak 317
roti with 402
sambal 354
sambal, ground onion and
  351
sauce, eggs in 299
savoury tempeh 436
stuffed 318
Thai green curry paste 454
Thai-style red curry paste 452
yoghurt and onion salad 176
Chinese cabbage
  braised, Chinese style 283
  Chinese vegetarian
    combination soup 251
  kim chi 350
  mixed braised vegetables 293
  pickled 350
  Shanghai egg pouch soup 250
  spring rolls 244, *245*
  sprout and water chestnut
    salad 167
  stir-fried bok choy 314
  stir-fried eggs with mixed
    vegetables 282
  stir-fried salad sprouts 302
  vegetarian dumplings 240, *241*
  *see also* cabbage
Chinese mushrooms
  and bean curd, braised 280,
    *281*
  braised gluten with
    vegetables 278
  braised vegetable
    combination 282
  braised vegetables with bean
    curd 290
  Chinese vegetarian
    combination soup 251
  combination fried rice 266
  heavenly braised vegetables
    296, *297*
  Korean pancakes 234
  pot stickers 237
  rice vermicelli with 268
  Shanghai egg pouch soup 250
  sushi rolled in seaweed 233
  Szechwan soup 256
  twelve varieties soup 257
  vegetarian dumplings 240,
    *241*
Chinese style braised broccoli
  292
Chinese style braised cabbage
  283
Chinese style eggplant 291
Chinese vegetarian
  combination soup 251
chirashi-zushi 248
chive sauce for walnut and
  rice loaf 112
chocolate
  cassata alla Siciliana 210
  croissants 387
  flake ice-cream 226
  hot malted 432
  Mexican 432, *433*
  mousse cake 191
  New York hot 431
  and pear loaf 419

choko
  mixed vegetables with
    coconut 334
  stir-fried vegetables 315
  stuffed, with mushrooms 146
  twelve varieties soup 257
chowder, corn 78
chutney
  coconut 359
  fresh coriander and coconut
    365
  fresh mint 356, *357*
  green mango 360
  tamarind 362
clafouti, cherry 200
cocktails, fruit and vegetable
  430
cocoa 431
coconut
  banana and yoghurt raita 363
  bean sprout sambal 349
  cakes, steamed rice flour and
    395
  and carrot salad 172, *173*
  chiffon pie 203
  chutney 359
  and fresh coriander chutney
    365
  pappadams with garnish 360
  with peanuts, crisp spiced 362
  rice with lentils and tamarind
    267
  roti 401
  roti with chillies 402
  sambal 355
  sambal, roasted 359
  shredded cabbage 299
  shredded leafy greens with
    302
  steamed vegetables with 312,
    *313*
  summer salad 178
coconut milk 443
  bean sayur 311
  chilli and peanut sauce 439
  coconut chiffon pie 203
  cucumber sambal 351
  curried vegetables in 325, *325*
  egg and coconut curry 306
  eggs in chilli sauce 299
  festive yellow rice 263
  fragrant rice 269, *269*
  fried bean curd with peanuts
    295
  fried eggplant salad 353, *353*
  garlic curry 318
  green banana curry 310
  lentil soup 254
  Malaysian curry 455
  milk rice 394
  mixed vegetables with 334
  okra curry 316
  peanut wafers 242
  pineapple coconut curry 319
  potato and cabbage curry 317
  pumpkin curry 304, *305*
  rice noodles with curried eggs
    275
  sago pudding 370
  savoury fried beans 324
  soup 255
  south sea island spinach 142
  spicy bean sprouts 306
  spicy cabbage in 303
  spicy coconut custard 372
  steamed and spiced eggplant
    304

steamed rice cakes 238
steamed rice in 270
Thai green curry 454
Thai-style red curry 453
using desiccated coconut 443
vegetable curry 308, *309*
vegetables in coconut gravy
  310
water convolvulus in sweet
  gravy 308, *309*
*see also* milk
coffee
  caffe latte 434
  ice-cream, rich 222
  iced 430
  mocha warmer 432
  and rum flip 384
coleslaw
  basic 158
  hot baked potato variety 42
confetti vegetable mould 127
cooler
  mango 423
  watermelon 428
coriander
  and chick pea pâté 54
  and coconut chutney, fresh
    365
  garam masala 456
  Indian curry paste 452
  mushrooms with tomato
    mousse and fresh 3
  Thai green curry paste 454
  Thai-style red curry paste 452
corn
  braised vegetables with bean
    curd 290
  chowder 78
  corn chowder 78
  fritters 247
  green and gold soup 67
  heavenly braised vegetables
    296, *297*
  mini-corn, snow peas and
    cucumber 288
  muffins 418
  rice and vegetable patties 106
  and spinach, creamed 52
  squash medley 88, *89*
  vegetable mosaic terrine 46
cos lettuce
  crunchy salad with garlic
    croûtons 156
  Greek country style salad 158
  *see also* lettuce
cottage cheese
  artichoke strudel 32, *33*
  corn chowder 78
  eggplant with cheese stuffing
    119
  hot baked potato variety 42
  savoury cheese dip 14
  savoury pecan loaf 95
  spinach and cheese pie 114
  tomato and mushroom mini
    quiches 7
  *see also* cheese
courgettes, *see* zucchini
couscous 116
  vegetarian 118, *117*
cracked wheat
  felafel 2, *41*
  rolls with rosemary 414
  tabbouli 172
cream
  asparagus soup 78
  avocado fool 188

blueberry wine soup 75
buckwheat crêpes with
   creamed leeks 35
butternut pumpkin soup 72,
   73
carrot and cauliflower
   timbales 27
carrot sweetmeat 374
champagne-glazed fruit 197
chick pea and cauliflower
   fricassée 110
chicory, leek and potato
   custard 43
cream of tomato soup 55
creamed spinach and corn 52
creamy onion soup 74
crème brûlée with grapes 188
Danish apple cake 194
fettucine in creamy capsicum
   sauce 52, 53
fettucine with rosy mushroom
   sauce 128
fresh pea soup 66
garlic custard for vegetable
   tarts 441
golden nuggets with
   vegetable ragoût 37, 37
herbed green peas 140, 141
leek and silverbeet soufflé 28
light custard 218
mushroom and hazelnut
   terrine 39
mushroom lasagne 90
New York hot chocolate 431
onion tartlets 9
pasta with mushrooms and
   peas 87
pumpkin caramel moulds 199
raspberry mousse 196
raspberry sherbet 216
rich pineapple ice-cream 217,
   219
sauce, saffron and 365
shortcake with berries 200,
   201
spicy parsnip soup 74
spinach and leek timbales 29,
   30
spinatspatzle 23
spring vegetable soup 60, 61
toast of the Shah 371
tomato and mushroom mini
   quiches 7
vegetable mosaic terrine 46
vichyssoise verte 80, 81
cream cheese
   blue cheese log with walnuts
      14
   camembert in port with green
      peppercorns 34
   mushroom canapés 7
   mushrooms with 12
   see also cheese
crème brûlée with grapes 188
crêpes
   basic batter 450
   with creamed leeks,
      buckwheat 35
   rainbow layer 26
croissants
   born again 387
   cheese 388
   chocolate 387
croquettes, almond-crusted
   potato 119
croûtons
   cheese 67

crunchy salad with garlic 156
   tomato filled with garlic 32
cucumber
   achar 352
   fattoush 162
   fried rice 262
   gazpacho Andaluz 70
   guacamole soup 64, 65
   hot baked potato variety 42
   Lebanese bread salad 162
   mini-corn, snow peas and 288
   Mischa's borsch 59
   mixed pickle 355
   mixed vegetables with
      coconut 334
   moulds, creamy 3
   pickle 354
   pineapple salad 168
   rojak 317
   salad 174
   salad, Scandinavian 170
   sambal 351
   sushi rolled in seaweed 233
   yoghurt soup 69
   yoghurt with 364
currants, vine leaves with rice
   chick peas and 8
curry
   dry potato 342
   egg and coconut 306
   eggplant and potato 322
   garlic 318
   green banana 310
   Indian pea pod 301
   okra 316
   pineapple coconut 319
   potato and cabbage 317
   puffs, potato and pea 238
   pumpkin 304, 305
   Thai green 454
   Thai-style red 453
   vegetable 308, 309
   yam 330
curry paste
   Burmese 451
   Indian 452
   Malaysian 455
   Thai green 454
   Thai-style red 452
custard
   garlic, for vegetable tarts 441
   light 218
   rich 219
   spicy coconut 372

## D

daikon, see Japanese radish
damper, herb 417
Danish apple cake 194
dates
   and pecan muffins 385, 385
   wedding pickle 366
desserts, frozen 213-27
dhal, see lentil purée
dieter's eggplant salad, Italian
   style 175
dill and garlic mayonnaise,
   fresh 181
dip
   hummus bi tahini 4, 5
   pesto 10, 13
   skorthalia 12, 13
dipping sauce
   for chilled noodles 290
   for fresh spring roll 231
   for Korean pancakes 235

dough
   no roll 447
   pizza 49, 446
   pot stickers 237
   ravioli with nut filling 99
   rich yeast 446
   tart 446
   see also pastry
dressing
   aioli 183
   balsamic vinegar 186
   basic French 184
   for cauliflower and broccoli
      salad 164, 165
   classic mayonnaise 180
   easy mayonnaise 180
   fresh herb 184
   garlic French 184
   green goddess 183
   Japanese salad 182
   kimizu 182
   for lentil salad 159
   for mushroom salad 168
   oil and vinegar 184-6
   orange and hazelnut oil 186
   Oriental 187
   for pineapple salad 168
   piquant salad 182
   for radish and apple salad 179
   raspberry vinaigrette 136,
      137
   for raw mushroom and
      zucchini salad 169
   for rojak 317
   sushi rice with vinegar and
      sugar 232
   walnut oil and raspberry
      vinegar 185
   yoghurt 187
   see also dipping sauce;
      mayonnaise; sauce
dried mushrooms, see Chinese
   mushrooms
dumplings
   caramel apple 211
   potato 143
   quince with 207
   vegetarian 240, 241

## E

egg noodles, see noodles
eggplant
   baba ghannouj 40, 41
   baked 98
   and bitter gourd, fried 322
   caponata 48
   with cheese stuffing 119
   Chinese style 291
   dieter's salad, Italian style
      175
   fritters 47
   and garlic tart 128
   lasagne 86
   mixed vegetables with
      coconut 334
   and onion fritters 46
   pickle 350
   pickle, Sri Lankan style 361
   poor man's caviar 148
   and potato curry 322
   purée 334
   rainbow layer crêpes 26
   ratatouille 96-7, 98
   salad, fried 353, 353
   salad, Spanish 170
   steamed and spiced 304

vegetarian couscous 116, 117
   yoghurt relish 314
eggs
   aioli 183
   artichoke strudel 32, 33
   asparagus with polonaise
      sauce 24, 25
   baked 395
   baked potatoes with spicy
      cheese filling 126
   bean curd omelettes 236
   beetroot pasta 86
   Benedict 392
   blueberry muffins 386
   broccoli and capsicum soufflé
      51
   Brussels sprouts and pecan
      flan with crumble topping
      103
   buckwheat crêpes with
      creamed leeks 35
   carrot loaf 420
   carrot ring with peas 155
   challah 402
   "cheese and crackers" loaf
      129
   cheese sauce 87
   cheese soufflés 92, 93
   cheeseboard pizza 49
   cherry clafouti 200
   chick pea and nut burgers
      110
   chicory, leek and potato
      custard 43
   chilli fried rice 264
   in chilli sauce 299
   Chinese vegetarian
      combination soup 251
   chocolate mousse cake 191
   classic mayonnaise 180
   coconut chiffon pie 203
   and coconut curry 306
   cold rice with vegetables 248
   confetti vegetable mould 127
   creamed mushroom roulade 18
   creamy onion soup 74
   crème brûlée with grapes 188
   easy mayonnaise 180
   frangipane fig tart 198
   French omelette 392
   French toast 390
   fresh spinach pasta 83
   fried rice 262
   gado-gado 340, 341
   garlic custard for vegetable
      tarts 441
   gazpacho Andaluz 70
   Hollandaise sauce 440
   hot strawberry soufflés 195
   Japanese salad dressing 182
   Japanese tempura-style batter
      449
   kimizu 182
   Korean pancakes 234
   lavosh 401
   leek and broccoli flan 91
   leek and silverbeet soufflé 28
   lemon delicious 212
   and lemon soup 60
   light custard 218
   lumpia wrappers 231
   marbled tea 244
   Mischa's borsch 59
   mushroom and hazelnut
      terrine 39
   mushroom puffs 20
   mushroom scallop 22

nut bread 419
omelette Normandy 205
onion tartlets 9
Parsi omelette 239
Parsi scrambled 249
pear and chocolate loaf 419
pecan pie 198
plain pasta 82
pumpkin caramel moulds 199
rainbow layer crêpes 26
raspberry mousse 196
ravioli with nut filling 99
rice and vegetable patties 106
rice noodles with curried 275
rice vermicelli with almonds
    and 276
rich custard 219
rotis with savoury filling 274
savoury pancake roll 246
savoury pecan loaf 95
scrambled 391
semolina gnocchi 31
Shanghai egg-pouch soup 250
soufflé omelettes 204
in soy sauce 326
Spanish eggplant salad 170
Spanish omelette 88, 391,
    393
spiced mushrooms and 19
on spinach 243
spinach and cheese pie 114
spinach and leek timbales 29,
    30
spinatspatzle 23
stir-fried, with mixed
    vegetables 282
sushi rolled in seaweed 233
Szechwan soup 256
three potato omelette 50
tomato and mushroom mini
    quiches 7
twelve varieties soup 257
vegetable mosaic terrine 46
vegetable spaghetti cheese 22
waffles 388, 389
walnut and rice loaf 112
wholemeal gougère 54
yeast-risen waffles 386
endive
    braised, Lebanese style 147
    Greek country style salad 158

F

Far Eastern menu 284-5
fattoush 162
felafel 2, 41
fennel
    braised, with onion 139
    salad 178
festive yellow rice 263
feta cheese
    cheese triangles 6
    Greek country style salad 158
    tomato and mushroom mini
        quiches 7
fettucine
    Alfredo 84
    in creamy capsicum sauce 52, 53
    with rosy mushroom sauce
        128
fig
    and honey bread 418
    tart, frangipane 198
    wedding pickle 366
filo pastry
    artichoke strudel 32, 33

baklava 210
cheese triangles 6
custard-filled pastries 207
spinach and cheese pie 114
see also pastry
flan
    Brussels sprouts and pecan,
        with crumble topping 103
    leek and broccoli 91
flat bread
    fattoush 162
    roti 401
    roti with chillies 402
    salad 162
    see also roti
flip
    banana 383
    coffee and rum 384
    vanilla 383
flour (plain)
    apple pie 194
    basic crêpe batter 450
    beetroot pasta 86
    caramel apple dumplings 211
    challah 402
    cheese casserole bread 407
    cherry clafouti 200
    chick pea and nut burgers
        110
    corn fritters 247
    couscous 118
    dough for pot stickers 237
    frangipane fig tart 198
    fresh spinach pasta 83
    Japanese tempura-style batter
        449
    Korean pancakes 234
    lavosh 401
    oatmeal cottage loaf 404, 405
    pecan pie 198
    pizza or tart dough 446
    plain pasta 82
    pocket bread 416
    pot stickers 237
    potato and pea curry puffs
        238
    potato dumplings 143
    potato gnocchi 36
    potato poppyseed rolls 413
    Punjabi leavened bread 411
    quick pastry 447
    rotis with savoury filling 274
    savoury pancake roll 246
    sesame loaves 410
    soft pretzels 416
    spinatspatzle 23
    Swedish rye bread 406
    tarte aux pommes 189, 190
    wholemeal rolls 415
    see also rice flour; rye flour;
        wholemeal flour
fondue with green
    peppercorns, cheese 46
fragrant ground spice blend
    456
fragrant rice 269, 269
fragrant seed mix 456
frangipane fig tart 198
frappé
    babaco 428, 429
    pawpaw 424
French beans, see green beans
French dressing 184
    garlic 184
French menu 192
French omelette 394
French onion soup 62

French toast 390
fresh spring roll – Lumpia 230
fried rice 262
    chilli 264
    combination 266
    simple 266
fritters
    bean sprout 234
    corn 247
    eggplant 46
    split pea 243
    see also patties
frozen desserts 213-27
fruit
    champagne-glazed 197
    cocktails 430
    feasts 384
    whole wheat and dried fruit
        compote 380

G

gado-gado 340, 341
garam masala 456
    see also Indian green masala
        paste
garlic
    aioli 183
    Armenian potatoes 148, 149
    baba ghannouj 40, 41
    Burmese curry paste 451
    butter, broccoli in 136
    butter, kohlrabi in 151
    chicory, leek and potato
        custard 43
    chilli and peanut sauce 439
    croûton filling, tomato with
        32
    croûtons, crunchy salad with
        156
    crumbs, grilled mushrooms
        with 31
    curry 318
    custard for vegetable tarts 441
    and eggplant tart 128
    French dressing 184
    and fresh dill mayonnaise 181
    harissa 118
    Indian green masala paste 454
    pesto sauce 442
    pizzaiola sauce 441
    and ripe olive tart 44, 45
    savoury tempeh 436
    skorthalia 12, 13
    zucchini with tomato and 132
gazpacho Andaluz 70
ghee rice 262
ginger
    Burmese curry paste 451
    Indian curry paste 452
    Indian green masala paste
        454
    Malaysian curry paste 455
    and rockmelon sorbet 215
gluten 435
    bean starch sheets and
        braised 307
    Korean pancakes 234
    minced 437
    pot stickers 237
    Shanghai egg pouch soup 250
    shredded, with cashews 287
    spring rolls 244, 245
    steaks 437
    stir-fried long beans and 286
    with vegetables, braised 278
    vegetarian dumplings 240, 241

gnocchi
    potato 36
    semolina 31
golden nuggets with vegetable
    ragoût 37, 37
golden raisins, see sultanas
gougère, wholemeal 54
Grand Marnier ice-cream 227
granita, watermelon and
    raspberry 216, 217
granola, almond 379
grapefruit, grilled 384
grapes, crème brûlée with 188
Greek country style salad 158
green beans
    asparagus soup 78
    bean sayur 311
    bean starch sheets and
        braised gluten 307
    braised 150
    braised gluten with
        vegetables 278
    chick pea and cauliflower
        fricassée 110
    Chinese vegetarian
        combination soup 251
    combination fried rice 266
    curried vegetables in coconut
        milk 325, 325
    fresh spring roll 230
    gado-gado 340, 341
    lima bean and vegetable stew
        122
    mixed braised vegetables 293
    mixed pickle 355
    mixed vegetables with
        coconut 334
    with mushrooms 138
    with pinenuts and raspberry
        vinaigrette 136, 137
    rice with lentils and tamarind
        267
    salad, white and 40
    sambal 356, 357
    savoury fried 324
    savoury pancake roll 246
    spicy diced vegetables 343
    spinach with mixed
        vegetables 338
    steamed vegetables with
        coconut 312, 313
    stir-fried vegetables 315
    twelve varieties soup 257
    vegetable mosaic terrine 46
    vegetable platter with sesame
        sauce 294
    vegetarian couscous 116, 117
    with walnut dressing 134
    see also beans (dried)
green curry paste, Thai 454
green masala paste, Indian 454
greens cooked Kashmiri style
    332
guacamole
    mushrooms with 4
    soup 64, 65
guava
    pie 206
    sorbet 215
Gujerati potatoes 331
Gula Malacca 370
gulab jamun 375

H

haricot beans
    bean soup 70

minestrone 76
white and green bean salad 40
*see also* beans (dried)
harissa 116
hazelnut
muesli 378
and mushroom terrine 39
praline ice-cream 223
hazelnut oil and orange dressing 186
herb
damper 417
dressing, fresh 184
Hollandaise sauce 440
honey and fig bread 418
hot chocolate
malted 432
New York 431
hummus bi tahini 4, 5
Hunza pie 102

**I**

ice-cream 218-27
banana 222
brown bread 227
chocolate flake 226
fresh peach 220
Grand Marnier 227
hazelnut praline 223
pecan brittle 223
pistachio 223
rich coffee 222
iced coffee 430
iced tea 424, *425*
inari-zushi 236
Indian curry paste 452
Indian green masala paste 454
*see also* garam masala
Indian menu 368-9
Indian milk sherbet 426
Indian pea pod curry 301
Indian-style batter for vegetable fritters 449
Indian style spicy fried cauliflower 300
Indian style spicy squash 300
Irish mashed potatoes 152, *153*
Italian menu 193
Italian style, dieter's eggplant salad 175

**J**

Japanese radish
and cabbage salad 167
Korean pancakes 234
radish and apple salad 179
Japanese salad dressing 182
Japanese tempura-style batter 449

**K**

kangkung in sweet gravy 308
karela, *see* bitter gourd
kasha with peas 130
Kashmiri tea 434
kemiri, *see* Brazil nuts
kim chi 350
kimizu 182
kiwi fruit sorbet 218
kohlrabi in garlic butter 151
Korean pancakes 234
kumara

glazed 152
three potato omelette 50
*see also* sweet potato; yam

**L**

lasagne
eggplant 86
mushroom 90
lassi 427
lavosh 401
Lebanese bread salad 162
Lebanese potatoes 144
Lebanese style braised endive 147
leeks
baked potatoes with spicy cheese filling 126
bean soup 70
and broccoli flan 91
buckwheat crêpes with creamed 35
cauliflower in green sauce 20, *21*
chicory, and potato custard 43
combination fried rice 266
fried with chilli 364
Hunza pie 102
mixed braised vegetables 293
pasta with mushrooms and peas 87
ravioli with nut filling 99
and silverbeet soufflé 28
spicy parsnip soup 74
and spinach timbales *29, 30*
vegetable mosaic terrine 46
lemon
delicious 212
and egg soup 60
fresh lemonade 421
spiced tea 422
lemon grass
Malaysian curry paste 455
Thai green curry paste 454
Thai-style red curry paste 452
lemonade, fresh 421
lentils 435
cakes in yoghurt 342
purée 339
rice with 264
rice with mixed 270
rice with tamarind and 267
salad 159
semolina pilaf 260, *261*
sesame and sunflower burgers 115
soup 254
sweet flaky bread 399
lettuce
crunchy salad with garlic croûtons 156
dieter's eggplant salad, Italian style 175
fresh spring roll 230
Greek country style salad 158
herbed green peas 140, *141*
mushroom and bean sprout salad 161
pasta with mushrooms and peas 87
Spanish eggplant salad 170
stir-fried 296
summer salad 178
lima beans
purée 10

salad 159
and vegetable stew 122
lime rickey 422
loaf
carrot 420
"cheese and crackers" 129
oatmeal cottage 404, *405*
pear and chocolate 419
savoury pecan 95
walnut and rice, with chive sauce 112
long beans
and minced gluten, stir-fried 286
quick-fried 295
savoury fried 324
*see also* beans (dried); green beans
lotus root
braised vegetable combination 282
cold rice with vegetables 248
lumpia 230
wrappers 231

**M**

Malaysian curry paste 455
mallung 302
malt vanilla yoghurt shake 426
malted hot chocolate 434
malted milkshake 383
malted rye bread 412
mangetout, *see* snow peas
mango
babaco frappé 428, *429*
buttermilk sherbet 423
chutney, green 360
cooler 423
milkshake 422
Moghul style 367
marrow fried in batter, white 231
mayonnaise
classic 180
easy 180
fresh dill and garlic 181
remoulade sauce 181
sauce andalouse 181
sauce noisette 181
sauce tartare 181
sauce verte 181
menus
autumn 104
breakfast and brunch 408-9
Far Eastern 284-5
festive yellow rice and accompaniments 263
fireside winter dinner party 124-5
French 192
hearty autumn fare 444
India 368-9
Italian 193
make-ahead 17
outdoor eating in spring 224-5
South East Asia 252-3
special occasions 105
spring 16
summer 16
summer alfresco luncheon 336
winter 104
Mexican beans with chilli 108, *109*
Mexican chocolate 432, *433*

mild soup, Burmese style 255
milk
almond 427
almond cream sweetmeat 371
balls in rose syrup, fried 375
banana flip 383
banana yoghurt shake 426
basic crêpe batter 450
broccoli and capsicum soufflé 51
buckwheat crêpes with creamed leeks 35
butternut pumpkin soup 72, *73*
caffe latte 434
cauliflower cheese 106
cheese sauce 87
cheese soufflés 92, *93*
cherry clafouti 200
chick pea and cauliflower fricassée 110
cocoa 431
coffee and rum flip 384
cold zucchini soup 58
confetti vegetable mould 127
corn chowder 78
corn muffins 418
cracked wheat rolls with rosemary 414
cream of broccoli soup 59
cream of mushroom soup 66
creamed spinach and corn 52
creamy carrot soup 71
creamy oatmeal porridge 382
frangipane fig tart 198
fresh pineapple yoghurt freeze 220
herb damper 417
hot chocolate malted 434
iced coffee 430
Indian milk sherbet 426
Irish mashed potatoes 152, *153*
Korean pancakes 234
leek and silverbeet soufflé 28
lemon delicious 212
light custard 218
malted milkshake 383
Mexican chocolate 432, *433*
mocha warmer 432
New York hot chocolate 431
nut bread 419
pasta with mushrooms and peas 87
pumpkin caramel moulds 199
raspberry mousse 196
rich custard 219
saffron and cream sauce 365
savoury pancake roll 246
semolina gnocchi 31
vanilla flip 383
vanilla malt yoghurt shake 426
waffles 388, *389*
watercress soup 58
*see also* coconut milk
milk rice 392
milkshake
malted 383
mango 422
millet pilaf with nuts 123
minestrone 76
mint
chutney, fresh 356, *357*
Indian green masala paste 454

tabbouli 172
Mischa's borsch 59
miso
lentil, sesame and sunflower burgers 115
mushroom soup with 69
spring vegetable soup 60, 61
mocha warmer 432
Moghul style mango 367
Moghul style rice with fresh cheese, nuts and vegetables 272, 273
mould
buttermilk 206
confetti vegetable 127
creamy cucumber 3
pumpkin caramel 199
mousse
cake, chocolate 191
mushrooms with fresh coriander and tomato 3
raspberry 196
mozzarella cheese
cheeseboard pizza 49
potato gnocchi 36
muesli
hazelnut 378
Swiss-style 380, 381
muffins
blueberry 386
corn 418
date and pecan 385
mushroom 386
mulberries, see berries
mulled wine 432
mung dhal, see lentils
mushrooms
and bean sprout salad 161
butter 450
canapés 7
and carrot 154
cheese fondue with green pepper corns 47
and cheese ramekins 15
with cream cheese 12
crunchy salad with garlic croûtons 156
devilled 143
and eggs, spiced 19
filling for omelettes 391
golden nuggets with vegetable ragoût 37, 37
green beans with 138
grilled, with garlic crumbs 31
with guacamole 4
and hazelnut terrine 39
hot baked potato variety 42
lasagne 90
marinated, and avocado salad 160
mild soup with cellophane noodles, Thai style 258
muffins 386
pasta with peas and 87
pilaf 259
puffs 20
risotto 100, 101
roulade, creamed 18
salad 168
sauce, fettucine with rosy 128
scallop 22
soup, cream of 66
soup with miso 69
stuffed chokos with 146
tempeh stuffed grilled 38
and tomato mini quiches 7

with tomato mousse and fresh coriander 3
walnut and rice loaf 112
and zucchini salad, raw 169
see also Chinese mushrooms
mustard cabbage
rice vermicelli with dried mushrooms 268
see also cabbage

N
naan 411
New York hot chocolate 431
noodles
cellophane 276
chilled 290
Chinese vegetarian combination soup 251
fresh rice noodle snack 235
mild soup with cellophane, Thai style 258
rice, with curried eggs 275
riz bi sh'arieh 135
Shanghai egg pouch soup 250
Szechwan soup 256
norimaki zushi 233
Normandy, omelette 205
nut bread 419
nutty nibbles 11

O
oat bran
almond granola 379
hazelnut muesli 378
oatmeal
cottage loaf 404, 405
porridge, creamy 382
porridge, Scots style 382
oil rice 267
okra
curry 316
fried 279
fried in batter 323
olives
baked capsicums with rice, pinenuts and 122
caponata 48
Greek country style salad 158
potato and artichoke salad 166
rice salad 171
Spanish eggplant salad 170
tart, garlic and ripe 44, 45
omelette
bean curd 236
filling for 394
French 392
Normandy 205
Parsi 239
soufflé 204
Spanish 88, 391, 393
three potato 50
onion
baked potatoes with spicy cheese filling 126
braised endive, Lebanese style 147
braised fennel with 139
braised green beans 150
Burmese curry paste 451
caponata 48
chilli con tempeh 121
chilli sambal 354
and chilli sambal, ground 351

cooked salad with sesame seed dressing 160
cream of tomato soup 55
cucumber achar 352
curried vegetables in coconut milk 325, 325
festive yellow rice 263
fried bitter gourd and eggplant 322
fried rice 262
garlic curry 318
gazpacho Andaluz 70
golden nuggets with vegetable ragoût 37, 37
hot baked potato variety 42
lentil, sesame and sunflower burgers 115
lentil salad 159
lima bean and vegetable stew 122
lima bean purée 10
Mexican beans with chilli 108, 109
mild soup, Burmese style 255
minestrone 76
Mischa's borsch 59
mushroom and hazelnut 39
mushroom puffs 20
oil rice 267
pizzaiola sauce 441
ratatouille 96-7, 98
red bean salad 169
rice salad 171
rice with mixed lentils 270
roasted coconut sambal 359
sambal 349
sambal, fried 360
savoury pancake roll 246
savoury pecan loaf 95
savoury tempeh 436
Sindhi style mixed vegetables 335
soup, creamy 74
soup, French 62
Spanish omelette 392, 393
spicy rice with cashews 265
spring vegetable risotto 131
stuffed chillies 318
tartlets 9
Thai green curry paste 454
Thai-style red curry paste 452
tomato and chilli salad 358
tomato sauce 86, 91
twelve varieties soup 257
vegetable stock 448
vegetarian couscous 116, 117
and yoghurt salad 176
orange
blintzes 202
in caramel 196
and carrot soup 79
glazed yams 152
and hazelnut oil dressing 186
juice, pear poached in 205
and orange soup 72
rice with pinenuts 138
spiced tea 422
and strawberry soup 76, 77
Oriental dressing 187
Oriental-style sprouts 292

P
pancakes 234
roll, savoury 246
savoury zucchini 135
see also crêpes

panch phora 456
panir 437
fresh cheese in tomato sauce 348, 348
peas with fresh cheese 328, 329
rice with nuts, vegetables and, Moghul style 272, 273
spinach with fresh cheese 347
papaya salad 166
pappadams with garnish 360
paratha 396
Parmesan cheese
artichoke strudel 32, 33
cauliflower cheese 106
cheese soufflés 92, 93
confetti vegetable mould 127
fettucine Alfredo 84
French onion soup 62
leek and silverbeet soufflé 28
minestrone 76
mushroom risotto 100, 101
pesto dip 10, 13
pesto sauce 442
rice with peas 44
risotta alla Milanese 100
semolina gnocchi 31
spinach ravioli 90
spinatspatzle 23
spirali with julienne of vegetables 130
spring vegetable risotto 131
stuffed artichokes 34
tomatoes with garlic croûton filling 32
vegetable spaghetti cheese 22
Parsi
omelette 239
scrambled eggs 249
parsley
Armenian potatoes 148, 149
fattoush 162
Lebanese bread salad 162
tabbouli 172
parsnip
in garlic butter 151
soup, spicy 74
vegetable mosaic terrine 46
pasta
asparagus with 84, 85
beetroot 86
fresh homemade 82
fresh spinach 83
green, with pumpkin and walnut sauce 94
with mushrooms and peas 87
pecan and bean salad 164
plain 82
salad, pink 175
salad with peas 163
spirali with julienne of vegetables 130
see also fettucine
pastry
Brussels sprouts and pecan flan with crumble topping 103
for curry puffs 238
custard-filled 207
frangipane fig tart 198
onion tartlets 9
pecan pie 198
quick shortcrust 447
tarte aux pommes 189, 190
tomato and mushroom mini quiches 7
see also dough; filo pastry

pâté, chick pea and coriander 54
patties
  barbecued tempeh 102
  rice and vegetable 106
  see also fritters
pawpaw
  frappé 424
  papaya salad 166
peach
  fizz 423
  ice-cream, fresh 220
  Swiss-style muesli 380, 381
peanut sauce for gado-gado 340, 341
peanuts
  and chilli sauce 439
  crisp spiced coconut with 362
  cucumber achar 352
  fried bean curd with 295
  nutty nibbles 11
  wafers 242
pear
  and chocolate loaf 419
  poached in orange juice 205
peas
  carrot ring with 155
  cauliflower in green sauce 20, 21
  cold rice with vegetables 248
  with fresh cheese 328, 329
  herbed green 140, 141
  Indian pea pod curry 301
  kasha with 130
  mixed vegetables with coconut 334
  pasta, pecan and bean salad 164
  pasta salad with 163
  pasta with mushrooms and 87
  and potato, savoury 333
  and potato curry 330
  and potato curry puffs 238
  rice vermicelli with eggs and almonds 276
  rice with 44
  rice with fresh cheese, nuts and vegetables, Moghul style 272, 273
  rice with mixed lentils 270
  Russian salad 174
  soup, fresh 66
  spinach with mixed vegetables 338
  spring vegetable risotto 131
  squash medley 88, 89
  vichyssoise verte 80, 81
pecans
  apricot nut bread 420
  brittle ice-cream 223
  and Brussels sprouts flan with crumble topping 103
  carrot and coconut salad 172, 173
  carrot loaf 420
  cauliflower with 288, 289
  and date muffins 385, 385
  fig and honey bread 418
  grilled mushrooms with garlic crumbs 31
  loaf, savoury 95
  millet pilaf with nuts 123
  nut bread 419
  pasta and bean salad 164
  pie 198

Pecorino cheese
  baked capsicums with rice, pinenuts and olives 122
  potato gnocchi 36
  stuffed artichokes 34
pepper, see capsicum
pesto dip 10, 13
pesto sauce 442
pickle
  cabbage 350
  chilli 352
  cucumber 354
  eggplant 350
  eggplant, Sri Lankan style 361
  kim chi 350
  mixed 355
  wedding 366
pie
  apple 194
  coconut chiffon 203
  guava 206
  Hunza 102
  pecan 198
  spinach and cheese 114
  see also flan; tart
pilaf
  brown rice and chick pea 111
  millet, with nuts 123
  mushroom 259
  rice and wheat 439
  semolina 260, 261
pineapple
  coconut curry 319
  ice-cream, rich 217, 219
  papaya salad 166
  rojak 317
  salad 168
  yoghurt freeze, fresh 220
pinenuts
  baked capsicums with rice, olives and 122
  green beans with raspberry vinaigrette and 136, 137
  orange rice with 138
  pesto sauce 442
pistachio
  almond cream sweetmeat 371
  carrot sweetmeat 374
  cassata alla Siciliana 210
  creamy rice blancmange 374
  creamy vermicelli pudding 375
  ice-cream 222
  mango, Moghul style 367
  rice with fresh cheese, nuts and vegetables, Moghul style 272, 273
  saffron and cream sauce 365
  toast of the Shah 371
pizza
  cheeseboard 49
  dough 49, 446
  pizzaiola sauce 441
pocket bread 416
porridge
  creamy oatmeal 382
  Scots-style oatmeal 382
port with green peppercorns, camembert in 34
pot stickers 248
potato
  Armenian 148, 149
  and artichoke salad 166
  baked 142
  baked, with spicy cheese filling 126

bean soup 70
  and cabbage curry 317
  chicory and leek custard 43
  croquettes, almond-crusted 119
  curried vegetables in coconut milk 325, 325
  curry, dry 342
  dumplings 143
  and eggplant curry 322
  eggplant with cheese stuffing 119
  filling for stuffed chillies 319
  fresh spring roll 230
  gado-gado 340, 341
  gnocchi 36
  golden nuggets with vegetable ragoût 37, 37
  Gujerati 331
  Hunza pie 102
  Indian pea pod curry 301
  Irish mashed 152, 153
  Lebanese 144
  lentil, sesame and sunflower burgers 115
  Mischa's borsch 59
  mushroom scallop 22
  omelette, three 50
  Parsi omelette 239
  and pea curry 330
  and peas, savoury 333
  poppyseed rolls 413
  pumpernickel 406
  rainbow layer crêpes 26
  rice vermicelli with dried mushrooms 268
  Russian salad 174
  savoury tempeh 436
  Sindhi style mixed vegetables 335
  Spanish omelette 88, 392, 393
  spicy diced vegetables 343
  spicy fried 338
  spicy steamed 327
  spinach with 332
  spring vegetable soup 60, 61
  variety, hot baked 42
  vegetarian couscous 116, 117
  vichyssoise verte 80, 81
  watercress soup 58
pretzels, soft 416
protein sources 435-6
pudding
  creamy vermicelli 375
  sago 370
  summer 208
puffs
  cheese 11
  mushroom 20
  potato and pea curry 238
  sweet potato 150
pumpernickel 406
pumpkin
  baked butternut 139
  butternut pumpkin soup 72, 73
  caramel moulds 199
  curry 304, 305
  golden nuggets with vegetable ragoût 37, 37
  green and gold soup 67
  mixed vegetables with coconut 334
  purée, for spinach and leek timbales 29, 30
  spiced 339

spinach with mixed vegetables 338
  vegetarian couscous 116, 117
  and walnut sauce, green pasta with 94
Punjabi leavened bread 411
Punjabi sourdough bread 398
puris 400

Q
quiches, tomato and mushroom mini 7
quince with dumplings 207

R
radish, see Japanese radish
raita, banana and yoghurt 363
raspberry
  avocado and watercress platter 176, 177
  champagne-glazed fruit 197
  delight 197
  mousse 196
  sherbet 216
  sorbet 214
  strawberry yoghurt sherbet 226
  summer pudding 208
  vinaigrette, green beans with pinenuts and 136, 137
  vinegar and walnut oil dressing 185
  and watermelon granita 216, 217
ratatouille 96-7, 98
ravioli
  with nut filling 99
  spinach 90
red cabbage
  with apples 132, 133
  basic coleslaw 158
  see also cabbage; Chinese cabbage
red currants
  summer pudding 208
red curry paste, Thai-style 452
red kidney beans
  chilli con tempeh 121
  hot baked potato variety 42
  Mexican beans with chilli 108, 109
  salad 169
  see also beans (dried)
relish, eggplant yoghurt 314
remoulade sauce 181
rice
  baked capsicums with pinenuts, olives and 122
  balls 242
  bean soup 70
  brown, and chick pea pilaf 111
  brown, baked with cheese 107
  cakes, steamed 238
  capsicum cups with toasted almond 38
  with cashews, spicy 265, 269
  chilli fried 264
  combination fried 266
  egg and lemon soup 60
  festive yellow 263
  fragrant 269

with fresh cheese, nuts and
  vegetables, Moghul style
  272, *273*
fried 262
ghee 262
how to cook 438
with lentils 264
with lentils and tamarind 267
milk 394
with mixed lentils 270
mushroom and hazelnut
  terrine 39
mushroom pilaf 259
mushroom risotto 100, *101*
oil 267
with peas 44
with pinenuts 138
risotta alla Milanese 100
riz bi sh'arieh 135
salad 171
with sesame seeds 274
simple fried 266
spring vegetable risotto 131
spring vegetable soup 60, *61*
steamed, in coconut milk 270
stuffed cabbage rolls 120
sushi, with vinegar and sugar
  232
and vegetable patties 106
with vegetables, cold 237
vine leaves with chick peas,
  currants and 8
and wheat pilaf 439
with yoghurt, South Indian
  style 271
rice flour
  and coconut cakes, steamed
    395
  peanut wafers 242
  roti 401
  roti with chillies 402
rice noodles
  with curried eggs 275
snack, fresh 235
rice vermicelli
  curried vegetables in coconut
    milk 325, *325*
  with dried mushrooms 268
  with eggs and almonds 276
ricotta cheese
  baked potatoes with spicy
    cheese filling 126
  cassata alla Siciliana 210
  cheeseboard pizza 49
  fresh cheese in tomato sauce
    348, *348*
  mushroom lasagne 90
  orange blintzes 202
  peas with fresh 328, *329*
  pesto dip 10, *13*
  rice with nuts, vegetables
    and, Moghul style 272, *273*
  spinach with fresh cheese 347
  *see also* cheese
risotto
  alla Milanese 100
  spring vegetable 131
riz bi sh'arieh 135
rockmelon and ginger sorbet
  215
rojak 317
rolled oats
  almond granola 379
  hazelnut muesli 378
  lentil, sesame and sunflower
    burgers 115

oatmeal cottage loaf 404, *405*
Scots-style oatmeal porridge
  382
Swiss-style muesli 380, *381*
rolls, bread
  cracked wheat with rosemary
    414
  potato poppyseed 413
  wholemeal 415
rolls, stuffed cabbage 120
Romano cheese
  cauliflower cheese 106
  cheeseboard pizza 49
  confetti vegetable mould 127
  spirali with julienne of
    vegetables 130
  spring vegetable risotto 131
  vegetable spaghetti cheese 22
  *see also* cheese
rose syrup 430
rosemary, cracked wheat rolls
  with 414
roti 401
  with chillies 402
  with savoury filling 274
roulade, creamed mushroom 18
rum and coffee flip 384
Russian salad 174
Russian tomato salad 171
rye flour
  malted rye bread 412
  pumpernickel 406
  Swedish rye bread 406

## S

saffron
  and carrot soup 63
  and cream sauce 365
sago
  pudding 370
  strawberry and orange soup
    76, *77*
  summer berry soup 56, *57*
salad
  bean sprout 163
  cooked, with sesame dressing
    160
  crunchy, with garlic croûtons
    156
  cucumber 174
  fattoush 162
  fennel 173
  fried eggplant 353, *353*
  Greek country style 158
  Italian style dieter's salad 175
  Japanese radish and cabbage
    167
  Lebanese bread 162
  lentil 159
  lima bean 159
  marinated mushroom and
    avocado 160
  mushroom 168
  mushroom and bean sprout
    161
  onion, tomato and chilli 358
  papaya 166
  pineapple 168
  pink pasta 175
  potato and artichoke 166
  radish and apple 179
  raspberry, avocado and
    watercress platter 176, *177*
  raw beetroot 162
  raw mushroom and zucchini
    169

red bean 169
rice 171
rojak 317
Russian 174
Russian tomato 171
Scandinavian cucumber
  170
Spanish eggplant 170
sprout and water chestnut
  salad 167
summer 178
tomato and basil 179
white and green bean 40
yoghurt and onion 176
salad dressing, *see* dressing;
  mayonnaise
salt and caraway sticks 414
sambal
  bean sprout 349
  bitter gourd 358
  chilli 354
  coconut 355
  cucumber 351
  fried onion 360
  green bean 356, *357*
  ground onion and chilli 351
  onion 349
  roasted coconut 359
sauce
  aioli 183
  andalouse 181
  for bean curd omelettes 236
  bean starch sheets and
    braised gluten 307
  cheese 15
  cheese, for eggplant lasagne
    87
  chilli and peanut 439
  chive, walnut and rice loaf
    with 112
  fettucine in creamy capsicum
    52, *53*
  harissa 118
  Hollandaise 440
  mornay 106
  noisette 181
  pesto 442
  pizzaiola 441
  polonaise, asparagus with 24,
    *25*
  remoulade 181
  saffron and cream 365
  sesame, for vegetable platter
    294
  sour cream, for baked
    potatoes with spicy cheese
    126
  for spinatspatzle 23
  for stir-fried long beans and
    gluten 286
  for stir-fried watercress with
    bean curd 286
  tartare 181
  tomato, for eggplant lasagne
    86
  tomato, for mushroom
    lasagne 91
  verte 181
  *see also* dipping sauce;
    dressing
scallions, *see* spring onions
scallop, mushroom 22
Scandinavian cucumber salad
  170
Scots-style oatmeal porridge
  382

scrambled eggs 391
semolina
  beetroot pasta 86
  couscous 118
  fresh spinach pasta 83
  gnocchi 31
  pilaf 260, *261*
  plain pasta 82
  potato dumplings 143
  ravioli with nut filling 99
  steamed rice flour and
    coconut cakes 395
sesame dressing
  cooked salad with 160
  for sprout and water chestnut
    salad 167
sesame seed paste, *see* tahini
sesame seeds
  cooked salad with sesame
    seed dressing 160
  cucumber achar 352
  dressing for radish and apple
    salad 179
  lentil and sunflower burgers
    115
  mushroom and bean sprout
    salad 161
  oil rice 267
  rice with 274
  sesame loaves 410
Shanghai egg pouch soup 250
sherbet
  Indian milk 426
  mango buttermilk 423
  raspberry 216
  strawberry yoghurt 226
sherry-glazed carrots 151
shiitake mushrooms
  cold rice with vegetables 248
  *see also* Chinese mushrooms
shortcake with berries 200, *201*
silverbeet
  Hunza pie 102
  and leek soufflé 28
  south sea island 142
  spinach and cheese pie 114
Sindhi style mixed vegetables
  335
skorthalia 12, *13*
snow peas
  Chinese vegetarian
    combination soup 251
  golden nuggets with
    vegetable ragoût 37, *37*
  mini-corn and cucumber 288
soda, strawberry 424
sorbet
  guava 215
  kiwi fruit 218
  raspberry 214
  rockmelon and ginger 215
  syrup 214
soufflé
  broccoli and capsicum 51
  cheese 92, *93*
  hot strawberry 195
  leek and silverbeet 28
  omelettes 204
soup
  asparagus 78
  bean 70
  beetroot and orange 72
  blueberry wine 75
  bread and almond 68
  butternut pumpkin 72, *73*
  carrot and orange 79

carrot and saffron 63
Chinese vegetarian
  combination 251
coconut milk 255
cold zucchini 58
corn chowder 78
cream of broccoli 59
cream of mushroom 66
cream of tomato 55
creamy carrot 71
creamy onion 74
cucumber yoghurt 69
egg and lemon 60
French onion 62
fresh pea 66
green and gold 67
guacamole 64, 65
lentil 254
mild, Burmese style 255
mild, with cellophane
  noodles, Thai style 258
minestrone 76
Mischa's borsch 59
mushroom with miso 69
Shanghai egg pouch 250
sour 258
sour, Burmese style 254
spicy parsnip 74
spring vegetable 60, 61
strawberry and orange 76, 77
summer berry 56, 57
Szechwan 256
twelve varieties 257
watercress 58
sour cream
  blue cheese log with walnuts
    14
  cold jellied borsch 63
  cold zucchini soup 58
  creamy cucumber moulds 3
  fresh pea soup 66
  green goddess dressing 183
  hot baked potato variety 42
  Mexican beans with chilli
    108, 109
  Mischa's borsch 59
  mushroom lasagne 90
  pasta, pecan and bean salad
    164
  raw beetroot salad 162
  Russian tomato salad 171
  sauce for baked potatoes with
    spicy cheese 126
sour soup 258
  Burmese style 254
sourdough bread, Punjabi 398
South East Asian menu 252-3
spaghetti squash
  Indian style, spicy 300
  squash medley 88, 89
Spanish eggplant salad 170
Spanish omelette 88, 391, 393
spice blends
  garam masala 456
  panch phora 456
spinach
  and cheese pie 114
  chick pea flour bread 400
  and corn, creamed 52
  eggplant and potato curry 322
  eggs on 243
  filling for omelettes 391
  with fresh cheese 347
  Hunza pie 102
  and leek timbales 29, 30
  with mixed vegetables 338

pasta, fresh 83
  potato gnocchi 36
  with potatoes 332
  rainbow layer crêpes 26
  ravioli 90
  sour soup, Burmese style 254
  south sea island 142
  spinatspatzle 23
  spring vegetable soup 60, 61
  yoghurt with 278
spinatspatzle 23
split peas
  fritters 243
  spiced pumpkin 339
  see also lentils
spring menus 16, 224-5
spring onions
  artichoke strudel 32, 33
  asparagus soup 78
  bean curd omelettes 236
  braised gluten with
    vegetables 278
  butternut pumpkin soup 72,
    73
  carrots and mushrooms 154
  cauliflower in green sauce 20,
    21
  "cheese and crackers" loaf
    129
  chick pea flour bread 400
  chilli fried rice 264
  Chinese vegetarian
    combination 251
  combination fried rice 266
  creamed mushroom roulade
    18
  fattoush 162
  fresh mint chutney 356, 357
  fresh pea soup 66
  fried bean curd with peanuts
    295
  fried rice 262
  green and gold soup 67
  guacamole soup 64, 65
  herbed green peas 140, 141
  kim chi 350
  Korean pancakes 234
  Lebanese bread salad 162
  Mexican beans with chilli
    108, 109
  Mischa's borsch 59
  mixed braised vegetables 293
  mushroom soup with miso 69
  papaya salad 166
  Parsi scrambled eggs 249
  pickled cabbage 350
  pot stickers 237
  rice with peas 44
  Russian tomato salad 171
  simple fried rice 266
  spicy parsnip soup 74
  spinach and cheese pie 114
  spring rolls 244, 245
  stir-fried eggs with mixed
    vegetables 282
  stir-fried salad sprouts 302
  stuffed cabbage rolls 120
  tabbouli 172
  vegetable platter with sesame
    sauce 294
  vegetarian dumplings 240,
    241
  vichyssoise verte 80, 81
  walnut and rice loaf 112
  watercress soup 58
spring rolls 244, 245

lumpia 230
spring vegetable soup 60, 61
spring vegetable risotto 131
squash
  Indian style, spicy 300
  medley 88, 89
Sri Lankan style eggplant
  pickle 361
sticks, salt and caraway 414
stock
  for carrot and orange soup 79
  for fresh pea soup 66
  vegetable 448
strawberries
  apple fizz 428, 429
  apple freeze 214
  champagne-glazed fruit 197
  and orange soup 76, 77
  shortcake with berries 200,
    201
  soda 424
  soufflés, hot 195
  summer berry soup 56, 57
  yoghurt sherbet 226
strudel, artichoke 32, 33
sultanas
  carrot and coconut salad 172,
    173
  carrot loaf 420
  hazelnut muesli 378
  rice with fresh cheese, nuts
    and vegetables, Moghul
    style 272, 273
  vine leaves with rice chick
    peas and 8
  whole wheat and dried fruit
    compote 380
summer berry soup 56, 57
summer menus 16, 336
summer pudding 208
summer salad 178
summer squash, see marrow
sunflower seeds
  almond granola 379
  almond milk 427
  chick pea and nut burgers
    110
  hazelnut muesli 378
  lentil and sesame burgers 115
sushi
  cold rice with vegetables 248
  in fried bean curd 236
  rice with vinegar and sugar
    232
  rolled in seaweed 233
Swedish rye bread 406
sweet potato
  fresh spring roll 230
  glazed 152
  three potato omelette 50
  see also kumara; yam
sweetmeat
  almond cream 371
  carrot 374
Swiss chard, see silverbeet
Swiss-style muesli 380, 381
Szechwan soup 256

**T**
tabbouli 172
tahini
  baba ghannouj 40, 41
  hummus bi tahini 4, 5
tamarind
  chutney 362

rice with lentils and 267
tapioca
  sago pudding 370
  strawberry and orange soup
    76, 77
tart
  apple 189, 190
  dough 446
  eggplant and garlic 128
  frangipane fig 198
  garlic and ripe olive 44, 45
  garlic custard for vegetable
    441
  onion tartlets 9
tartare sauce 181
tarte aux pommes 189, 190
tea
  iced 424, 425
  Kashmiri 434
  marbled eggs 244
  spiced 422
tempeh 435
  almond-crusted potato
    croquettes 119
  chilli con 121
  patties, barbecued 102
  savoury 436
  stuffed grilled mushrooms 38
terrine
  mushroom and hazelnut 39
  vegetable mosaic 46
Thai green curry paste 454
Thai style mild soup with
  cellophane noodles 258
Thai-style red curry paste 452
timbales
  Brussels sprouts 94
  carrot and cauliflower 27, 29
  spinach and leek 29, 30
toast
  crisp spicy 15
  French 390
  of the Shah 371
tomato
  Armenian potatoes 148, 149
  baked capsicums with rice,
    pine nuts and olives 122
  and basil salad 179
  braised green beans 150
  cheese fondue with green
    pepper corns 47
  chilli con tempeh 121 .
  dieter's eggplant salad, Italian
    style 175
  eggplant and potato curry 322
  eggs in soy sauce 326
  fattoush 162
  fettucine in creamy capsicum
    sauce 52, 53
  fresh cheese in tomato sauce
    348, 348
  with garlic croûton filling 32
  gazpacho Andaluz 70
  guacamole soup 64, 65
  hot baked potato variety 42
  Indian pea pod curry 301
  Lebanese bread salad 162
  Mexican beans with chilli
    108, 109
  minestrone 76
  mousse and fresh coriander,
    mushrooms with 3
  and mushroom mini quiches
    7
  onion and chilli salad 358
  Parsi scrambled eggs 249

pink pasta salad 175
pizzaiola sauce 441
potato and pea curry 330
Provencale 154
purée, spicy 324
ratatouille 96-7, 98
salad, Russian 171
sauce for eggplant lasagne 86
sauce for mushroom lasagne 91
savoury chick peas 344, 345
Sindhi style mixed vegetables 335
soup, cream of 55
sour soup, Burmese style 254
spicy diced vegetables 343
spring vegetable risotto 131
stuffed artichokes 34
stuffed chillies 318
tabbouli 172
vegetables in coconut gravy 310
vegetarian couscous 116, 117
yoghurt and onion salad 176
zucchini with garlic and 132
toor dhal, see lentils
twelve varieties soup 257

**U**

urad dhal, see lentils

**V**

vanilla
  flip 383
  malt yoghurt shake 426
vegetable spaghetti
  cheese 22
vegetables
  braised, with bean curd 290
  braised combination 282
  braised gluten with 278
  cheese fondue with green peppercorns 47
  Chinese vegetarian combination soup 251
  cocktails 430
  in coconut gravy 310
  in coconut milk, curried 325, 325
  cold rice with 237
  confetti vegetable mould 127
  cooked salad with sesame seed dressing 160
  curry 308, 309
  filling for omelettes 391
  gado-gado 340, 341
  greens cooked Kashmiri style 332
  heavenly braised 296, 297
  Indian-style batter for fritters 449
  and lima bean stew 122
  mild soup, Burmese style 255
  mixed, Sindhi style 335
  mixed braised 293
  mosaic terrine 46
  platter with sesame sauce 294
  ragoût, golden nuggets with 37, 37
  and rice patties 106
  rice with fresh cheese, nuts and, Moghul style 272, 273

semolina pilaf 260, 261
shredded gluten with cashews 287
shredded leafy greens with coconut 302
soup, spring 60, 61
spicy diced 343
spinach with mixed 338
spirali with julienne of 130
spring vegetable risotto 131
steamed, with coconut 312, 313
stir-fried 315
stir-fried eggs with mixed 282
stock 448
Thai green curry 454
Thai-style red curry 453
with coconut, mixed 334
vegetarian combination soup, Chinese 251
vegetarian couscous 116, 117
vegetarian dumplings 240, 241
vermicelli
  pudding, creamy 375
  riz bi sh'arieh 135
vichyssoise verte 80, 81
vinaigrette, see dressing
vine leaves with rice, chick peas and currants 8

**W**

wafers, peanut 242
waffles 388, 389
  yeast-risen 390
walnut oil and raspberry vinegar dressing 185
walnuts
  apricot nut bread 420
  baklava 210
  blue cheese log with 14
  carrot loaf 420
  "cheese and crackers" loaf 129
  chick pea and nut burgers 110
  dressing, beans with 134
  nut bread 419
  and rice loaf with chive sauce 112
  sauce, green pasta with pumpkin and 94
  skorthalia 12, 13
  Spanish eggplant salad 170
water chestnut
  braised vegetable combination 282
  spring rolls 244, 245
  and sprout salad 167
  vegetarian dumplings 240, 241
water convolvulus in sweet gravy 308, 309
watercress
  with bean curd, stir-fried 286
  gado-gado 340, 341
  raspberry and avocado platter 176, 177
  soup 58
  stir-fried vegetables 315
watermelon
  cooler 428

and raspberry granita 216, 217
wedding pickle 366
wheat
  how to cook 438
  and rice pilaf 439
  see also cracked wheat; whole wheat
wheatgerm
  almond granola 379
  hazelnut muesli 378
  Hunza pie 102
  ravioli with nut filling 99
  yeast-risen waffles 386
white radish, see Japanese radish
whole wheat and dried fruit compote 380
wholemeal bread
  flaky 396
  paratha 396
  rolls 415
  tomatoes with garlic croûton filling 32
wholemeal flour
  barbecued tempeh patties 102
  blueberry muffins 386
  chapatis 398
  chick pea flour bread 400
  date and pecan muffins 385, 385
  deep-fried wholemeal bread 400
  gougère 54
  Hunza pie 102
  pastry for Brussels sprouts and pecan flan 103
  pizza dough 49
  pizza or tart dough 446
  pocket bread 416
  pumpernickel 406
  Punjabi sourdough bread 398
  puris 400
  rainbow layer crêpes 26
  savoury zucchini pancakes 135
  shortcake with berries 200, 201
  spinach and cheese pie 114
  sweet flaky bread 399
  yeast-risen waffles 386
  see also flour (plain)
wine
  mulled 434
  soup, blueberry 75
winter menus 104, 124-5
wongah bak, see Chinese cabbage
wood fungus
  braised gluten with vegetables 278
  braised vegetable combination 282
  braised vegetables with bean curd 290
  Chinese vegetarian combination soup 251
  heavenly braised vegetables 296, 297

stir-fried eggs with mixed vegetables 282
Szechwan soup 256
twelve varieties soup 257

**Y**

yam
  curry 330
  glazed 152
  see also kumara; sweet potato
yeast dough, rich 446
yeast risen breads 402-13
yeast-risen waffles 386
yoghurt 435
  and banana raita 363
  banana shake 426
  cold jellied borsch 63
  cucumber soup 69
  with cucumbers 364
  dressing 187
  drink 427
  eggplant relish 314
  and fresh pineapple freeze 220
  hot baked potato variety 42
  lentil cakes in 342
  and onion salad 176
  potato and pea curry 330
  Punjabi leavened bread 411
  Punjabi sourdough bread 398
  savoury black-eyed beans 346
  sesame loaves 410
  Sindhi style mixed vegetables 335
  sour cream sauce 126
  South Indian style rice with 271
  spicy parsnip soup 74
  spicy steamed potato 327
  with spinach 278
  spinach with fresh cheese 347
  strawberry sherbet 226
  vanilla malt shake 426

**Z**

zucchini
  cheese fondue with green peppercorns 47
  confetti vegetable mould 127
  gado-gado 340, 341
  golden nuggets with vegetable ragoût 37, 37
  Korean pancakes 234
  mild soup with cellophane noodles, Thai style 258
  minestrone 76
  mixed vegetables with coconut 334
  and mushroom salad, raw 169
  pancakes, savoury 135
  rainbow layer crêpes 26
  ratatouille 96-7, 98
  rice and vegetable patties 106
  rice salad 171
  soup, cold 58
  spirali with julienne of vegetables 130
  spring vegetable risotto 131
  with tomato and garlic 132
  vegetarian couscous 116, 117